NO RELIGION WITHOUT IDOLATRY

NO RELIGION

WITHOUT

IDOLATRY

Mendelssohn's Jewish Enlightenment

GIDEON FREUDENTHAL

University of Notre Dame Press

Notre Dame, Indiana

Manufactured in the United States of America

Library of Congress Cataloging-in-Publication Data

Freudenthal, Gideon.
No religion without idolatry : Mendelssohn's Jewish Enlightenment /
Gideon Freudenthal.
p.   cm.
Includes bibliographical references and index.
ISBN 978-0-268-02890-9 (pbk. : alk. paper) —
ISBN 0-268-02890-7 (pbk. : alk. paper)
E-ISBN: 978-0-268-07975-8
1. Mendelssohn, Moses, 1729–1786.   2. Judaism and philosophy.
3. Jewish philosophy.   4. Faith and reason—Judaism.
5. Haskalah.   6. Idolatry.   I. Title.
B2693.F69   2012
296.3092—dc23

2012005300

לְנֹעָה,

בְּאַהֲבָה רַבָּה

CONTENTS

ACKNOWLEDGMENTS

I discussed my ideas concerning idolatry and enlightened Judaism with friends and colleagues. I am grateful for their suggestions and criticism. In an early stage of my work, Ursula Goldenbaum, Rachel Livneh-Freudenthal, and Reinier Munk encouraged me to turn my initial ideas into a more comprehensive study.

I am particularly grateful to Hannah Kasher, who has been my permanent consultant and challenging interlocutor but above all helpful in innumerable ways.

Israel Fischer, Ariel Furstenberg, Avi Warschavsky, and Ynon Wygoda read an early version of the manuscript and discussed it with me in a very supportive and mildly critical spirit. Discussions with Maoz Kahana, Martin Schüle, Hartwig Wiedebach, and Klaus Hamberger helped me clarify my final conclusions.

The research for this book was done in part in Berlin. As always, I enjoyed there the hospitality of the Max-Planck-Institute for the History of Science. I am grateful to the director of Department I, Jürgen Renn, for the opportunity to work in this inspiring setting. I am also deeply indebted to my friends in Berlin for their support in good and bad times.

Finally, I owe much to my grandfather Siegfried (Shimon) Freudenthal z"l (Breslau, September 28, 1877–Jerusalem, December 26, 1960). His personality taught me more about Mendelssohn's spirit than I could have learned from books. Fifty years ago he also gave me some volumes of Mendelssohn's *Netivot ha-Shalom*, which I used when writing this book.

ABBREVIATIONS

AA   Kant, Immanuel. *Gesammelte Schriften*. Königlich Preußische Akademie der Wissenschaften. Berlin: Reimer; later Walter de Gruyter, 1900–. (Cited by volume and page.)

AT   Descartes, René. *Discours de la Méthode*. In *Oeuvres de Descartes*, vol. 6, ed. C. Adam and P. Tannery. Paris: J. Vrin, 1983.

Bi'ur   Mendelssohn, Moses (Solomon Dubno, Aaron Jaroslav, Naftali Herz Weisel, Herz Homberg). Commentary to the biblical text in *Netivot ha-Shalom* (Hebr.). Berlin: G. F. Starcke, 1780–83. Reprint, *JubA* 15–18. (Cited by biblical chapter and verse.)

CpR   Kant, Immanuel. *Critique of Pure Reason*. Ed. and trans. P. Guyer and A. W. Wood. Cambridge: Cambridge University Press, 1998.

GM   Maimon, Salomon. *Giv'at ha-Moreh* (1791). Ed. S. H. Bergman and N. Rotenstreich. Jerusalem: Publications of the Israel Academy of Sciences and Humanities, 1966.

GP   Leibniz, Gottfried Wilhelm. *Die philosophischen Schriften von G. W. Leibniz*. Ed. C. I. Gerhardt. Berlin, 1849–55. Reprint, Hildesheim: Georg Olms, 1978.

GW   Maimon, Salomon. *Gesammelte Werke*. Ed. V. Verra. Hildesheim: Olms, 1965–76. (Cited by volume and page.)

JubA   Mendelssohn, Moses. *Moses Mendelssohn: Gesammelte Schriften–Jubiläumsausgabe*. Ed. I. Elbogen, J. Guttmann, and E. Mittwoch et al. Berlin: Akademie-Verlag, 1929–; continued by A. Altmann et al. Bad Cannstatt: Frommann-Holzboog, 1971–. (Cited by volume and page.)

Tr   Maimon, Salomon. *Versuch über die Transzendentalphilosophie*. Berlin: Christian F. Voß und Sohn, 1790.

Introduction

> True Judaism is no longer found anywhere. Fanaticism and
> superstition exist among us to a most abhorrent degree.
> Were my nation not so stupid, it would stone me on account
> of my *Jerusalem,* but people do not understand me.
>   —*Mendelssohn*[1]

This book has a direct and an indirect topic. Its immediate subject
matter is Moses Mendelssohn's conception of enlightened Judaism; its
indirect topic is the very possibility of enlightened religion. Drawing
conclusions concerning the possibility of enlightened religion in general on the basis of the analysis of one historical episode may seem far
too ambitious, even misguided on principle. "All religion is positive
and particular. Any attempt to speak without speaking any particular
language is not more hopeless than the attempt to have a religion that
shall be no religion in particular," George Santayana famously said.[2]
However, having a religion is one thing, analyzing it another. It may be
the case that a person cannot simultaneously confess more than one
religion, although I will also qualify this statement in a moment. But at
least the related monotheistic religions (Judaism, Christianity, Islam)
and the different confessions within these have enough in common to
be named "religions" and also to justify some generalization. Moreover,

the work of Mendelssohn itself is a comparative study of religions. His presentation of Judaism is primarily based on a comparison of religions according to one criterion: their closeness or distance to idolatry—as he conceives it—on the one hand and to "natural religion" on the other. His touchstone is the nature of religious symbols. These can be understood as "symbols" that signify by convention only and that merely help to recall the religious content intended. According to this understanding, the ascription of holiness to the body of the symbol itself is idolatry: holiness is necessarily transcendent. But a symbol may also be considered sacred in itself in some sense, such as are sacraments, icons, and holy sites. In this case, a religious service may in some sense be a genuine religious experience, an encounter or communication with the divine that is not only transcendent but also present in some way and degree in the symbols. Religions can be allocated in the span between these opposite ends. Mendelssohn's discussion of Judaism thus also draws the coordinates by which not only Judaism, but all comparable religions can be located.

Mendelssohn's perspective is semiotic, and he concentrates on religious practice. Concentrating on religious practice is an alternative to the focus on theology on the one hand and on belief on the other. Mendelssohn excludes from his discussion all codified confessions of faith, as well as the beliefs of the practitioners. These are all attempts to fix in precise formulas something that by its very nature is allusive and changing in time. Mendelssohn rather concentrates on religious practice that comprises a form of life, the fulfillment of precepts, rites, and objects (sites, symbols, ritual articles). Practices are often communal, and they involve no intellectual subtleties. Practice, therefore, builds and preserves a community, and avoids useless intricacies. It also avoids an inquisitorial invasion of people's private, unclear, and changing thoughts. For Mendelssohn, it is also the preferred way to study religion.

Nevertheless, religious practices are not severed from faith. They are meaningful acts testifying to the beliefs of the practitioner. Therefore they imply and exclude some notions of God. This is displayed in the discussions over religious practices since the Hebrew prophets' criticism of animal sacrifice. To say that some practice is or is not adequate implies a rudimentary theology. Participating in such practice therefore expresses some beliefs, but even more it shapes them. "The hearts follow the deeds," is an old observation. Religious communal practice thus provides a privileged access to religion, as Mendelssohn understands it. Concentrating on religious practice from this perspective means that Mendelssohn studies religion as a symbolic system. Semiotics, so I argue, is also the foundation of Mendelssohn's general philosophy. Mendelssohn's philosophy of religion is an integral part of his general philosophy, and both are rooted in semiotics.

•   •   •

The intimate dependence of religion and idolatry on the interpretation of religious symbols is manifest in an inscription on the pedestal of the Kornmarkt-Madonna in Heidelberg (1718). This statue shows the Holy Virgin as queen of heaven with baby Jesus on her arm. The inscription (in Latin and German) reads:

> Non statuam aut saxum sed quam designat honora.
> (Honor neither statue nor stone but what they designate.)
> Noch Stein noch Bild noch Säulen hier das Kind und Mutter lieben wir.
> (We love here not stone nor image nor columns but child and mother.)

Whereas the inscription does not testify to a poetic talent in either language, it may claim priority on the paradox that became famous through René Magritte's "Ceci n'est pas une pipe" (written under a picture of a pipe). But whereas Magritte's picture strikes us as paradoxical, the inscription of the statue does not. The difference consists in this: No matter how blurred the distinction between picture and depicted may be, no pipe smoker is likely to mistake the picture for a real pipe or try to feed it with tobacco and light it. The case is different with the statue of the Madonna. The real Madonna is currently not existent in space and time. The real duality of the pipe and its picture, and the duality of actions involving them, does not exist here: only the picture is present; its referent is not, and there is no observable difference between the overt behavior of a practitioner who intends the absent, real Madonna—although he physically turns to the statue—and an idolater who intends the statue itself. Moreover, we believe that a practitioner does not intend the statue only because we understand symbols and symbolic action. In contradistinction to ordinary activities, worship is meant to be essentially different from what it appears to be. It appears to be an adoration of a statue; in fact it is the adoration of an absent divine person that is different from the statue in its very nature, although it resembles it in its assumed appearance. According to Catholic doctrine, the honor paid to the statue or other representations is referred to the divine person depicted, the prototype. This is also what the inscription expresses. The problem is that whether the practitioner intends the sculpture itself or the divine person, whether he "honors" the former but "adores" the latter (as he should) or adores the sculpture itself (as he should not), does not show in his or her overt behavior. It is not even clear that the practitioner understands the subtle theological distinctions between giving honor, worshiping, and adoring. The ambiguity inherent in religious symbols and the lack of an observable difference between the commanded and forbidden worship is the reason for the inscription on the pedestal: it reminds practitioners and observers that the marks of reverence visibly directed towards the sign should refer in intention to the real object of reverence—the thing signified. A similar move to adding the inscription to the statue was undertaken by Hermann Cohen in his discussion of animal sacrifices in the temple in Jerusalem: The Israelite who watches the ritual, so Cohen comments, looks up above priest and altar to God.[3] One wonders how Cohen knows that the Israelite is looking up to God when his gaze is fixed on the concrete demonstration of the ritual, which, so it seems, offers God food and scent that are known to please him and dispose him graceful (Genesis 8:21). Cohen and the German inscription on the pedestal of the statue in Heidelberg use the indicative mood in the sense of an imperative.

And yet there is an important difference between the threat of idolatry in Christianity (especially Catholicism) and in Judaism. The Madonna and Jesus were once both (also) visible human beings, hence of human likeness that may be depicted. However, God himself cannot be perceived by the senses in principle. A picture of God is hence a theological misconception, and according to Catholic doctrine,[4] God himself ("God-Father") should not be represented in statues that are venerated in religious service. This very difference between the permissible and even recommended use of pictures of the Madonna and Jesus ("Pictures are the books of the ignorant") and the forbidden use of a picture of God is mutatis mutandis the dividing line between the Christian and the Jewish notion of idolatry. Judaism rejects the idea that God may become also human or a human also divine. In Judaism only the unique invisible God is worshiped and adored, and therefore all pictures are forbidden. And yet Judaism too knows some of the problems mentioned. Ritual articles, especially Torah scrolls and articles containing passages of the holy text (phylacteries, mezuzot), should be treated with special reverence; some are even considered sacred and venerated. Here too distinctions between respect, veneration, worship, and adoration, as well as between the physical script, the text in some particular language, and its meaning, are necessary.

This ambiguity concerning the addressee and the nature of worship cannot easily be dissolved. Moreover, religious ceremonies (consecration) confer a special status on religious symbols and sites, and irreverence towards them is a religious offense (blasphemy). It seems that the ambiguity of the symbol is especially due to the similarity to the divine personae represented, and yet the idea to substitute conventional symbols for iconic representations immediately strikes us as inadequate, and it often forms part of a critique of (traditional) religion. Consider Christian Wolff's (1679–1754) elaboration of the meaning of the crucifix and a Jewish medieval critique of the phylacteries. First Christian Wolff:

[I]t is understood that a perspicuous sign should be introduced, so that we may remember our general purpose the whole day.

Since the meaning of artificial signs (as are those of which we speak here) is arbitrary (see *Ontologia*, §958); everybody may introduce for himself signs *ad libitum*. The ancient Christians used the sign of the cross, to remind themselves permanently that Christ was crucified (according to the admonition in 2 Timothy 2:8) and that they should conduct a life worthy of a Christian, and therefore, in preparing an action, one should observe what befits a Christian. Hence, those who condemn the sign of the cross as a superstitious rite, err greatly. Similarly, the image of the crucified Christ that is continually exposed to your look in a room can be given the meaning of the general purpose. The same meaning can be given to words written in golden letters: "What are you doing?" And why not also to the form of a snuffbox or some other object, which is frequently used during the day, especially if you wanted to conceal the meaning?[5]

Now the medieval Jewish source:

> When asked why [they don't put on phylacteries] they respond, "*Tefillin* (Phylacteries) are only intended to be 'a reminder between your eyes'" (Exodus 13:9). Since they are intended as a reminder, it is better to mention the Creator with our mouths several times a day. That is a better and more fitting reminder![6]

Now, these particular symbols were evidently suggested in order to exclude the possibility that they be ascribed inner religious value. But a snuffbox is so mundane and strange to any religious practice that the suggestion to use it as a religious symbol sounds blasphemous. Language, on the other hand, is the best-known system of purely conventional signs. "What's in a name? / That which we call a rose / By any other name would smell as sweet."[7] However, the fact that Christianity did not forsake symbols or Judaism ritual articles or Islam holy sites speaks for itself. Religion evidently needs symbols that are not merely conventional but partake in some way and to some extent in the divine nature they purport to represent.

The very nature of religious practice implies explicitly or tacitly some presence of the divine. It makes little sense to address a God in prayers who does not listen to them in principle, or to perform ceremonies of which he takes no notice. As an act of communication with the divine (and a fortiori as an action that influences the divine), a religious practice is at the same time also a religious experience: it is an encounter with the divine. In the human world this encounter takes place in the symbol that unites the corporeal nature of a worldly object and its non-material meaning and referent. I believe that the following suggestion of Gerardus van der Leeuw captures the essentials, although it is formulated in very emphatic language:

> In the cult man speaks and acts, but also God. This can only happen
> when divine and human action assumes form, when it becomes visible,
> audible, tactile. And this is possible only by means of a *tertium quid*
> which is of this world, but sanctified and removed from this world. We
> name this *tertium quid:* symbol. Not in the attenuated, modern sense of
> the word, but in the genuine, ancient sense: two realities coincide in the
> symbol, God and Man encounter each other.[8]

Religious practice may be a religious experience because the Holy is
present in it. In order to be "visible, audible, tactile," the Holy must be
material, present in some sense in an object or an event, and at the
same time it must carry a meaning that transcends its material nature;
it thus becomes a symbol.[9]

Looking back at the suggestions above, we can see that the various
religious conceptions mentioned may be characterized by their understanding of symbols: from the understanding (which is not part of the
Judeo-Christian-Muslim lore) that a material object is itself the deity to
the conception that nothing worldly is sacred and that religious symbols
are merely conventional signs by which we express and communicate
thoughts about the transcendent Godhead. However, many symbols in
extant religions are on neither of these opposite ends but somewhere in
between them. In fact, these religions themselves are clusters of practices
and symbols in which myth and idolatry, enlightenment and abstract
signification are intertwined. This is not merely a contingent state of affairs. In this book I suggest that a mixture of myth and enlightenment is
inherent to religion. No religion without idolatry.

I discuss the different kinds of symbolic signification in more detail
in the body of the book. Here I wish only to emphasize that the ambiguity of religious symbols does not correspond to different kinds of symbols, for example, pictures and language. The very same symbol (the
material object, or the "sign-vehicle") can be understood in different
ways. Following Peirce, we can distinguish three major kinds of signification: the "symbolic," in which the sign is purely conventional (e.g.,
the Hindu-Arabic numerals or punctuation marks); the "iconic," in
which the signifier resembles the signified (i.e., an architectural model, a
statue of the Madonna); and an "indexical," in which the sign is directly

connected to the signified (e.g., "natural signs": smoke signifies fire; the symptom an illness, a part a whole, the relicts the deceased saint). Most signs will feature more than one kind of signification. A photograph, for example, is certainly "iconic," but it is also "indexical" because it is produced by a process in which the object photographed is involved as a causal agent. If, moreover, we consider the conventions leaving their imprints on a photograph and on its observation, then we may say that they also involve a conventional signification. The equivocal nature of the sign implies that it can be interpreted according to these different modes by the same person at different times, or by different persons both at the same and at different times. Because the same object or action can signify in more than one way, the very same observable religious practice can be understood differently by different practitioners or observers. Moreover, the same person can understand his own practice in different ways at different times. A practitioner may not even be aware of the distinctions between different modes of signification of the sign he is using and, if asked, would smoothly move from one mode to the other. When we point to the sign-vehicle, that is, the material body or action—say, a cross—and demonstrate its proper use in a ceremony, we do not resolve the ambiguity.

We should therefore complement Santayana's statement that it is impossible to have a religion that is no religion in particular with the statement that a person can believe in more than one particular religion within a very short time span. Certainly, as a rule, a believer will not simultaneously be Christian and Jewish or Moslem but stick to the traditions of one religion only, but it is not certain that all practitioners of the "same" religion understand their practice in the same way, nor that a practitioner will not believe at some point something that he or she will deny at another time. It is not even clear that at the same time a person will consistently interpret a religious symbol in one definite way and not mix different conceptions. It is the fact that the very same sign-vehicle (the sensuous object or practice serving as a sign) can signify in different ways that makes it possible to practice without making up one's mind on the alternatives involved, and hence also not choosing between them. What is here said of one person holds a fortiori for a community.

These suggestions concerning the role of "symbol" in religion are here offered in my name (although they rely strongly on predecessors). Nevertheless, I believe that they largely coincide with Mendelssohn's views. In a nutshell, Mendelssohn's thesis is this: Jewish religious law is a "ceremonial law," and ceremonies are a "living script," meaningful, transient acts that disappear after their performance. Permanent signs are conducive to idolatry. This is so because people might fail to properly distinguish between the sensuous sign, a physical object (the sign-vehicle), and the signified itself; that is, they attribute properties of the signified to the sign. This may lead to the veneration of the signs and thus to idolatry. The full argument for this seemingly strange thesis is found in Mendelssohn's works in general philosophy, in a survey of his views on language and signs in general in the second part of his *Jerusalem,* and in his biblical commentary where his semiotics is applied to explain idolatry. I gave above an example for the semiotic characterization of idolatry: If a particular statue is believed to be more than a material object that signifies by similarity or convention, if it is believed to have intrinsic metaphysical properties or to be itself holy, or if one acts in a form suggesting that it is, then the sign (the "signifier") is attributed properties of the signified; and this is idolatry in Mendelssohn's terms.

There are of course also Jewish examples, and Jews were in fact accused of idolatry because of the respect or veneration or adoration they show to the Torah scroll. By the criterion mentioned, God's message is holy but not the spoken or written or thought words themselves. Here again we should distinguish between the sign-vehicle, the sounds, the scroll or the book, and the sentences in some particular language on the one hand and the meaning, the content represented on the other. However, the difference does not show in the representation used: the same object may be seen by one person as nothing but a material sign-vehicle of the content and considered holy by his co-practitioner. It is not clear that an observer of their overt behavior and words could tell the difference between their views. Both show the same respect to the Torah scroll (overt behavior); one intends the holy content, the other the scroll itself. Mendelssohn's philosophy of Judaism and idolatry is hence rooted in semiotics. This, however, does not at all square with the received view of Mendelssohn's philosophy. My own understanding of Mendelssohn's philosophy—and my esteem for it—differ so much from the received view that I want to first briefly report Mendelssohn's reputation and discuss its reasons.

•   •   •

The reputation of few persons has changed so radically as Mendelssohn's. Once the "German Socrates," he is now considered only a shallow popularizer of philosophy. Once called "Rambaman" and compared to "Rambam," to Maimonides himself,[10] three generations later even the founder of modern orthodoxy, Rabbi Samson Raphael Hirsch (1808–88) slandered him as a destructor of Judaism.[11] Hermann Cohen, certainly a liberal, acknowledges Mendelssohn's historical accomplishment but criticizes his "theoretical weakness," although his own philosophy of Judaism is clearly an elaboration of Mendelssohn's ideas.[12] Less surprising is that Mendelssohn's work was condemned by Rabbi Moses Sofer ("Chatam Sofer") (1762–1839), perhaps the most influential leader of Jewish "ultra-orthodoxy" in the nineteenth century.[13]

In modern scholarship, Mendelssohn's philosophy of Judaism is considered an inconsistent project, doomed to lead to the abolishment of Judaism. Julius Guttmann concluded his impressive concise presentation of Mendelssohn's philosophy of Judaism with the statement that there is an insurmountable duality in Mendelssohn's thought. It is the duality of natural religion and Judaism, of a universal system of beliefs that depends on reason alone and, therefore, common to all human beings, and a particular Jewish religion, that depends on revelation. Mendelssohn the enlightener cannot accept that eternal life and felicity will be the heritage of Jews only, excluding all other human beings irrespective of their merit. Instead, Mendelssohn maintains with other enlighteners that whoever upholds the basic principles of natural religion (belief in one God, providence, and the immortality of the soul, including reward and punishment), and lives morally, deserves felicity here and in the hereafter. But if so, what was revelation, what is Judaism good for? And yet at the end of *Jerusalem*, Mendelssohn does not advocate a unified religion of reason but the toleration of a plurality of particular religions, and even maintains that not unity but diversity is the purpose of providence. But if so, what is the office of universal reason and natural religion? Sound reason and revelation work towards the same end, and therefore "what Mendelssohn gives here to revelation, he evidently must take off reason," says Guttmann.[14] Suggesting that Mendelssohn's trust in reason dwindled in his late years allows Guttmann to turn the blatant contradiction between universal reason and particular revelation into a development from the former to the latter. With this move Guttmann also acknowledges Mendelssohn's personal sincerity in spite of the inconsistent final product.[15] More recent scholarship did not improve on this assessment. Alexander Altmann, the foremost Mendelssohn scholar in recent decades, did not think much of Mendelssohn's Jewish philosophical project. Mendelssohn's views were held together, so he tells us, more by "personal convictions and loyalties" than by internal consistency.[16]

However, Mendelssohn advances one decisive argument for adhering to Judaism and the commandments in spite of universal reason and natural religion: the ceremonial law renders Judaism a safeguard against idolatry. The ceremonial law consists in transient actions. It is a "living," not a written, script, and, moreover, it prohibits representations that lend themselves to idolatry. On the other hand, it also does not depend on a codified doctrine, which, due to the imperfections of language, is in principle inadequate to express metaphysical and religious truth. There is no contradiction between the assertion that natural religion suffices for eternal felicity and the recommendation of a special form of life that guards this very religious truth from corruption.

The core of Mendelssohn's philosophy of religion is hence a philosophy of representation or semiotics that is applied both to religious practice (ceremonies) and to theology. The ambiguous nature of religious symbols is the reason for idolatry, and the imperfection of language is the reason for the uncertainty of metaphysics and a fortiori theology. Natural language was formed in the contexts of everyday practices with sensible objects. When applied to the metaphysical realm, which by definition is not accessible to the senses, language necessarily turns metaphorical and unreliable. Metaphysics is, therefore, irremediably uncertain and, when in conflict with sound reason, most probably in error. I already mentioned that a critique of linguistic and other representations is also the core of his philosophy of Judaism. Moreover, I argue below that Mendelssohn's entire philosophy, from his philosophy of mathematics to his philosophy of Judaism, revolves around semiotics. This and his reliance on common sense give coherence to his thought in all the different areas of study.

Mendelssohn's unique contribution, which distinguishes him from other critics of idolatry, consists in that he did not criticize this or that religious practice as idolatrous, or this or that *theolegoumenon,* but rather examined the (semiotic) principle by which they are all formed. In its tendency and ambition, Mendelssohn's philosophy is indeed comparable to Maimonides' project; in fact their critiques of idolatry and superstition are analogous. However, on the basis of his semiotics, Mendelssohn developed a general theory of religion and idolatry, whereas Maimonides offered only circumstantial explanations for individual idolatries and precepts. Based on these fundaments, Mendelssohn's philosophy of Judaism—and of religion in general—can be defended and, in fact, still deserves contemporary interest.

Most readers of *Jerusalem* ignored Mendelssohn's semiotics or glossed over it. They also ignored the commentary on Exodus where this semiotics is applied to explain idolatry. Therefore also the discussion of idolatry in *Jerusalem* was not understood. Alexander Altmann decisively dismissed it, and later commentators followed Altmann:

> Mendelssohn's "hypothesis" that "the need for written signs was the first cause of idolatry" is the least substantiated of all theories he ever advanced. (*Moses Mendelssohn: A Biographical Study,* 546)[17]

With this disregard for Mendelssohn's semiotics, and with his classification as a Wolffian rationalist, the way to understanding his philosophy in general and his philosophy of Judaism in particular was blocked. In this book I attempt to show that—interpreted from the semiotic perspective—Mendelssohn's philosophy of common sense is consistent and his philosophy of religion highly enlightening. Mendelssohn's general philosophy was also misunderstood. One reason for the disregard for it may lie in the sweeping acceptance of Kantianism in the years following Mendelssohn's death. In Kant's conception, Mendelssohn belonged to the "Leibniz-Wolffian" philosophy. In his own judgment, Kant not only refuted this specific philosophy but also proved that its "dogmatic metaphysics" consisted of judgments that cannot be argued to be either true or false. Later historiography followed suit and adopted Kant's view of the "prehistory" of Kant's "critical philosophy." It seems to me that this picture is utterly wrong. It can first be doubted whether Kant really proved that he has definitely overcome both "dogmatic metaphysics" and "skepticism" and that "[t]he critical path alone is still open" (*CpR* B 884). Of course, this question cannot be discussed here. However, I argue here that Mendelssohn was not a "dogmatic metaphysician" at all but developed his own version of philosophy of sound reason or "common sense." This shows not only in specific epistemological discussions but also and above all in the respective functions he ascribed to sound reason and metaphysics: it is sound reason that determines truth; metaphysics is called upon only to further buttress the judgments of common sense. Moreover, Kant paid little attention to semiotics in general or to philosophy of language in particular. Kant and the historiography of philosophy in the tradition of Neo-Kantianism therefore had no interest in Mendelssohn's semiotics and, more generally, contributed to the decline of interest in it. In various respects, Kantianism hence significantly contributed to the lack of understanding for Mendelssohn's philosophy.

It is, however, also no wonder that Mendelssohn has the reputation of a Wolffian. Mendelssohn earned the name "the German Socrates" with his *Phaedon oder über die Unsterblichkeit der Seele* of 1767. He did not translate this Platonic dialogue but adapted it to the dominant philosophy of the time, Wolffian metaphysics, which he used also in other writings. Mendelssohn often referred to himself as a follower of this school. And yet readers cannot ignore his repeated advocacy of common sense or sound reason and his reservations concerning metaphysics as such. Scholars wished to attenuate this inconsistency and suggested that at first Mendelssohn was a Wolffian metaphysician but that he grew ever more skeptical regarding metaphysics and more inclined to common sense.

However, Mendelssohn's major philosophical work, *Morgenstunden* (Morning Hours), mainly presents metaphysical proofs for the existence of God in Wolffian style and yet was written a few months before Mendelssohn's death; he was hence a "metaphysician" to the end of his life. But in this very work we also find his most vivid partisanship for common sense. The thesis that a change in Mendelssohn's philosophical views can explain the seeming inconsistency of adhering first to Wolffian metaphysics and then to common sense simply does not square with obvious facts.

How can Mendelssohn philosophize in the Wolffian framework and yet not be a dogmatic metaphysician? The answer is metaphilosophical and concerns the role of metaphysics in Mendelssohn's thought, of philosophy in human life. Mendelssohn welcomed metaphysical underpinning of his commonsensical views. But he never made the acceptance of a truth dependent on metaphysical demonstration, or relied on it to guide his conduct. This is the domain of common sense. In case of conflict between metaphysics and common sense, he trusted the latter. The seeming inconsistency in Mendelssohn's philosophical views is resolved once we realize that he indeed upholds both "sound reason" and Wolffian metaphysics but that he attributes to them different functions and clearly determines the relative priority of "sound reason" in cases of conflict between them. Mendelssohn philosophizes to buttress positions he already holds independently of metaphysics, to fend off the critique of skeptics, and to lend his thought a systematic, axiomatic structure. A good example is the existence of God. Mendelssohn maintains that the existence of God can be known by everybody, educated or not, by means of sound reason alone. Nevertheless, he invests much effort in metaphysical (Wolffian) proofs of the existence of God. Whether or not the proofs are successful, Mendelssohn's belief in the truth of the proposition does not at all change. This, so I argue below, is the root of his disagreements and misunderstandings with Salomon Maimon, for whom theoretical reasoning alone determines truth and conduct.

Salomon Maimon, for some time supported by Mendelssohn, embodies in all respects a radical alternative to Mendelssohn: in general philosophy, in philosophy of religion and particularly of Judaism, finally also in his way of life. In philosophy, Mendelssohn follows common sense in his epistemology and philosophy of language, whereas Maimon combined in a unique way rationalism with skepticism. They are opposed also in their ways of life. Mendelssohn was a well-to-do, respected member of the Jewish community and also of the non-Jewish enlightened circles; Maimon, a clochard, living outside of all community, later on the premises of his non-Jewish benefactor and buried in the Jewish cemetery in disgrace. They also clearly differ in character. Mendelssohn was renowned for his kindness and amicability; Maimon, for his offensive behavior and ingratitude towards benefactors. These differences bear on the very different conclusions they draw from their similar views on religious practice: Mendelssohn grants Judaic traditions trust reserved to "familiar" informers; Maimon demands rational proofs. Mendelssohn is willing to accept religious representations as adequate to humans, although not to their referent; Maimon does not, and he rejects, moreover, all merely symbolic action. Mendelssohn brings into consideration human needs; Maimon maintains that all conventional religious practice implies at least anthropomorphism if not idolatry and superstition. To him the only legitimate religious practice is genuine religious experience, and this can be attained only in pure intellectual apprehension. Knowledge is also a religious experience. Finally, conceiving God not only as an "idea" that can never be reached but also as an idea that merely expresses a human "drive," not an objective reality, undermines also this concept of religious experience. The controversy between common sense, religion (religious practice), enlightenment, and community on the one hand (Mendelssohn) and strict philosophy, Enlightenment, autonomy, and aloneness on the other (Maimon) cannot itself be adjudicated by philosophy, which is here not objective but partisan. This is rather the choice of a way of life en bloc. However, elaborating the alternatives is certainly the task of philosophy, and this is what I attempt to do in this book.

In conclusion, I argue that religion consists in the tension between Enlightenment and myth or idolatry. In a religious community, these interdependent poles may be represented by more and less enlightened and idolatrous members of a community. This structure of a community often corresponds to the ambiguity in its practitioners' minds, who either combine idolatrous and enlightened views or consciously or unconsciously waver between them. It is therefore that I qualified at the beginning of this introduction my agreement with Santayana: As a rule, people do not endorse more than one codified confession, but within the same confession they may and do hold beliefs that, upon analysis, prove incompatible, or quickly switch back and forth between such views.

In the appendix, I attempt to apply this view to one episode that is of special concern here. I juxtapose Mendelssohn and Alexander Altmann, the foremost Mendelssohn scholar and biographer in the twentieth century. I show that they are mirror images of each other: Mendelssohn enlightens religion; Altmann reinvests Enlightenment with mystery (idolatry in Mendelssohn's view) to revive religion. Both hence combine enlightenment and idolatry but with opposed tendencies. No wonder that Altmann is very close to Mendelssohn and yet shows no understanding for his semiotic critique of idolatry or for its philosophical underpinnings.

•   •   •

I will now briefly outline my argument as it unfolds in the book. In the first chapter, I elaborate Mendelssohn's general philosophy of common sense and his skepticism concerning metaphysics. I argue that Mendelssohn's preference for practices as adequate representations of belief is supported by his linguistic skepticism. He distrusts the ability of language to adequately represent and to help generate truth transcending commonsense knowledge of the empirical world. Language, so Mendelssohn believes, arises in everyday practice of humans, and when applied to abstract concepts is necessarily metaphorical and ambiguous. Knowledge derived from long chains of arguments in natural language is not reliable without additional immediate support. Metaphysics is therefore dubious beyond the first steps in which propositions are almost direct inferences from commonsense knowledge.

In the second chapter, I portray Salomon Maimon, Mendelssohn's younger protégé, as an alternative to Mendelssohn. Maimon is a strict rationalist. In fact, he accepts only logical inference as true: neither presuppositions nor conclusions are completely transparent to reason and therefore cannot be known to be true. Objectively true and certain are logic, pure metaphysics, and, to a lesser degree, arithmetic but not even geometry, and even less so physics. These are severe demands on truth, and Maimon is therefore skeptical concerning most purported human knowledge: with him strict rationalism and skepticism are two sides of the same coin. Maimon also develops a philosophy of language that is the exact opposite of Mendelssohn's in *Jerusalem*: he does not proceed from names referring to objects of experience and show how abstract terms develop from these by metaphors but, on the contrary, claims that the most abstract and general concepts (categories) come first and that names of individual objects are constructed from these by specification. Language is not necessarily metaphorical but can be rendered adequate to philosophical purposes by exact definitions. With these alternative epistemologies and philosophies of language, we have the foundations for their opposite philosophies of religion within (Jewish) Enlightenment.

Readers who are not interested specifically in epistemology, philosophy of language, or metaphysics, but only in philosophy of religion, can skip these chapters and begin with the third chapter, keeping in mind that, in spite of his opposite reputation, Mendelssohn is a commonsense philosopher and skeptic in metaphysics and that the basis of this skepticism and of his philosophy in general is his semiotics. He therefore conceives of religion in two ways. On the one hand, there is "natural religion," which is common to all people and consists of simple, almost self-evident truths that do not require long chains of arguments. It consists of three short propositions: God is the creator of the universe; there is afterlife; and there is providence. Religions, however, say much more than this, and whatever is said beyond immediate or almost immediate truths is either dependent on authority (revelation) or requires arguments (natural theology). Natural religion is dependent on experience and common sense. Revealed religion is dependent on tradition. The truths revealed must also be transmitted to the next generations that did not witness revelation. The differences between these kinds of truths and their respective dependence on language are studied by Mendelssohn (chapter 3).

Belief in revelation and skepticism concerning language are contrary to each other since the lore is couched in language. Mendelssohn mitigates this opposition in emphasizing that the Bible itself uses descriptions of a "language of action." The "language of action" is a form of expression that uses gestures, mimickry, ostension, and spoken language. Following influential contemporary philosophers, Mendelssohn argues that such language of action is the primordial language from which our merely spoken and written language developed. Later languages are more refined and subtle but therefore also too speculative and their reference often uncertain. In key episodes (e.g., the bond between God and Abraham) the Bible reports that God and Man used the language of action, not only spoken language. This prevents the application of linguistic skepticism to the foundations of revealed religion: What God and Man expressed on such occasions is unambiguous. And since the Bible reports and describes these actions, our understanding of this text is least liable to misunderstanding. The basis of religious life should therefore be natural religion and religious practice (analogous to the language of action) (chapter 4).

Religious ceremonies that are as it were a residual of the primordial language of action have not only the advantage of their clear meaning and reference, but also of their transitory character. Once performed, they are over and gone and leave nothing behind. This is crucial to forestall idolatry. Whether an object (e.g., a site) is ascribed holiness and gives occasion to religious service, or whether the very practice itself imbues as it were the objects involved with holiness (e.g., in the case of ritual articles), in both cases their very permanence facilitates idolatry. Similar considerations apply to language. Spoken language vanishes as soon as the pronunciation of the phrases ends. Written language endures. Mendelssohn studied in depth the foremost biblical case of idolatry, the sin of the golden calf, and developed a comprehensive theory of idolatry, as the adoration both of objects and of linguistic signs (chapter 5).

As an antidote to idolatry, Mendelssohn recommended the "ceremonial law" of Judaism, a "language of action" of sorts, which, allegedly, uses conventional signs only and, once performed, leaves no objects behind that would lend themselves to idolatry. Moreover, the ceremonial law also positively contributes to religion: It serves as the social bond of the community; it enables a unity of action without imposing monolithic thought; it prompts reflection on and instruction in religious truths (chapter 6). Mendelssohn's presentation of Judaism is a reform project rather than a description of extant Judaism. He passed in silence phenomena in Judaism that answer his criteria of idolatry such as veneration of religious articles and sacred sites, texts, or the Hebrew letters, or the understanding of prayer in magical terms (chapter 7).

Furthermore, drawing on some scattered observations of Mendelssohn, I argue that religious practice need not necessarily be judged as adequate or inadequate to its divine referent but may be considered as an adequate or inadequate *human response to the divine*. Thus, for example, beauty and goodness may be considered as responding to divine perfections, not as representing them. From this perspective, a religious symbol may be conventional and yet subject to constraints: it must share the value—but not other properties—of the perfection it purports to address. This significantly changes the criteria of adequacy. A practice judged inadequate in respect to God may pass for an adequate human response to him.

In support of Mendelssohn's position, I also emphasize the epistemological role of accepting the religious community into which one is born as into a family: it explains trust, and this in turn strengthens belief in one's own tradition. I also develop an interpretation of the nature of the ceremonial law and religious service that can be justified according to Mendelssohn's criteria (chapter 8).

In the last chapter, I argue in my name that religion consists in the tension between myth and enlightenment, and that it ceases to exist when coinciding with either of these extremes. Practitioners whose views are more enlightened or more mythical consider one another as foes, but in fact each side is essential to the existence of the other, and the existence of both is essential to the subsistence of the community. No religion without myth and enlightenment; in short: no religion without idolatry. Religious symbols cannot signify in a purely conventional manner; an iconic or indexical manner of significations must also obtain.

I consider finally the entrenchment of the controversy between Mendelssohn and Maimon in a more comprehensive framework. I argue that they assume opposed positions vis-à-vis worldly life. Mendelssohn's values "all natural impulses, capacities and powers" (which are human finite representations of the divine infinite "highest perfection"); Maimon's values strict "reason" only. Mendelssohn is a committed member of his community to which he irrevocably belongs as to his family; Maimon lives for himself, and community is to him a voluntary association based on a contract that can be terminated at any time—and in fact he did terminate his membership in the Jewish community. The corresponding values are loyalty and trust on the one hand, independence and loyalty to pure truth on the other. The corresponding drawbacks may be lesser consistency on the one hand and the confinement of human life to reason alone on the other. Mendelssohn's and Maimon's respective positions form clusters of attitudes to many facets of human life. The choice is between these clusters en bloc and depends on what forms of life are historically possible, as well as on our scale of values and on what form of life we wish to endorse.

CHAPTER 1

Mendelssohn

Common Sense, Rational Metaphysics, and Skepticism

Mendelssohn's philosophy of religion depends on an argument on what can and cannot be known. It is therefore necessary to elaborate his basic epistemological and metaphysical views prior to a discussion of his views on religion. Mendelssohn's reputation has been that he is the last representative of the Leibniz-Wolffian school and his *Morgenstunden* a summary of its metaphysics and of "dogmatic rationalism" in general. Kant's *Critique of Pure Reason* marks the end of this "dogmatism." However, Mendelssohn also advocates "commonsense" philosophy, which is incompatible with so-called dogmatic rationalism. The resolution I suggest is that the function of both these philosophical orientations is different. Common sense determines what is true, what false. Metaphysics attempts to systematize true knowledge (produced by common sense), base it on first principles, and defend it against skeptics. Metaphysics is of secondary importance compared to common sense.

As a "dogmatic rationalist," Mendelssohn is supposed not to restrict knowledge to the realm of sense experience (as Kant did) but to maintain that we can know objects of sense experience as they are "in themselves" (and not merely as they appear to us) and that we can also know objects that are in principle not within the reach of our sense experience: metaphysics should therefore be possible as a science. So much for our preconception. In what follows, I argue that the very opposite is true. Mendelssohn believed in common sense and was a skeptic about metaphysics. This has consequences: In cases of conflict between the judgments of common sense and metaphysics, common sense has the last word. Mendelssohn also considers the reasons for the difference in the reliability of entirely theoretical disciplines such as metaphysics and mathematics. His answer is pathbreaking also for the discussion of religion: the difference lies in the symbolic means of the various disciplines. This idea tightly connects epistemology as well as religion to semiotics.

The "Wonderful Harmony" between Deduction and Experience

In 1763 Mendelssohn won the Berlin Royal Academy of Sciences prize for his essay "On Evidence [i.e., perspicuous apodictic truth] in Metaphysical Sciences,"[1] in which he claimed that metaphysical truths are "capable, to be sure, of the same certainty but not the same perspicuity as geometrical truths" (*JubA* 2, 272; Dahlstrom, 255). Moreover, twenty years later, in his *Jerusalem,* Mendelssohn said of himself that he was "perhaps one of those who are the farthest removed from that disease of the soul" called skepticism (*Jerusalem,* 66–67). The affirmation of strict knowledge in metaphysics and the negation of skepticism suffice, so it seems, to qualify Mendessohn not only as a rationalist philosopher but also as opposed to skepticism.

The commonplace that Mendelssohn was a "rationalist" in this sense has never been doubted.[2] It has rather been repeated innumerable times in subsequent scholarship.[3] Nevertheless, readers could not ignore his partisanship for common sense. Some of them concluded that in later years Mendelssohn changed sides from rationalism to common-sense philosophy or that he was an empiricist in psychology and aesthetics and a rationalist in logic and metaphysics.[4] Others maintained that since common sense itself is a faculty of reason, the difference between these persuasions is not so great. The former suggestion is at odds with Mendelssohn's writings; the latter waters down "rationalism" to a simple use of reason. True, with Tetens, Mendelssohn maintains that it is the same faculty that is active in "common sense" and in speculation or metaphysics, but this does not remove their differences.

"Rationalism" means that all truth is, in principle, based on logical truth. In Mendelssohn's time, this was understood to mean that all truth can be reduced to identical or partially identical propositions: "AB is AB," "AB is A," "AB is B." This conception was best expressed in Leibniz's principle *"praedicatum inest subjecto"*—the predicate is contained in the subject.[5] Mendelssohn endorses this conception of truth:

> Each individual proposition . . . is true if, on the basis of a consideration of the subject, it can be intelligibly explained either absolutely or under certain assumed conditions that the predicate is part of the subject. (*JubA* 2, 302; Dahlstrom, 283)[6]

This metaphysical notion of truth (as God knows it) has little to do with epistemology. It does not teach us what criteria justified true belief must satisfy. Consider, for example, Mendelssohn's words at the very beginning of his essay on "evidence":

> The certainty of mathematics is based upon the general axiom that nothing can be and not be at the same time. In this science each proposition such as, for example, "A is B," is proven in one of two ways. Either one unpacks the concept of A and shows "A is B," or one unpacks the concepts of B and infers from this that non-B must also be non-A. . . . In fact, since geometry lays nothing else as its basis than the abstract concept of extension and derives all its conclusions from this single source . . . there is no doubt that all geometric truth . . . must be encountered all tangled up in it. (*JubA* 2, 273; Dahlstrom, 257)

There has never been a geometry book that begins with a concept of extension and derives all theorems by its analysis. On the contrary, Euclid's *Elements,* to which Mendelssohn repeatedly refers, begins with definitions of elementary objects, introduces axioms and postulates, and then constructs more complex objects and proves theorems about their properties. It is a synthetic, not an analytic, science; it proceeds by means of constructions and diagrams, not by means of concepts and their logical analysis. This, however, is immaterial to Mendelssohn's project. Already Leibniz was cautious to write that *predicatum inest subjecto* refers to the concepts "as God understands them." But in most cases this also remains God's prerogative. We humans know most of the few true propositions we know at all in a different way. However, there is no contradiction between both claims. We know a true geometrical proposition, say, that the sum of the internal angles of a triangle equals two right angles (Euclid, *Elements,* I, 32), by means of the synthetic construction of a diagram and the application of the definitions, axioms, and postulates. But that this proposition is true means that the predicate "equals the sum of two right angles" is somehow contained in the concept of a triangle, although we humans do not see how—evidently because we do not understand these concepts as God does.

The duality of truth and our knowledge of truths does not coincide with the difference between God and man. There are also true propositions that we humans know both logically and empirically. Consider for example the "first law of nature," the supreme maxim for all our actions (and note that for Mendelssohn imperatives can be immediately derived from propositions):

> Make your intrinsic and extrinsic condition and that of your fellow human being, in the proper proportion, as perfect as you can. (*JubA* 2, 317; Dahlstrom, 297)

This maxim can be formulated on the basis of experience: "Simply consider human beings' actions and omissions, their diverse inclinations and passions, amusements and worries and abstract the one thing on which they all ultimately agree" (*JubA* 2, 316; Dahlstrom, 296). "The same natural law," says Mendelssohn, "can be proven a priori from the mere definition of a being with free will" (*JubA* 2, 317; Dahlstrom, 297). The very same law of nature is hence arrived at in both ways, and the difference between its empirical or metaphysical justifications lies simply in the "degree of their insight" (*JubA* 2, 316; Dahlstrom, 296). In spite of the entirely different logical and empirical ways of reaching the conclusion, the maxim itself is precisely the same, and Mendelssohn twice formulates verbatim the same principle in the contexts of the relevant discussions (*JubA* 2, 317, 318; Dahlstrom, 296, 297).

But the same maxim can be derived also "by the most irrefutable reasons" in a third way:

> As soon as one assumes that a God, who cannot act without the wisest intentions, has produced the world, no proposition in Euclid can be proven with more rigor than this one, that the cited law of nature must be the will of God. (*JubA* 2, 318; Dahlstrom, 298)

This "wonderful harmony," the coincidence of the result reached by analysis of the concept of a free agent, or by abstraction from behavior of people, or finally from the concept of God in natural theology, shows in this case that the way of experience, "bottom up," reaches the same result as the way of deduction, "top down." This is no exception.

> Infinitely many additional basic definitions, or also correct experiences, can be premised in this way, leading us all on a sometimes shorter, sometimes longer route to the same result. In this wonderful harmony one recognizes the truth! . . . For the all-seeing eye, the whole of nature is one painting, the sum total of all possible knowledge is one truth. (*JubA* 2, 321; Dahlstrom, 300)

This is a very optimistic view of human knowledge and reason. Its practical import is the confidence that a well-established empirically known truth is, in fact, a logically necessary truth (even if we cannot infer or prove it as such), and that it will harmoniously integrate with other true propositions, logical and factual, metaphysical and empirical, to form a comprehensive worldview.

SYSTEMATIC REASON, METAPHYSICS, AND COMMON SENSE

The "wonderful harmony" between all parts of our knowledge irrespective of the experiential or deductive way on which they were established, shows that "the sum total of all possible knowledge is one truth." It teaches us not only that God created a world governed by reason but also that it is accessible to our reason, even though in most cases not deductively. Moreover, human reason is one and the same in all the different forms of its employment. The reason governing syllogisms is not different from the reason that argues inductively, and it is also the same in those forms of reasoning called "common sense" or, better, sound reason. The differences rather lie in the *means* reason employs and in the degree of the explicitness and systematicity of the arguments.[7] Most of our knowledge is generated by common sense.

Descartes opens his *Discourse on Method* with reference to this faculty: "Good sense [*bon sens*] is of all things, the most equally distributed among men"; it is "the power of judging properly and of distinguishing truth from falsity [*la puissance de bien juger, et distinguer la vraie d'avec le faux*]."[8] Mendelssohn, too, defines *bon sens* as proficiency in distinguishing truth from falsity (*JubA* 2, 325; Dahlstrom, 303).

Sound reason works in the entire range of human knowledge and is not confined to reasoning. Mendelssohn also conceives sense perception as involving "unconscious inferences." This shows in perceptual illusions. When we see a tower from afar we see it as round. We then judge that the tower is round. This may be an error. The tower may be square and only appear round from afar. Such mistakes in judgment are based on "incomplete induction"; in fact they are "mistakes in logical inference." We infer from the sameness of two sensual impressions the sameness of the objects, from the sameness of the signs that of the signified. Of course, we are not conscious of such inferences. They are repeated so often, and our habits were formed so early that the inferences are automatic and not consciously executed but become "quasi-immediate sensations" (*Morgenstunden* 3.2, 30–32). However, commonsense judgments are not really "immediate sensations," nor do they display unmediated inferences (e.g., *cogito ergo sum*); they only so appear because they are quick and effortless. But there is all the difference in the world between *cogito ergo sum,* which cannot and need not be further explicated, and the commonsense inference "where there is smoke there is fire," or, analogously, the inference from the existence of the world to the existence of its creator. The latter judgments may be even quicker than the first (which belongs to professional philosophy and is rarely considered in daily life), but they involve a notion of causality that is not at all "evident," although in daily life we constantly apply it.

Mendelssohn's idea can be explicated thus: In principle, there is only one human reason, and whether it is called "reason" or "common sense" depends on whether or not it is applied systematically and what means are used. The lower degrees of explicitness and clarity are reached when only natural language is used. This is called "common sense." Explicit, reflective arguments are called "reason," and they apply at least some specific terminology, often also formal arguments or mathematical representations. Judgments of common sense are implicit logical inferences; arguments "in form" explicate them. This is Mendelssohn's view of common sense from the first to his last publication. It is the difference in the kind of language used and in the dependence on formal arguments that was not taken into account by later readers and facilitated the misunderstandings of Mendelssohn's philosophy.

In his early *Verwandtschaft des Schönen und Guten*, Mendelssohn writes:

> In respect of *bon sens,* we are fully convinced that its judgments may be analyzed into syllogisms; *bon sens* is well-trained reason. Reason and *bon sens* operate according to similar rules; the former slower, such that we become aware of the middle terms, the latter so fast that of the whole succession of concepts we retain nothing but the beginning and the end. (*JubA* 2, 183)[9]

And at the end of his life, Mendelssohn still maintains the same view: "Sound human reason (*gesunder Menschensinn; gesunder Menschenverstand*) and reason (*Vernunft*) flow both from the same source, they are one and the same faculty of knowledge. The latter proceeds slowly[,] . . . whereas the former rushes as if winged to the goal" (*JubA* 3.2, 50). Building on the Leibnizian hierarchy of "confused" and "clear" representations, Mendelssohn also concludes that "sense" and "reason" do not differ essentially but only gradually.

> Having a sensation, [sound] human reason proceeds in quick pace and hastens forward and does not waver because it fears to fall. Reason, on the other hand, taps around with the staff before it dares take a step; she totters the same way, indeed more carefully, but not without fear and trembling. Both may lose their way, both may stumble and fall; but if this happens, then at times it is more difficult for reason to get back on its feet. (*Morgenstunden, JubA* 3.2, 33–34)

Analogously, we judge beauty by a "sense" of beauty without adducing arguments, and we judge morality by our "conscience," a sense of "right and wrong." On principle such arguments could be spelled out—and so they in fact are in the specialized disciplines of aesthetics and moral philosophy. Mendelssohn, therefore, analogously introduces the term *sense for truth.*

> A refined taste in no time finds what sluggish criticism only gradually casts light upon. Just as quickly, conscience decides and the sense for the truth judges what reason does not reduce to distinct inferences without tedious reflection. (*JubA* 2, 325; Dahlstrom, 303)

Note that the question does not at all arise whether "reason" and common sense reach the same conclusion. This is clear, because common sense is not different from reason. But if so, what is then the role of systematic thought and what the contribution of specialized disciplines like metaphysics and natural theology?

In his last publication, Mendelssohn brings an enlightening analogy:

> I am an ardent admirer of demonstrations in metaphysics, and firmly convinced that the main truths of natural religion are as capable of apodictic proof as any proposition of mathematics. Nevertheless, even my conviction of religious truths is not absolutely dependent on metaphysical arguments such that it must stand and fall with them. . . . Petrus Ramus raised many doubts concerning the axioms and postulates of Euclid, but remained nevertheless completely convinced of the truth of Euclid's *Elements.* (*An die Freunde Lessings, JubA* 3.2, 197)

The important distinction introduced here is between knowing a fact and systematically proving it from the axioms of reason alone. These are different projects, as I will now elaborate. The truths of mathematics are established on the basis of mathematical axioms and postulates; these are accepted presuppositions in the relevant mathematical theory or discipline. In addition to such disciplinary principles, we have philosophical principles that are universal (e.g., the laws of logic or metaphysical principles). Philosophers may engage in the justification of disciplinary presuppositions on the basis of philosophical universal principles. However, as philosophers, they accept the body of mathematics as valid, whether justified philosophically or not.[10] Thus for many centuries philosopher-mathematicians attempted to prove that exactly one straight line connects two points and that it is the shortest between these points, although the cynics provoked them with the observation that this is known to every dog chasing prey.[11] To know the fact is the business of sound reason in mathematics, a so-called mathematical common sense; to prove the fact from first principles—that is, on the basis of logic and metaphysical principles only—is the business of philosophy.[12] Although mathematicians did not yet succeed in proving these propositions in Mendelssohn's time, nobody doubted the truth of the geometrical propositions dependent on them, least of all Mendelssohn.[13]

It also follows that what is "sound reason" in one context may be "theoretical reason" in another and vice versa. Consider again the question whether the straight line is the shortest line between two points. In choosing our way from one place to the other, we take the straight rather than the zigzag or curved path without further thought. On the basis of Euclid's *Elements* it can be proven that a zigzag line between two points is longer than the straight line. This is mathematical common sense. But that a *curved* line is longer than the straight line between the same points is not proven by standard means and, therefore, not part of this mathematical "common sense." It belongs to everyday "common sense" by which we live, and, in mathematics, it belongs to "theoretical reason" that goes back to mathematical or philosophical first principles.[14]

Similar considerations are valid in religion. Whenever possible, Mendelssohn wishes to demonstrate truths of religion philosophically, but their truth and a person's knowledge that they are true do not depend on these philosophical underpinnings. I believe—says Mendelssohn—that the evidence of natural religion is as brightly obvious and as incontrovertibly certain to unspoiled human reason that has not been led astray, as any proposition of geometry. Mendelssohn quotes a story of a Greenlander who pointed to dawn and said, "See, brother, the young day! How beautiful must be its author!" And he ascribes to this "natural, foolproof conclusion" the same "evidence" as to a geometrical demonstration.[15]

So what do we need demonstrations of reasons for? From Mendelssohn's very early writings to the very last we find one and the same answer: such demonstrations are helpful when common sense is attacked by skepticism and sophistry, by an "Epicurus or a Lucretius, a Helvétius or a Hume." Once criticized by the skeptics, refined metaphysical arguments are called for to reinstall truth:

> At bottom, the material is always the same, — there endowed with all the raw but vigorous juices which nature gives it, here with the refined good taste of art, easier to digest but only for the weak. (*Jerusalem*, 95)

This is so in general philosophy, in natural theology, and also in practical philosophy (*JubA* 2, 313; Dahlstrom, 293; *JubA* 2, 328–29).[16] It is because of confusion of common sense by superstition, clerical deceit, and sophistry that philosophy is called upon to rectify what sophistry has spoiled. Its purpose is to restore our peace of mind that was disturbed by sophistry. It should produce an ordered series of reasons and consequences that can be easily recalled when needed and reaffirm the basic truths of natural religion required for tranquility (*Phaedon, JubA* 3.1, 81).[17] Rigorous demonstration of the truths already known by common sense helps to refute the skeptic, but in finding truth it is inferior to common sense. In his *Phaedon*, Mendelssohn argued for the immortality of the soul in an "exoteric" fashion, using "merely *bon sens*" and avoiding the "esoteric" jargon of the Leibnizians—with no loss of substance.[18]

If a conflict arises between reason and common sense, there are two lessons to remember. First, since they are but different forms of applying the same reason and both normally lead to truth, it must be possible to resolve the conflict. Second, in cases when a quick decision is necessary, trained sound reason is to be preferred.[19] Mendelssohn recommends his method of "orientation" for cases of conflict between philosophical reasoning and common sense. This simply means looking for the last point of agreement and carefully checking every step from there on. Carefully inspected, error will be detected. In most cases common sense should be preferred, unless there is not only a perfect demonstration to the contrary but also an explanation why common sense came off track.[20]

This is also the lesson of Mendelssohn's metaphysical epitome, the *Morgenstunden*. Mendelssohn there narrates an allegorical dream in which a group is guided in the Alps by a young, coarse native of moderate intelligence and a gaunt woman of "enthusiastic physiognomy." At a crossroad, the guides head in opposite directions, leaving the group undecided whom to follow. An elderly lady representing reason (as such) comes by and reassures the hesitant wanderers that their guides, common sense and speculation, disagree at times but only for a short while and for trifling reasons. She usually decides in favor of common sense. So does Mendelssohn. Moreover, reason must "speak most decisively in favor of speculation if I am to abandon common sense." Finally, reason must also explain the error of common sense if he, Mendelssohn, should follow it, but not vice versa. The *onus probandi* is not equally distributed, because common sense is in principle more reliable than metaphysics (*Morgenstunden, JubA* 3.2, 81–82). With the same arguments and wording, Mendelssohn supported "friends of common sense who attacked the Bishop" (Berkeley) and were not led astray by the "subtleties" of speculation.[21]

Mendelssohn's partisanship for common sense is likely to be misunderstood and was often misunderstood, both sincerely and not. As we have seen, the dilemma is not between reason and another faculty, different in kind, or between reason and belief or faith.[22] Rather, it is the alternative between well-established knowledge both practical and theoretical and a gapless logical proof *ex principiis*. This duality of truth and philosophical justification, common sense and philosophical reason, the independence of certainty from demonstration from first principles, has important implications for Mendelssohn's philosophy. Mendelssohn did not believe in religious, moral, or metaphysical progress in the sense of extending our positive knowledge. Religious, moral, and basic metaphysical truths are accessible at all times to people with common sense. But Mendelssohn did believe in refinement of arguments. Truth and knowledge may remain unchanged, but demonstrations change. Our ancestors were not less pious or moral than we are, nor did they know fewer metaphysical truths. In fact, "new metaphysical truths, if you wish, were not invented since centuries. . . . In order to say something entirely new, you must almost say nonsense (*Ungereimtes*)" (*JubA* 7, 45–46). But the arguments for the truths we know may be refined in history.

When presenting in his *Phaedon* Plato's true doctrine of the immateriality of the soul, Mendelssohn replaced Plato's arguments with modern ones, be it to pay tribute to "the taste of our times," or because Plato's demonstrations "seem, to us at least, so shallow and bizarre that they hardly deserve a serious refutation." "But I cannot decide," he wrote, "whether this follows from our better insight into metaphysics or from our bad insight into the philosophical language of the ancients" (*JubA* 3.1, 8). Whatever the answer concerning the ancient philosophical arguments may be, the doctrine itself that the soul is immaterial (and therefore immortal) did not at all change. Another example clearly shows what Mendelssohn had in mind when he mentioned the difference in language used to express or demonstrate a doctrine. Arguing that mathematical truth is a priori, Mendelssohn first refers to Plato's doctrine of learning as "recollection" in the *Meno,* then to "more recent philosophers" (Leibniz and followers) and their principle that "No new concepts that have not already been in the mind enter there by learning"; finally he refers to "oriental sages" who maintain "that the soul grasped the entire world prior to this life but then forgot everything when it entered this world." The oriental and the modern views are one and the same, believes Mendelssohn. The moderns "have merely removed the mystical aspect that lends it [the oriental view] so absurd an appearance" (Dahlstrom, 258–59; *JubA* 2, 275–76).[23]

The same reservation concerning progress in metaphysics, perhaps with a differently inclined prejudice, is repeated in the preface to the *Morgenstunden.* Mendelssohn reflects there on the decline of the Leibniz-Wolffian school, he admits that his philosophy is no longer "the philosophy of these times," and he modestly suggests that "better forces," especially Kant, should undertake the reformation of metaphysics (*JubA* 3.2, 4–5). Whether he thought that this time, too, it is more fashion than real progress that makes his arguments seem outdated, or indeed meant what he said, in any case he did not refrain from publishing the book, hence did not believe that his arguments were wrong or worthless. The truths of metaphysics have been well known for centuries thanks to common sense, and it is only their specialized demonstration from principles that changes in history.

Moreover, common sense is superior to metaphysics in yet another respect. Although they are not strict, commonsense arguments for the existence of God are more persuasive than philosophical demonstrations. Whereas strict metaphysical demonstrations are "the fortresses that protect a country against enemy [i.e., skeptics'] attacks," they are "not the most comfortable and pleasant places in which to live." Commonsense knowledge of God—say, the arguments from the beautiful design of the world or from its purposiveness—give us "the sweetest comfort, the most refreshing consolation as well as the very fire and animation of knowledge that transfers into the capacity to desire and occasions decisions that break out into actions," and this, after all, "should be our foremost purpose in contemplating divine properties" (*JubA* 2, 313; Dahlstrom, 293). Mendelssohn returns to this topic in his *Jerusalem*. He distinguishes there between "reasons that motivate the will" and "reasons that persuade by their truth" (*JubA* 8, 110; *Jerusalem*, 40), but the arguments of common sense fulfill both functions. He ascribes to them the power of geometrical demonstrations, and at the same time they also motivate to action.

The result of these elaborations is simple, and it contradicts Mendelssohn's reputation. Mendelssohn was not at all a "rationalist" who trusted pure reason only and suspected that the senses and everyday knowledge deceive us. On the contrary, he trusted "sound reason" in everyday life, in the sciences, and in natural theology. In judging truth, metaphysics is inferior to sound reason. Metaphysics serves two purposes: its main purpose is to fend off the attacks of the skeptics; its second purpose is the explication and systematization of knowledge of common sense.

This result raises a question. If sound reason is so successful, why is metaphysics—which applies the same reason in a more systematic way—inferior to it? Whence the errors in metaphysics? And why can also common sense fall into error?

Common sense can err either when it transgresses the limits of its competence or when it is purposefully deceived. Truth and certainty of our commonsense knowledge are not in doubt as long as it judges within the respective domains, that is, in the sphere of our experience or by means of an appropriate symbolic system, as in mathematics. In metaphysics, however, we have no specialized symbolic means but depend on natural language. However, natural language reflects our experience with physical objects in our immediate environment, whereas metaphysics deals with objects that are in principle not in the realm of our experience. Our language as well as the body and models of our everyday knowledge are adequate to the empirical world and exactly, therefore, may be inadequate to metaphysics. This is similar and yet different in the sciences. In cosmological matters, for example, the uneducated views of the man in the street, also called commonsensical views, may be misguided. But they can be corrected by science on the basis of new empirical knowledge and the employment of specialized means of scientific research.[24] In science we remain in the domain of experience. This is different in metaphysics. Although metaphysics deals with objects that are essentially different from those of everyday practice, we nevertheless apply to both the same means of natural language. There is no special philosophical language adequate to its specific enterprise. Mendelssohn does not formulate the general conclusion arising from his discussion of this topic, but his following discussion of the difference between mathematics and metaphysics leaves little doubt about it: The difference between reasoning in everyday life (including natural theology), in mathematics, and in the sciences on the one hand and metaphysics on the other does not lie in the organ of thought (it is reason in all these cases) but in the material and symbolic means on which they depend.

THE SUPERIORITY OF MATHEMATICS TO METAPHYSICS, ESSENTIAL AND ARBITRARY SIGNS, POSSIBLE AND REAL OBJECTS

What, then, are the means employed in the various disciplines? Mathematics uses "real and essential signs" (*reelle und wesentliche Zeichen*). These "agree in their nature and connection with the nature and the connection of the thoughts" (*JubA* 2, 281; Dahlstrom, 264). In geometry the simple and composite signs correspond to simple and composite objects (lines and figures). It is therefore that in geometry nothing can be represented *in abstracto,* but everything is represented *in concreto.* The sign of the class of triangles is itself an individual triangle (*JubA* 2, 282; Dahlstrom, 265). In arithmetic and algebra the simple signs—numbers, letters, and combinative signs—are arbitrary. "Yet in the composite signs and formulas and equations, everything is determined [i.e., not arbitrary] and agrees exactly with the thoughts" (*JubA* 2, 281–82; Dahlstrom, 264).

Not so in metaphysics. Here the objects are represented by language, and "[e]verything in the language of philosophers is still arbitrary. The words and the connections among them contain nothing that would essentially agree with the nature of thoughts and the connections among them" (*JubA* 2, 290; Dahlstrom, 272). Since mathematical signs agree either in their nature and connection or at least in their connections with the nature and the connection of the thoughts, we can reason according to the rules of the symbolic system and need not refer to the signified subject matter before applying to it the conclusions of our reasoning. Following Lambert, Mendelssohn therefore characterizes a "scientific" symbolic system such that the symbolic system can be substituted (*verwechselt*) for what it stands for:

> The signs of concepts and objects are scientific when they agree with the signified with such precision that the theory of the subject matter and the theory of its signs may be substituted for each other, i.e., when from the observation of the signs with respect to what we wish to know follows exactly what would follow from the observation of the subject matter.[25]

Operating with such a symbolic system is what Leibniz called "blind thoughts" (*cogitationes caecae*), and the power of a good symbolic system lies exactly in this blindness, in that we mechanically operate with signs without a thought about what they represent.[26] Not so in natural language. The meaning of composite terms and of whole sentences is not composed of the meaning of their constituents, and "blind thoughts" are therefore not possible. We cannot operate with natural language without semantic considerations. Natural Language has no algorithm. Rather, "there is nothing in the designation by means of which [the soul] could be guided to the nature of the designated subject matter. . . . Hence the soul must constantly fix its attention on the arbitrary combination of signs and what is designated" (*JubA* 2, 290; Dahlstrom, 272).

Besides the differences in the nature of their objects and of the symbolic systems that serve them, there is another important difference between mathematics and metaphysics. Both metaphysics and geometry raise claims concerning necessary connections among concepts. However, in geometry they refer to possible objects, in metaphysics to real objects. Geometrical truths remain valid irrespective of the existence of material triangles in the world. Metaphysical assertions should refer to real, not merely possible, objects. An atheist may concede that a being endowed with all perfections must also possess the perfection of existence and therefore exist, but he can still doubt that there is a being endowed with all perfections and therefore also that it exists.

> We do not owe the philosopher thanks for the mere possibility of something if he does not know how to render it actual. Hence, far more is demanded of the philosopher than of the mathematician. (*JubA* 2, 293; Dahlstrom, 275)

Therefore, the attack of the idealists may be lethal for metaphysics, but it has no import at all for mathematics. The mathematician may be content as long as this mere "appearance" is constant and unchanging (*JubA* 2, 284–85, 292–93; Dahlstrom, 266–67, 274–75). Not so metaphysics; and this explains why the claims of metaphysics are not merely less conspicuous than those of mathematics but also less certain. As long as metaphysics limits its claims to analytic conceptual relations, it is as certain as mathematics; as soon as it claims the existence of its objects— and this claim is essential to metaphysics—it has to shoulder a burden of proof of which mathematics knows nothing, and it often fails. Surely there is one exception. From the concept of God a direct argument leads to the reality of its referent, but this (in addition to *cogito ergo sum*) is specific to this object, the existence of which is independently established by common sense, and does not apply generally in metaphysics.

Can we compare the claims of metaphysics to those of applied mathematics? After all, the latter also makes claims concerning real objects in the world and not merely about conceptual connections. Here a further difference shows that further buttresses Mendelssohn's skepticism concerning metaphysics, in fact all knowledge of objects other than those of the five senses. Take, for example, a geometrical theorem concerning triangles. Does it apply to any object in the world? All we need to answer the question positively is to ascertain that a given material object is a triangle. It then follows that all true theorems about triangles are true of this object too. Can we be sure that an object is a triangle without a *petitio principii,* that is, without presupposing that all the relevant theorems are true of it? Mendelssohn affirms that we can.

> I regard, for example, a figure that is present and notice that I can regard each of its sides from an angle at which it appears to vanish completely or to be similar to a mere point. From this I infer that it is a rectilinear figure and thus the figure at hand possesses all the properties which are inseparable from the concept of a rectilinear figure. I count its sides and ascertain that there are three of them; this figure is thus a triangle, and I can assert everything of it that is connected with the concept of a triangle. (*JubA* 2, 283; Dahlstrom, 266; cf. *JubA* 3.2, 82–83)

We can thus escape the tautology that all properties of a triangle apply to a material triangle if and only if all the properties of a triangle apply to it. The requirement is weaker. It suffices that an object has the essential properties named in its definition, and then all its proven properties may be ascribed to it. A triangle is defined in Euclid as a rectilinear figure enclosed by three straight lines. Since the given figure was found to satisfy this definition, all propositions concerning triangles are applicable to it. We know that geometrical propositions apply to their ideal objects because the signs we use (or their combinations) are "essential" and not arbitrary signs, and they apply to physical objects because our senses and common sense are reliable and show us whether a material object possesses the properties named in the definition. This is different with metaphysics: We practice metaphysics with the arbitrary signs of natural language, and since the objects of metaphysics are not empirical, we cannot ascertain that our concepts apply to them.

The result of this discussion is hence this: In metaphysics, no less than in mathematics, we have strict inferences that are evident. However, in mathematics we also have a system of representation and algorithms that allow the replacement of thought by mechanical operations (Leibniz's "blind thoughts"). We have no similar means in metaphysics, and yet our expectations from metaphysics are higher than those from mathematics. Metaphysics should present knowledge of real, not of merely possible, objects (as in mathematics). Metaphysics is hence similar to applied and not to pure mathematics. However, applied mathematics is based on the one hand on "blind thoughts" (of pure mathematics) and on the other on sense perception, and on the coordination of these two sources of knowledge. Metaphysics lacks "blind thoughts," and the very nature of her objects excludes sense perception. No wonder, then, that metaphysical knowledge falls short of mathematical.

Epistemic and Linguistic Skepticism: Metaphysics and Common Sense

Let us now look at the consequences from Mendelssohn's stance for some metaphysical questions. Our perceptions teach us of the inter-actions of bodies, and from these we infer their properties—but also not more than this: we cannot know their inner essences, and Mendelssohn argued that we should not get entangled in hopeless speculations over this. Kant referred to these arguments as mere "feats" or "tricks" (*Kunststücke*) adduced to evade a controversy. At stake was the fundamental controversy between "idealists" and "dualists." In lecture 7 of the *Morgenstunden* Mendelssohn argues that this controversy will finally turn out to be merely a *logomachia,* a quarrel over words (*JubA* 3.2, 61). He presents the contest as follows. We perceive phenomena. The idealist argues that these perceptions are merely "accidents of the human mind"; the dualist argues that real objects correspond to our perceptions. He argues that the agreement among our perceptions and between those of our fellow men is grounded in that they are all evoked by their common real objects. Perceptions are copies of things. The properties excited in our mind are copies of the original (*Urbild*), for example, extension, motion, figure, impenetrability, for material bodies; thought, sentiments, passions, and so on, for the soul (*JubA* 3.2, 59). The idealist maintains that we know our perceptions but not whether anything corresponds to them, simply because we have no access to this objective world other than through these perceptions. Mendelssohn himself believes that the disagreement is pointless because the issue transcends human knowledge. Similarly, the question what something is in and for itself (*an und für sich selbst*) is meaningless. It consists of "empty words, which have no meaning" (*JubA* 3.2, 60). What we know of material or immaterial objects are their actions and passions, that is, how they act and react—and from these we directly infer their properties, but we do not know their "essences," which are allegedly "beyond" that. Let me illustrate the point. When pressing on a body, the resistance we experience teaches us that it is "impenetrable." And conversely: the assertion that the body is "impenetrable" merely means that this body moves as a whole when pushed and does not coexist in the same space with another. The wish to transcend this knowledge and ask what corresponds to impenetrability in the essence of a substance in and for itself is meaningless.

Now, intentionally or not, it seems that Mendelssohn adopts the Kantian distinctions between phenomena and "things in themselves" and also Kant's critique of metaphysics. It is, therefore, quite surprising to read Kant's critique of these views of Mendelssohn. In fact, we witness a complete reversal of the expected roles: Mendelssohn is the philosopher who emphasizes the limitations of knowledge and refuses to engage in idle speculations, while Kant assumes the role of the "dogmatic" metaphysician and insists that we can determine some properties of things in themselves. Kant refers both to the concept of a material body (and to his *Metaphysical Foundations of Natural Science*) and to the concept of the soul to argue that with both kinds of objects,

> if we were to know effects of a thing that could indeed be properties of the thing in itself, then we would not be allowed to ask anymore what the thing is outside of these properties; for then it is exactly that which is given through these properties.

But how do we know what properties are those that "could indeed be properties of the thing in itself"?

> Consider only how you bring about the concept of God as highest intelligence. You think in it nothing but *true* reality, i.e., something that is not only opposed to negations (as one commonly maintains) but also and primarily to realities in the *appearance* (*realitas Phaenomenon*), such as all realities that have to be given to us through the senses and are therefore called *realitas apparens* . . . and you will have properties of the things in themselves that you can apply to other things outside of God.[27]

Now, the concept of "true reality" and of God as *summa realitatis* in which all objects are comprised or in which they partake, can be read as Kant's turn to Spinozism, or as a relict from traditional Wolffian metaphysics, to which Kant was committed before the "Copernican turn."[28] This question is of no importance in the present context. Essential to our discussion is that Mendelssohn argues in the typical fashion of empiricists, "bottom up," from experience to the properties of things—and refuses to transcend the limits of experience; whereas Kant argues like rationalists, "top down," from the concept of God as "the sum of reality" (*summa realitatis*), the single source of beings, to the properties of "things in themselves." What is most important, however, is that Kant clearly recognized Mendelssohn's rejection of metaphysics and adherence to common sense.[29]

The limitation Mendelssohn puts on knowledge refers to all non-empirical objects: God, souls, the inner nature of material bodies, and beliefs. This latter kind of objects is essential to his understanding of the place of faith in religion. Consider what Mendelssohn says concerning "principles of faith":

> The perceptions of the internal sense are in themselves rarely so palpable that the mind is able to retain them securely and to give them expression as often as it may be desired. . . . Many things for which I would suffer martyrdom today may perhaps appear problematic to me tomorrow. If, in addition, I must also put these internal perceptions into words and signs, or swear to words and signs which other men lay before me, the uncertainty will be still greater. My neighbor and I cannot possibly connect the very same words with the very same internal sensations, for we cannot compare them, liken them to one another and correct them without again resorting to words. We cannot illustrate the words by things, but must again have recourse to signs and words, and finally, to metaphors; because, with the help of this artifice, we reduce, as it were, the concepts of the internal sense to external sensory perceptions. But, given this fact, how much confusion and indistinctiveness are bound to remain in the signification of words, and how greatly must the ideas differ which different men, in different ages and centuries, connect with the same external signs and word! (*Jeursalem*, 66)[30]

We cannot precisely know the proper meaning of formulas of belief, or that we all share the same one. We cannot penetrate the metaphors. Mendelssohn, therefore, argues that the alleged opposition between Leibniz's and Spinoza's philosophy is due to a different "misinterpretation of one and the same metaphor" (*Morgenstunden, JubA* 3,2, 124). But if neither the meaning of terms nor that we share the same meaning is certain, then skeptical conclusions seem called for. Whereas Mendelssohn says on the one hand that metaphysical demonstrations from principles are necessary to refute skepticism and idealists, he also concedes that metaphysics is rather the problem than the answer to skepticism. In the first part of *Jerusalem* Mendelssohn remarks that he was "perhaps one of those who are the farthest removed from that disease of the soul" called skepticism (*Jerusalem*, 66–67), and yet in the same breath he also admits that he had to cure himself repeatedly from this disease and has "become aware of how difficult it is, and what little hope one has of success (*Jerusalem*, 67).

In *Jerusalem*, as well as already in his prize-winning essay, Mendelssohn hence presents a skeptic's position regarding beliefs about objects of the inner sense and metaphysics. He nevertheless rejects the title "skeptic," presumably both because he never doubted common-sensical knowledge and because he associates skepticism with the doubt concerning the existence of the external world. In the *Morgenstunden* of 1785 he names the latter position together with so-called Spinozism from which it follows that I am not an existing substance but merely a thought of God and concludes: "I cannot believe that any of these absurdities was ever seriously asserted. It seems that some wanted to put reason to the test whether it can keep pace with common sense; whether it can incontrovertibly demonstrate according to the laws of thought what common sense takes for granted" (*Morgenstunden, JubA* 3.2, 79; see also 82).

We know already that the office of metaphysics is to "incontrovertibly demonstrate" what common sense already knows and that in case of disagreement between metaphysics and common sense the latter overrules the former. But now we also learn that error is indigenous to metaphysics. Entire schools, skepticism, Spinozism, idealism, are fundamentally misconceived. However, "[t]hough this be madness, yet there is method in't," and such a widely spread phenomenon needs not only correction by common sense but also an explanation of its existence. Mendelssohn's suggestion comes as no surprise now: metaphysics is often misguided because it must apply language that reflects worldly experience to transcendent objects. The remedy is also clear: distrust metaphysics, distrust natural language when applied to nonsensual objects, hold fast to commonsense knowledge of the empirical world.

Commonsense knowledge of our physical environment is embodied in natural language, which is also used in the production of new knowledge of the same kind. But here a social and temporal differentiation must be introduced: learned and unlearned people naturally attach somewhat different meanings to words, and with the change in the state of our knowledge and culture the socially accepted meanings of terms also change. This, however, does not happen simultaneously in all strata of society: "But the common man still clings to the meaning to which he is accustomed and still adheres to his usual mode of speaking, which has given rise to much confusion in religious matters" (*Jerusalem,* 59 n.).[31] The "common man" hence lags behind the educated, because he knows only what is embodied in natural language, and natural language embodies past commonsensical views. Linguistic meanings change slowly, such that they necessarily lag behind science and philosophy. Educated people keep abreast with development. The mechanism of progress shows for example in this. The reflection triggered by Hobbes's provocative theory resulted in an improved understanding of some metaphysical concepts and the introduction of new distinctions between them (the differences between physical and moral ability, between might and right): "These distinctions have become so intimately fused with our language that, nowadays, the refutation of Hobbes's system seems to be a matter of common sense, and to be accomplished, as it were, by language itself" (*Jerusalem,* 36). Thus natural language does not reflect most advanced knowledge, but it is the best indication for the state of culture and *Bildung* of a nation. It develops with science and culture and reflects the current stage of a nation.[32]

In conclusion, it is clear, I believe, that Mendelssohn was so skeptical concerning metaphysics and objects of the "inner sense" that he had to repeatedly cure himself of this disease of the mind—evidently with little success. And yet he also said that metaphysics should defend us against skepticism. The seeming inconsistency is easy to resolve. The metaphysics Mendelssohn recommended was a systematic presentation of the views that were also accepted by common sense.

Metaphysical Controversies as Disputes over Metaphors

Mendelssohn's skepticism concerning knowledge of nonempirical objects justifies to some extent his view that philosophical controversies are mostly mere *logomachiae,* disputes over words. Moreover, this was commonplace in philosophy in his time.[33] And yet it earned Mendelssohn the reputation of a hypocrite. Condillac, Mendelssohn, and others believed that controversies would be resolved if we could substitute "ideas" for our words; we would then see that we think the same and differ only in expression.[34] This is especially so in metaphysics. On the one hand, metaphysics cannot avail itself of the senses, nor, on the other hand, rely on formal language with well-defined terms and algorithms. Its objects are not tangible, and it depends, like all abstract thought,[35] solely on natural language with all its imperfections.

We saw above that Mendelssohn considered the controversy between some metaphysical systems "absurdities" and the controversy between materialists, idealists, and dualists but a dispute over words, of more interest to the linguist than to the philosopher. In the beginning of his discussion of Spinozism in his *Morning Hours* (Morgenstunden), Mendelssohn admonishes the reader:

> We hover here in a region of ideas that are too far removed from immediate knowledge; where we express our thoughts only by means of the silhouettes of words; and even attain knowledge merely with the help of these silhouettes. How readily can an error occur here! How great the danger to take the silhouettes for the things. You know how much I am inclined to say that all quarrels of the philosophic schools are mere disputes over words, or at least that they originally derive from such disputes. (*Morgenstunden, JubA* 3.2, 105)[36]

The claim that a philosophical controversy is, in fact, a *logomachia* must be substantiated. It is the task of philosophical analysis to show that behind the different words stand the same ideas. Thus the main bone of contention between the Wolffians and Spinoza was their respective concept of substance. Mendelssohn suggests that his analysis will show whether the differences between Spinoza and "our common concepts" differ in *re* or only in *verbis* (*Morgenstunden, JubA* 3.2, 106). Spinoza's view that there is only one substance follows cogently only because the ambiguities of the terms *infinity, independence,* and therefore *substance* were not clarified. If Spinoza wishes not to name those beings "substances" that are independent in his specific sense of "independence"— "then the dispute is merely over words" (*JubA* 3.2, 107). Mendelssohn also applies the same technique to the word *necessity* (*JubA* 3.2, 109) and to other terms. Finally, he discusses the alleged opposition between Leibniz and Spinoza, namely, whether God created the world (the best of all possible worlds) or whether—since there is only one possible/ necessary world—it makes no sense to distinguish possibility from reality, and "creation" is therefore meaningless. Mendelssohn reduces the difference to the question whether

> God caused the thought of the best contingent world to radiate, to emanate, to pour forth—or what metaphor shall I use? (for the subtlety can scarcely be expressed save by means of metaphors); whether he caused the light to fulgurate from him, or simply to shine within himself; whether the source remained a spring, or whether it became a wellspring which poured itself forth into an overflowing flood. . . . The consequences of the two systems still seem to be far apart, and in fact this is due to a misinterpretation of one and the same metaphor: at times God is placed too figuratively in the world; at times the world is placed too figuratively in God. Sincere love of the truth soon leads us back to our point of departure and shows that we have simply become entangled in words. Do without words, friend of wisdom, and embrace thy brother![37]

The difference lies in the interpretation of "in," a spatial metaphor for God's relation to the world. If we think with Leibniz of creation, then the "world" is thought first as being "in" God's understanding, then, as real, "outside" of it. With Spinoza, we think of God as immanent, that is, as "inside" the world. Now, the inference from the world as we experience it to the existence of its unique omniscient and omnipo-

tent author belongs to sound reason and is secure. Problems arise when
we speak of this author himself or when we attempt to understand how
this unique author relates to (produces? appears in?) the experienced
plurality of his world. Here only metaphors of light and liquid are at our
disposal, all of them inadequate. Moreover, these limitations of our
knowledge are not temporary; they necessarily arise because of the nature of our knowledge and the subject matter involved. In principle,
such controversies cannot be resolved, and therefore it makes no sense
to engage in them. This is so because the analysis of concepts to their
alleged last primitive constituents is infinite and, therefore, in principle
not the lot of humans. Thus, whereas in some cases the analysis of terms
can settle the dispute, in other cases we cannot penetrate the ideas but
must stop at the level of metaphors. Here it is essential to constantly remember the difference between sign and signified: "How great the danger to take the silhouettes for the things," said Mendelssohn (*Morgenstunden, JubA* 3.2, 105). When metaphors represent the immaterial
realm with pictures taken from the material world, sign and signified
are essentially different. Inferences from the properties of the representation to those of the represented are likely to lead to error, and in the
case of the divine they are bound to lead to idolatry. God cannot and
should not be imagined as our pictorial metaphors suggest. Rather than
engage in controversies over such metaphors, it is more reasonable to
treat them all with great reservation.[38] Skepticism concerning metaphysics on the grounds that it is in fact based on metaphors is a permanent
theme in philosophy.[39]

In his review of Lambert's *New Organon,* Mendelssohn summarizes Lambert's discussion of metaphors and their contribution to controversies over words. Most susceptible to misunderstandings are abstract concepts of the second degree, that is, those that are composed
of abstract concepts of the first degree, which, in their turn, are formed
from words referring to sensible objects and actions. This is exactly
how Mendelssohn explains the impossibility of adequately referring
to objects of the inner sense. These concepts are metaphors of the second degree: "We cannot illustrate the words by things, but must again
have recourse to signs and words, and finally, to metaphors" (*Jerusalem,* 66).

The Semantic Triangle and Metaphysics

Why is metaphysics dependent on vague and ambiguous metaphors? The reason is that most words are conventional signs and that they are not proper names. A pictogram directly signifies an object, and also a proper name directly refers to an object without mediation of a "meaning." But most spoken or written words signify meanings (concept, mental image), which in their turn signify objects. A pictogram refers to an object by similitude. Words of natural language, both oral and written, are conventional and do not depict their objects. A picture of a lion refers directly to the lions in the world due to the resemblance of the picture and the pictured.[40] The picture can be compared with the object and the similarity recognized. This reference is independent of my mental representation of a lion. The advantage of pictorial representation is hence that the reference of the signs can be determined independently of their meaning, that is, on different linguistic and individual conceptualizations.

This is different with natural language. Since Aristotle, linguistic representation has been explained by a triad: the sign, the mental representation (or idea), and the object (the signified). (This was later called the "semantic triangle.") The sign—for example, a word whether written or spoken—is said to evoke the representation in the mind, and this representation refers to the object in the world. When I say "lion" the word evokes my concept or my mental image of a lion, and this refers to the lions in the world. But here misunderstandings are possible because we cannot know that in using the same word I and my interlocutor mean the same concept or mental image and hence refer to the same object.

Nevertheless, we can exclude ambiguities also from basic words of natural language by pointing to the intended object or action and naming it. In the twentieth century, this possibility was cast in doubt,[41] but in most cases it is nevertheless helpful. From this conception it follows that when we want to refer to abstract objects, we must refer to concrete objects and use their name figuratively. But the speaker's figurative meaning cannot be compared and adjusted to that of another speaker. Mendelssohn does not provide an example of metaphors of the second degree, which form the metaphysical vocabulary, but they are not difficult to find. Take, for example, Mendelssohn's coinage "living script" for the ritual. It is a mixed metaphor that cannot be understood verbatim. Script does not belong to the kind of things that can be either alive or dead; it is not animated. As a metaphor for the cult, the expression uses both "script" and "living" metaphorically, "script" for ritual, "living" for its meaning (in contradistinction to the "dead letter"). The first metaphor likens the ritual to language, the second to an organism. In the next step we realize that Mendelssohn uses "organism," a living body, as a metaphor for language or words. The word is likened to a living body consisting of "body" and "soul." "Body" is a metaphor for the physical linguistic sign (script, spoken word), "soul" a metaphor for its meaning.[42] In *Jerusalem* he says that ritual (script, word, body) without religious intention (meaning combined with emotions and will) is "dead puppetry" (another metaphor). These metaphors are further elaborated in the introduction to his commentary on Maimonides' *Millot ha-Higayyon* (*JubA* 15, 25). A word without its sense is like a dead body without a soul, and a soul without a body is invisible. Mendelssohn continues: "And this connection between the spiritual (רוחני) and the corporeal (גשמי) is very wondrous and on this we say a daily benediction 'He who acts wondrously.'"[43] Mendelssohn gives a reference to a commentary of Rabbi Moses Isserles (1520–72) on *Shulchan Arukh* (*Orach Chayyim*, §6) where this benediction is discussed.[44] But the point of the benediction is not the corporeal and the spiritual but literal corporeality, the fragility of the human body. The phrase commented on likens the human body to a water skin full of air from which, if pierced, the wind/spirit/soul (רוח) escapes, thus causing death. And yet, though full of holes, the human body nevertheless retains its wind/spirit/soul, thanks to God's "acting wondrously."[45]

Now, working our way bottom-up, we begin with the motion of air, "wind," meaning also human breath and metaphorically the soul.[46] "Soul" and "spirit" (literally, "wind") are then used as a metaphor of the second order for the meaning of a spoken or written expression. The audible tone and the written letters are named metaphorically its "body." In the third degree, "life" (evoking the association of a living body compounded of body and soul but abstracting from the body) is used (like "soul" and "spirit") as a metaphor for the meaning of the physical action of the ritual. Here a specific ambiguity opens up: We often distinguish the "literal meaning" of an expression from its "spirit," which refers to the author's intention as opposed to the literal meaning of an expression ("the dead letter"). "Life" can hence stand for "meaning" as "soul" for the author's intention as opposed to the lexical meaning. We hence have a metaphor of the fourth degree. A precise discussion of Mendelssohn's expression "living script" would first have to unpack, if at all possible, the different components of the meaning and connotations of wind/spirit/soul/meaning and ascribe them to the proper layer.

We thus see that Mendelssohn's skepticism concerning all knowledge of objects other than those of the senses is essentially dependent on his philosophy of language in particular and of representation in general, as he elaborated it in his first essay on the evidence in metaphysics. We also see that Mendelssohn and Lambert thought along similar lines about the cardinal question of the dependence of abstract concepts on metaphors. No wonder, therefore, that a short time after the publication of his review of Lambert's book, Mendelssohn wrote to Abbt, "Had I read Herr Lambert's *New Organon* some years ago, my prize essay would certainly have remained in my drawer."[47]

The result of all these considerations is this. It is easy to reach consensus concerning matters of fact; it is difficult in metaphysics. Education, prejudices, and so on, suffice to incline our judgment in this rather than the opposite direction in these abstract and intricate questions, and even more so because our most vital interests are involved. Here the "slightest impetus" suffices to bring reason off track. This is no reason to despair if we remember the respective roles of metaphysics and sound reason. Therefore, when we finally attain certainty in metaphysics, we should stick to it but never forget that this is our conviction and that others may reach opposite conclusions.[48] Needless to say that the tolerance shown here in spite of certainty, a tolerance that would not have been shown in the case of science, testifies to the fact that this is subjective certainty, not objective necessity.

Whatever we may think of Mendelssohn's motives for endorsing the suggestion that many philosophical controversies are but disputes over words, it is clear that the arguments for his view are serious and important: the elusive nature of metaphysical objects and the unreliability of natural language in philosophical matters. And this also is clear: Mendelssohn's reputation as a dogmatic metaphysician has little to recommend itself. Indeed, Mendelssohn philosophized in the framework of the then-predominant Wolffian metaphysics but did not trust it when it did not agree with common sense. His philosophy of language is mainly indebted to the empiricist Locke and to the sensualist Condillac. He trusted empirical knowledge and mathematics (and their synthesis in mathematical science), as well as the power of reason in general; but he distrusted human knowledge of objects that are not accessible to sense experience (objects of the inner sense and of metaphysics), especially when it depends on long chains of argument in natural language. Blindly following such chains of reasoning is what Mendelssohn critically named "consequenzerey."

CONSEQUENZEREY

Salomon Maimon and later readers suggested that Mendelssohn compromised intellectual integrity for the sake of his cherished (conservative) socioreligious stance. There seems to be much to support this interpretation. In fact, Mendelssohn himself says that he would give precedence to morals and welfare over theoretical truth, and at the end of his life he also explicitly named personal "happiness" as a valid consideration in deciding on religious practices. Nevertheless, some questions deserve a closer look. First, the very question of consistency needs clarification, or, more specifically, differentiation according to branches and kinds of knowledge. Second, does the commitment to the truth of a proposition imply the obligation to confess or even disseminate it? Or does it imply the obligation to criticize its false opposite proposition? Further, is our commitment to the truth of a proposition independent of our obligation to disseminate it, or is perhaps a good reason not to propagate a proposition also a good reason to doubt its truth? Moreover, are reason and cognitive consistency the exclusive considerations in decisions concerning religious matters, or do emotions and other human considerations and needs play a role? Finally, are these questions of the sort that can have exactly one answer, or is there a kind of rationality involved that allows for more than one answer?

Truth and Morals; Philosophy and Politics

In *Jerusalem* and the *Morgenstunden* Mendelssohn explicitly opposes blind commitment to valid implications of true propositions. He derogatorily names such commitment *"Consequenzerey."*
     Mendelssohn's critic, Mörschel, challenged him:

> Ecclesiastical law armed with power has always been one of the principal cornerstones of the Jewish religion. . . . How, then, can you, my dear Mr. Mendelssohn, remain an adherent of the faith of your fathers . . . when you contest the ecclesiastical law . . . ? (*Jerusalem*, 85)

In response, Mendelssohn concedes that "this objection cuts me to the heart," and he also concedes that "the notion given here of Judaism" is accepted by many Jews (*Jerusalem*, 85). His own answer to the question is the rejection of *Consequenzerey.*

> Demanding blind acceptance of implications (*Consequenzerey*) like this ought to be banished forever from the intercourse of learned men. Not everyone who holds a certain opinion is prepared to accept, at the same time, all the consequences flowing from it, even if they are ever so correctly deduced. (*Jerusalem*, 86)[49]

One is tempted to ask: Why should the demand of consistency be banished? Should not rather those people be criticized who refuse to accept correctly deduced consequences? A few pages earlier, Mendelssohn himself took to task an opponent who refused to accept the conclusion from accepted principles: "but there must be some hidden flaw in the conclusion, if the result is not to be necessarily true" (*Jerusalem*, 80).
     What then? Should we consistently follow reason or not? Or does the answer depend on whether reason leads to the cherished conclusion of the scholar?[50] Here is what Mendelssohn explicitly said on this:

> I please myself at times with the thought, that everything which would bring the whole human race true comfort and benefit, if it were true, already for this reason has a great probability that it is true. If zealous skeptics (*zweifelsüchtige*) turn against the doctrine of God and virtue,

and object that it is a mere political device, which had been thought up
for the well-being of human society: then I always wish to call out to
them: . . . The human race is destined (*berufen*) to sociality (*Geselligkeit*)
just as every member is destined to happiness. Everything which will
lead to this end in a general, certain and constant manner, was indis-
putably chosen and produced by the Wisest Creator of all things as a
means to it. (*JubA* 3.1, 88)

This is analogous to the method of orientation. If the result of a metaphysical speculation (conducted by reason by means of language) leads
to a result that is repugnant to common sense, if "overly subtle" speculation leads us away from the way known by experience, we judge that we
must have erred in our reasoning even before we can put our finger on
the mistake. We may apply this principle not only to the relation between
theory and practice in general but also to the relation between theory
and morals in particular. We may not judge that a proposition is false
because its consequences seem to contradict morals, but we can take this
as an indication that there is a mistake somewhere: either in the derived
proposition itself, or in the decision on its dissemination, or in the assumption that it would be detrimental to morals, or, finally, in the moral
principle itself. And also in the contrary: If a belief is essential to human
felicity, this in itself is an indication that it is true. Mendelssohn's Socrates
is, therefore, willing to bet that doctrines that are so "indispensable" to
human society as the immortality of the soul are true.[51]

The same principle is behind Lessing's parable of the ring in *Nathan
the Wise*. The father gave his three equally beloved sons the ring that
"had the hidden virtue to render of God and man beloved" and two
imitations that could not be distinguished from the original one. The
rings stand here for the three monotheistic religions. It is impossible to
decide which of the rings is the original, which the imitations. The
clever judge acknowledges his inability to pronounce a sentence, but he
offers advice:

> Let each
> vie with both his brothers in displaying
> The virtue of his ring; assist its might
> With gentleness, benevolence, forbearance,

With inward resignation to the godhead,
And if the virtues of the ring continue
To show themselves among your children's children,
After a thousand thousand years, appear
Before this judgment-seat—a greater one
Than I shall sit upon it, and decide. Go!
So spake the modest judge.[52]

The point is not to determine the most beneficial ring (religion) but historical truth and the original ring *by means* of the beneficial effects. Although in this case the historical truth cannot be directly discovered, that is, by historical research, we can nevertheless identify the original ring indirectly, by means of its effects. We thus change domains from history to morals and observe the degree of being "of God and man beloved," which is a causal effect of the ring. This now serves as an indication of the truth of the historical narrative involved and, therefore, also as an indication as to which of the rings is genuine.[53] Of course, Lessing postpones the final verdict almost to eternity and thus avoids a decision in this life, but he also advances the principle that beneficial moral effects serve as an indication of historical and metaphysical truth.

Similarly in Mendelssohn. Negative implications for the well-being of human society serve as an indication of the falsity of the metaphysics of which they are the consequences. If the negative effect on morals is certain and the proposition itself is metaphysical and its truth, therefore, on principle doubtful, we should act on the evident moral considerations (and as if the metaphysical proposition is false) even though we may not judge that the metaphysical proposition is false. This consequence follows from the view that "For the all-seeing eye, the whole of nature is one painting, the sum total of all possible knowledge is one truth" (*JubA* 2,321; Dahlstrom, 300).

This is the rationale of Mendelssohn's criticism of *Consequenzerey* in the *Morgenstunden*. The locus in question is the last sentences of lecture 15, the end of Mendelssohn's discussion of Lessing's alleged Spinozism.

"You see," I added in conclusion, "that Lessing envisaged pantheism in the totally refined manner I have ascribed to him: in complete harmony with whatever has a bearing on life and happiness; indeed, that he was on his way to link pantheistic concepts even with positive religion. This linking is in fact as possible with pantheism as with the Ancients' system of emanation which, throughout the centuries, was accepted by religion and held to be the only orthodox doctrine. On the long road which takes one from these overly subtle speculations to the praxis of religion and morality, there are many points where one can effortlessly reenter the open highway from a by-way. . . . [O]ne small digression which might, in the event, have led us far from our goal can be rectified by an equally small turn, and we are back on the road. Hence the contemptibility of blind acceptance of implications (*Consequenzerey*) which from time immemorial has spawned, or at least nourished, all the persecutions and religious hatred of the human race. (*JubA* 3.2, 136–37; Vallée, 77)

Mendelssohn shows in this passage first his interest in the practical consequences of religious thought, in "whatever has a bearing on life and happiness" on the one hand and little regard for theological "overly subtle speculations" on the other. Pantheism and emanation and creation finally all lead to "the practice of religion and morality," which is not only what really counts but is also certain. A "small digression" in the subtle argument may lead to a very different theological position, but it "can be rectified by an equally small turn." All these subtleties are unreliable and also of little practical importance. Important are religious practice (and a religious intention) and morality that require natural religion, and these considerations are clear. They have here the function of common sense elsewhere. They may discern, at least: help discern between correctness and error of the relevant religious position. What, then, is metaphysics good for? Metaphysics systematizes and refines our "natural religion," but it does not lead the way.[54] Its abstract objects, which are not sensible, and its medium, natural language, which is ambiguous, cannot guarantee reliable knowledge independent of the guidance of common sense. Just as conscience discerns as quickly and reliably good from evil so common sense is "a sense for the truth" (*JubA* 2, 325; Dahlstrom, 303). In conclusion: moral practice is more important and moral judgment is more reliable than metaphysical speculations.

Note, however, that this is not a justification for sacrificing truth for the sake of morals or societal life. Truth and morals cannot get into conflict. Mendelssohn ends his *Jerusalem* with the call: "Love truth! Love peace!" (*Jerusalem,* 139). He was deeply convinced that no real conflict can arise between the two: both are perfections of God.

Consider, finally, the case in which a proposition is certain; does it follow that one should confess it, or that it should be disseminated? In his *Phaedon,* Mendelssohn explicates the reasons to abstain from criticism or enlightenment in such cases: "There is no religious system so corrupt that it does not sanctify at least some duties of humanity that the friend of mankind venerates and the moral reformer must leave untouched, if he is not to act against his own insight" (*JubA* 3.1, 15).

Socrates, therefore, did not challenge doctrines that were "merely theoretically false" and less detrimental to mores than was to be feared of their reform (*JubA* 3.1, 19). Mendelssohn applied the lesson to himself and refrained from attacking Christian dogmas in the course of his controversy with Lavater since he believed that Christianity played a positive role in enhancing morality.[55]

Mendelssohn hence believes first that in cases of collision between metaphysical speculation and its unacceptable moral consequences, there is good reason to suspect that the metaphysical premise is wrong. Moreover, even if its truth is certain, it doesn't follow that one had to confess and a fortiori disseminate it. Judging the truth or falsity of a proposition is a theoretical issue, confessing or propagating it a practical issue; and the decision in the latter case involves in addition practical considerations. The decision depends on the balance between its expected positive and negative outcomes for perfection. Is the latter consideration hypocritical? In his "What Does It Mean to Enlighten?" Mendelssohn explicitly considers this question.

> If certain useful and—for mankind—adorning truths may not be disseminated without destroying prevailing religious and moral tenets, the virtue-loving bearer of enlightenment will proceed with prudence and discretion and endure prejudice rather than drive away the truth that is so closely intertwined with it. Of course, this maxim has become the bulwark of hypocrisy. . . . Nevertheless, the friend of man-

kind must defer to these considerations, even in the most enlightened times. It is difficult, but not impossible to find the boundary that separates use from misuse.[56]

The problem lies in the fact that the values involved have no common measure and there is no "balance of reason" to weigh them against each other. This is why the decision taken cannot be demonstrated and may be—or may seem to be—hypocritical. And yet common sense may still be quite certain as to the appropriate action, as it can often determine whether hypocrisy is involved. It is hypocrisy if we suppress truth to maintain the existing social order in our own interest, but it may be judged responsible behavior if it is done to avoid near-certain major turmoil for truth of minor importance.

Consider a case in point. Mendelssohn believes that the dissemination of enlightenment may endanger the constitution of the state. Here the vital interests of man as man, that is, the development of his understanding, may come into conflict with the vital interests of man as a citizen, namely, when enlightenment "cannot be disseminated through all the estates of the realm without risking the destruction of the constitution. Here philosophy should lay its hand on its mouth! Here necessity may prescribe laws, or rather forge the fetters that are applied to mankind, to force them down and hold them under the yoke!"[57] Evidently the destruction of the state endangers the very existence of human beings, and Enlightenment has therefore to be sacrificed.[58] Nevertheless, no public institution is called upon to determine the permitted measure of enlightenment: this is rather given to the discretion of the enlightener himself.[59]

As the phrase "disseminated through all the estates of the realm" suggests, Mendelssohn, in fact, does not think in general of "mankind" but more specifically of the "common people."[60] It thus seems that he openly supports the deception of the common people in the interest of peaceful social life (or class rule). This would not have been a very original position, neither in general nor in particular, at that time and place. After all, only thirteen years before Mendelssohn answered the question "What Is Enlightenment?" (1783), the Royal Prussian Academy in Berlin announced an essay competition on the question, "Est-il utile au peuple d'etre trompé, soit qu'on l'induise dans les nouvelles erreurs, ou qu'on l'entretienne dans celle où il est?" This formulation was chosen under the pressure of Friedrich II, who made no secret of his own view on the matter. In response to Holbach's and du Marsais's *Essai sur les préjugés* (1770), in which the authors claim that all religious and political views of common men are but prejudices, judgments accepted without examination (chapter 1), the king published his own *Examen de l'essai sur les préjugés* (1770), in which he argued that not truth but rather prejudices are the "reason of the people" (Les préjugés sont la raison du peuple) and condemned the critique of religious and political prejudices as subversive.[61]

Read on this background, Mendelssohn seems to agree with Friedrich II. The allegation that he compromised truth for prejudices in the interest of social peace seems well established. This would indeed be so if truth and prejudice were clear alternatives and unless Mendelssohn could argue that the possible detrimental effects of enlightenment are an indication of the falsity of the view advanced. In Mendelssohn's view both conditions are not fulfilled. The argument presupposes, on the negative side, Mendelssohn's view on the limitations of the intellect, especially concerning long chains of abstract inferences by means of language; and on the positive side, the unity of God, the inseparability of his wisdom and goodness (and all other perfections), and in consequence the "wonderful harmony" of all truths. "For the all-seeing eye, the whole of nature is one painting, the sum total of all possible knowledge is one truth" (*JubA* 2, 321; Dahlstrom, 300).

Certainly, if unconditional commitment to liberalism is presupposed, there is no justification to suppress any truth whatever (although there may be no obligation to disseminate it). But is Mendelssohn committed to such liberalism, and is anyone committed to liberalism in this form? Not at all. In *Jerusalem* Mendelssohn argues for the separation of state and church and thus earned the epitaph "liberal." But he is also willing to call upon the state to cautiously interfere if religious freedom endangers the political constitution or morals. In *Jerusalem,* for example, Mendelssohn recommends that atheism and fanaticism should be (indirectly) checked by the state "from a distance," "and only with wise moderation" (63). The state should promote mainstream religion, and concerning atheism and enthusiasm Mendelssohn clearly compromises his alleged pluralistic-liberal evenhanded toleration of religious persuasions.[62] The motivation is his belief that atheism and fanaticism may be detrimental to morality and social order. This does not mean that Mendelssohn subscribes to the view that individual atheists cannot be moral, but on a social scale religion is a guarantee of morals.

> Without God, providence and a future life, love of our fellow man is but an innate weakness, and benevolence little more than a foppery into which we seek to lure one another so that the simpleton will toil while the clever man enjoys himself and has a good laugh at the other's expense. (*Jerusalem*, 63)

Mendelssohn repeatedly remarks that the appropriate constitution for a society depends on the particular historical situation. Even the separation of state and church is not a principle for him, on the contrary. Their separation is at the same time a solution to a problem and its source. The very problem whether the dissemination of truth or the preservation of the political constitution should be preferred arises because "[t]he enlightenment of man can come into conflict with the enlightenment of the citizen" (*On the Question: What Is Enlightenment?* 55). Such conflict cannot arise before these aspects of human life fall apart. Just as in God all truths are but one truth, so also in God's reign all aspects of human life cohere in one constitution. And such constitution was the Mosaic constitution.

> In this original constitution, state and religion were not conjoined, but one; not connected, but identical. Man's relation to society and his relation to God coincided and could never come into conflict. God, the Creator and Preserver of the world was at the same time the King and Regent of this nation; and his oneness is such as not to admit the least division or plurality in either the political or the metaphysical sense. (*Jerusalem*, 128)

The existence of "state" as distinct from "church" or "religion" (Mendelssohn does not distinguish between religion and church) is a contingent

historical fact: "Some thought it proper to separate these different relations of societal man into moral entities, and to assign to each a separate province, specific rights, duties, powers, and properties"—says
Mendelssohn at the beginning of *Jerusalem* (33). This is neither necessary nor Mendelssohn's choice. Liberalism is Mendelssohn's choice
faute de mieux. His ideal was without doubt the Mosaic constitution in
which "state and religion were not conjoined, but one; not connected,
but identical" (*Jerusalem*, 119).[63] In fact, Mendelssohn considered the
anointment of King Saul (the separation of religious and worldly rule
in Israel) as an act of rebellion against God. (See below, chap. 7, "The
Idolatry of Worldly Kingdom.") Moreover, it is questionable whether
such liberalism with complete separation of state and church ever existed; in fact, Mendelssohn's restrictions on liberalism concerning "fanaticism" would presumably find wide support today.[64]

In conclusion, we see that if indeed there is one comprehensive truth
and one supreme value, namely, perfection (*JubA* 2, 317; Dahlstrom,
297), then truth and beneficial social order are not independent realms.
Every disagreement between them indicates a mistake somewhere. Ig-
noring such indications and strictly drawing consequences from accepted presuppositions in one's own discipline is narrow-minded *Consequenzerey*. In lack of absolute knowledge, we must—also in the interest
of truth!—use whatever indications we have to achieve a harmonious
worldview and thus approach as much as possible that one truth that
reflects the most perfect world order.

Truth and Happiness, Philosophy and Pleasure

In an early stage of his philosophical career, Mendelssohn widened his
horizon, became "infidel" to speculative metaphysics, and added to his
interests belles-lettres. Contrary to what he believed at the time, he remained occupied with the arts all his life and not "for some time" only.[65]
Following the Leibniz-Wolffian understanding, Mendelssohn presents
in his juvenile *On Sentiments* (1755) a concept of beauty and aesthetic
pleasure that will remain central to his philosophy and to his views on
religion. He proceeds from the definition of beauty: "Beauty rests, in the
opinion of every philosopher, on the indistinct representation of a per-

fection," and perfection is "a multiplicity that is in harmony and refers to a unity."[66] Neither fully distinct nor fully obscure concepts are compatible with sensing beauty. Sensuous pleasure is common to man and animal; intellectual pleasure is common to man and God; aesthetic pleasure is man's only. Certainly, intellectual perfection stands higher than beauty, but beauty is distinctly human.[67] Analyzing a work of art and reducing it to rules resembles analyzing "dried-up remains of worms." "If you do not want to feel without thinking, then I am in danger of embracing in you a lukewarm friend."[68]

Now, placing man between the beasts and superior intellects, like the angels or God, is rather traditional. What is new is Mendelssohn's attitude to this position of man. He fully accepts and approves of the constitution of the universe and of the intermediate position man occupies in it between the beasts and God. He conceives it as the specific human perfection, not as the human predicament. Mendelssohn, therefore, does not wish to analyze every sensual apprehension to concepts, on the contrary. "We would be unhappy if all our sentiments were all at once elucidated and made into clear and distinct representations." "At that very moment your pleasure would perish and you would have, instead of a sweet rapture, a set of arid truth."[69]

This view of young Mendelssohn elucidates an important statement on religion that he made two weeks before his death. On Christmas Eve, December 24, 1785, his friend Sophie Becker (a Christian) wrote Mendelssohn that she cannot anymore experience the "sweet delirium" (*süßer Taumel*) that she experienced as a child on that day. Reason tells her that there was no truth in her juvenile religious sentiments, but it leaves her with an emptiness in the heart. "Dearest friend," she addresses Mendelssohn, "how did you manage, with your feeling heart, to overcome the first false religious sentiments without having become in any way colder?"[70]

Mendelssohn's answer is worth quoting in extenso.

My maxim is to let no pleasure slip by that is bound up with any sort of representation. My reason must not act prudishly in spoiling my pleasure in the innocent enjoyments of this life. Philosophy is meant to make me happier than I would be without it. . . .

This is rather epicurean, you will say. Perhaps it is! I also choose from the systems of philosophy that which can make me happier and better at the same time. A philosophy that makes me disgruntled or indifferent to other people or to myself, or frosty toward the sentiment of the beautiful and good, is not my philosophy.

So far as popular concepts of religion are concerned, it seems to me that the pleasant sentiments that they evoke are, for the most part, founded upon an underlying truth that has been merely obscured by a false accretion. . . .

I rejoice in every religious custom that does not lead to intolerance and hatred of men. Like my children, I am happy with every ceremony that has something true and good underlying it. I seek to cut out the untrue as much as I can, [but] I abolish nothing until I am able to substitute something better for its good effect.[71]

Delight and aesthetic and cognitive pleasure all contribute to the perfection (and happiness!) of human beings. They are marks of perfection. Reason is not the critic of moral or aesthetic common sense but rather their collaborator. Reason is not the way to flee the material world and the bodily nature of man but rather integrates harmoniously with them. All faculties contribute to human perfection, which is part of the perfection of the universe and its creator.

The philosophical underpinning of this view is the notion that knowledge derived from sensual perception and from understanding is continuous. Knowledge ranges from "obscure" to "clear" but not "distinct" to "clear" and "distinct." However, knowledge of the senses and of the understanding is not conceived as different in kind or so heterogeneous that its mediation becomes a central problem of epistemology (Kant) or altogether negated (Maimon).

The consequences of Maimon's epistemological stance for religion are immediate. Maimon proceeds from the definition of man as an *animal rationale* and conceives both theoretically and practically contemplation as the only worthy form of life. This is true also in religion. Normal religious service is for the multitude; metaphysics is the proper religious service for philosophers, those "who have apprehended the true realities."[72] He repeats this ideal in all his writings as the "calling of man" (*Bestimmung des Menschen*), and in practice he dedicates himself entirely to studies and never seriously attempts to permanently earn his living by work. From the time he arrived in Berlin, Maimon never belonged to any religious (or other) community.

Mendelssohn is the exact opposite. Not only does his notion of perfection include moral, aesthetic, and other perfections relating to the social and bodily nature of man as ends in themselves,[73] and not only does he earn his living and is a member of a community to which he contributes much, and also observes the religious law, but he also justifies his religious practice with reference not to a philosophical concept of God but to human *needs,* which he accepts without further ado as a valid justification: "The most common man, I believe, does not sing, so that God may hear him and enjoy his melodies. We sing for our own sake, and the wise does so as much as the simpleton."[74]

Borrowing the expression from Heine, we may surely say that Mendelssohn and Maimon differ from each other not only in the content of their philosophy but also as "Menschennaturen"—they represent diametrically opposite conceptions of life within Jewish enlightenment. Salomon Maimon saw this clearly.

Perfection and Common Sense; the Balance of Reason

Maimon characterized precisely Mendelssohn's position as well as his own and diagnosed in their difference the source of his disagreements with Mendelssohn:

Perfection was the compass which he had constantly before his eyes, and which directed his course, in all these investigations. . . . I made the highest destination of man to be the maintenance of his differentia specifica, the knowledge of the truth. . . . The knowledge of the good was not distinguished by me from the knowledge of the true; for, following Maimonides, I held the knowledge of the truth to be the highest good of man. Mendelssohn, on the other hand, maintained that the idea of perfection, which lies at the basis of ethics, is of much wider extent than the mere knowledge of the truth. All natural impulses, capacities and powers, as something good in themselves (not merely as means to something good), were to be brought into exercise as realities. The highest perfection was the idea of the maximum, or the greatest sum, of these realities. (Maimon, *Lebensgeschichte, GW* 1, 480–82; Murray, 226–28)

The conflict between Mendelssohn's and Maimon's views does not pertain only to the subject matters involved, but also to the very concept of rationality, to logical reason versus sound reason. On the one hand, Mendelssohn argues for multifarious "perfection," whereas in Maimon "perfection" is tantamount to "true knowledge." On the other hand, Mendelssohn's "idea of the maximum, or the greatest sum," of perfection requires transformation rules to equate different degrees of various perfections to units of a single measure of perfection. Neither Mendelssohn nor any other philosopher suggested such rules. This is not surprising. Such rules may refer to a common property of different objects (as length, surface, or volume is measured by the same standard unit of length in the first, second, and third power) or by their power to cause a common effect (as "work" for all kinds of energy). Both possibilities do not apply here. We do not know of a common property or substance "perfection" of which, for example, moral, knowledge, and beauty are but forms of appearance, nor can we transform one into the other. Certainly, we can speak of such a common substance, "supreme reality" (*summa realitatis*), of which all existent beings are but manifestations, but this does not help us to estimate the relative perfection of any two existing beings of different nature.[75]

And yet reasoning seems involved. In deciding on our preferences concerning various "perfections" in everyday life, we often put much effort into deliberations and also discuss the matter with others; we do not act instinctively. How do we do this? Do we in fact use such a unified "scale of perfections," and consciously or unconsciously transform different degrees of various ends to this unified scale and then compare them? Since we are unable to explicate the alleged rule, this suggestion is merely an hypothesis ad hoc. It seems therefore that Mendelssohn would have to rely on unspecified, global "sound reason" if he were to justify such decisions, relying on life experience, traditions, and other prejudices. Indeed, in his praise of logic, Mendelssohn refers to the metaphor "balance of reason," as if all values involved here have in fact a common magnitude ("weight"), but rightly opposes this obscure evaluation to strict and clear logic. Logic is preferred to all other studies, "since it is not dependent on discretion and on the balance of reason, but is clear and necessary without any doubt and controversy as occur in the natural and metaphysical sciences and in morals where controversy never ceased and common sense and assessment always change."[76] When several "perfections" are involved, we must turn to the "balance of reason"—but this metaphor resists clarification.

The situation has not really changed since Mendelssohn's time and not in everyday life alone. In the justification of court decisions, for example, a comparison between magnitudes of various values is explicitly referred to. These magnitudes, too, are complex. They are products of the rank of the values involved (which are often conceived as opposites: "freedom" and "equality," "freedom of press" and "privacy") and the grades of each of the values involved in the particular case. Some lesser grade of a higher value is supposed to balance some higher grade of a lower value. Here, too, no measure has been hitherto explicitly introduced. Leibniz, who emphasized the complexity of the relevant magnitudes in medicine and jurisprudence, expressed his hope to further improve on the methods of jurisprudence, and Mendelssohn shared his view: "I do not think that your friend, the seeker of truth, wishes to collect votes, in order to count. These should be weighted, not counted."[77]

Indeed, both in medicine and in jurisprudence opposing values are often estimated to reach a combination that is optimal in terms of maximum positive value. This is done without explicating the relevant transformation rules and the common measure involved. Not surprisingly, the results reached differ from one physician to the other and from one judge to the other. The lack of explicable rules of reasoning is often expressed positively. Judicial discretion is said not to be "mechanical" such that the judge may exercise his "freedom."[78] In conclusion, multifarious perfection requires that a single conclusion be drawn from various lines of reasoning and calculation, although they cannot be transformed into each other. It thus requires reason that is wider than logic alone—and is rather opaque.

CHAPTER 2

Salomon Maimon

The Radical Alternative to Mendelssohn

One chapter in Maimon's autobiography is titled "Mendelssohn—A Chapter Devoted to the Memory of a Worthy Friend." And yet, in spite of the expression "worthy friend" and the many positive things Maimon has to say about Mendelssohn, he also twice calls him a "hypocrite" (*GW* 1, 470; 497) and accuses him of compromising philosophy out of political considerations. On the basis of Mendelssohn's views on the harmony of truth, morals, and beauty, which together constitute perfection, and Maimon's own notion of "perfection," we can understand this ambivalent judgment. Maimon opposed Mendelssohn's much more comprehensive notion of perfection to his own, which was restricted to truth (*GW* 1, 480–82; Murray, 226–28). Indeed, intellectual perfection was Maimon's sole ideal from his youth to the end of his life.

In his juvenile manuscript, *Cheshek Shlomo* (Salomon's Desire), as well as in his commentary on *The Guide of the Perplexed* by Maimonides or in his *Versuch über die Transcendentalphilosophie*, Maimon opens with a discussion of the supreme good of man, which is acquiring "perfection." However, this is not Mendelssohn's perfection. It is exclusively the perfection of the intellect, to which perfection of the body, property, and also morals is subordinated. Aesthetics is never even mentioned. Reason does not cooperate with the senses but is rather an alternative to them. Mendelssohn's "maxim," never to miss an innocent pleasure of any form of representation, and his rejection of a philosophy that would make him "frosty to the sentiment of beauty and goodness," are strictly incomprehensible to Maimon. Maimon's turning to philosophy and turning his back to the world are one and the same act. Of pious philosophers, Maimon says that they "despise" worldly affairs and human pleasures and turn to the acquisition of knowledge and science—and the same thing he says of himself, too, and also repeats the word *despise*.[1] It is not merely this view; it is the very attitude to life that is entirely different from Mendelssohn's.

Nevertheless, on the basis of their entirely different philosophies, they share skepticism concerning metaphysics, and also one major reason for this skepticism, namely, the metaphoric character of natural language. But from here their ways part. Their differences show not only in their philosophies but also in their ways of life. Maimon is a radical polemicist and a clochard, Mendelssohn moderate, conciliatory, and a bourgeois.

The most important difference between Maimon and Mendelssohn in our context concerns common sense. Maimon's skepticism applies also to common sense. In fact, from this stance, "common sense" does not appear as a philosophical position at all but merely as a pre-philosophical, naive view of the "man on the street." Maimon does not accept the certainty of immediate experience: all knowledge dependent on the senses is suspicious to him. Certain are only logical inferences, neither their premises nor their conclusions. "Fire consumes wood," says the common person, respectively common sense. "That the common person (*der gemeine Mann*) expresses this assertion in the form of a necessary and universal judgment is due to "*want of philosophical knowledge* and insight into the difference between rightly so-called necessary and universal judgment and judgments erroneously so considered," comments Maimon (*GW* 4, 74; original emphasis). The judgment "fire consumes wood" rests on an association of ideas based on experience and is not a necessary truth, says Hume, with whom Maimon sympathizes here. Causality is an a priori category of the understanding, says Kant, and it produces synthetic judgments a priori, not empirical generalizations. Maimon objects: Indeed, the conceptual connection between "cause" and "effect" is necessary (and, in fact, analytic!) but not its application, not the judgment that a specific cause produces a specific effect.

It is essential to remember that the discussion is not over trivial judgments of this kind but over the epistemic status of the epitome of Western science: Newtonian mechanics. Kant takes mathematical physics to be certain knowledge, and even attempts to show that its basis—so-called pure natural science—is synthetic a priori, whereas Maimon insists that it is nothing but a highly probable, almost certain generalization of experience.[2] Kant, as also Mendelssohn and Reinhold, "profound philosophers of standing," "take refuge" in common sense as if they were merely "popular philosophers." Common sense is based on a fallacy, on either self-deception or intentional deception. It consists in applying a judgment on the representation, for example, necessary relations between concepts to the objects themselves. Moreover, common sense and the common man rely on the senses, on the association of ideas, and so on, not on what is distinctly human: reason. What Maimon thinks of this is very clear from an example he gives. A child who takes his mirror image to be a second child and plays with it mistakes appearance for the real object, but this is harmless. However, if a horse sees its image in the water, believes that it is another horse, which hinders it from drinking, and kicks it until the image disappears, it will drink murky water. It "demonstrates in doing so that to its own mischief it is a horse" (GW 4, 250–55).

MAIMON ON MENDELSSOHN
THE PHILOSOPHICAL HYPOCRITE

Common sense, says Maimon, is due either to self-deception or to deception, and Mendelssohn was as distant from simplemindedness as one can wish. In fact, Maimon bestows on Mendelssohn's intellectual abilities the highest compliments: he was a "good Talmudist," he "possessed a thorough acquaintance with mathematics," and his intellect was both deep and acute (*Lebensgeschichte*, GW 1, 472, 474; Murray, 221–22). Maimon, of course, praises here those gifts of Mendelssohn's in which he also excels. This is no wonder. Their initial intellectual formation was quite similar, and they both retained some of its practices all their lives, for example, developing their views in commentaries on the more or less canonical works of others.[3] He goes on to praise Mendelssohn for his knowledge of human nature, for his morals, and so on, but this is of no concern here. If Mendelssohn nevertheless adhered to common sense, so Maimon believes, then he must have done so for ulterior reasons. Mendelssohn belonged to the dominant philosophical school of his day, says Maimon, and he "was very political and dealt with some persons and issues very delicately, and all this cannot be said of the present author [i.e., Maimon]" (*GW* 7, 629).[4]

In his autobiography, Maimon goes into details. He believed he had refuted Mendelssohn's (i.e., Wolff's) refutation of Spinoza, but Mendelssohn refused to acknowledge it.

> Moreover, I could not explain the persistency of Mendelssohn and the Wolffians generally in adhering to their system, except as a political dodge and a piece of hypocrisy, but which they studiously endeavored to descend to the mode of thinking common in the popular mind; and this conviction I expressed openly and without reserve. (*GW* 1, 470; Murray, 220)[5]

Maimon mentions more philosophical controversies with Mendelssohn, but the conclusion of them all is the same. Because of the political import of these philosophical questions, Mendelssohn compromised his intellectual integrity and accommodated his views to the accepted views. He was therefore a "philosophical hypocrite." This view has been endorsed by some scholars. However, neither Maimon nor later scholars considered Mendelssohn's arguments discussed in the previous chapter to the effect that views which endanger public morals are in all likelihood also false; not only harmful, but erroneous. These arguments, which are based on the conviction that all truths and goodness must cohere, that the capacities of the human intellect are modest, may convince or not, but they are certainly part and parcel of Mendelssohn's entire philosophy.[6]

RATIONAL DOGMATISM, EMPIRICAL SKEPTICISM

Maimon presented his "rational dogmatism and empirical skepticism" as an alternative both to Mendelssohn's commonsense philosophy and to

Kant's apodictic synthetic judgments a priori. However, as he himself admitted, he was the sole philosopher to endorse this position (*GW* 2, 436).

Maimon proceeds from a distinction between "objective necessity," "subjective necessity," and purely sensual "knowledge." Strict logical implications are objectively necessary truths. Not even geometry fulfills the requirements of objective knowledge because (synthetic) geometry depends on diagrams, and hence not on the understanding (logic) alone but also on pure intuition. Indeed, we cannot doubt the truth of a geometrical proof, but "necessity" means here merely that the truth is imposed on our intuition. A three-sided figure has three angles, but we don't know this truth adequately since it is merely imposed on our intuition; we have no logical insight or conceptual understanding of its necessity. We "see" that this is so, but this knowledge belongs to intuition, to sensibility, not to understanding. Understanding is universal, sensibility particular; what in our sensibility is necessary need not be so for other rational beings with different senses. Only the "infinite intellect" knows all truths adequately, that is, without intuition, by pure understanding.[7]

The uniqueness of Maimon's position is obvious if we compare it to Mendelssohn's (or Wolff's) on the one hand and to Kant's on the other. Mendelssohn believed that the proposition, "A three-sided figure has three angles," is analytic (i.e., depends on logic), its negation a contradiction.[8] This is Mendelssohn's understanding of Leibniz's view that all properties of a substance are virtually contained in its concept.[9] Kant suggested that it is a synthetic judgment a priori, a judgment based on constructing a concept in intuition. He maintained that it is not an analytic truth of reason but that this does not detract from its necessity; on the contrary: it is necessarily true and moreover synthetic; that is, it enlarges our knowledge.[10]

Maimon accepts Mendelssohn's (in fact, Leibniz's) stance that only analytic judgments are necessary, and he accepts Kant's claim that the judgment, "A closed three-sided figure in the plane has three angles," is synthetic and depends on intuition. Exactly therefore he maintains that the proposition is not objectively necessary. He beautifully makes the point.

> The Understanding prescribes the productive imagination a rule to produce a space enclosed by three lines. The imagination obeys and

constructs the triangle, but lo and behold! three angles, which the understanding did not at all demand, impose themselves. Now the understanding suddenly becomes clever since it learned the connection between three sides and three angles hitherto unknown to it, but the reason of which remains unknown to it. Hence it makes a virtue of necessity, puts on an imperious expression and says: A triangle must have three angles!—as if it were here the legislator whereas in fact it must obey an unknown legislator.[11]

True, we feel that this connection is necessary, perhaps not less than if its negation were a contradiction, but it is nevertheless merely subjective necessity imposed on us and not objective necessity established by the understanding. Nevertheless, in the *degree* of certainty, we may approach objective necessity ever closer (*GW* 4, 450; *GW* 3, 198–200).

Now, objectively certain knowledge is thus confined to logic and algebra, less so to arithmetic, that is, to those branches of knowledge in which the objects are produced according to a law of reason. In all cases in which the objects are first given and the understanding attempts to discover the laws, there is also no certainty. As an alternative to rationalism and Kantianism, Maimon presents the results of his own philosophy: "our knowledge has something pure to it and something real, but unfortunately the pure is not real and the real is not pure. The pure (formal) is the idea which we may approach ever closer in the use of the real, but which we can never reach" (*GW* 1, 576).

But what about commonsensical knowledge, knowledge dependent on sense perception and not on specialized reason? Empirical knowledge based on sense perception (considered by Mendelssohn to be indubitable) is in Maimon's view not only uncertain, but not at all knowledge. When we say, "The body is red," this merely means that we perceive in a certain area of space at the same time some properties (say, extension, impenetrability) and also some others (say, red) and therefore combine them to an object of which we then judge: The body is red.[12] However, such synthesis is not "real": we do not understand how "red" applies to "body," nor can a new proposition be inferred from it. Moreover, we have no criterion that would distinguish this allegedly meaningful predication from a meaningless predication like "The body is happy," "The line is sweet."

Besides conceptual entailment, all knowledge is uncertain. No wonder that Maimon is skeptical concerning most of our scientific knowledge. The rationalist ideal of pure conceptual knowledge that excludes
all intuition and experience implies that most so-called knowledge falls
prey to skepticism. Strict rationalism and skepticism are therefore interdependent.[13] Mendelssohn and Kant are not skeptics because their criteria of valid knowledge are far more liberal than Maimon's.

MAIMON'S RATIONALIST PHILOSOPHY OF LANGUAGE

We have seen that Mendelssohn's reliance on common sense and his
restriction of knowledge claims to knowledge of the empirical world,
to science and elementary metaphysics (especially "natural religion"),
depend on his empiricist philosophy of language. And yet this view of
language that develops from the concrete to the abstract is so "commonsensical" that it seems difficult to deny. And can we acknowledge
the obvious metaphoric nature of language and nevertheless evade
Mendelssohn's conclusions concerning common sense on the one hand
and metaphysics on the other? Salomon Maimon thought we can.
Maimon does not deny the truth of the empiricist view of language but
adds to it a rationalist alternative. He therefore distinguishes between
"barbaric" languages of the "primitives" (Wilde), similar to the language
usage of children, and "developed" (*ausgebildete*) languages (GW 3, 135,
139). All "developed" languages were once "barbaric" (GW 2, 329), and
it therefore is important whether we wish to study these languages historically or as they are today. Moreover, we can analyze and interpret
contemporary "real languages" from the point of view of an "ideal language" (GW 2, 297–98). This is but one form in which his philosophy of
"rational dogmatism" and "empirical skepticism" appears. However, the
alternatives are not equal. The rationalist version is the basis on which
it is possible to reform language and render it adequate to scientific
and philosophical usage, and it has a normative advantage. Following
Leibniz and others, Maimon believes that by strict definitions of the
terms, language can (on principle) be rendered precise and structurally adequate to represent our knowledge of the world.[14] Polemicizing
against Mendelssohn's friend Johann Georg Sulzer, who claimed that

the greatest part of language consists of tropes that are taken for proper expressions, Maimon maintains that this view is both wrong and "opposed to the interest of reason and true morality": "it enables the imagination to triumph over reason" (*Tr*, 302–3). The philosophy of language of Sulzer (and Mendelssohn, who is not mentioned by name) threatens rationality. For Maimon, there are normative reasons to prefer the rationalist philosophy of language, and for counter-enlighteners there were normative reasons to prefer the opposed alternatives.[15]

Maimon recounts how he proceeded in his own philosophical development from the empiricist (Maimonidean, which is also shared by Mendelssohn) to the rationalist alternative of Wolff. In fact, the insight that natural language is figurative and not adequate to metaphysics was Maimon's initiation into philosophy with the help of Maimonides; the second step in his development was the adoption of Wolff's solution to that very problem. Maimon writes of himself in the third person:

> From Maimonides [Maimon] learned the difference between proper and improper expression in language and that those loci of the Scripture whose proper meaning is contrary to reason, should be understood figuratively. . . . Reason could now proceed toward perfection, and faith become ever more reasonable. (*GW* 7, 639)

Reason was liberated from the letter of the script by assuming that its true meaning was different from its literal meaning. But in what language can true knowledge be thought and communicated? And how can we generate new knowledge if the language we use is figurative and unreliable? This was the content of the second "revolution" in Maimon's thought, his encounter with Wolff's philosophy.

> From Wolff he learned the formal difference between concepts (obscure, clear, distinct, etc.). . . . Only now he discovered that almost not a single of the inventory of the concepts he collected hitherto fulfilled the requirements of a clear and distinct concept. He attempted to overcome this deficiency by definitions which would endow the concepts with this formal perfection. (*GW* 7, 639–40)

The necessary reform has to occur within natural language itself. Turning natural language into a precise philosophical tool requires exact definitions of almost all terms, hence almost the invention of a new specialized philosophical language within the ordinary. In retrospective, Maimon judges his efforts as a "mania of definitions" (*Definitionswut*) (*GW* 7, 641). However, the basic tenet, that is, eradicating figurative language and securing unambiguous meaning, remained essential to Maimon.

However, Maimon's development does not imply that he adopted the latter view instead of the former. In a long footnote to his presentation of Maimonides in his autobiography, Maimon informs us of his change of mind. In his commentary on *The Guide of the Perplexed* (*Giv'at ha-Moreh*), he still explained the ambiguity of terms as the result of their figurative meaning when transferred from one domain to another. In a later published paper ("Was sind Tropen?"), which was integrated into the appendix "On Symbolic Cognition" to his *Transcendentalphilosophie* (which, alas, appeared one year earlier than the commentary on *The Guide of the Perplexed*), he already presented his new view. Now Maimon presents these views as coexistent possibilities: an ambiguous expression could have been formed either because a general term is applied without further distinction to two species of the same genus or because it was proper to one species and has been figuratively transferred to the other. Maimon does not take a position on this alternative and leaves both possibilities open.[16] However, the rationalist version is the basis of his attempt to further develop language and philosophy.

He gives there the example of the word אכל which I will discuss in the following (see *GW* 1, 322–23 n.; *GM*, 22, 60; *Tr*, 303–17, esp. 309).[17] In *The Guide of the Perplexed*, Maimonides explains that the original and proper meaning of the word is "the taking in of food by living beings." "Subsequently the Hebrew language saw two notions in the action of eating. One of them was the destruction and disappearance of the thing eaten. . . . The other notion is that of the growth of the living being due to the food he takes." Then the first meaning (destruction of food) is "figuratively applied to all destruction," and the second meaning (growth of the living being) "is applied figuratively to knowledge, learning, and, in general, the intellectual apprehensions through which the permanence of the human form endures in the most perfect of states, just as the body endures through food in the finest of its states" (*The Guide of the Perplexed*, I, 30; Pines, 63).[18]

Maimonides gives several biblical examples for each usage. In his *Transcendentalphilosophie* and in his autobiography, Maimon, however, denies that the concrete meaning is original, the others figurative. Proceeding from general categories and their application to objects, he suggests that the original meaning is "sustaining something by destroying another"; it applies to objects as such, and therefore both to empirical and abstract objects, both to nurture and to intellectual apprehension. This dual applicability does not result from the transference of terms from one domain to the other, and therefore it does not depend on an analogy between these domains; it is rather the application and differentiation of an abstract term in different specific contexts (*GW* 1, 322–23).

On this interpretation, the inadequacy of language results from lack of distinctions, not from figurative transference.[19] And language should mirror these distinctions. This means that primitive, irreducible objects should be represented by primitive, irreducible signs; and derivative, composite objects by derivative, composite signs. Moreover, signs should indicate the degree of composition of their objects by assigning each concept its proper place in the system of genera and species (*GW* 2, 296). Thus we would not use the term *man*, which does not convey any information about its place in our conceptual system, but *animal rationale*, in which "animal" is the *genus proximum* and "rationale" the *differentia specifica* (*GW* 2, 320). The entire fabric of philosophical language would thus present a Porphyrian tree that mirrors our knowledge of the world. It is therefore that Maimon says that philosophy, properly understood, is "a universal doctrine of language" (*eine allgemeine Sprachlehre*) (*GW* 2, 296). But this conception also sheds light on the paramount importance of Maimon's "principle of determinability" (*Satz der Bestimmbarkeit*). This is a grammatical-logical-metaphysical principle that governs the compositions of terms: it presents rules according to which we may predicate a determination of a genus but not vice versa and thus produce a new concept. But not every predication is permitted: "square table" is permitted, but "tabled square" is excluded. And the analysis of "The body is red" (see above) would show that there is no conceptual connection between the terms and that the predication does not represent knowledge. The correct subject-predicate relation mirrors the substance-property structure. The Porphyrian tree of genera and species mirrors the ontology of the world or our knowledge of it.[20]

In addition to the words standing for objects, we should consider the linguistic means referring to relations. "The ideal of a developed language is that all relations and ratios of the objects can be expressed in it in the most precise manner" (GW 3, 139). These relations are transcendental forms (GW 3, 140). This is another formulation of what Mendelssohn says of algebraic formulas: the letters represent their referents by convention, but the signs for algebraic operations agree with their referents, that is, with the mental operations. For natural languages this means that the *partes orationis* must correspond exactly to the system of categories (GW 2, 299–300, 305, 317–18). But such a general language may also be empty and fail to refer to experience. The main job of philosophy is therefore to secure "that the concepts contain reality and nevertheless be universally valid," hence develop both specific and general concepts (GW 2, 12–13). Certainly, this language is not yet constructed, but we can approach ever more this ideal of a "general or philosophical language." However, we do not know the inner essence of things and therefore whether our conceptual system captures the objective structure of the world. We certainly cannot claim that it is the only system that would fit it (GW 2, 317–18).

Further details and problems of Maimon's philosophy of language are not of interest in this context. It is important to see that the very same empirical phenomenon, the improper meanings of linguistic expressions, and basically the same intellectual heritage (biblical commentaries, Maimonides, Locke, Wolff; reflections on the language of the deaf and mute, on primitive language and pantomime) occasion two very different philosophical responses. In the wake of empiricism, Mendelssohn conceives a philosophy of language that proceeds from alleged primitive human experience with material objects, involving sense perception and bodily gestures, to the construction of tropes of ambiguous meaning. Whereas he trusts commonsense knowledge of empirical objects, he doubts abstract knowledge, which depends on natural language (and not, for example, on mathematical symbolism). Mendelssohn limits, therefore, the domain of human knowledge to empirical objects and rudimentary metaphysics and is skeptical concerning metaphysics proper. It all depends on metaphors.

Maimon goes a different way. He acknowledges the merits of the empirical approach but is more interested in the rationalist alternative, because this can serve as the basis of the construction of an adequate philosophical language. This does not proceed from individual to abstract terms but, on the contrary, from the most general concepts of relations (categories) and genera to their subsequent differentiation into genera and species. The result of such analysis should be a reconstruction of knowledge by means of clear and distinct primitive and composite terms and their relations. If these requirements are not met, then the entire fabric of knowledge is not objectively necessary, and falls prey to skepticism. Maimon therefore characterizes his philosophy as "rational dogmatism and empirical skepticism." He pursues rationalism and hopes that the progress of knowledge approximates ever more the true structure of the world as conceived by the "infinite intellect," but he also knows that what appears to be true may prove to be nothing more than custom and habit. Metaphysics and skepticism on Maimon's side, common sense and limitations of knowledge on Mendelssohn's side. There can hardly be a deeper disagreement between philosophers. However, Mendelssohn, too, has ideas concerning a less ambiguous language than normal written or spoken natural language (see chapter 5). But first let us look at the differences between Mendelssohn's and Maimon's views of religion.

CHAPTER 3

The Truth of Religion

In discussing the truth of religion, the distinction between "natural religion" and "revealed religion" is essential. Natural religion comprises a body of elementary knowledge about God and his relation to man. This is universal, known to all people at all times and in all regions of the world by reason alone. Revealed religion is a direct message of God to man; it can comprise a body of knowledge and also promises, commandments, precepts revealed at some point in time to some people in a specific place. By its very nature, it cannot be universal at the time of revelation, since not all human beings live at the right time and place to witness it.

THE TRUTH OF NATURAL RELIGION

Mendelssohn's epistemic and linguistic skepticism does not affect his trust in natural religion. Its essentials—the belief in God, providence, and afterlife—are accessible to sound reason on the basis of empirical observation of the world anywhere and at all times. It is independent of revelation and therefore does not involve historical events and reports. This is especially true of the first and third principles, the existence of God and afterlife. It is doubtful whether providence can be known by reason, and some versions of deism deny this. Mendelssohn invested much effort in providing metaphysical proofs of the existence of God (*Morgenstunden*) and the immortality of the soul (*Phaedon*); he usually passed in silence over providence. He may have believed that the truths of providence, reward and punishment, are implicitly contained in the notion of God as the most perfect being (i.e., also of supreme goodness). The argument is this: Since God is most perfect, perfect justice must obtain in the universe. This is evidently not the case. The contradiction vexes the believer. The Book of Job testifies to this, as does the question that the Babylonian Talmud puts in Moses's mouth: "Lord of the Universe, whence the suffering of the righteous and the prospering of the wicked" (צדיק ורע לו, רשע וטוב לו) (Berakot 7a.)? The traditional answer is that all apparent injustice in this life is compensated for in afterlife (see *Jerusalem*, 98). The notion of God as the most perfect being is thus tightly associated with providence, afterlife, reward and punishment. And these indeed are Mendelssohn's words in his introduction to Ecclesiastes: "The believer in the existence of God and his providence must choose one of these alternatives: either believe that the souls have an afterlife, and that the time of trial for each deed, good or bad, will come; or—God forbid!—attribute evil and violence to the holy God himself" (*JubA* 14, 154). The basic truths of natural religion are established by simple common sense, by an inference from creation to the creator. The Psalmist says: "The heavens declare the majesty of God, And the firmament announceth the work of his hands. . . . No teaching no words, Without their voice being heard (Psalms 103:2–4; quoted in *Jerusalem*, 126).[1]

The commonsense inference from experience is short and immediate: it does not require language, at least not in any essential way (*Jerusalem*, 90, 93, 94). God can be known in different depth, but to know the essentials it suffices to hear and see "the all-vivifying power of the Deity everywhere" (*Jerusalem*, 95). A consideration of the nature of human beings and the difference between their bodies and souls suffices to establish the immortality of the latter, and the notion of God as the most perfect being suffices to establish providence, reward and punishment. Certainly, the metaphysician does important work in clarifying our concepts, in systematizing our views, and in forging proofs to fend off the skeptics and sophists. But the truths of natural religion themselves, which are necessary for our eternal felicity, are equally accessible to the learned and unlearned.

Mendelssohn had a vital personal interest in the truth of natural religion. In his youth Mendelssohn seems to have experienced an existential crisis: He was close "to being completely ruined": "Like hellish furies, cruel doubts about providence tortured me; indeed I can say without skittishness, that they were doubts about the existence of God and the blessedness of virtue" (*JubA* 1, 64; Dahlstrom, 27). Doubts in providence and in reward and punishment threatened to deprive life of meaning. This remained Mendelssohn's conviction: "Without God, providence, and immortality all the goods of this life have in my eyes a contemptible value" (*JubA* 3.2, 68; Arkush, 110–11). The reason is spelled out in *Phaedon*, in a long introduction to the second dialogue, which is not in Plato's original dialogue. This introduction reads like the desperate outcry in the face of nihilistic consequences that would follow if the soul were mortal:

> If our soul is mortal, then our reason is a dream, sent to us by Jupiter to deceive us; then virtue is without any splendor, that makes it divine in our eyes; then the beautiful and sublime, the moral as well as the physical, is not an imprint of divine perfections (since nothing perishable can contain the weakest ray of divine perfections); then we are like cattle, put here to search for fodder and to die; . . . If our mind is perishable, then the wisest legislators and founders of human societies deceived us or themselves; then the whole human race has conspired to contrive untruth as it were and to venerate the deceivers who have devised this; then a state of thinking beings is nothing more than a flock of cattle without reason, and Man—I am horrified to look into this abyss! and Man, deprived of his hope of immortality, is the most miserable animal on Earth, who can think about his situation to his own misfortune, fear death and must despair. (*JubA* 3.1, 79–80)

Basing religion on common sense is not peculiar to Mendelssohn, or to deists. It is an elementary demand of religious enlightenment that religion be as much as possible of the same kind as other parts of the *globus intellectualis* and equally accessible to all human beings. Philosophers of Enlightenment in general share, therefore, the conviction that "sound reason" can and should establish the basic truths of "natural religion" as far as possible. Kant certainly did not share Mendelssohn's philosophy or his partisanship for Judaism as a much more rational religion than Christianity. But Kant writes about the role of common sense in religion as if he copied the text from Mendelssohn.[2] And Bernard Bolzano, himself a Catholic priest, and as anti-Kantian as one may wish, voices very much the same views.[3]

Although the means of attaining the truths of natural religion are "as widespread as mankind itself" (*Jerusalem*, 94), these truths are in fact not universally acknowledged. Here the ambiguity of "common sense" shows. "Common sense" means a faculty of judgment, but it also means the views accepted by common people in a certain society at a certain time. All people are endowed with this faculty of reason, but the socially accepted "commonsensical" views at a certain time need not be those common sense reaches if undisturbed.

Whatever the reasons (some will be discussed below), societies neither steadily progress nor stay on the level they once attained in their cultural development. "Rather do we see the human race in its totality slightly oscillate; it never took a few steps forward without soon afterwards, and with redoubled speed, sliding back to its previous position" (*Jerusalem*, 96; see also 97). At times there are "wise men" who communicate their better insights to their fellow men (*Jerusalem*, 94–95), and within the same society some people are at times more advanced than others (*Jerusalem*, 97). As we shall see, this "sliding back" on the one hand and the more advanced status of individuals and peoples compared to their neighbors on the other set the ground for enlightenment, as well as for the special destination of the Jewish people. The special mission of the more advanced individuals and people, especially the Jewish people, is to defend true "natural religion" against idolatry.

THE TRUTHS OF REVELATION

The epistemological status of revealed religion is different from that of natural religion. All revealed religions depend on historical truths. They derive their authority from the report of the event of revelation.[4] Now, most contingent (empirical) truths, whether laws of nature or historical truths, cannot be known by personal experience. For most contemporary and historical truths we are dependent on other people's reports, which we accept on their reputation and authority. We trust the reports of experiments done by others, the reports of expeditions, the reported observations of astronomers. There is, however, an important (epistemological) distinction between these different kinds of reports. With historical truths (and astronomical observations) we are *in principle* dependent on the credibility of other observers. Experiments can in principle be replicated and the results affirmed or falsified. But reports of historical or astronomical events cannot be checked because the events are no longer observable. We have only one additional criterion of their credibility: they must be consistent with other truths.

Mendelssohn accepts the authenticity of the Sinaitic revelation as a historical event, and also the authenticity of the five books of Moses, which, according to him, were recited by God to Moses. He is well aware of modern skepticism that sees in Moses a legislator who invoked God to give his laws absolute authority.[5] And exactly therefore Mendelssohn insists on its authenticity. Essentially he endorsed the argument of Judah Halevi, namely, that the event was witnessed by the entire nation and that the concordant testimony of six hundred thousand people is reliable.[6]

> The whole nation, at which this mission was directed, saw the great divine manifestation with their own eyes and heard with their own ears how God installed Moses as his emissary and spokesman. All the Israelites were therefore eye- and ear-witnesses of the divine calling of this prophet, and they required neither further testimony nor further proof. (*JubA* 7, 324)

Mendelssohn simply applies here the principles of common sense and of his epistemology: "men can swear only to what they know by the evidence of their external senses, to what they saw, heard, touched" (*Jerusalem*, 71). And this exactly is the basis of the testimony of the Israelites confirming the authenticity of revelation.

> In the same way as two witnesses, who observed a deed with their own eyes, need not further adduce more proofs [to convince] each other; so Moses needed not prove his mission by miracles, since the entire nation were his witnesses. (*JubA* 7, 87; cf. *JubA* 7, 43)[7]

The Israelites do not directly testify to the authenticity of the Torah. They witnessed (heard) the voice proclaiming only the first or the first two commandments, but they witnessed Moses's appointment. The authenticity of the Torah is mediated: God authenticated Moses's mission, and Moses authenticated the Torah. God promised Moses in public to install him as his spokesman so that the people will believe in Moses forever (Exodus 19:9), and so he did (Exodus 24:16–17). In his commentary, Mendelssohn speaks for God (commentary [*Bi'ur*] on Exodus 19:9):

> They will hear with their very ears, not by hearsay and not only by signs and wonders, but by hearing from my mouth that I send you to them to present them my Torah and they will therefore believe in this and in you for ever. And if a prophet or someone who had a dream, will give a sign and perform a wonder to abrogate even a single word of the Torah, they will not listen to him and will promptly contradict him, since your mission has already been authenticated by a proof that leaves no room for revocation and doubt, namely the testimony of the senses in great publicity.

The truth of the revelation on Sinai is hence better corroborated than any historical event. If we were to doubt its authenticity, we would have to doubt a fortiori all historical truths. We believe that "King Frederic the Second waged many great wars and was the pride of kings" because it was known to many people at the time, and their testimonies—partly credible, partly not—reached us. "So much more will we believe the signs and wonders done to our ancestors in great publicity and to a great number of spectators and handed down to us by honorable people, prophets and servants of God, lovers of truth and enemies of deceit." "Whoever demands an apodictic proof for their truths is but mistaken, since a proof cannot be given for past events."[8]

The truth of the event of revelation is hence ascertained by the general criteria of empirical truth (*Jerusalem*, 93)—and even more because of the great number of witnesses. However, these testimonies do not yet suffice to substantiate the divine origin of the Torah. Mendelssohn established the truth of natural religion and also the truth of the manifestation on Mount Sinai, but these two truths still have to be integrated. It has to be shown that the marvelous spectacle on Mount Sinai was an authentic appearance of the unique God who is the creator and ruler of the universe as well as the God of Israel, and not the making of another agent, human or superhuman. True, if we did not believe in the existence of God of natural religion, we would not believe that the voice heard on Mount Sinai is his; but it does not follow that if God of natural religion exists, then the voice heard was his. God may exist, and the miraculous events on Mount Sinai may nevertheless be fraud, staged by the worldly lawgiver Moses in order to confer on his legislation divine authority, or they may be the making of a being or several beings capable of performing supernatural events that make one believe that one witnesses such events, and not of the God of which revealed religion speaks: the "unique, eternal Deity that rules the entire universe according to its unlimited will, and discerns men's most secret thoughts in order to reward their deeds according to their merits, if not here, then in the hereafter" (*Jeursalem*, 98).

To Mendelssohn, miracles may "verify testimonies, support authorities, and confirm the credibility of witnesses and those who transmit tradition" (*Jerusalem*, 99). The doubts of the skeptic or of the sophist are of a person who can "no longer hear the voice of common sense" but demands "rational proofs, not miracles" (*Jerusalem*, 97–98).[9] This demand is out of place with historical truths. Here "common sense" is responsible. This is Mendelssohn's answer. I believe that there is another reason, based on an argument known to Mendelssohn. Indeed, there is no rational proof that it is the unique God who revealed himself on Sinai and not indefinitely many supernatural beings, or one or more extremely talented magicians. But sound reason endorses a version of the principle of Occam's razor: *Dii non sunt multiplicanda praeter necessitatem*. Gods should not be multiplied beyond necessity. We cannot prove that one entity only stands behind all these phenomena, but the principle of parsimony requires that if the existence of one God suffices to explain all phenomena, we should not introduce more Gods or semigods without compelling reasons.[10] We should choose the simplest explanation—and this is the convergence of the truths of natural religion with the truths of revelation. Moreover, since the evidence supporting the existence of God of natural religion is—as Mendelssohn says—entirely independent of the evidence supporting the existence of God of revelation, we have here a perfect case of "consilience of induction" that strongly supports the truth of the conclusion.[11] The hypothesis developed to explain the existence of our well-designed world also accounts for revelation. Moreover, the contrary assumption requires the introduction of an ad hoc hypothesis, namely, that God of common sense and metaphysics, the most perfect being, has chosen to deceive all Western nations, or at least allowed it. There is no ground for such a strange assumption.

This is not an apodictic proof, but it is a persuasive argument that can be believed bona fide in spite of the critique of Spinoza and others. This is especially so because it is not an isolated argument but an integral part of Mendelssohn's philosophy.[12] Neither revelation nor natural religion are deductively demonstrated from evident principles: they are not apodictic truths as are those of logic and mathematics. However, this is also not necessary: We entrust our lives to sound reason; we may entrust to it also our convictions concerning natural and (in the case of Judaism) also of revealed religion.

The Burden of Proof

It has been argued that Mendelssohn did not do justice to the power of modern arguments against the authenticity of revelation from Spinoza onwards and that he "resorted, on occasion, to some less than straightforward rhetorical strategies, all designed to make his own position seem more cogent than it actually was."[13] I attempted to show above that Mendelssohn had very good arguments for his position. But it should also be noted that the opposite, critical position was far from cogent itself. No side had or could have had compelling evidence or arguments, and on both sides it was necessary to weigh the pros and cons and reach a decision that could be supported with arguments but not proven. This is not surprising. If we attempt to fully account for the reasons to accept or reject the report on the revelation on Mount Sinai (or, to take Mendelssohn's example, that "King Frederic the Second waged many great wars and was the pride of kings"), we will soon discover that very extended parts of the entire fabric of our convictions are involved, some of them very remote from the subject matter at hand. Most of these convictions are simply prejudices that happen to be widespread in our society, or historical reports that we accepted without ever reflecting on their justification. The possibility or impossibility of so-called miracles is another important issue. In a science-credulous society the majority of people will deny their possibility but will not have compelling arguments for their position. We should bear in mind that the *Weltanschauung* in which such beliefs are embedded changes through history. Views that were once self-evident require a proof today, and such a proof cannot always be given. And vice versa: what once required justification is today an accepted prejudice, a presumption of all further discussion. This clearly shows in the case of "natural religion" for which Mendelssohn hardly argues but almost takes for granted. Mendelssohn accepts that revelation can be doubted and therefore argues for it. He may not have cogently proven the fact, but his arguments have certainly also not been disproven.

A most important decision in cases of disagreement is the allocation of the burden of proof. The proponent of the received view has an advantage over the opponent. The opponent has to refute the received view and prove his own position in order to win the controversy. The proponent of the received view merely needs to ward off the critique. If the critique is not conclusive, the received view remains by default in place, even though the arguments supporting it may be no better than those of the opponent. Note that the roles of the proponent and opponent are distributed on the basis of what is accepted in society; the distribution is not itself the outcome of a rational procedure.

Indeed, the sociocultural atmosphere has radically changed since Mendelssohn's times. In some societies the burden of proof is now with the believers. The same arguments that were sufficient in the eighteenth century to defend revelation against skeptics are insufficient today (among intellectuals in so-called Western cultures). Until an argument to the contrary is adduced, this is a contingent historical fact and does not necessarily testify to the quality of the arguments. In fact, the change in historical atmosphere distorts the assessment of the arguments in Mendelssohn's time. Moreover, we should also remember that in *Jerusalem* Mendelssohn argues in the first place with Christians, who avow revelation themselves, not with atheists or deists who may deny revelation.[14]

We should also remember that our perspective is biased in favor of the critics of (Jewish) revelation for yet another reason. We read the critical works of Spinoza, Eichhorn, and others as predecessors of biblical criticism at the end of the nineteenth century. This discipline acquired high prestige and authority that reflect back on its heralds. In the eighteenth century, however, these were single critical works that questioned the received view with some good but certainly not conclusive arguments. It was by no means unreasonable to stick to the received view. Finally, also today, many people believe in some version of revelation, and it seems to me misguided to consider all of them either irrational or hypocritical. The renowned biblical scholar Mordechai Breuer even developed a theory ("the aspect approach") that reconciles modern biblical criticism with the belief in the divine origin of the Torah.

THE TRUTH OF JEWISH REVELATION AND RELIGIOUS PLURALISM

Mendelssohn asserted his belief in the revelation on Mount Sinai and endorsed the Jewish tradition referring to this origin. How does this tally with genuine religious pluralism, that is, with accepting the other's same claim to truth as mine, although both contradict each other? It is possible to accept religious pluralism in the political sense, and it is possible to accept a common denominator of different creeds (as is indeed natural religion), and yet the belief in different revelations seems to be mutually exclusive. Mendelssohn wishes no "compromise between the faiths" that would be an agreement over symbols and words. "In reality, everyone would then attach to the same words a different meaning of his own," and "universal hypocrisy" would be the result. He accepts that "diversity is evidently the plan and purpose of Providence" (*Jerusalem*, 136–38). How can he maintain this together with his firm belief in the exclusive truth of Judaism?

The resolution of the seeming contradiction is this: The credibility of a historical proposition (in this case, the report of revelation) is dependent on trust in the informers. Trustworthiness may be substantiated, but trust is granted. The former is a judgment; the latter is an attitude and an action. We may have reasons to trust one person, group, or tradition rather than another, but a full justification of trust is an inconsistent notion: Trust consists in transcending the evidence justifying it.[15] Since we acquire our language and the basic fabric of our worldview by appropriating the social knowledge of the society in which we grow up, we are likely to trust this tradition more than others. And since trust cannot and need not be fully epistemically justified, and also involves affectionate moments, everybody is entitled to trust "familiar" (!) witnesses more than foreigners. In Lessing's *Nathan the Wise* (third act, seventh entry), Nathan (Mendelssohn) adduces this argument. In whom are we likely to put trust? Surely in our own people, in those whose blood we are and who have taken care of us when we were children. All other circumstances being equal, everybody is entitled to believe more the traditions of his own society than others.

But the very same argument for the credibility of one's own tradition—trust in witnesses akin to one—substantiates the claim of adherents of another creed to believe in *their* tradition. In spite of inclination, fairness demands therefore that we grant our opponents and ourselves the same right to truth concerning all truth claims dependent on trust, not on proof. Strict trust in our own tradition goes here hand in hand with the acknowledgment of the equal right of others to trust their own. This is a philosophical stance concerning epistemic pluralism, not political pluralism or tolerance based on indifference concerning religion and philosophy. The maxim "In meinem Staat soll ein jeder nach seiner Façon selig werden" (In my state everyone should find salvation after their own fashion), attributed to Mendelssohn's contemporary, Friedrich II of Prussia, is a political one, not a religious or philosophical statement.

In short, Mendelssohn's belief both in natural religion and in Jewish revelation and his granting Christianity the same claim to validity are consistent with his epistemology. And his religious pluralism distracts nothing from his conviction that Judaism is the true religion.[16]

CHAPTER 4

The Language of Action
in Biblical Times

The truths of natural religion are revealed "through nature and thing, but never through word and script" (*Jerusalem*, 90). However, Judaism is revealed through word and script, and moreover, it is so transmitted to later generations. Three questions must be answered to buttress the authenticity of contemporary Judaism.

First, if, as Mendelssohn believes, language is ambiguous, how can we be certain that the historical addressees of revelations understood them properly? Second, how can we know that the texts we have are identical to those revealed thousands of years ago? How can the mere body of the text be faithfully preserved, a certain number of words, sentences, passages? And third, how do we know that the sense of the text has been preserved, that today we properly understand the ancient text?

The second question is easy to answer, and the problem it addresses is easiest to solve. Once script was invented, the conservation of an unaltered text is in principle possible. *Verba volant, scripta manent.* A written text on durable material preserves the body of the text. Of course, we know how difficult it is to safeguard from corruption a text handed down in tradition, but in principle the problem is solved once a lasting representation is available. In Jewish tradition many means were used to "freeze" the text of the Torah. With meticulous care, the verses, the pericopes (פרשות), and so on, of the authoritative version of the text (*Massorah*) are counted, and an inventory is added at the end of each book.

Wrongly written words are kept as they are, and the correct form is merely added in the margins; even the form of some oddly written single letters is mandatory. Mendelssohn not only was well informed of these means but also practiced them himself in his edition of the Torah.[1]

More difficult are the two other problems. How do we know that the addressees of revelations understood them properly? The answer lies in the special kind of language used in revelation: a language of action that is least prone to misunderstanding. The last problem, the preservation of the sense of the text over thousands of years, is solved by the special medium of Jewish tradition: ceremonial law.

THE ADVANTAGE OF ORAL OVER WRITTEN LANGUAGE: THE LEGACY OF JUDAH HALEVI

Mendelssohn believes that commonsense knowledge of objects of the five senses and represented in natural language is reliable. However, language also refers to objects that are not external objects of our senses, namely, abstract and metaphysical objects as well as our thoughts, feelings, and intentions. Moreover, language is used not only to make assertions on matters of fact, but also on possibilities and to pronounce wishes and orders. How can natural language be adequate to these tasks?

To secure unambiguous meaning of the biblical language, Mendelssohn adopts various ideas of medieval Jewish and contemporary philosophy to conceive a "language of action," a language in which physical performance is accompanied by spoken language as well as gestures and mimicry. An expression in which the different media refer to the same content greatly reduces the possibility of misunderstandings. A contemporary philosopher, Condillac, suggested that all language and even all arts used to express our thoughts originated in the language of action:

> It will be shown how it [the language of action] produced all the arts that pertain to the expression of our thoughts: the arts of gesture, dance, speech, declamation, the art of recording it, the art of pantomime, of music, of poetry, eloquence, writing, and the different characters of language.[2]

Inversely read, Condillac implies that the language of action combines the power of expression of all these arts and techniques of communication; he also implies that the power of expression of language alone, especially of written language, is very poor when compared to the language of action.

Consider first the advantages involved in oral language when compared with its written form. Speech is much more variegated than its written representation. The "same written sign is read and pronounced differently in different combinations and positions." Intonation, prosody, and finally mimicry and gestures reduce ambiguities (*Jerusalem*, 109–10). Mendelssohn surely encountered this idea in Judah Halevi's *Kuzari*, which he studied with his mentor, Israel b. Moses ha-Levi of Zamosc, whose commentary on this book he copied with his own hand.[3]

Judah Halevi writes:

> The Rabbi said: "The purpose of language is to allow that which is within the soul of the speaker to enter into the soul of the listener. This purpose cannot be accomplished properly unless the two are face-to-face. This is the advantage that the spoken word has over the written word, as people say, "From the mouths of the scribes and not from the mouths of the books."[4] One can better understand oral communication, because the speaker will pause at the break points, will speak continuously when the sentences should be connected, and will use harsh or soft intonation. The speaker can also use body language—eye movement, mouth gestures, and so on—to indicate when he is amazed, inquisitive, providing plain information, hopeful, fearful, or submissive. These gestures convey the message much more efficiently than a message without them. The speaker can be aided by the movement of his eyes and eyebrows, his head, and his hands, in order to portray anger, desire, submissiveness, or arrogance to the desired degree." (*Kuzari*, II, 72; Korobkin, 112–13)

Moreover, Jewish lore knows a system of signs that may partially compensate for facial expressions and gestures, prosody and intonation when a text is not spoken but is communicated in writing. This is the system of the "cantillations," the signs serving as punctuation marks and musical notes, supplying a melody for chanting or reciting the Hebrew text of the Bible as well as indicating the prosodic structure of the sentences. No wonder that Halevi emphasizes the importance of the cantillations:

> They indicate where to pause and where to continue reading; they distinguish the question from the answer, the subject from the predicate, that which is said hastily from that which is said slowly, that which is commanded from that which is requested—books can be written on the subject. (*Kuzari*, II, 72; Korobkin, 113)

Mendelssohn, even more than previous commentators, stressed the importance of the cantillations for a correct exegesis of the biblical text.[5] He explicitly refers to Halevi and adopts his view (*Kuzari*, III, 30–31) that although the written biblical text was originally given by Moses to the people of Israel without cantillations, Moses himself heard the entire Torah recited by God himself with the proper vocalization, intonation, and cantillations and declaimed it in his turn to Joshua, who recited it to the elders of Israel, from whom the tradition continues.[6]

> The child learning from his father or the pupil listening to his teacher would hear these announciations with whatever was appropriate for their proper pronunciation, just as he had also received it from his father or teacher. He would similarly rehearse it with his children and pupils. . . . [T]hey would not give their children the Holy Script and leave it to them to read the written text only, because this would be to them as a sealed book, but they read it to them and rehearsed it with them, outloud and chanting. They would thereby transmit to them the Torah's cantillation notes, and would sweeten its words like honey, so that the words might enter their hearts and remain there as firmly implanted goads and nails.[7]

THE LANGUAGE OF ACTION AND SPOKEN LANGUAGE IN THE PHILOSOPHY OF THE ENLIGHTENMENT

Obscurity and ambiguities specific to written language can be diminished by the cantillations or spoken language, in personal contact. However, the very meaning of single linguistic expressions, even words, may be doubtful and misleading. In order to conceive appropriate remedies, it is necessary to understand how meaning is constituted in the first place. In the philosophy of the Enlightenment this question is answered by the narration of a real or possible development of language from its origin onwards. Mendelssohn was well versed in these discussions. In fact, the rudimentary conceptions of the *Kuzari* and the philosophy of the Enlightenment and even much later conceptions in the nineteenth and twentieth centuries are so close to each other that it is rather difficult to see the differences.[8]

Condillac begins the section of his book devoted to the origin and development of language with a caveat that he had already introduced in the first chapter. There he wishes to establish that we have no ideas other than those received from the senses. If not restricted, his principle implies that a soul separated from the body cannot have ideas. Condillac therefore reminds the reader that his principle applies only to the human condition after the original sin (*Essai sur l'origine des connaissances*, I.1 #8; Aarsleff, 13–14). Addressing now the origin of language, Condillac introduces a similar warning: Adam and Eve were of course in command of language thanks to a *concursus extra ordinarius* of God. Suppose, however, that after the deluge, two children of different sex were wandering in the desert and that a people originated from them. Could they have developed a language, and if yes, how?[9]

Condillac now outlines a process of development of language from a language of action (*langage d'action*) to an articulated spoken language. At first, an isolated child is governed by sporadic imagination: the perception of a need evokes the perception of the objects that last satisfied it, and if it arouses a strong emotion, it will also trigger a vocal expression that thus becomes its natural sign. This child not only expresses his need vocally, but attempts to reach the object satisfying the need, that is, moves his limbs and head in its direction. When in company, his companion follows the motion and looks at this object. With time, they begin to associate these cries and bodily motions with the perceptions that evoke them, then to produce the actions in order to communicate their feelings and needs to one another (*Essai sur l'origine des connaissances*, II.1.1; Aarsleff, 113–19).

In the next step they give things names, conventional vocal signs. Needless to say, at first only simple objects of everyday practice were named: tree, fruit, water, fire—all substantives. The names for the objects' parts follow later, then names for the properties and circumstances, that is, adjectives and adverbs. Objects of the inner sense, for example, emotions, can be expressed only indirectly: by pointing to the object to which the emotion refers, indicating by action one's purpose, and pronouncing the name of the object in a specific intonation that expresses one's attitude and state of mind (II.1.9; Aarsleff, 156–63).

With time, spoken language is found to be as comfortable as the language of action, and both are used alternately. Finally the use of spoken language replaces the language of action. However, there was an epoch when a mixture of both was used. The Bible testifies to this epoch. Here Condillac quotes Warburton at length:

> Language, as appears both from the records of Antiquity, and the Nature of the Thing, was at first extremely rude, narrow, and equivocal; so that Men would be perpetually at a loss on any new Conception or uncommon Adventure to explain themselves intelligibly to one another. This would naturally set them upon supplying the Deficiencies of Speech by apt and significant Signs. Accordingly, in the first Ages of the World, mutual Converse was upheld by a mixed Discourse of Words and ACTIONS; and Use and Custom, as in most other Circumstances of Life improving what arose out of Necessity, into Ornament, this Practice subsisted long after the Necessity had ceased; especially amongst the Eastern People, whose natural Temperature inclined them to a Mode of Conversation which so well exercised their Vivacity, by Motion; and so much gratified it, by a perpetual Representation of material Images: Of this we have innumerable Instances in Holy Scripture: As where the false Prophet pushed with Horns of Iron, to denote the entire Overthrow of the Syrians (1 Kings 22); where Jeremiah, by God's Direction, hides the Linen Girdle in a Hole of the Rock near Euphrates (Jeremiah 8); where he breaks a potter's Vessel in Sight of the People (ch. 19); puts on Bonds and Yokes (ch. 27), and casts a Book into Euphrates (ch. 51); where Ezekiel, by the same Appointment, delineates the Siege of Jerusalem on a Tile (Ezekiel, ch. 4); weighs the

Hair of his Beard in Balances (ch. 5); carries out his Household-stuff (ch. 7), and joins together the two Sticks for Judah and Israel (ch. 37:16). By these Actions the Prophets instructed the People in the Will of God, and conversed with them in Signs.[10]

In Condillac, the language of action does not only supplement spoken language, but is also its origin. Moreover, spoken language was modeled after the language of action (*Essai sur l'origine des connaissances,* II.1.9; Aarsleff, 156–62). The interpretation of Scripture in which both languages or a mixture of them were used can rely on both. But the biblical examples quoted above already indicate why people in biblical times reliably understood each other and divine messages: they used not merely spoken language but also the language of action. This is shown in the next section.

The language of action as well as spoken language could at first only point or refer to singular sensual objects. From words referring to such objects, words for abstract objects were derived, and they are, therefore, necessarily metaphorical (*Essai sur l'origine des connaissances,* II.1.10, #103 n.; Aarsleff, 165). Above we encountered these views as Mendelssohn's, but here they receive a philosophical justification and a historical explanation. In addition, operations of the mind were metaphorically named after actions of the body (#103). This extension of the use of language was hence achieved at the cost of certainty of reference and meaning. People never understand each other better than when they refer to sensual objects of experience. Problems arise as soon as there is no empirical model for the use of a word. In transcending the limited area of singular empirical objects, two complementary problems arise: different speakers understand the same words differently without realizing the fact; and people disagree because although they think the same ideas (meanings), they use different words to express them. Remedy is again offered by the language of action: when people share the circumstances of living, they can resolve equivocations with the help of ostension (II.1.9, # 80; Aarsleff, 156). Severed from common practice in a community, the use of language results in misunderstandings and logomachies that lead to errors, as even the works of philosophers show (II.1.10–11; Aarsleff, 164–72).

Mendelssohn's views on the metaphorical nature of all terms refer-ring to intangible objects and his repeated conviction that philosophical and theological controversies are rooted in misunderstandings perfectly agree with this account of Condillac.[11] If read only in the context of Men-delssohn's elaborations on religion, one is inclined to interpret his stance on controversies as expressing his mild character or his opportunism. On the background of contemporary philosophy of language, a sincere philosophical concern appears, perhaps even a justification for his view.

Finally, it should also be noted that the "language of gestures" was not only held in high esteem by Mendelssohn and his contemporaries, but successfully put to practice precisely in these years. Travelers often reported that they communicated with the natives by means of ges-tures, and in 1776 l'Abbé de l'Epée's book appeared in which he pre-sented his "language of gestures." It is remembered as a language for the deaf and mute, but its inventor thought of it also as a "universal language," as the book's title explicitly states.[12] This language could be understood as inspired by a philosophical program: abstract ideas were analyzed into elements that have affinities to material objects that in their turn were rendered by gestures. To understand an abstract idea in this language was to understand its composition of simpler ones, in fact its possible emergence from concrete actions and objects.

MENDELSSOHN ON THE BIBLICAL LANGUAGE OF ACTION: THE LORD'S COVENANT WITH ABRAM

Mendelssohn's skepticism concerning natural language and his em-phasis on the biblical language of action are two aspects of his view on the necessary conditions of successful representation. These conditions are fulfilled by the specific biblical synthesis of spoken language and language of action much better than by one of its components alone. The fundamental truths of Judaism are trustworthy because they were revealed either by means of such synthetic representation or by lan-guage emulating the language of action. This reliable representation will serve Mendelssohn also as a model for his understanding of the "ceremonial law." Consider first the foundational bond of God and his people. In the account of the Lord's covenant with Abram it says:

בַּיּוֹם הַהוּא, כָּרַת יְהוָה אֶת-אַבְרָם--בְּרִית לֵאמֹר: לְזַרְעֲךָ, נָתַתִּי אֶת-הָאָרֶץ הַזֹּאת, מִנְּהַר
מִצְרַיִם, עַד-הַנָּהָר הַגָּדֹל נְהַר-פְּרָת.

In the King James Version:

> In the same day the LORD made a covenant with Abram, saying, Unto thy seed have I given this land, from the river of Egypt unto the great river, the river Euphrates. (Genesis 15:18)

And in Luther's translation in the version of 1545:

> An dem Tage machte der HERR einen Bund mit Abram und sprach: [etc.]

And now Mendelssohn:

> Damals zerschnitt der Ewige mit Awram einen Bund, und sprach: [etc.]

Note the expression "zerschnitt einen Bund." It means literally "cut" or "cut to pieces" a bond. This expression does not exist in German. You may say, as Luther and Zunz do, "einen Bund machen" (make a bond), or "einen Bund stiften" (establish a bond) as Mendelssohn says on another occasion, or "einen Bund schließen" (Ludwig Philipsohn), or "einen Bund knüpfen," or similar expressions. However, Mendelssohn's "einen Bund zerschneiden" is not only nonexistent; it is strictly impossible and irritating. This is so, because *Bund* means "bond," knot, something that you tie, connect, not something that you cut up. This is so in English, and this is so also in German.

So why did Mendelssohn use *zerschneiden?* Evidently because he wanted to translate literally the Hebrew *karat brit* (כרת ברית) and *karat* indeed means "to cut." German and Hebrew use different metaphors for the same content. However, Mendelssohn is a very reflective translator, and in his introduction titled *Or la-Netiva* (אור לנתיבה) he dedicates more than ten pages to a discussion of the problems of translation. He there discusses the difference in the semantics of words in different languages and the differences in meaning due to different syntax, and so on, and then concludes with an explicit *votum* against literal translation.

Thus languages differ from each other in the way of expression and each of them has its own proper ways which the other has not. And if, therefore, you would translate the text word for word into another language, the speaker of that language will sometimes not understand it at all, and even if he does, he will understand the main intention of the text only, but will not sense its loveliness of expression and the text will lose in comparison to the original language. (*Or la-Netiva* 32b; *JubA* 15.1, 32)

And yet in our example Mendelssohn not only translated verbatim, but even used an expression that does not exist in German. So why did he translate כרת ברית as "zerschnitt einen Bund"?

We do not have to guess. In his commentary on verse 10 of the same chapter, Mendelssohn explains his decision in a long passage in his *Bi'ur*. But first the verse itself. God commands Abram to cut three different animals into halves:

וַיִּקַּח-לוֹ אֶת-כָּל-אֵלֶּה, וַיְבַתֵּר אֹתָם בַּתָּוֶךְ, וַיִּתֵּן אִישׁ-בִּתְרוֹ, לִקְרַאת רֵעֵהוּ;

In the King James translation:

And he took unto him all these, and divided them in the midst, and laid each piece one against another. (Genesis 15:10)

And in Mendelssohn:

Awram brachte ihm alle diese Stücke, zerschnitt sie in der Mitte, und legte jedes Stück dem andern gegen über.

Note that Mendelssohn uses the same word, *"zerschnitt,"* for cutting the animals and making the *"Bund,"* the covenant, although in the Hebrew original two different words are used: b.t.r.; k.r.t. כרת, בתר! Now, in the *Bi'ur* to this verse, Mendelssohn explains at length "the distress in translating the expression כריתת הברית into German since it was necessary to translate 'ein Bündnis zerschneiden,' and this is a strange and wrong expression (מליצה זרה ובלתי נכונה) since *kritah* כריתה (*zerschneiden* [to cut]) is the opposite of tying." So why did he nevertheless use it?

Mendelssohn explains:

> The meaning of a covenant between humans is that they oblige them-
> selves to help one another to reach a certain goal . . . and since a promise
> cannot be made by means of an oral expression alone without a deed
> (ואחרי שאין הבטחה בבטוי שפתים לבד בלי מעשה) people were accustomed to
> validate and confirm their words with a deed proper to this purpose. . . .
> And in order to validate and reinforce the words of a covenant between
> men, it was the custom in ancient times to take a whole animal, cut it
> into two and walk through in between the halves, and it seems that they
> chose this deed because each part of it denotes (מורה על) something.
> Cutting refers to the fact that the issue is judged and determined as if
> already done and that nothing may be changed in it,[13] and passing be-
> tween the parts denotes the unity of intention and will of those who
> enter the covenant, and as one half is not complete without the opposite
> half, so the will of one of them is not complete without the will of his
> partner . . . and in analogy to this deed it is said in Hebrew that they "cut
> a convenant" (ומן המעשה הזה הושאל בלשון הקודש לאמר שכרתו ברית).

And Mendelssohn continues to interpret the analogies between the action and the words in the covenant, but these are of no further interest
to us. What is important is Mendelssohn's principle:

> a promise cannot be made by means of an oral expression alone with-
> out an action (אין הבטחה בבטוי שפתים לבד בלי מעשה).

"Making a covenant" (ברית) hence refers to the actions involved in
the ceremony and to the verbal expression accompanying them, as well
as to the establishment of the mutual obligation. Moreover, the "covenant" may also refer to the results brought about by the action and later
serving as a sign of the bond. Thus God uses the word *bond* (ברית) to
refer both to this covenant and to its sign in the flesh of the circumcised
male (Genesis 17:13):

וְהָיְתָה בְרִיתִי בִּבְשַׂרְכֶם, לִבְרִית עוֹלָם.

and my covenant shall be in your flesh for an everlasting covenant.

The unity of the language of action, spoken language, and obligation established appears not only in this covenant and in others (Jeremiah 34:18–21; Exodus 24:1–8), and not only in Jewish tradition. Mendelssohn correctly refers to "ancient times" in general.[14] Thus in Latin the expressions "foedus facere" or "foedus icere" refer to making a bond by slaying an animal and smearing blood onto the partners.

There are more examples of covenants that consist in some action that also leaves behind a sign (אות), representing the covenant. Not only covenants, but all agreements consist in word and deed. The agreements between Jacob and Laban (Genesis 31:51–53), between Abraham and Avimelekh (Genesis 21:27–30), and so on, involve an action, as does also the solemn promise that Abraham's servant gives his master when he leaves to search for a bride for Isaac (Genesis 24:1–2), or when Joseph promises Jacob to bury him in Canaan (Genesis 47:29). An oath, too, cannot be made by means of an oral expression alone without an action. Let just two of many examples suffice: God's promise to Noah was accompanied by the sign of the rainbow (Genesis 9:8 ff.); God's solemn oath is described as if he raises his hands (e.g., Deuteronomy 32:40; Exodus 6:8; Numbers 34:30), in analogy to human oath and prayer (Genesis 14:22; Psalms 28:2; 63:5).

The same principle, the unity of action and linguistic expression, is deeply entrenched also in Halakhah, Jewish religious law. Of course, I cannot enter this vast field. I would like only to point out that the acquisition and transfer of proprietary rights—a model of other agreements between persons—beautifully exemplifies this principle. The acquisition of proprietary rights requires a deed, an action demonstrating the actual transfer, be it "lifting" or "pulling" the goods, the presence of the goods in one's courtyard (ארבע אמות), or an act of taking possession (חזקה). With perhaps one exception (קנין סודר), all these actions do not symbolize anything other than themselves: they are the act of acquiring property.[15]

The same is true in reverse: the mere action of transfer of goods is valid as transfer of property rights only if it can be taken to testify to the will of the persons involved. In his *Jerusalem,* Mendelssohn writes:

Everything depends solely upon the declaration of will, and even the actual transfer of movable goods is valid only insofar as it is taken to be a sign of a sufficient declaration of will. The mere transfer, viewed by itself, neither gives nor takes away a right, whenever this intent is not connected with it. (54)

To sum up: In the Bible a covenant and other agreements are a unity of action and verbal expression. In the case of the Lord's covenant with Abram (significantly named the "covenant between the parts," ברית בין הבתרים) the verbal expression mirrors the action; in the covenant of circumcision, the action itself leaves behind the sign of the covenant. Only the unity of action and expression is a reliable testimony to the intentions of the agents. This unity of action and expression was so important to Mendelssohn that he chose to use a "strange and wrong" expression in German rather than lose the point that cannot be translated into correct German. The same unity of action and verbal expression is also ubiquitous in Halakhah. And it is this unity of action and verbal expression that guarantees that the biblical actors properly understood the intention of their interlocutor and that we can better understand the divine messages reported in such language than if they were made by spoken or written language only.

From a later point of view, we observe that all examples mentioned are "performative utterances." They do not state facts (and are not true or false) but are "speech acts": they perform an action (make an oath, establish a bond, etc.).[16] However, as if out of distrust in the power of words to accomplish this by themselves, words and physical actions were coordinated. In the biblical tradition and later Jewish ceremonial law, words alone do not suffice. To do the things in question, you need words, but also a physical action with material objects. Now, although no spoken language can do things or adequately represent when severed from action, not all languages are equally deficient. Of all natural languages, Hebrew is the most appropriate. In fact, it shares to some degree the advantages of mathematical symbolism. I will elaborate this now.

THE LANGUAGE OF CREATION
AND THE LANGUAGE OF THE BIBLE

Mathematical symbolism explains the superiority of mathematics, especially geometry, over other areas of human knowledge. It is "essential."

The symbols and the rules of their manipulation conform to the objects and the rules of their combinations (*JubA* 2, 281–82). Not so in natural language. Words may be simply conventional and reveal nothing of their referents' nature, and grammatical rules may be entirely different from the real connections between the objects represented. This restricts the use of language to representation of the known and excludes its possibility to generate new knowledge. Natural language cannot even show that "the line is sweet" or "Nothingness nothings" are not proper expressions. Words may indeed serve as name tags attached to their objects, but if most words are metaphors, then we cannot even know whether the tag is attached to its proper object: Maimonides' critique of anthropomorphic conceptions of God in the first part of *The Guide of the Perplexed* addresses exactly this problem. The Bible is replete with expressions attributing to God sensual perceptions, emotions, and corporeal properties. Natural language hence is not only of little help in conceiving abstract truth, but in some areas it positively misleads us.

Consider the notion of Man. Its definition and essence is *animal rationale,* a living being endowed with reason. This not only shows what it is but also shows its place in the "Great Chain of Being." But the word *man,* as Maimon remarked, is not composed of the words for "animal" and "reason." It hence conveys no information on the nature of its referent and is of little help in learning about the structure of the world. It also cannot distinguish possible from impossible predications.

In these respects, Hebrew is preferable, believes Mendelssohn, because it is the language of creation and agrees with the nature of things. Mendelssohn quotes in the introduction to his translation of the Pentateuch a rabbinic saying: "Just as the Torah was given in the Holy Tongue, so also the world was created in the Holy Tongue" (*Bereshit Rabbah,* 31:8; quoted in *Or la-Netiva,* 22b). Being also the language of creation, Hebrew reflects to some degree the essence and essential relations of things. This shows in Hebrew proper names, not all of which are arbitrary but express a significant property of the object named. *Adam* is derived from *adamah* (soil, earth), which in turn is derived from *adom* (red), related to *dam* (blood); Eve (*Chava*), the mother of all humans, is derived from *chai* (alive), and so on. In Hebrew, but not in Greek or Latin, the names for male and female animals are often closely related (e.g., *ish, isha* for man and woman). Mendelssohn does not consider modern languages (e.g., man, woman) since they evidently could not have been God's language in creation. This means that the semantics of single Hebrew words and their relations convey knowledge of their objects.[17]

Another unique advantage of Hebrew is that it is the language of revelation. Moses heard the entire Torah spoken by God himself with the proper vocalization, intonation, and cantillations. Thanks to the cantillations, Hebrew prosody and intonation are so perfect that speech best agrees with inner speech, with thought (24b).[18] Because of this agreement between speech and thought, grammar reflects logic, as it were, and Mendelssohn devotes an extensive part of his *Or la-Netiva* to a discussion of the logico-grammatical categories of Maimonides' *Millot ha-Higayyon* (Treatise on Logic) on which he also wrote an extensive commentary (43a–55b). Mendelssohn's discussion of Hebrew as a system of representation hence ranks it somewhere between natural language and mathematics.

In a comprehensive synthesis of arguments from various traditions, Mendelssohn thus attempts to substantiate the trustworthiness of the revelation on Sinai, and also that the text revealed can be reliably understood. However, these arguments also emphasize his basic skepticism concerning language, his doubts that in general language can reliably represent meaning. Hebrew is not free of these faults and yet is best among existing natural languages. Some of its substantives reflect the essence of their referents, its syntax reflects logic, and its cantillations represent the proper prosody. The Hebrew Bible is hence least prone to misunderstandings, especially if the content is represented not only by language but also by a description of the language of action, as in the key episodes discussed above, and studied not in isolation but in living intercourse with a mentor. Thus we have at our disposal more than only the lexical meaning of single words or expressions to understand the biblical narrative. This and continuous oral tradition explain why the biblical text has remained alive and understood through the ages, whereas the contemporary Egyptian hieroglyphics have become proverbial for obscurity. Another most important difference is that hieroglyphics are particularly conducive to idolatry.

We can now answer all three questions raised at the beginning of this chapter. The biblical language of action and its representation in figurative language are appropriate to guarantee the proper understanding of revelation; the technique of transmission by writing and declamation, in addition to specialized measures of precaution, safeguard the text from change and corruption; and biblical exegesis that pays attention to the biblical language of action and the cantillations assures as much as possible a proper understanding of the text's meaning.

CHAPTER 5

Idolatry

Egyptian and Jewish

In *Jerusalem* Mendelssohn discusses the threat of idolatry inherent to the use of script and other permanent signs. His foremost example is Egyptian hieroglyphics. He also remarks that the Hebrew alphabet derived from hieroglyphics. Not only Egyptian hieroglyphics but also Egyptian idolatry are highly important for Judaism. According to the biblical report, Judaism was constituted in an act of physical and religious opposition to ancient Egypt: the Exodus and the indubitable revelation on Sinai. And yet, soon thereafter, in the sin of the golden calf, the Jews relapsed into Egyptian idolatry.

If Mosaic religion is understood as a "counterreligion" to the Egyptian, then its practices can be understood as means of drawing a dividing line between the Jews and the nation that hosted them for centuries. All the more reason that the relapse into idolatry immediately after revelation on Mount Sinai seems inexplicable. The Egyptian religion appears here as both the repulsive and the attractive opposite pole to Judaism.

There is even an immediate and specific connection between Egyptian hieroglyphics and Judaism. Mendelssohn believed—as we do today, too—that the Hebrew alphabet developed out of hieroglyphics. In his *Jerusalem* Mendelssohn goes into the details: א, aleph, is derived from the pictogram of *elef* or *aluf*, אלף: an ox; ב, beth, is derived from the pictogram of *bayit*, בית: house; ג, gimel, derives from the pictogram of *gammal*, גמל: camel; and so on (*Jerusalem*, 110).[1]

Were the hieroglyphics conducive to the Hebrews' relapse into Egyptian idolatry in the adoration of the calf? And did the transition from the pictorial representation of the hieroglyphics to the conventional representation of the alphabet eventually safeguard the Hebrews from relapsing again into Egyptian idolatry? Or does it also generate new dangers? These are important themes in Mendelssohn's thought, both in his *Jerusalem* and in his commentary on the Bible. However, a major issue is the distinction between Gentile and Jewish idolatry. Mendelssohn argues with many others that Jewish monotheism is more restrictive than the monotheism of natural religion. This is the ultimate justification for the continued separate existence of the Jewish people and Jewish religion: Judaism is a safeguard of monotheism free of idolatry.

HIEROGLYPHICS AND IDOLATRY: THE SIN OF THE GOLDEN CALF

In the second part of *Jerusalem,* Mendelssohn sketches his theory of the connection between representation and idolatry. This theory is based on the best ethnographic and historical scholarship of his day. In fact, Mendelssohn displays considerable erudition and judgment concerning ancient Egyptian history and pre-alphabetic representations of the Indians.[2] Most of Mendelssohn's knowledge of hieroglyphics derives directly or indirectly (via Condillac and Meiners) from Warburton, who was the main authority in this field. However, Mendelssohn had additional sources of information on the ancient history of Egypt, and he did not fully adopt Warburton's view on the function of hieroglyphics.

Mendelssohn sketches a progressive development of representation from the concrete to the abstract. Abstract concepts were at first represented by individual "things themselves." Note, however, that these "things themselves" do not represent themselves but rather abstract concepts! Thus, for example, a lion represented courage, a dog faithfulness, and so on (*Jerusalem,* 107–8). "Things themselves" hence means in this context that the symbols were not designed as symbols but are real objects, and that they are used as synecdoches: the lion does not only represent lions or the concept of a lion but also the lion's characteristic property: courage. Similarly, the dog does not only represent dogs but also their property: loyalty.[3] Later, "images" of these things replaced them, and then "outlines" of the images substituted the images. This very much resembles the way we use today an outline of a schematic pictogram of a man to signal a public toilet for men. Finally, a combination of such outlines formed so-called hieroglyphics (*Jerusalem,* 108), and on the basis of hieroglyphics alphabetic script was invented.

The problem with representations that are not entirely arbitrary and recognizable as mere symbols is that they may be believed to have intrinsic meaning. If its symbolic function is not understood, an object or an icon may be taken to be "the thing itself." Mendelssohn's idea is this: a good symbol is "transparent." We look "through" it to what it stands for. A good symbol does not itself attract attention, is often not "seen" at all, as when we don't remember whether the sign on the door said "No Entry!" in words or was the traffic sign "No Entry"; or when bilingual people do not remember whether the word on the traffic sign in Canada was "Stop" or "Arrêt." A symbol is problematic when the "sign-vehicle," the sensuous object, attracts attention to itself instead of to the referent, and is believed to have intrinsic meaning, not a mere sign for something entirely different from itself. This is what Mendelssohn says of hieroglyphics:

> Misunderstanding, on the one hand, and misuse, on the other, transformed what should have been an improvement of man's condition into corruption and deterioration. . . . On the one hand, misunderstanding: the great multitude was either not at all or only half instructed in the notions which were to be associated with these perceptible signs. They saw the signs not as mere signs, but believed them to be the things themselves. (*Jerusalem,* 110–11)

I will return to the expression "the things themselves" at the end of this section. But first to the hieroglyphics. Suppose that simple hieroglyphics are pictorial, icons, and resemble the signified. In this case they may be believed to share properties with the things they represent. In fact, they obviously do. The question is, however, what properties they do and do not share and whether they share only traits of their appearance or others as well. Now, compound hieroglyphics, combinations of simple icons, often show no resemblance to what they represent, often with nothing existent. Since they are not "essential" signs and may, therefore, be compounded in arbitrary ways, complex hieroglyphics were "misshapen and preposterous figures which had no existence of their own in nature." However, in this case it was exactly their enigmatic character that fed superstition (*Jerusalem*, 110–11).[4] They were recognized as signs, but their meaning was not known. Therefore, imagination imputed to them some fantastic meaning. Moreover, "if the strange hieroglyphics were not understood by the common people, they were likely to be abused by the ruling learned" (110–11).

Mendelssohn hence suggests that the "multitude" is not able to understand the arbitrary, purely conventional nature of signs, as it cannot understand abstract concepts or accept invisible entities as real. The multitude wishes images that stand for real, physical entities, and it interprets conventional signs or signs for abstract concepts as if they were pictograms that represent concrete objects.[5] He also believes that there is a learned class that profits from the deception of the common people and uses hieroglyphics for this purpose, ascribing to them a mysterious nature, even holiness. It should be stressed that this is not Mendelssohn's original idea but rather was commonplace for centuries.[6] However, with the needs of common people on the one hand, the interests of the learned class on the other, monotheism is never safe. And exactly here lies the special mission of the Jewish people: their ceremonial law provides the means to forestall idolatry and defend pure monotheism.

But before they finally received the law, and perhaps strengthened by the hieroglyphic tradition, the people of Israel, even after the Sinaitic revelation, relapsed "into the sinful delusion of the Egyptians," into the idolatry of an image, of which they finally said, "These are your gods, Israel, who brought you out of Egypt" (*Jerusalem*, 120). The association of idolatry with the Egyptians is hence twofold. The Egyptians engaged in the worship of images of animals (not of living animals),[7] and the hieroglyphics are themselves images that are likely to be misunderstood as sacred in themselves.

These are the outlines of the theory that seemed incredible to many readers. Indeed, how could anybody mistake a picture for the pictured, the image of a lion for a lion? Is there any sane person who fears that the image of a lion may bite? And Mendelssohn says so much himself—in his commentary on the sin of the golden calf that was not consulted by his critics:

> There is no such fool on Earth who believes that the gold that was on their ears until today and was made today a cast calf, is he who delivered them from Egypt. But they said that the power [כח] of this form and the spirit [רוח] that is in it delivered them from there. And this is really the mistake of all worshippers of wood and stone, creations of human hands. (Commentary on Exodus 32:4)[8]

Believing that the signs are the things themselves hence does not mean that they are identical or share all properties; it means that *the sign partakes in the power and spirit of what it represents.* As we will see, this theory is much more plausible when read together with Mendelssohn's and his predecessors' commentary on the sin of the golden calf; moreover, Mendelssohn put his finger on the very nature of religious symbols in general. "The symbol," says a renowned phenomenologist of religion, "is a *participation of the sacred in its veritable, actual, form:* between the sacred, and its form, there exists community of essence."[9] This is exactly what Mendelssohn means when he says of idolatry that in it the sign is taken "not as mere sign" but as endowed with power and spirit, or conceived as "the things themselves" (*Jerusalem,* 110–11). However, before we turn to Mendelssohn's interpretation of the sin of the golden calf, we have first to consider why the incident was a sin at all.

Gentile Idolatry, Jewish Idolatry

Suppose that the people of Israel were not informed of the commandments before they produced the golden calf. Did they nevertheless sin at a time when only the existence of the unique God and the Laws of Noah were known to them?

All human beings, says Mendelssohn, can apprehend the eternal truths of natural religion; these do not depend on revelation, nor can eternal truths be commanded. He maintains that the first sentence of the commandments ("I am the LORD thy God" [Exodus 20:2]) is not itself a commandment.[10] Gentiles are obligated by the first Law of Noah to acknowledge one and only one deity as creator and supreme ruler of the entire universe. But, so Mendelssohn continues, the adoration of other "heavenly rulers" (שרי מעלה) or stars or heroes, and so on, who are subordinated to God cannot be forbidden to the Gentiles.[11] "Reason cannot forbid such worship if [the worshiper] does not intend to exempt [himself] from the authority of the supreme God, since by what is he obligated to designate worship and prayer exclusively to God?" Indeed, as long as Gentiles acknowledge that all heavenly rulers are subordinated to the supreme God, even praying, and sacrificing to these beings, even the installation of images and idols cannot be considered a revolt against the eminence of God. The Gentiles may also believe that such service accords with God's will. Indeed, so much is said in the Torah in the same breath in which such service is forbidden Jews:

> Take ye therefore good heed unto yourselves. . . . And lest thou lift up thine eyes unto heaven, and when thou seest the sun, and the moon, and the stars, even all the host of heaven, shouldest be driven to worship them, and serve them, which the LORD thy God hath divided unto all nations under the whole heaven. But the LORD hath taken you, and brought you forth out of the iron furnace, even out of Egypt, to be unto him a people of inheritance, as ye are this day. (*Deuteronomy* 4:15, 19)

Mendelssohn translates "divided unto all nations" (אֲשֶׁר חָלַק יְהוָה אֱלֹהֶיךָ אֹתָם לְכֹל הָעַמִּים תַּחַת כָּל-הַשָּׁמָיִם) as "permitted for all nations" (für alle übrige Völker . . . zugelassen), and the commentary (by Homberg) *ad locum* repeats what Mendelssohn has written in his commentary on Exodus 20:2: "provided that they acknowledge and know that God may He be blessed is the supreme cause and supervisor since the association of God with others [שיתוף] was not forbidden to the Noahides." What counts as idolatry with Jews after revelation is not necessarily idolatry for Gentiles and for the Israelites before the revelation. This notion has implications for the afterlife of Gentiles and also for the interpretation of the sin of the golden calf.[12]

This restricted notion of Gentile idolatry implies that Gentiles can earn afterlife without any recourse to revelation, and also if they venerate images in some form. This is true of the inhabitants of America and India, and this is true of Christians, provided of course that they obey the Noahitic laws. In this Mendelssohn opposes Maimonides and major authorities of his own day who maintained that the afterlife of righteous Gentiles is contingent on their living morally out of obedience to God's decree and not upon their own discretion.[13] In his letter to Jacob Emden, Mendelssohn counters Maimonides' view both on the basis of Jewish lore and philosophically. He points out that already Rabbi Joseph Karo remarked that here Maimonides voices his own opinion only (סברא דנפשי). The source of Maimonides' position, so Mendelssohn suggests, is his view that ethical principles are not based on reason (*muskalot*) but are widely accepted conventions (*mefursamot*). As conventions, they could not be justified by the understanding, and Maimonides, therefore, turned to tradition to justify them. He suggested that they were reliable traditions (*mekubalot*) originating with Adam but that their source has been forgotten. Thus they could both be justified as true, although not as truths of reason. Mendelssohn finds Maimonides' view that the principles of morals are not truths of reason "very strange." He believes that he has "clear and correct proofs" that they are truths of reason.[14] For Mendelssohn morals and the prohibition of idolatry (in the sense of revolting against the rule of God) are truths of reason. These truths, therefore, require no revelation, and the "righteous of the nations" are entitled to the afterlife without any reference to the revelation on Sinai.

The Jews did not know that only the supreme God is worthy of worship before they were explicitly "admonished by God in the Torah" to this effect. Indeed, when forbidding the adoration of other gods and the making of "graven image, or any likeness of any thing that is in heaven above, or that is in the earth beneath, or that is in the water under the earth," God is not speaking as the creator of the world but introduces himself as "God, which have brought thee out of the land of Egypt, out of the house of bondage" (Exodus 20:3–4). God speaks here as the God of Israel, and the prohibition is valid for his people only:

But we, His people, since He delivered us from Egypt, from the house of bondage and did us all these wonders in order that we should be His property and chosen people from all peoples and that He Himself should rule over us without mediation of an angel or a ruler or a star, therefore we, His servants, are obligated to accept the Yoke of His kingdom and rule and to fulfill His decrees; and he decreed that we should serve none but Him alone. (Commentary on Exodus 20:2).

We see that the term *idolatry* is ambiguous. Gentiles and the Israelites before revelation are bound to accept the kingdom of God. They may engage in worship of "intermediaries" as long as this is not done with the intention of revolting against God's rule. However, we cannot attain certain knowledge even of our own intentions, a fortiori of other people. Therefore, the presumption that all people accept God's kingdom cannot be refuted. This, of course, exculpates Gentiles and the Israelites before the proclamation of the Ten Commandments from the sin of idolatry, and thus assures that Gentiles who live morally merit afterlife.

The prohibition of images in the Second Commandment does not follow from reason. The sin of the golden calf was hence idolatry in the sense valid for Jews after revelation but not idolatry in terms of Gentiles. Precisely in this more restrictive notion of monotheism lies the special mission of the chosen people. We cannot say whether a Gentile who worships images or stars revolts thereby against the rule of the supreme God, because we can never know the intentions of another person. It is, however, obvious that from the worship of "subordinated" Gods one can easily slip into the notion that these are Gods per se. With Jews, who may not at all worship images or stars, neither doubts nor this danger arises. The further extended prohibition of idolatry serves as a "fence," as a safeguard around the Torah laws (סיג לתורה). The Jewish people and their ceremonial law continually "call attention to sound and unadulterated ideas of God and his attributes" (*Jerusalem*, 118). Judaism serves, therefore, as a guarantee of true monotheism against the threat of polytheism, fetishism, anthropomorphism, and so on.[15] It has a special mission that does not grant its practitioners any privileges and yet singles them out from other people. Mendelssohn's interpretation thus makes sense of two seemingly mutually exclusive notions—that Jews have no privilege over Gentiles concerning afterlife and that Jews have a special religious mission and may not forsake their heritage. It is therefore that the making of the golden calf, understood as a mediator, would not count as a sin in the case of Gentiles but is a sin in the case of Jews.

In what, then, consisted the sin of the golden calf? It was not the preparation of a picture but the revolt against God when they called out, "These be thy gods, O Israel" (Exodus 32:4). But they had already rebelled earlier against God. In the first verse of the narrative, when it says, "And when the people saw that Moses delayed to come down out of the mount, the people gathered themselves together unto Aaron" (Exodus 32:1), Mendelssohn translates "da liefen die Leute über Aaron zusammen," and he comments that the verb *gathered*, when used with the preposition *unto* (וַיִּקָּהֵל הָעָם עַל-אַהֲרֹן), means "mutiny" (מרידה). Indeed, Mendelssohn's interpretation of the sin of the golden calf shows that if the restrictive Jewish notion of idolatry, that is, the prohibition of images, is not kept, the way is paved to idolatry also in the sense valid for Gentiles, that is, a revolt against God.

The Golden Calf and Astral Magic

In the beginning of his commentary on Exodus 32, Mendelssohn explicitly announces that he adopts the reading of Halevi (*Kuzari*, I, 92–98) and the commentaries of Nachmanides and Ibn Ezra (commentary on Exodus 32:1). All three commentators in whose name Mendelssohn speaks interpret the sin of the golden calf as an attempt at forbidden astral magic—and presumably favor permitted forms of such magic![16] When Moses ascended Mount Sinai, Halevi explains, the people expected him to return with new visible signs of the newly revealed God, as he was later to bring: the tablets in the shrine were to be put in the tabernacle, on which the cloud would rest. All these are visible objects. People felt the need for something to which they may point when narrating the wonders of their God.[17] The Israelites hence did not renounce God, nor was the use of a perceptible sign per se an offense—such signs were also introduced by God and Moses. Their offensive act was to introduce on their own discretion an image and ascribe to it divine power. This transgression came about under the influence of astrologers and writers of talismans (*Kuzari*, I, 97)—the "learned" in Mendelssohn's *Jerusalem*.

Another explanation of the sin that can be integrated with the first is that the people wished a replacement for Moses, the guide through the desert who did not return on time from the Mount. The Israelites first demanded of Aaron: "Make us gods, which shall go before us; for as for this Moses, the man that brought us up out of the land of Egypt, we know not what is become of him" (Exodus 32:23). In his commentary, Mendelssohn offers in Aaron's name the following answer to Moses's later allegations: "At the beginning they intended to make themselves a guide instead of my lord, but then they bowed to it and brought sacrifices to it."

The important distinction is between "at the beginning" and "then." At the beginning, the Israelites did not worship an image of a calf; they believed "that the power of this form and the spirit that is in it, guided them out of there." Later on, the Israelites regarded the calf as a sensual correlate (מקביל מוחש) for God and turned to it when they recounted his marvels, "and thus they drifted from one thing to the next, from thought to thought until they began to direct their prayers and offerings to the figure as all idolaters do."[18] Thus pictorial representation and the ascription of intrinsic value to it may eventually lead to the result no fool would have wished in the beginning.

Israel Zamosc, Mendelssohn's teacher, interpreted Halevi's reference to "astrologers and writers of talismans" as to those who attempt to "draw divine affluence" (הורדת שפע אלהית) with the aid of "an image done for the cult of Heavens" (*Otsar Nechmad, ad locum*).[19] Maimonides, too, associates the Egyptian veneration of animals, or rather, their images, with the corresponding constellation. The Egyptians, he explains with reference to Onkelos, "used to worship the sign of Aries and . . . therefore forbade the slaughter of sheep" (*The Guide of the Perplexed*, III, 46; Pines, 581). Their high respect for cattle is presumably also connected—directly or indirectly—to star worship (see *The Guide of the Perplexed*, III, 30; Pines, 522–23). There is much to support such interpretations in the biblical text itself.

"Calf" and "ox" may be used synonymously. This is natural enough, and concerning the sin of the calf it even has support in the psalm to which Mendelssohn refers here.[20] Second, calf or ox is associated, of course, with the constellation Taurus, be it by shape, be it by the common name.[21] Rabbi Abraham, son of Maimonides, indeed relates the interpretation of his father that the people of Israel adhered to the opinion of astrologers that the Exodus occurred in the sign of Taurus.[22]

Mendelssohn first adopts the view of some commentators that the original intent of the Israelites was not idolatry in the sense of worshiping stars instead of God. When Moses did not return for forty days, the people did not wish another god but "another Moses," "another guide," a "permanent thing that will not perish and die like him," to serve as their guide. They wished to have something to which divine power adheres: "since in those days it was widespread knowledge that the divine adheres to the idols and makes them prophesy" (Mendelssohn, commentary on Exodus 32:1).[23]

Once they had this image, they were tempted to try practices of astral magic and draw the forces of Taurus to the image of the calf. Like other commentators before him, Mendelssohn explains the sin as the outcome of a process.[24] It begins with the wish to turn to something visible when referring to the invisible God; it leads to the ascription of divine powers to this idol; it may end with worship of the idol itself. True, people conceded that there is only one supreme God but maintained that there are also other "godly" rulers next to him. In short: idolatry begins with the ascription of "intrinsic meaning" or supernatural properties or holiness to what should have been regarded as a sign only. What began as an innocent need for a perceptible sign may lead over astral magic to the denial of the unique God or at least to adoring other gods next to him.

We can now better understand Mendelssohn's claim that idolatry consists in the misunderstanding of the representational function of an image. The basis of different kinds of idolatry is not that the image is taken to be the divine but that it is ascribed divine power, that it is supposed to share in "force" and "spirit" with the divine or that the divine "adheres" (ידבק) to it. At the beginning of the story of the golden calf, Mendelssohn remarks that in those days people believed that divine essence (ענין אלהי) adheres to certain "images" or house gods (תרפים)—such as those stolen by Rachel from Laban—which can, therefore, be used for divination.[25] This view depends on conceiving the relation of such sign to the signified, not as purely conventional, but as real, such that the sign partakes in the properties of the represented. Thanks to its form or to human action performed on it, a real connection is supposed to exist between the divine and the material object serving as a sign, such that the object receives divine properties. From here the way may lead to the negation of God, but this is not even necessary; it suffices that the symbol is ascribed divine powers to make its referent, God, lose his singular place or even recede into the background: "thus they drifted from one thing to the next, from thought to thought until they began to direct their prayers and offerings to the figure as all idolaters do." This, however, does not yet explain the association of this sin with hieroglyphics. Here Warburton comes in.

Warburton: Hieroglyphics and Idolatry

Warburton develops in great length a series of arguments to support the thesis that "the true original of animal worship in Egypt was an improved kind of hieroglyphics, called symbols." His arguments are, first, that this kind of idolatry was peculiar to the Egyptians; and second, that the Egyptians didn't worship icons of animals only but also plants "and, in a word, every kind of Being that had qualities remarkably singular or efficacious." Such qualities stand for a characteristic property of a person and represent the person in the same way in which animals represent specific human characters in fables. Third, the Egyptians also adored Chimeras, fantastic compounds of several parts of humans or beasts or mixtures of both that certainly did not exist in nature. It is therefore clear that such beliefs did not arise from the observation of nature but from the manipulation of symbols. The fact that different cities venerated representations of different animals although the Egyptians had "one national religion" shows that these were representations of a deity or of lesser Hero Gods "of whom Animals were but the Representatives" (*The Divine Legation of Moses Demonstrated*, vol. 2, 165–68). Warburton concludes:

> But to put the matter yet further out of question, it may be observed that the most early Brute-Worship in Egypt was not an Adoration of the Animal, but only of the Picture or image of it. . . . From the Second Commandment, and Moses's Exhortation to Obedience, it appears that the Egyptians at the time of the Exodus, worshipped no living Animal, but the Picture or Image only:—"Thou shalt have no other

Gods before me. Thou shalt not make unto thee any graven image, or any Likeness of any thing that is in Heaven above, or that is in the Earth beneath, or that is in the Water under the Earth. Thou shalt not bow down thyself to them, nor serve them" (Exodus 20:3, 4, 5). The consequence was, that Hieroglyphics were forbid; a plain Proof of their being the Source of that Idolatry in question.[26]

In Warburton the Second Commandment is hence a measure against the hieroglyphic idolatry of the Egyptians. So it is in Mendelssohn. With him, the association between idolatry and hieroglyphics is so strong that it enters into his translation of the Pentateuch, not only into his commentary. Leviticus 26:1 reads:

> Ye shall make you no idols nor graven image, neither rear you up a standing image, neither shall ye set up any image of stone (אֶבֶן מַשְׂכִּית) in your land, to bow down unto it: for I am the LORD your God. (King James translation)

Mendelssohn translates:

> Macht Euch keine Götzen, errichtet kein Bild, kein Denkmal, und duldet in eurem Lande keinen Stein mit Bilderschrift zur Verehrung.[27]

Bilderschrift, pictorial script, is German for "hieroglyphics." Moreover, Mendelssohn refers to this locus in his commentary on Exodus 20:20 and hence follows Warburton and interprets the Second Commandment as referring explicitly to hieroglyphics (*Bilderschrift*). In a note to the locus in *Leviticus,* added to the commentary of Herz Weisel, Mendelssohn remarks that hieroglyphics served the sages of Egypt to write down those things that they wished to conceal from the people and of which they said that they are sublime figures that should be venerated and worshiped in order to induce people to respect them (and, of course, respect the learned themselves).[28] We find here both causes of idolatry mentioned in *Jerusalem*: the inclination of the multitude towards the imagination and mysteries and the interest of the sages in deceiving the common people and securing their own superiority and rule.

This interpretation of hieroglyphics as involved in idolatry in Leviticus is supported in Mendelssohn's translation and explanation of the word *chartom* (חרטם) used in Genesis and Exodus. The King James translation renders the plural, *chartumim* (חרטמים), "magicians of Egypt." Mendelssohn translates חרטמים as "*Bilderschriftkundige*," "experts in hieroglyphics" (see Genesis 41:8; Exodus 7:11, 22) and "magicians."[29] The explanation is given in the commentary on the first locus: חרטם (*chartom*), says Mendelssohn, is derived from *cheret* (חרט), and this is the instrument with which you produce engravings on hard surfaces—and this instrument also served in the creation of the golden calf:

> And it is known that at the beginning of writing all things and ideas were written by means of pictures and engravings called hieroglyphics or pictorial script (*Hieroglyphen oder Bilderschrift*) and this writing was practiced by the sages of Egypt and by its means their priests and sages concealed their scientific knowledge and mechanics and magic (חכמת התולדות והתחבולות ומעשה הכשפים) from the multitude since only the priests and the leaders of the people understood it, and until today nobody can interpret these engravings and pictures, and it is therefore possible that chartom (חרטם) was the person who understood these pictures and engravings and knew how to use them and adequately interpret them, and these were the sages and the magicians and the interpreters of dreams in Egypt.

This explanation of *chartom* is repeated in brief in the context of the story of the golden calf and is directly associated with it. In Exodus 32:3–4 we read that the people of Israel brought their golden earrings to Aaron:

> And he received them at their hand, and fashioned it with a graving tool (*cheret*, חֶרֶט), after he had made it a molten calf: and they said, These be thy gods, O Israel, which brought thee up out of the land of Egypt.

In his translation, Mendelssohn omits the word *cheret* (חרט) (engraving tool) but returns to it in his commentary: "A tool of goldsmiths with which one engraves and notches forms in gold, as the pen of the scribe that engraves letters in tablets and books."[30] Thus Mendelssohn moves from the tool of the goldsmith to the pen of scribes, from a three-dimensional figure to pictograms and letters engraved in tablets.

The *chartumim* (חרטמים) are hence scribes, sages, and magicians who use a *cheret* (חרט; engraving tool), after which tool they are named, to engrave or delineate the hieroglyphics. They may use magic to draw the "divine affluence," for example, by preparing an image of a calf and thus draw divine powers from the constellation of "Taurus," bull. Consider the sign of Taurus ♉, and compare it with the ancient aleph, ▷, or with a later א. These are all pictograms of a bull, or "outlines" of such a pictogram, whether they derive from one another or from a common source or, finally, are independent of one another. Mendelssohn suggests that the time of revelation was the time of transition from hieroglyphics to alphabetic script and that the Hebrew alphabet derives from hieroglyphic pictograms. The pictogram of the calf first directly represented a calf (which, in turn, may represent a property of heroes or gods); later the same pictogram (or its simplified variant) represented the syllable with which the word for calf or bull begins. Now, "bull" in Hebrew is *eleph* or *aluph*, both written אלף, as also the name of the letter "aleph" is written (see Deuteronomy 7:13; 28:4, 18, 51). Note that in Hebrew the difference between the syllable "e" and "a" does not show in writing, since aleph is a consonant only and the vocal is not written. The sign in question is hence either a pictogram referring to a bull or already the alphabetic letter "aleph" representing the syllable "א" with which the word *eleph* or *aluph* (אלף), meaning bull, begins. The sin of the calf hence consisted in using either a pictogram of a calf or an aleph (if the two can be distinguished), an image (צלם) of the constellation Taurus (or of the word *eleph*, or *aluph*, "bull," referring to Taurus) in order to draw divine powers by means of the affinity between the star group and this representation and put them into human service. No wonder that two of the few markings in Mendelssohn's copy of Maimonides' *The Guide of the Perplexed* emphasize two loci in chapter 29 of the third part, in which Maimonides describes the idolatrous practices of astral magic of the Sabians![31]

The difference between Aaron and the Egyptian magicians is that in the latter case the intentional deception of the multitude is stressed, whereas Mendelssohn (with other commentators) does not accuse Aaron of ill intentions but rather blames the desire of the multitude to have a pictorial idol, not only an abstract God (more on this below). Mendelssohn summarizes his theory thus:

> I already told you about the custom of ancient nations (that did not yet know the art of writing) to engrave shapes and pictures and different figures, each denoting something of which they wished to inform posterity. And the sages knowledgeable of history knew the reference of each and every figure and, as we already said in our commentary, among them were the chartumim of Egypt and the sages who knew the interpretation of these figures and announced what was to be seen in them. And in the beginning these forms were nothing but signs of script referring to something, similar to the letters of the alphabet which we use that have no intrinsic meaning but signify only (שאין בהם הוראה עצמית כי אם הוראה סימנית). But in the course of time and the deterioration of the Ages, these chartumim deceived the multitude with corrupt views and falsities and said that these figures have an intrinsic meaning and attributed to them occult qualities and false effects. And from there stems the error of idols and talismans which lead most people astray on crooked paths and to revolting deeds, as is well known, except the patriarchs and their sons whom God, blessed be He, has singled out as His special people and gave them Torah and Mitsvot to safeguard them from those revolting things.[32]

The Torah forestalls idolatry because the Second Commandment forbids representations that can be abused in idolatry. The gist of Mendelssohn's theory is this: the use of lasting representations carries with it the danger of idolatry. This is so because a representation may be understood as a manifestation of the represented, a conventional sign as an index. This understanding is so tempting because it confers meaning and importance on the religious practice that otherwise would be merely symbolic and conventional, and because it makes an abstract entity accessible to human imagination. Mendelssohn's short sketch of his semiotics and the role of hieroglyphics in idolatry in *Jerusalem* seemed unconvincing to Altmann:

It cannot be said that Mendelssohn made a very plausible case for the idea that abuses of script led to idolatry. Even if one conceded his point that men tend to take the sign or image for the thing itself, the question of why the worship of animals should have developed via the corruptive influence of hieroglyphic writing, and not more directly, would still remain. Mendelssohn's "hypothesis" that "the need for written signs was the first cause of idolatry" is the least substantiated of all theories he ever advanced. (*Moses Mendelssohn: A Biographical Study*, 546)

On the background of semiotics and his interpretation of the sin of the golden calf, Mendelssohn's hypothesis appears rather as a remarkable synthesis of semiotics, biblical scholarship, and—as we will see later—ethnology.

The Script on the Tablets: Maimon versus Mendelssohn

In what script were the tablets written? It makes little sense to suppose that the Second Commandment forbidding hieroglyphics was itself written in hieroglyphics; but if it was written in alphabetic script and yet addressed the use of hieroglyphics, were both scripts used simultaneously as Warburton suggests?

Warburton believed that the Egyptians invented an alphabet but that hieroglyphics remained in use "particularly on their public monuments of stone" (*The Divine Legation of Moses Demonstrated*, vol. 2, 138) and that Moses "brought Letters with the rest of his Learning from Egypt," although he presumably "enlarged the alphabet and altered the shape of the Letters" (139).

Mendelssohn, too, believed that at the time of the revelation on Mount Sinai different scripts were simultaneously used, alphabetic and pre-alphabetic. In his *Or la-Netiva*, Mendelssohn discusses at length and with astounding erudition the frequently discussed question in what alphabet Moses wrote the Torah.[33] Mendelssohn adopts the traditional view that the Torah of Moses was written in the Hebrew language and in the Hebrew alphabet still used today (see *Or la-Netiva*, *JubA* 15.1, 25–28).

Mendelssohn's explanation of the Second Commandment as directed against hieroglyphics and their abuse by the Egyptian sages prompts the question whether Moses and Aaron themselves were Egyptian sages who deceived the common people. The question is of course especially urgent regarding Aaron, who collaborated with the Israelites in preparing the figure of the golden calf or, as Mendelssohn implies, the hieroglyphics referring to Taurus. This question is reinforced by a solution to yet another problem concerning the revelation on Mount Sinai. In Exodus it says that the tablets were "written with the finger of God" (Exodus 31:18; 32:16). In order to frustrate possible anthropomorphic interpretations, Mendelssohn explains in his *Bi'ur* that the expression is modeled after human affairs, whereas the meaning of the expression is

> to attribute the script of the tablets to God may He be exalted alone, since it was not done by art nor by natural causality, but by the will and wish of God alone . . . and no force of the created forces partook in it; and already our sages of blessed memory counted the script of the tablets among those things created at the eve of Shabbat at sunset. (Mishna *Abbot,* 5:5(6))[34]

Mendelssohn more or less rehearses here Maimonides' interpretation in *The Guide of the Perplexed,* I, 67. Commenting on Exodus 31:18 and 32:16 ("And the tables were the work of God, and the writing was the writing of God, graven upon the tables"), Maimonides says that this means that they were natural and not artificial and that they were created by God's word, as we also say that the Heavens are the work of God's hands.

Mendelssohn of course knew this chapter and also the traditional commentaries that were printed in the 1742 edition of *The Guide of the Perplexed.* Both Efodi and Shemtov quoted Narboni that on Mount Sinai there are

> stones with the bush drawn on them . . . and I saw one of the stones from that mountain on which the bush was perfectly drawn, a divine drawing, and I broke the stone into halves, and the bush appeared on each piece, and I broke this piece again into halves and the bush re-

appeared on the surface of each inner part and so many times more, until the pieces were as big as peanuts and the bush still appeared on them, and I was very astonished and delighted, since this is a way to understand the meaning of the Rabbi [Maimonides].

Narboni can be read as insinuating that on the tablets natural patterns and not alphabetic script were seen, and in the context of the eighteenth century these patterns could be interpreted as hieroglyphics! Mendelssohn does not draw this conclusion, but Salomon Maimon did. In his commentary on *The Guide of the Perplexed*, I, 66, Maimon quotes Narboni at length and then adds (German words in parentheses appear in German, also in the original Hebrew):

It is known that the alphabetical script we use now was invented approximately at the time of the writing of the tablets because previously figures denoting individual things were used (Hieroglyphen). And these figures were forms of minerals, plants and animals and referring to things similar to them in some respect. But in our script the figures of the letters are merely conventional and do not refer to the things meant themselves, but to the syllables that form the names of the things meant. And the ancient nations and specifically the Egyptians used the natural figures mentioned. . . . And if we assume that the script on the tablets was the ancient hieroglyphic script or the new script mentioned, in both cases the words of the Rabbi, his memory for a blessing [Maimonides] will be properly understood. If we assume that it was the ancient script mentioned, then it is clear that because it was difficult to understand, it was known only to the priests and sages and unknown to the multitude of people (and in fact we know that the Egyptian priests alone and not the simple people used that script). And if we assume that it was the new script as it shows in the words of our Rabbis their memory for a blessing that the letters Mem and Samech [ס, ם] in the tablets remained miraculously in place,[35] then it is also clear that it was necessarily known only to the sages since it was then newly invented. Now, according to the mentioned testimony of the sage r' Moses Narboni, and as is well known to the reader of Natural History (Natur Geschichte), there are many stones in nature with different patterns, and I myself saw such special marble, and since the stones at Mount Sinai are also of this kind, it is clear that after Moses our Teacher, may he rest in peace, hewed the two stone tablets from the mountains and found on them the Divine script mentioned, he explained to the people how to understand that script that was unknown to them hitherto. (*GM*, 99)

Also in Maimon's reading, hieroglyphic and alphabetic script overlapped at the time of the revelation on Mount Sinai. However, Maimon combines this view with the naturalistic explanation of the origin of the tablets. He suggests that Moses showed the people rare stones with natural figures that he presented either as hieroglyphics or as inscriptions in a new and unknown alphabetic script. Moses presented the laws he wished to proclaim as if reading them off the tablets. Maimon's suggestion is in line with the deistic interpretation that presented Moses as one of the great legislators of mankind but not as a prophet. In a less friendly manner, radicals suggested that Moses together with Jesus and Muhammad were the Three Impostors, as the title of the infamous book claimed. Concerning Moses, this is the view against which Warburton wrote his book *The Divine Legation of Moses.*

JEWISH IDOLATRY

The sin of the golden calf is a special case in more than one respect; two of them are of special interest to us. The first is that the sin occurred a short time after the delivery from Egyptian slavery and can be considered a "relapse." This cannot be said of later cases. The second is that in Mendelssohn's interpretation it involved the whole gamut of representations, from three-dimensional figures to hieroglyphics and alphabetic script, from natural to man-made signs. It is rather obvious that this series corresponds to more or less aptitude for idolatry: even letters of the alphabet may be ascribed magical efficacy, but it is not likely that it will be said of them, "These be thy gods, O Israel, which brought thee up out of the land of Egypt"—as it was said of the three-dimensional golden calf. Why is this so? I suggest that this difference depends on the kind of symbol (sign-vehicle) involved and its analogy to normal physical efficacy. Consider first the difference between the golden calf and a hieroglyphic pictogram of an ox. The efficacy of a sacred three-dimensional object may be independent of its interpretation. When God comes down upon Mount Sinai, "whosoever toucheth the mount shall be surely put to death . . . whether it be beast or man, it shall not live" (Exodus 19:11–13). The beast certainly knows nothing of the prohibition to touch the Mount, nor does it understand holiness, but the sanctity of the Mount is an existing power irrespective of understanding. Similarly, the Ark of the Covenant has power to bring about success in war and destroy other gods.[36] This is less so with iconic, two-dimensional, man-made representations.

Hieroglyphics may be believed to be efficacious thanks to astral magic. However, they are not likely to be considered efficacious independently of a human performer or interpreter. Finally, with language, spoken and written, not even similarity between the symbol and its referent obtains. Language is mostly conventional, either when it has been invented as such, or if its mimetic origin in the language of action is forgotten and plays no part anymore in its understanding. The same holds for alphabetic script. No student of Hebrew associates the letters with hieroglyphics, and their actual usage is independent of this origin: they signify syllables, not things. Nevertheless, as we will see below, given an interpreter, language can be believed to be a "real symbol" and can even be efficacious in some usage. This graded closeness to idolatry from the three-dimensional object to the conventional, man-made sign is not absolute, but the analogy to normal physical efficacy seems to play a role.

In what follows I want to briefly look at two other biblical cases of idolatry. The first, the case of the brasen serpent, corroborates Mendelssohn's view that the involvement of permanent objects in religious affairs is conducive to idolatry. The second, the Urim and Thummim, shows Mendelssohn's attempt to attenuate biblical reports of magic. He interprets magic by means of permanent three-dimensional figures as referring to less offensive practices with script and excludes the use of the tetragrammaton — which is often ascribed magical powers. All these are not merely historical observations. In important currents of

Judaism, in Mendelssohn's day but also before and after, indexical representations, icons, and abstract symbols were and are conceived as "real symbols" to a greater or lesser degree. The task of the enlightener is hence clear: He should render as much as possible indexical representation into conventional representation and emphasize the subjective contribution to the interpretation of symbols. This is the line Mendelssohn takes. Consider first this practice in his biblical commentary.

The Brasen Serpent

God once punished the people of Israel for their sins and "sent fiery serpents among the people, and they bit the people; and much people of Israel died." When Moses prayed for the people, God said to him, "Make thee a fiery serpent, and set it upon a pole: and it shall come to pass, that every one that is bitten, when he looketh upon it, shall live. And Moses made a serpent of brass, and put it upon a pole, and it came to pass, that if a serpent had bitten any man, when he beheld the serpent of brass, he lived" (Numbers 21:7–9). Here it seems that an image of an animal is introduced for magical purposes. In fact Ibn Ezra reports that many believe that the brasen serpent served—as did the golden calf!—in astral magic to draw upon its celestial powers. Mendelssohn quotes both ibn Ezra and Rashi to exclude this: "God forbid! God forbid!"—writes ibn Ezra—"since it was done upon God's command, and we shouldn't ask why [the image was] in the form of a serpent for otherwise [we could ask] to be shown whether there is a tree that sweetens bitter water that even honey cannot sweeten [referring to Exodus 15:25], or why put a lump of figs on boils [referring to 2 Kings 20:7] since it is not the nature of figs to heal boils. And the truth is that we cannot fathom Heaven's thought." And Rashi refers to the sages who turn magic into piety: "Could a serpent kill or bring to life?! Rather, when the Israelites looked upward to heaven and subjected their heart to their Father in heaven they were healed, but when they did not they perished."[37] We see that Mendelssohn consistently opposes all kinds of supernatural efficacy of the cult (magic), if possible with the traditional commentators, if not against them, as we shall see below. What appears as a causal relation between the object and its efficacy is not really so. Rashi here explicitly turns magic into prayer.

The installment of the brasen serpent was commanded by God himself, and an ill intention of Moses is therefore excluded. And yet by the time of Hezekiah, king of Judah, the magical device was already venerated as an idol. The righteous king destroyed it together with other means of idolatry:

> He removed the high places, and brake the images, and cut down the groves, and brake in pieces the brasen serpent that Moses had made: for unto those days the children of Israel did burn incense to it: and he called it Nehushtan. (2 Kings 18:4)

Note that the connection between symbol and its referent is double: the snake heals the snake's sting (*similia similibus curentur*) and was traditionally associated with magic (e.g., Exodus 4:3, 7:15), but it works also by means of a linguistic connection: "serpent" in Hebrew is *nachash* (נחש), "copper" is *nechoshet* (נחושת), and "divination" is also *nakhash* (נחש). Note also that the case of the brasen serpent corroborates Mendelssohn's thesis that the very existence of a permanent object in service is prone to idolatry. As he said of the golden calf: "and thus they drifted from one thing to the next, from thought to thought until they began to direct their prayers and offerings to the figure as all idolaters do."[38]

Urim and Thummim

In another case of the fabrication of a device apparently for divination, Mendelssohn argues both against the simple meaning of the text itself and against his favorite commentators.

In pericope *Tetsaveh* ("And thou shalt command") in the Book of Exodus, God himself gives orders for the arrangement of the service in the tabernacle. The garments of Aaron and further utensils are also described, among them a *choshen* (חשן), translated as "breastplate." Then Moses is ordered as follows:

> And thou shalt put in the breastplate of judgment the Urim and the Thummim; and they shall be upon Aaron's heart, when he goeth in before the LORD: and Aaron shall bear the judgment of the children of Israel upon his heart before the LORD continually. (Exodus 28:30)

What are the Urim and the Thummim? In Numbers 27 we read that God announces to Moses that he will die and not enter the Holy Land. God commands Moses to appoint Joshua as his successor. Joshua should consult Eleazar the priest, "who shall ask counsel for him after the judgment of Urim before the LORD: at his word shall they go out, and at his word they shall come in, both he, and all the children of Israel with him, even all the congregation" (Numbers 27:21). The Urim and perhaps also the Thummim are hence involved in divination. This is also what Ibn Ezra suggested in his long commentary on Numbers 28:30: "the reason of judgment, the laws of God and his future discretions, since this is what the Urim and Thummim are consulted for." In his short commentary he adds an explanation of how the Urim and Thummim serve for divination by astrology.

Needless to say, this must be unacceptable to Mendelssohn. Astral magic is to him "association of God with others" (שיתוף), a transgression of the Second Commandment, and astrology presumably falls under the same verdict. This cannot be what God ordered. Mendelssohn turns to Ibn Ezra's critic, Nachmanides, and summarizes his comment with significant omissions.

> The Urim and the Thummim. The script does not explain what these are, nor did He order their production as He did with all other vessels, but mentioned them here for the first time with the definite article, the Urim and Thummim, and [speaking of] practice (מעשה), no craftsman has been mentioned but Moses alone since He [God] said that he [Moses] shalt put in the breastplate of judgment the Urim and the Thummim, and this shows that they were not the making of an artisan and craftsmen did not make them (לא היי לבעלי המלאכה בהם מעשה) and the congregation of Israel did not donate for them, but they are a secret revealed by God to Moses and he wrote it in holiness, and they are the making of Heavens, and therefore they are referred to without any specification and with the definite article, as it is written *and He placed at the East of the garden of Eden the Cherubim*[39] (Genesis 3:24), and God commanded Moses to put in the folds of the breastplate the inscription of the Urim and Thummim, and it is so called since by its means he lightens [*Urim*, "lights"] his words and makes them invulnerable [*th.m.m.*, "perfect," "faultless"], and it is called judgment after

the same script, as it is said *shall ask counsel for him after the judgment of Urim* (Numbers 27:21), since by its means he chooses and verifies his words, as it is said supra in the name of Rashi, his memory for blessing, (from Nachmanides' words in his commentary on Rashi): "The judgment of the children of Israel" are the Urim and Thummim, something by means of which they are judged and admonished on whether to do something or not (Rashi).[40]

Now, the emphasis on the fact that the Urim and Thummim were not manufactured aims at excluding the plausible reading that they were idols. Nachmanides argues the point explicitly against Ibn Ezra. Thus the way is open for the suggestion that they are a script written by Moses, although the text uses no word associated with "writing" or "script." Having established this, the question arises: what was written by Moses? Mendelssohn suggests "a secret" and quotes Rashi's suggestion why the Urim were so named. However, Mendelssohn omits the beginning of Rashi's sentence, "This is the inscription of the Explicit Name [שם המפורש, the tetragrammaton], which he placed into the folds of the breastplate, by means of which . . ." Evidently Mendelssohn did not wish to suggest that the Urim and Thummim were talismans. Be this as it may, in his commentary on Leviticus 8:8, where the Urim and Thummim are mentioned again, Naphtali Herz Weisel referred to Rashi, said explicitly that the script was the tetragrammaton (שם המפורש), and added that this was discussed by Mendelssohn in his commentary on pericope "And thou shalt command" (תצוה) from which the text above has been taken.

But Mendelssohn omits even more. He relies on Nachmanides for the arguments that the Urim and Thummim were not idols, but he does not even mention Nachmanides' own exegesis. Nachmanides suggests that the inscription was of "holy names" and proceeds with a description of the magical technique used in divination. It does not come as a surprise that Mendelssohn ignores it all. He merely says that Aaron carried an inscription on his heart. Mendelssohn does not say more, but the reader associates, of course, this practice with God's command, "And these words, which I command thee this day, shall be upon thy heart" (Deuteronomy 6:6), which is understood as the precept of phylacteries,[41] and as such it is legitimate and not idolatrous. Be it as it may, whereas in the case of the golden calf Mendelssohn was happy to endorse Ibn Ezra's and Halevi's suggestion that the Jews attempted astral magic—because the golden calf is the exemplary case of idolatry—he rejects this possibility here: what was ordained by God may not be understood as a dubious practice involving talismans, magic, or even idolatry.

The lesson from looking at this exegetical exercise is that Mendelssohn wishes to exclude the reading that idols or any figures are permitted in "ancient, original" Judaism. In full sovereignty he agrees or disagrees with his famous predecessors: he endorses their view when they oppose a magical interpretation of a practice, and he opposes their stance when they favor it. Since he cannot ignore the biblical text, he prefers to interpret Urim and Thummim as a conventional symbolic representation (script) of a secret rather than as any kind of idols or even innocent iconic representations, and rather as a two-dimensional than as a three-dimensional representation. In the case of the brasen serpent, the image could not be interpreted away, but here, too, Mendelssohn argues against magic—and adopts the excuse that actually pious intentions or prayer rather than magic explains the healing of the people. The later fate of the serpent—or the interpretation of the Urim and Thummim by both Ibn Ezra and Nachmanides—confirmed Mendelssohn's understanding that permanent objects promote superstition and idolatry. Indeed, John Spencer's *De legibus Hebraeorum ritualibus,* which Mendelssohn owned, suggested that the Urim and Thummim were idols. Moreover, a few years after the publication of *Jerusalem* and of his Pentateuch, Carl Leonhard Reinhold adopted Spencer's interpretation in his anonymously published *Die Hebräischen Mysterien oder die älteste religiöse Freymaurerey.* Reinhold dedicated a special chapter to the Urim and Thummim and quoted Spencer. The gist of his book was that ancient, original Judaism was not a counterreligion to the Egyptian but rather, on the contrary, the very same religion, which was secret with the Egyptians, and this religion has been strongly tinted with Spinozism![42]

The Fringes (Tsitsit) and the Quipu

We know that at the time of the revelation on Mount Sinai more than one system of symbolic representation was used: hieroglyphics and an alphabetic script. In a note added to the commentary on Numbers (15:37(8)–41), Mendelssohn expresses his view that in Moses's time, in addition to hieroglyphics and the alphabet, yet another form of representation was in use. His discussion of this form is especially important because it has been preserved as part of the "ceremonial law" up to today. Mendelssohn's interpretation is hence a contribution both to biblical exegesis and to an interpretation of the "ceremonial law" in a way that forestalls idolatry. The explanation pertains to the precept to wear a *tsitsit*, fringes worn on the corners of four-cornered garments, including the tallith, or prayer shawl.

First the biblical verses:

> Speak unto the children of Israel, and bid them that they make them fringes in the borders of their garments throughout their generations, and that they put upon the fringe of the borders a ribband of blue: And it shall be unto you for a fringe, that ye may look upon it, and remember all the commandments of the LORD, and do them; and that ye seek not after your own heart and your own eyes, after which ye use to go a whoring: That ye may remember, and do all my commandments, and be holy unto your God. I am the LORD your God, which brought you out of the land of Egypt, to be your God: I am the LORD your God.

Mendelssohn's commentary on verse 39:

> *and remember all the commandments of the LORD* [The commentator said: The *peshat* commentators search for an explanation in what way all the commandments will be remembered when seeing the fringes, and I will alert you to something they did not mention. . . .
>
> Some of the peoples made signs of script by means of strings of different colors and knots in them, and according to the colors and the number of knots which served them as signs, they knew all the narratives of the past. Seafarers and sailors of ships reported that when they conquered all the lands of the New World called America, they found in the royal courts of the southern part, called Peru, locked chests filled with colored strings with different numbers of knots, and didn't know what these were. But the inhabitants of that country said that all

these were antique signs of the narratives of their history, and by the number of knots and by the colors they knew everything correctly. And God may He be blessed who singled us out from those who go astray forbade us those pictures and figures which perplex and confuse the minds of people and gave us Torah and Mitsvot to purify our hearts from the impurity of idolatry and to alert us always by means of specific actions and deeds to the corner stones and fundaments of true belief and ordered us to put signs and marks in our flesh and on our houses and in everything we see and feel, so that those sublime things will be in front of our eyes all days, and these are the commandment of circumcision and the commandment of Mezuzah on the openings of our houses and courts, and He commanded us to put the sign of Tefillin [phylacteries] on our heads and on our left arm, and the commandment of Tsitsit [fringes] on our clothes so that we remember Him every time we look at them; and thus we see that in the commandment of Tsitsit remembering is according to the second manner mentioned that was common with the ancients, i.e. according to color and shade and according to the calculation of the knots and the strings.]

In Mendelssohn's understanding, the Torah—written in the Hebrew alphabet—ordered the *tsitsit,* which was a pre-alphabetic script! In the time of the revelation on Mount Sinai not only alphabetic scripts and hieroglyphics were used, but also another pre-alphabetic representation—*tsitsit*—similar to Peruvian quipus. Note that in this interpretation the *tsitsit* does not fall under the prohibition of hieroglyphics in the Second Commandment: it is not a pictorial script. The difference in hieroglyphics is exactly that the latter are pictograms of which each refers to a singular "entire concept (or object)" (ענין שלם) by means of similarity or a combination of such pictures or their outlines. Not so the Peruvian quipu and the *tsitsit.* In Mendelssohn's interpretation, the hieroglyphics and the *tsitsit* also shared a similar fate: both were ancient systems of signs whose meaning was lost. However, in Judaism, the *tsitsit* remained a singular case. With this exception, Judaism succeeded in finding mechanisms of tradition immune to the loss of meaning and at the same time not conducive to idolatry.

Note that Mendelssohn particularly mentions the following commandments: circumcision, the mezuzah, tefillin (phylacteries), and *tsitsit.*

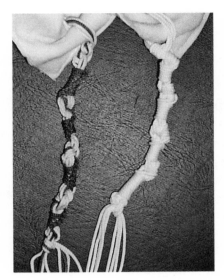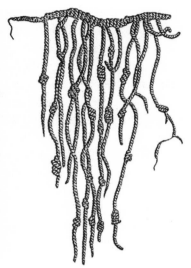

Tsitsit (left), http://en.wikipedia.org/wiki/Tzitzit, Creative Commons license. Peruvian quipu (right), *Meyers Konversationslexikon, 1885–1892* (Leipzig, 1892), vol. 13, 522.

All these commandments are memorials. The circumcision (ברית, "covenant") is a "sign" (אות) of the covenant between God and Abraham and his posterity (Genesis 17:11), and the mezuzah and tefillin are also introduced as memorials for the covenant between God and his people, referring specifically on the one hand to the exodus of the Jews from Egypt and on the other hand to God's Torah that was received by the Israelites.[43] Now the *tsitsit*, the quipu of the Israelites, serves the recollection of "narratives of the past." It is not difficult to guess what narratives: the exodus of the Israelites from Egypt, the revelation on Mount Sinai, and the assumption of the commandments by the people of Israel. This is Mendelssohn's answer to the question asked by the commentators offering the literary meaning of the text (*peshat*). The question is why do we remember "*all* the commandments of the LORD" by looking at the *tsitsit* and not this commandment only? The answer: because with the help of the fringes, we tell the story of the revelation in which all the commandments were proclaimed. All commandments mentioned by Mendelssohn and also others mention signs that serve a mnemonic function:

they refer to the covenant between God and his people before (circumcision) and after revelation (mezuzah, tefillin, *tsitsit*, Sukkot). Circumcision is a simple sign; *tsitsit* is a nonalphabetic representation of spoken language; mezuzah and tefillin contain written texts, narrating the making of the covenant between God and the Israelites; Sukkot reenacts as it were the wanderings of the Israelites in the desert after their Exodus from Egypt. Passover—discussed below in more detail—is dedicated entirely to commemorating this event.

The tendency of Mendelssohn's interpretations is emphasized when compared to the commentary of Aaron Jaroslav (or Friedenthal) (who penned the commentary on Numbers in Mendelssohn's *Netivot ha-Shalom*) into which he inserted his note. Jaroslav interpreted the representation of the *tsitsit* as iconic or mystical! He first refers to the Babylonian Talmud (*Menachot*, 53b) where the color *tekhelet* (azure) of the *tsitsit* is said to be the color of the sea, which is similar to the sky, and the sky similar to the Lord's throne. Then Jaroslav refers to Rashi, who answers the question why the single commandment of *tsitsit* reminds us of all the commandments, as follows (based on *Midrash Tanchumah*, 128:12): the numerical value of the letters of the word *tsitsit* equals 600; add to this eight strings and five knots (as prescribed), and you obtain 613—which is the number of the Godly commandments (Mitsvot). Mendelssohn's interpretation is a clear alternative to these iconic and mystical interpretations that ascribe to the *tsitsit* an intrinsic meaning and not only a conventional meaning of a sign. But even more than that: In Mendelssohn's interpretation, the *tsitsit* does not directly represent anything that may be considered holy; it is a conventional representation of conventional language in which we tell the story of Exodus, during which God announced—again in conventional language—certain precepts. An indexical connection between the holy essence and the *tsitsit* does not exist.

CHAPTER 6

The "Ceremonial Law" of Judaism

Transitory Hieroglyphics

Mendelssohn's best-known pronouncement in *Jerusalem* is that Judaism has no specific theology of its own, and it is this view that raises the question why he nevertheless insisted on remaining Jewish.

> It is true that *I recognize no eternal truths other than those that are not merely comprehensible to human reason but can also be demonstrated and verified by human power.* . . . I believe that Judaism knows of no revealed religion in the sense in which Christians understand this term. The Israelites possess a divine legislation—laws, commandments, ordinances, rules of life, instruction in the will of God as to how they should conduct themselves in order to attain eternal felicity . . . but no doctrinal opinions, no saving truths, no universal propositions of reason. (*Jerusalem,* 89–90; original emphasis)[1]

Judaism shares with other religions the three basic beliefs of "natural religion" (the existence of God, afterlife, and providence), and the revelation on Mount Sinai consisted in commandments and precepts, not in articles of faith. But if so, why adhere to Judaism, why keep the precepts? Why not be content with "natural religion"? Although Mendelssohn insisted that Judaism has no special theology of its own, he remained staunchly faithful to it. This tension has not yet been resolved. Scholars agree that Mendelssohn's conception is inconsistent but differ in their interpretation of his motives: some believe that he did not see that his views are inconsistent, others that he was hypocritical.

In what follows I wish to show that Mendelssohn's conception is in fact consistent and insightful. The gist of my thesis is very simple: "Natural religion" is not at all a religion. Religion is not merely a system of beliefs concerning the nature or purpose of the universe and its connection with God and with a moral code but also a social institution of devotional and ritual practices. Natural religion is not a *practiced* religion but stands for those religious *beliefs* that every person can reach with his sound human reason. In different words, deism, theism, or natural religion is a kind of "natural theology" but not a religion. All these names refer to beliefs, not to a social institution or to practices or religious service and the emotions arising in them. "Natural religion" refers to the beliefs common to different religions, all consisting also in ceremonies. Borrowing from Nicholas of Cusa, we could say, *Una est religio [naturalis] in varietate rituum.*[2]

Certainly, we may ask why religion (not specifically Judaism) is at all necessary if moral conduct and the beliefs supporting it ("natural religion") suffice for eternal bliss? The answer is twofold: As Mendelssohn argued, beliefs must be represented. The question therefore is not whether to represent but merely by what means. As we will see below, Mendelssohn has many good arguments for the superiority of cultural techniques of Jewish tradition and ceremonies over others: they forestall the dangers of dogmatic fixation of belief and idolatry, and they foster communities. The second answer stresses the difference between religion and cognitive content, between social practice and individual conviction.

In fact, the most essential purpose of religious society is mutual edification. By the magic power of sympathy one wishes to transfer truth from the mind to the heart; to vivify, by participation of others, the conceptions of reason, which at times are lifeless, into soaring sensations. (*Jerusalem*, 74)

Religion is an integral component of social life, and this requires, in addition to knowledge of truth, the motivation and societal organization for acting upon it. Belief without practice is not religion, and conversely, religious ceremonies cannot do without belief. Religion "commands actions only as tokens of convictions" (*Jerusalem*, 73). Although the advantage of Judaism is that it has no "articles of faith," Mendelssohn maintains that religious beliefs are indispensable for the performance of the religious law. Without proper beliefs, we may practice the law of the state but not the religious law.

> The state will . . . be content, if need be, with mechanical deeds, with works without spirit, with conformity of action without conformity in thought. Even the man who does not believe in laws must obey them, once they have received official sanction. . . . Not so with religion! It knows no act without conviction, no work without spirit, no conformity in deed without conformity in the mind. Religious actions without religious thoughts are mere puppetry, not service to God. (*Jerusalem*, 44)[3]

And yet the Hebrew language, so Mendelssohn says in a different context, does not even have a word for "religion." Indeed, *Dat* or *Din*, and *Torah* mean law and teaching respectively, neither religion nor belief.[4] And the word usually used to translate *Glauben* (belief and faith) into Hebrew actually means "trust," "confidence" (א.מ.נ.) (*Jerusalem*, 100). This seems to be an obvious contradiction: On the one hand, Mendelssohn insists that Judaism consists in prescribed actions only, and on the other, he demands that they be guided by religious thoughts to count as religious actions. This seeming contradiction can be easily resolved: Mendelssohn demands religious thoughts, but he also demands that no specific thoughts be prescribed. Religious actions are prescribed; religious thoughts are free—as long as they are there, and as long as they do not contradict the simple truths of natural religion. Judaism has no authoritative theology beyond the natural religion of reason.

But if so, what is the ceremonial law good for? Why do we need it in the first place? The answer is simple: All beliefs must be connected to signs. At first we form concepts without the mediation of signs, but as soon as concepts are formed, man "becomes aware of the necessity to attach them to perceptible signs, not only in order to communicate them to others, but also to hold fast to them himself, and to be able to consider them again as often as necessary" (*Jerusalem*, 105).

Why, then, are actions, ceremonies, the adequate representation of religious thoughts? Ceremonies have two major advantages compared to other means of representation: they are a "language of action" and as such much less ambiguous than purely conventional spoken language, and they are transient and leave no permanent objects behind that are conducive to idolatry. The ritual ceremonies revive as it were the "language of action" in the midst of modern life. Solemn actions accompanied by speech represent the truths of natural religion and the most important events in the history of revelation and the bond between God and his people. Certainly, the language of action is basic and is not apt to express subtle metaphysical or arcane truths,[5] but it also need not be. Metaphysics is a source of misunderstandings and controversies over words. Religion should be based on certain basic truths of common sense. Mendelssohn himself was evidently fond of metaphysical speculations. But he did not wish to base the religious life of a community on common metaphysical and theological views.[6]

The language of action combines the advantages of hieroglyphics and spoken language. It is unambiguous, as are hieroglyphics,[7] but hieroglyphics are conducive to idolatry. Spoken language leaves no objects that could be venerated, but it is ambiguous. The language of actions is both transitory and unambiguous. Francis Bacon named gestures "transitory hieroglyphics." Like hieroglyphics, they have "an affinity with the things signified," but unlike hieroglyphics, they are not permanent.[8] The language of action is hence the ideal medium for religious ceremonies in Mendelssohn's eyes: "Man's actions are transitory; there is nothing lasting, nothing enduring about them that, like hieroglyphic script, could lead to idolatry through abuse or misunderstanding" (*Jerusalem*, 119).[9]

To emphasize this difference between hieroglyphics and ceremonies, Mendelssohn adopted his teacher Israel Zamosc's idea that the golden calf was made of gold in order to make it permanent, "since Gold is lasting longest of all things in the world, and as the naturalists know it does not suffer corruption and some even thought that it cannot corrupt in all eternity." When the multitude saw that Moses did not return from the mountain, writes Mendelssohn, they believed he died and resolved, "Let us now make something *lasting* that will not corrupt and die like him."[10] An emphasis should be put on Zamosc's word *eternity*. As is well known, Mendelssohn introduced for the tetragrammaton, YHWH, the expression "der Ewige" or "das ewige Wesen," the Eternal or the eternal Being. This, he says, best captures God's nature as "being" in the past, present, and future tense, as expressed in the verse וַיֹּאמֶר אֱלֹהִים אֶל-מֹשֶׁה אֶהְיֶה אֲשֶׁר אֶהְיֶה. ("And God said unto Moses, I AM THAT I AM"), which Mendelssohn translates as "Ich bin das Wesen, welches ewig ist"—I am the being that is eternal (Exodus 3:14). This name also expresses that God is the necessarily existing being, and exercising providence.[11] But here we see another aspect of idolatry. Everything worldly is corruptible and transient. Eternal is God alone. When the Israelites prepared the idol, they also wished to have a guide or a god who is lasting—compared to the human Moses who disappeared—and is eternal like God. Idolatry (like astral magic) consists also in the wish to blur the difference between worldly beings that belong to the world of "coming to be and passing away" and the divine, eternal, transcendent, and holy. Moses's reaction was therefore to prove that even gold is not incorruptible: "And he took the calf which they had made, and burnt it in the fire, and ground it to powder, and strawed it upon the water, and made the children of Israel drink of it" (Exodus 32:20). Mendelssohn, however, wanted to emphasize the point such that it would be acceptable also to the scientifically minded modern reader of his day who knew that gold does not burn. He therefore translated "burnt" as "calcinated" and added in the *Bi'ur* the proper chemical explanation.[12]

Actions, the most transient of all things, are diametrically opposed to the allegedly incorruptible gold of the calf. This is arguably the most important difference between Jewish ceremonial law and other religions: It is not only that the ceremonial law does not use images, but Mendelssohn presents it as if it did not employ anything lasting, and this can be taken further to open an insurmountable hiatus between the worldly and temporal and the transcendent and eternal. This is a very rigorous notion of idolatry and a radical practice to forestall it.

In *Jerusalem* Mendelssohn tacitly equates the "prescriptions and ordinances" of Judaism, the "ceremonial law," with ceremonies, that is, with solemn rule-governed actions performed in the framework of a religious rite and serving as memorials. He passes over in silence hundreds of commandments of Judaism that pertain neither to religious ceremonies nor to moral and social order but regulate the minute details of the daily conduct of observant Jews: the dietary laws, prescriptions regulating clothes, purity and impurity, and so on.[13] These "ceremonial laws" form a way of life specific to the community of its practitioners and is its social bond. This has two aspects: it is the medium in which the community exists, and it segregates this community from others.

Speaking of establishing a community of theists (necessary as long as polytheism, anthropomorphism, and religious usurpation rule over the globe), Mendelssohn characterizes the bond to be established among them: "And in what should this bond consist? In principles and opinions? These, like articles of faith, symbols, formulae, keep reason in fetters. Hence [it should consist] in acts, i.e. ceremonies."[14]

More will be said below on the function of ceremonies in forming a community, but first to its segregating function. In *Jerusalem* Mendelssohn addresses the Gentiles and mentions also the second function: "we are outwardly distinguished from you by the ceremonial law, do not eat with you, not marry you" (135). The Jewish people must remain distinct from the surrounding people in order to defend pure monotheism. This function of the ceremonial law hence serves the installment of the Jewish people as "a kingdom of priests, and a holy nation" (Exodus 19:6) and will be discussed later in more detail. Here it suffices to note that Mendelssohn's adherence to the ceremonial law is consistent with his stance that Judaism has no specific theology of its own. In order to represent the content of "natural religion" in a form that frustrates idolatry the ceremonial law must be practiced.

RELIGIOUS DOCTRINES AND CEREMONIES:
ONE AND THE SAME

Beliefs are not merely "deposited" in ceremonies. Mendelssohn cautiously said that we may perhaps form a concept without signs, but he insisted that we cannot retain it over time or "think" without signs (*Jerusalem*, 105). The medium of thought, of abstraction, inferences, comparisons, and so on, are signs, not ideas. But ceremonies are more than simple signs. They are a "living script," and they trigger activity.

The ceremonial law was the bond which was to connect action with contemplation, life with theory. The ceremonial law was to induce personal converse and social contact between school and teacher, inquirer and instructor, and to stimulate and encourage rivalry and emulation. (*Jerusalem*, 128)

How does this happen? I will analyze below in detail the ceremony of Passover, but here only the general function is of interest. Ceremonies are known to be religious signs even though their exact meaning may not always be known. They refer to religious truths directly and indirectly. They refer directly when their proclamation explicitly introduces them as memorials:

They should remind us that God is a singular God (*einziger Gott*), that he created the world, that he governs it according to His wisdom and is an absolute ruler over entire nature, that he liberated the nation from the oppression of the Egyptians by extraordinary deeds, that he gave the nation laws, etc. (*JubA* 7, 98)

How can "rational truths and religious doctrines" be so "intimately connected with the laws that they form but one and the same" (*Jerusalem*, 99)? We know that the ceremonies are signs. But how exactly do they function? Is it merely by association of ideas that we think of the signified content when we perceive the sign? How can the fringes, the phylacteries, or the Sabbath remind us of the religious truths mentioned above? A part of the answer, I believe (Mendelssohn does not suggest this), is answered by the text quoted above: the signified content is often quoted as part of the ceremony. The religious truths Mendelssohn names there are proclaimed on Friday evening in the benediction of the Sabbath, said as part of the ceremony sanctifying the Sabbath (קידוש). First, the verses from Genesis (1:31–2:3) in which the completion of creation and God's rest on the seventh day are narrated, and after the blessing on the wine, the following text is recited:

Blessed are You, Lord our God, King of the universe, who has sanctified us with His commandments, has desired us, and has given us, in love and good will, His holy Shabbat as a heritage, in remembrance of the

work of Creation; the first of the holy festivals, commemorating the
Exodus from Egypt. For You have chosen us and sanctified us from
among all the nations, and with love and good will given us Your holy
Shabbat as a heritage. Blessed are You, Lord, who sanctifies the Shabbat.

Here God is addressed as governor of the world (natural religion) and
as the redeemer of his people from Egyptian slavery who has also chosen Israel of all peoples (Judaism). All the religious truths mentioned
by Mendelssohn are contained in this single and short ceremony. Finally, the precept to sanctify the Sabbath is named. And this, I believe,
explains why Mendelssohn suggested that the ceremony and the truths
it stands for are almost "one entity." The blessing is a "speech act," but
it contains also propositional truth, truth of reason and of history:
Creation and delivery from Egypt. To sanctify the Sabbath means among
other things to say exactly these verses that command the sanctification
of the Sabbath and remind us that he is the creator of the world and the
redeemer of Israel.

However, if here sign and signified are really but "one entity," it
seems that the blessing fits Mendelssohn's definition of idolatry that sign
and signified are identified! We will indeed see that linguistic practices
can give rise to idolatry. However, whether this recitation is idolatrous or
not depends on the understanding of the practitioner. If he believes that
by uttering these words he changes the metaphysical status of time from
that minute onwards, this is certainly idolatrous. But if he understands
the recitation as a sign, reminding us of the truths of natural and revealed religion, and of the beginning of a special time in which special
rules of conduct are to be followed, then it is not.

THE INVARIANT BODY AND THE CHANGING SOUL OF THE RITE

An advantage of ceremonies as symbols is that they represent basic
core meanings and leave much room for individual differences in connotations. Mendelssohn likens a ceremony and its meaning to a body
and its soul. However, the same body need not always host the same
soul. Moreover, this is always uncertain.[15] The objects of the "internal

sense" are not palpable. Nobody knows precisely what he believes, and "many things for which I would suffer martyrdom today may perhaps appear problematic to me tomorrow" (*Jerusalem*, 66). Therefore, no oaths should be demanded concerning beliefs. And yet beliefs are indispensable for the performance of the religious law, even though their specific meaning is uncertain and changing.

Now, the fact that an action needs a "soul" to count as a religious rite does not mean that each rite must have exactly one soul or meaning. On the contrary, it is not very likely that different people will ascribe exactly the same meaning to a ceremony, much less so if this meaning has to be conjectured because it was not explicitly revealed together with the details of its performance.

At the end of Exodus, Mendelssohn reflects on the detailed description of the sanctuary and the cult. His commentary is telling. He mentions that "our ancestors may their memory for a blessing commented in various places scattered in the Talmud and Midrash on the purpose of commandments and the service ordained in the sanctuary, on what is meant or hinted at by them, and why these things were [ordained] in this measure and in this shape and no other." He then gives a few examples of symbolic meaning ascribed to the sanctuary and the service and refers to the interpretations of Maimonides, Ibn Ezra, Nachmanides, Isserles, Albo, and Gersonides. Now, he adds, the reader should not be bewildered to see that these commentators do not agree with each other, that one explains these issues with reference to physics, the other to arcane wisdom, that one sees in them a reference to celestial bodies and the properties of stars, the other to the organs (limbs) of man, the third to sublime spiritual issues that no eye ever saw.

> You should not wonder and you should not reject the opinion of any of them because of this diversity, and remember the difference between diversity and contradiction . . . because all these opinions may be true together, although they are different and diverse, as long as there is no contradiction, since it is known of the supreme wisdom and its properties that it aims at many ends with one action.[16]

There is no one-to-one but a one-to-many correlation between sign and signified. The cult requires that all members of the community share its practice and give it the same religious core meaning, that is, the meaning ascribed to it in practice. But they may disagree on its theological interpretation.

Consider, for example, the ritual signifying the beginning of Sabbath discussed above. The members of the community must agree that the ritual introducing the Sabbath signifies the beginning of this holy day (and change their conduct accordingly). Upon the question of the novice or a stranger, why this day is singled out from the days of the week, the unanimous answer is given as it appears in the blessing sanctifying the Sabbath (קידוש): Sabbath is a memorial of creation and a day of rest commemorating that God "rested on the seventh day from all his work which he had made" (Genesis 2:2, recited in the ceremony) and also of Exodus (also mentioned in the ceremony). However, how "creation" is understood, whether as a historical event that happened less than six thousand years ago in the form described in Genesis, or whether the current scientific view is adopted and the story of creation is given some metaphorical meaning—these are the theological issues that Mendelssohn wished to leave to the discretion of the individual members of the community. The Sabbath as a day of rest and its referent—God's rest after the creation of the world and the Exodus—hence belong to the core meaning of the ritual; the theology of creation does not.

Of course, the core meaning of the Sabbath includes also the content of key texts referring to it and the precepts of conduct on this special day as practiced in the community. These texts show what Mendelssohn meant when he said that "religious and moral teachings were to be connected with men's everyday activities" (*Jerusalem,* 118).[17] In addition to the text recited in the ceremony on Sabbath eve and referring to God as the creator of the world and redeemer of Israel, innumerable "everyday activities" are different on the Sabbath from their regular form. The prohibition against lighting a fire, cooking, or traveling, the prohibition against bringing anything to completion, and countless other prohibited activities single out the Sabbath. All of them fall under "keeping the Sabbath holy"—and this immediately refers to the following text.

Remember the Sabbath day, to keep it holy. Six days shalt thou labour, and do all thy work: But the seventh day is the Sabbath of the LORD thy God: in it thou shalt not do any work, thou, nor thy son, nor thy daughter, thy manservant, nor thy maidservant, nor thy cattle, nor thy stranger that is within thy gates: For in six days the LORD made heaven and earth, the sea, and all that in them is, and rested the seventh day: wherefore the LORD blessed the Sabbath day, and hallowed it. (Exodus 20:8–11)

This impressive collection of "religious and moral teachings," including the obligation to allow servants, animals, and strangers to enjoy equal rights, are all referred to by the altered "everyday activities."

The great advantage of a ceremony compared to a written text is that a sequence of actions and a text recited by heart are remembered "bodily" and acoustically, like riding a bicycle and like whistling a tune, not mediated by their meaning. "Knowing how" is independent of "knowing that," but the meaning of the rite can be reproduced by reflection on the actions performed and the texts recited on the occasion. Moreover, embodied in actions, in perceptible events, this religious content is rendered public and shared by the community. The rite is analogous to a word that has a shared "core" meaning and very different connotations. But different from a written word, this "body" of thoughts does not last and therefore does not promote idolatry as do permanent objects. Mendelssohn condensed all this in a short sentence:

> The ceremonial law itself is a kind of living script, rousing the mind and heart, full of meaning, never ceasing to inspire contemplation and to provide the occasion and opportunity for oral instruction. (*Jerusalem*, 102–3)

This "oral instruction" is best exemplified by the Seder ceremony of Passover.

ALERTING TO HISTORICAL TRUTHS, PASSOVER, FIRSTLING

Reflecting on practices brings to mind the religious and moral teachings. But what prompts reflection and gives opportunity for oral instruction?

The great maxim of this [the Mosaic] constitution seems to have been:
Men must be impelled to perform actions and only induced to engage
in reflection. There, each of these prescribed actions, each practice,
each ceremony had its meaning . . . and was an occasion for man in
search of truth to reflect on these sacred matters or to seek instruction
from wise men. (*Jerusalem*, 119)[18]

Ceremonies alert us to the foundations of true belief and give occasion
for instruction simply because they have no practical purpose. This is
what marks such practices as ceremonial and raises the curiosity of the
uninitiated as to their purpose. This is above all important for the religious socialization of children. They are initiated into the practices
and ask, Why do we do this? What for? The answer introduces them to
the foundations of religion.

Mendelssohn's idea of communal reflective practice as the basis of
Judaism is so happy because it is not original. In fact, some suggestions
concerning the reasons for the commandments (טעמי המצוות) go half-
way in this direction, and the codified rite of Passover exemplifies it
beautifully. Passover is celebrated in the extended family or the community, and the feast is arranged differently than the habits on other
days of the year. One of the children asks, "Wherefore is this night distinguished from all nights?" and then the elder people recite the story of
the Exodus of the Jews from Egypt. The motto of the celebration is "And
thou shalt shew [tell] thy son in that day" (והגדת לבנך ביום ההוא) (Exodus 13:8; see Deuteronomy 6:20–24), that is, instruct the next generation. Here, too, the religious rite that induces the instruction is also this
very instruction itself. Indeed, the codified rite represented in the text
recited on that evening (Haggadah, הגדה) obviously mimics a dialogue.
The child notices a strange practice introduced on purpose to raise his
curiosity and asks for its meaning, and thus prompts an answer that
informs him of the special bond between God and the people of Israel,
of the Exodus from Egypt, and also gives detailed explanations of the
symbolic religious meaning of the different practices and dishes of the
evening.[19] But Passover is not a singular case. Consider, for example,
one of the four sections of the Torah contained in the phylacteries and
referring to "firstlings":

And every firstling of an ass thou shalt redeem with a lamb; and if thou wilt not redeem it, then thou shalt break his neck: and all the firstborn of man among thy children shalt thou redeem. And it shall be when thy son asketh thee in time to come, saying, What is this? that thou shalt say unto him, By strength of hand the LORD brought us out from Egypt, from the house of bondage: And it came to pass, when Pharaoh would hardly let us go, that the LORD slew all the firstborn in the land of Egypt, both the firstborn of man, and the firstborn of beast: therefore I sacrifice to the LORD all that openeth the matrix, being males; but all the firstborn of my children I redeem. (Exodus 13:13–15)

It is all here again: a rather strange practice, the question of the son and the narration of Exodus. Mendelssohn was on firm Jewish ground. But not only on Jewish ground; the idea, to raise the curiosity of children by deeds, not by dead letters, was also suggested by Rousseau.[20] However, the Passover ceremony and the phylacteries exhibit another important feature: the narrative explaining the rite and recited as part of it also commands its performance. Religious instruction and practice are inseparable. The practice derives its meaning from the narrative, and the narrative also commands the practice and, at times, is recited in its course.

Indeed, the Passover Haggadah does not teach a theology but a historical truth, that is, the covenant between the Lord and the people of Israel. The Passover rite serves as a mechanism of tradition, of handing down unaltered and uncorrupted the testimony of the revelation on Sinai. Here we have a direct analogy to the historical narratives of the inhabitants of Peru remembered by the colored strings with knots.

APOSTASY FROM NATURAL RELIGION AND
THE ROLE OF THE COMMANDMENTS

We saw that the ritual law concerning Passover and the firstling are both there to prompt the narration of Exodus, the delivery from Egypt. The phylacteries, the mezuzah, the *tsitsit*, and the holiday of Sukkot are also signs of this event. It is immediately following his commentary on the verse quoted above (Exodus 13:13–14) that Mendelssohn quotes two full pages from the commentary of Nachmanides *ad locum* in which the reasons for the commandments in general are elaborated.

> And now I shall declare to you a general principle in the reason of many commandments. Beginning with the days of Enosh [see Genesis 4:26] when idol-worship came into existence, opinions in the matter of faith fell into error. Some people denied the root of faith by saying that the world is eternal; they denied the Eternal, and said: It is not He [Jeremiah 5:12]. Some admit His knowledge but deny the principle of providence and make men as the fishes of the sea, [Habakkuk 1:14] [believing] that God does not watch over them and that there is no punishment or reward for their deeds, for they say the Eternal has forsaken the land [Ezekiel 8:12]. Now when God is pleased to bring about a change in the customary and natural order of the world for the sake of a people or an individual, then the voidance of all these [false beliefs] becomes clear to all people, since a wondrous miracle shows that the world has a God who created it, and who knows and supervises it, and who has the power to change it. And when that wonder is previously prophesized by a prophet, another principle is further established, namely, that of the truth of prophecy, that God doth speak with man [Deuteronomy 5:28], and that He revealeth His counsel unto His servants the prophets [Amos 3:7], and thereby the whole Torah is confirmed.
>
> Accordingly, it follows that the great signs and wonders constitute faithful witnesses [Isaiah 8:2] to the truth of the belief in the existence of the Creator and the truth of the whole Torah. And because the Holy One, blessed be He, will not make signs and wonders in every generation for the eyes of some wicked man or heretic, He therefore commanded us that we should always make a memorial or sign of that which we have seen with our eyes, and that we should transmit the matter to our children, and their children to their children, to the generations to come. (Nachmanides on *Exodus* 13:16)[21]

Mendelssohn concludes with praise for Nachmanides' explanations: "and his pronouncements are so very pleasing and the learned (משכילים) will understand them."

The argument hence runs thus: at some point in history, natural religion has deteriorated, be it that creation has been negated or providence. Prophesied miracles prove the falsity of these views and the truth of prophecy, hence—speaking in Mendelssohn's language—the truth of both natural and revealed religion. However, as Nachmanides says, since God would not redo miracles for the sake of each and every villain or heretic, he ordered that the Israelites testify to the miracles they have witnessed, such that the heretic will immediately be refuted. We now see another reason why the Torah includes "an inexhaustible treasure of rational truths and religious doctrines which are so intimately connected with the laws that they form but one entity" (*Jerusalem,* 99). Recounting biblical events in which the truths of natural religion manifestly show reconfirms their truth and may help the person perplexed by the arguments of the heretics to hold fast to the truth, which he also knows by common sense. Practicing ceremonies presupposes and therefore reminds of the truth of revelation; revelation implies the existence of God and his providence, hence natural religion. Eternal truths, historical truths, ceremonies: each refers to the former. The ceremonies of Judaism have a practical function similar to philosophy: they help buttress truths of reason against doubts.

It is now clear why Mendelssohn recurrently claims both—that natural religion is independent of revelation and that nevertheless Judaism is a guarantee of monotheism and that the people of Israel have a unique mission. Whenever the commandments reminiscent of Exodus and the Sinaitic revelation are performed, also the basic truths of natural religion are evoked. Thus the practice of Judaism consolidates natural religion among the Jews, and the Jewish people itself is a symbol of the revelation on Sinai, which may remind other peoples of these truths. The truths of natural religion can be known independently of Judaism. In fact, the existence of the unique God had to be known before the manifestation on Sinai could be recognized as his revelation. But the exercise of the rite evokes exodus; it also alerts to the truths of natural religion and thus to true monotheism.

Another connection between the practice of the ritual law and morality is not explicitly mentioned by Mendelssohn, but the notion is so widespread in Jewish tradition that we can safely ascribe to him acquaintance with it. It is the maxim "The hearts follow the deeds" (אחרי המעשים נמשכים הלבבות). The fulfillment of the mitzvoth should form the character of the practitioner in that it trains him to act according to rules aimed at doing good. The sincere fulfillment of the mitzvoth, that is, exercising them with the intention to fulfill them as religious acts, eventually produces the corresponding attitude.

Sefer ha-Chinukh (ספר החינוך) says:

> Know that a man is influenced in accordance with his action. His heart and all his thoughts are always [drawn] after his deeds in which he is occupied, whether [they are] good or bad. Thus even a person who is thoroughly wicked in his heart, and every imagination of the thoughts of his heart is only evil the entire day—if he will arouse his spirit and set his striving and his occupation, with constancy, in the Torah and the mitzvoth, even if not for the sake of Heaven, he will veer at once toward the good, and with the power of his good deeds he will deaden his evil impulse. For after one's acts is the heart drawn.[22]

Thus, whereas natural religion and morality are independent of Judaism, Judaism supports them. First, the practice of the ritual law alerts to the meaning of the practice and to its revelation on Sinai and to natural religion. Second, practice forms the character of the practitioner and supports moral behavior.

SUBJECTIVE AND OBJECTIVE FULFILLMENT OF THE COMMANDMENTS

A ceremony requires religious thoughts if it is not to be "empty puppetry." And yet the beliefs of a person should not be of concern to his coreligionists, says Mendelssohn. Does his skeptical tolerance hold also if the private religious thoughts of a practitioner are *very* skeptical?

A critic raised the following question, answered by Mendelssohn in *Jerusalem.* A circumciser (mohel מוהל) appointed by the Berlin community has doubts after a while about the precept of circumcision;

suppose that he denies it was ordained by God. He says nothing about his doubts and continues to exercise his office, but his act lacks the proper religious intention. Did he nevertheless fulfill the precept, the mitzvah, of circumcision? It seems clear that from the point of view of the circumciser, an act was performed without the proper intention and was therefore "empty puppetry," not the fulfillment of the precept of circumcision. This is different from the perspective of the objective result of this action. The child is circumcised:

> A foreskin is cut off: the circumciser may think and believe whatever he pleases of the practice itself. (*Jerusalem*, 83)

So, does the intention count or not? I suggest that this seeming inconsistency can be resolved if we introduce a distinction between the subjective and the objective fulfillment of the religious law,[23] or with Mendelssohn a distinction between "actions which are demanded as actions and those that merely signify convictions" (*Jerusalem*, 83; see also 72). From the point of view of the actor, an action according to the precepts of the rite becomes a religious act if it is done with the proper religious intention. However, from the point of view of the circumcised child and the community, only the overt action and its result count.

The case Mendelssohn discusses is ideal for his purpose since his position agrees with the religious law.[24] Every Jew (including a woman, if no man is available) may circumcise. A Gentile may not, but if he did, the circumcision is valid. Nevertheless, a community will usually appoint to this office a person who is not only Jewish but also known to be pious. However, Mendelssohn forbids investigations into the religious convictions of religious functionaries. This may be interpreted in the following way: Our presumption is that an action is what it seems to be. If the circumciser performs the act, says all the blessings required, and so on, then we presume that he performs the prescription of circumcision with the proper intention. Moreover, since on principle we have no access to the thoughts and intentions of another person, we take the overt action to signify what it conventionally signifies in our community. Hence the exercise of an action according to the precepts of the rite is by presumption taken to be done with the proper religious intentions and hence a proper religious act of the actor. However, whether this is true or not, objectively, from the perspective of the child and the community, the religious precept has been fulfilled and the child has been circumcised.

Personal Instruction

A common way of life, common ceremonies, and personal instruction create social ties and have an important part in the formation of a socioreligious community. But Mendelssohn recommends Oral Law and oral traditions also as the way to secure a continuous insensible adjustment of tradition to changing culture. In personal transmission of religious knowledge, we never encounter without mediation an ancient and strange text that may be either entirely incomprehensible—as the hieroglyphics—or alien to our time, as, say, Babylonian mythology is to today's reader. We always face a text interpreted throughout its history in living discourse by the older generation. At most, the interpretation may be "old-fashioned," as everything is that belongs to the generation of our parents. But the gap is not greater than one generation. Indeed, this is the mechanism of progress: when new "moral truths" become accepted, they gradually become so "intimately fused with our language" and part of "common sense" that "they become evident even to ordinary minds" (*Jerusalem*, 36). In short, personal instruction enables continuous updating of religious beliefs; and this practice also helps reproduce the religious community:

> Doctrines and laws . . . were not connected to words or written characters which always remain the same, for all men and all times, amid all the revolutions of language, morals, manners, and conditions, words and characters which invariably present the same rigid forms, into which we cannot force our concepts without disfiguring them. They were entrusted to living, spiritual instruction, which can keep pace with all changes of time and circumstances and can be varied and fashioned according to a pupil's needs, ability, and power of comprehension. (*Jerusalem*, 102–3)

This is not an accidental result of these religious practices but the purpose of their design:

> For this reason there were but a few written laws, and even these were not entirely comprehensible without oral instruction and tradition; and it was forbidden to write more about them. But the unwritten laws, the oral tradition, the living instruction from man to man, from mouth to heart, were to explain, enlarge, limit and define more precisely what, for wise intentions and with wise moderation, remained undetermined in the written law. (*Jerusalem*, 119)

Mendelssohn can rely on a long Jewish tradition in which was often quoted the biblical phrase, "ask thy father, and he will shew thee; thy elders, and they will tell thee" (שְׁאַל אָבִיךָ וְיַגֵּדְךָ זְקֵנֶיךָ וְיֹאמְרוּ לָךְ) (Deuteronomy 32:7).

We know that Mendelssohn himself drew consequences from this view. He himself taught his children Torah—and he says that we owe his translation of the Torah into German to this practice—and Mendelssohn also instructed his son and other children in theology and metaphysics—and he says that we owe his metaphysical magnum opus, his *Morgenstunden,* to this practice.[25]

Even if we accept Mendelssohn's view of Judaism, shouldn't there be at least a minimal core of the essentials of Judaism? Mendelssohn refers to Maimonides' thirteen articles of faith with quite obvious reluctance (although he translated them into German for the instruction of children). What have these articles contributed to Judaism? Well, not much: the morning hymn *Yigdal,* and some good writing by Chasdai Crescas, Albo, and Abrabanel.

> These are all the results they have had up to now. Thank God, they have not yet been forged into shackles of faith. Chasdai disputes them and proposes changes; Albo limits their number and wants to recognize only three basic principles. (*Jerusalem*, 101)

Judaism thrives when the coherence of the community is safeguarded by common rites and by discourse over their precise religious meaning.

Of course, the community also shares a rich common tradition that directs and put constraints on future development, but it does not determine it. An authoritative and unchanging theology is not to be desired. It is better to observe unity of action and pluralism of interpretations.

ROYAL DECREE

We have seen above some of Mendelssohn's reflections on the nature and use of the precepts. There are, however, hundreds of other precepts to which these considerations do not easily apply. Do we have to justify all the precepts to follow them, and is obedience to the law at all dependent on our insight into its justification? Mendelssohn's answer follows his basic stance concerning the relation between metaphysics, common sense, practice, and law. The "reasons of the commandments" (טעמי המצוות) and other philosophical justifications of religion stand to our religious practice in the same relation as our metaphysics to our practice in general. As a rule, our daily practice is guided by sound reason and law, be it the law of the state or the religious law of our community. Acting on common sense and abiding by the law are not dependent on their philosophical justification. We may, of course, wish to justify common sense metaphysically and also understand the reasons for a specific law, but our compliance is not contingent on our insight. It is merely dependent on our acceptance of the form of life of our community, which implies our acknowledgment of the legitimate authority that ordained the law. The words in Leviticus 18:4 were traditionally understood in this way:

> You shall fulfill My laws and you shall keep My statutes to follow them, I am the Lord, your God.[26]

The canonical commentator, Rashi, comments on the verse (phrases commented on are emphasized) thus:

> *And keep My statutes,* matters which are a royal decree, against which the evil inclination raises objections: Why should we keep them? And the nations of the world raise objections against them; such as [the law

against] eating of pork,[27] the wearing of *sha'atnez*,[28] and the purification [power] of purifying water (מי חטאת).[29] Therefore, it is said: *I am the Lord*, My decree is upon you, you are not allowed to evade [it].[30]

Mendelssohn adopts this view in the discussion of the prohibition to cook a kid in the milk of its mother (Exodus 23:19). We do not know the reasons for many commandments. It is permitted to surmise what the reasons for the commandments are, but their fulfillment is not dependent on understanding.

[A]nd it suffices for us to know that they were ordained by Him, may He be blessed, and once we accepted the yoke of His kingdom, we are bound to do His will, and the benefit of the commandments lies in performing them rather than in knowing their reason.

Then Mendelssohn quotes the sages on inexplicable precepts: "I ordained them and you are not allowed to ponder them."[31] The very same view is repeated in *Jerusalem*. Here, however, Mendelssohn draws far-reaching conclusions pertaining to his adherence to Jewish law:

We are permitted to reflect on the law, to inquire into its spirit, and, here and there, where the lawgiver gave no reason, to surmise a reason which, perhaps, may be liable to change in accordance with time, place, and circumstances—if it pleases the Supreme Lawgiver to make known to us His will on this matter, to make it known in as clear a voice, in as public a manner, and as far beyond all doubts and ambiguity as He did when He gave the law itself. As long as this has not happened, as long as we can point to no such authentic exemption from the law, no sophistry of ours can free us from the strict obedience we owe to the law; and reverence to God draws a line between speculation and practice which no conscientious man may cross." (*Jerusalem*, 133)[32]

Mendelssohn hence follows a Jewish tradition in accepting inexplicable commandments as legitimate "royal decrees." But note also Mendelssohn's allusion to the distinction between speculation and practice, which is at the core of his philosophy. Mendelssohn's own thoughts concerning the law aim at demystification and critique of idolatry. But these thoughts pertain to the philosophical underpinnings of the law, not to its validity. The validity of the law depends only on its legitimate source, and this was guaranteed by the revelation on Sinai.[33] Moreover, its divine source also guarantees that these precepts are meaningful, indeed holy, whether understood by us humans or not.

This is different with the rabbinic law presented as the interpretation of the biblical law. In principle, Mendelssohn argued that the tradition of rabbinic lore is the legitimate interpretation of the law. However, at times he was willing to challenge the rabbis' interpretation. We have seen that Mendelssohn suggested reforming burial precepts in order to meet the state's demand that the dead not be buried on the day of passing and that he referred to biblical sources to buttress his view. He was also willing to reconsider dietary precepts and even to delegate jurisdiction (according to the Jewish law) to non-Jewish state judges.[34] These seemingly opposing attitudes to the authority of the rabbis are not inconsistent. On the one hand, the need to interpret the law and to arbitrate in cases of the "collision" of rights and duties (an important topic in the first part of *Jerusalem*; see *Jerusalem*, 48–49) justifies the status of rabbis in society. However, this does not exclude discussions, even struggles, over their interpretation, especially since Mendelssohn also emphasized that the "learned" in every society tend to willfully disseminate superstition in order to consolidate their rule. This is analogous to the attitude of many citizens to courts in democratic societies: Their function and authority are accepted without further ado, but some of their rulings are criticized and debated.

The Alleged Injustice of Revelation

I discussed above Mendelssohn's reasons to adhere to Judaism in spite of his view that all moral human beings who believe in natural religion merit afterlife. However, if Judaism is beneficial to monotheism, why were all other human beings deprived of its blessings? Were people who lived prior to revelation or in parts of the world where knowledge of revelation never arrived arbitrarily discriminated against?

If, therefore, mankind must be corrupt and miserable without revelation, why has the far greater part of mankind lived without true revelation from time immemorial? Why must the two Indies wait until it pleases the Europeans to send them a few comforters to bring them [the?] a message without which they can, according to this opinion live neither virtuously nor happily? (*Jerusalem*, 94)[35]

Eternal felicity cannot be made dependent on revelation. God's goodness and omnipotence guarantee that the eternal truths required for eternal felicity can be grasped by everyone everywhere. Natural religion depends on simple common sense, not revelation. But if indeed revelation supports the truths of natural religion, if the existence of the Jewish people and its ceremonial law are supportive of true monotheism (as will be argued below)—then it seems to follow that the Jews enjoy an unfair advantage over other peoples. It seems that Mendelssohn is in a dilemma: he may uphold either equal access of all peoples to eternal felicity or a special status of the Jews as the "chosen people"—but not both.

This conclusion is too hasty. Jews may have an advantage over other people. The same holds for the difference between "wise men" "looking with a clearer eye" compared to their ordinary fellow men (*Jerusalem*, 94–95) or between religious functionaries (rabbis and priests) who are permanently concerned with ultimate questions compared to their fellow men. There hence obtains liberal equality of opportunities notwithstanding differences in the real conditions of their realization. This is certainly consistent with Mendelssohn's semiliberal but certainly not egalitarian social views. Jews are religious functionaries, "a kingdom of priests, and a holy nation" (Exodus 19:6), permanently concerned with the ceremonial law and therefore alerted to religious matters. However, this possibility is open to all who wish to devote themselves to the service of God. Since the days of Abraham and reinforced since the revelation on Sinai, the mission of Judaism is "to preserve . . . pure concepts of religion, far removed from all idolatry" (*Jerusalem*, 118). Judaism has a special mission but no privilege other than this mission itself. It would be wrong to accuse God of injustice because he did not appoint all individual people to be rabbis and priests, and it would be equally wrong to doubt his justice because he chose one people only to form a "a kingdom of priests."[36] Concerning God's justice, there is another important consideration: would the world be more perfect if all peoples were strict monotheists like the Jews? I will return to this question in the conclusion of this book. Here it suffices to note that Mendelssohn's view is diametrically opposed to such a view: "Brothers, if you care for true piety, let us not feign agreement where diversity is evidently the plan and purpose of providence" (*Jerusalem*, 138). This is true within the Jewish community, and it is true within the human race as a whole.

The Wolves' System of Union

If the beliefs of Judaism do not go beyond natural religion, why not profess these instead of Judaism with its very specific and rich heritage? I argued above that "natural religion," "deism," and "theism" do not denote religions but merely beliefs that are but a component of religion. But if so, what exactly did Mendelssohn's contemporaries mean when they called on him to forsake the burden of the ceremonial law? Significantly, he was not invited to become a deist or theist and yet free of any specific denomination. Rather, his opponents called on him to convert to Christianity, presented as universal. Now, Christianity is universal, Judaism particular in the ethnic/national sense: every human being of whatever ethnicity is called to be Christian; only Jews are called to live according to Jewish law. But as confessions, as religions of revelation, both are equally particular. Establishing a genuine confession of all monotheists without Jewish or Christian leanings was not considered by either party. Mendelssohn was by all means justified in his remark that the offer to convert was "the wolves' system of union." Wolves were so desirous of union with sheep that they liked to transform the flesh of lambs into wolves' flesh.[37]

The case in point is David Friedländer, Mendelssohn's follower. As is well known, Friedländer proposed in 1799 that Protestants and Jews unite around basic principles of monotheism, rejecting Christian dogma and Jewish ceremonial law—but under the flag of Christianity! Friedländer's initiative failed. At the end of the eighteenth century in Germany, all inhabitants were "by default" taken to be Christians, unless they were Jewish and had "good reasons" to remain so. The demand that Mendelssohn renounce Judaism was tantamount to the demand to endorse Christianity, hence to convert from one religion of revelation to another, from a religion that was not repugnant to reason (in his eyes) to one that was.

Mendelssohn repeatedly emphasized that Judaism is more congenial to Enlightenment than Christianity. The truths of Judaism were based merely on "expressions and judgments of simple common sense that looks straight at things and reasons calmly."[38] It demands the fulfillment of the law but not the belief in dogmas, least of all in the Christian dogmas that he considered offensive to reason—"fetters to my reason!" as he said.[39] There is little wonder that he chose as he did. The seeming contradiction between the belief he advances in natural religion, or deism or theism, and his loyalty to Judaism is simply the difference between mere belief and real religion.[40]

CHAPTER 7

_____

Idolatry in
Contemporary Judaism

Mendessohn defends Jewish ceremonial law with the argument that it alerts the practitioner to the truths of natural religion and that it does not promote idolatry. The Jewish service consists only in actions that are transitory: "[T]here is nothing lasting, nothing enduring about them that, like hieroglyphic script, could lead to idolatry through abuse or misunderstanding" (*Jerusalem*, 119). Once enduring objects are involved, the "great multitude" (encouraged and deceived by priests) is likely to understand the signs "not as mere signs" but as "the things themselves" (*Jerusalem*, 110–11).

The claim that in Jewish ceremonies "there is nothing lasting, nothing enduring," is simply false. Mendelssohn passes in silence over the existence of ritual articles that are used in ceremonies. He discusses the *tsitsit* as a conventional sign, as prealphabetic script, but not the Torah scrolls, the phylacteries, the mezuzah,[1] the shofar, or the Four Species taken during the holy day of Sukkot (Leviticus 23:40). This confronts us with a dilemma: either these ritual articles are conducive to idolatry in Judaism, so that Mendelssohn's recommendation of the ceremonial law as a bulwark against idolatry is ill founded; or these ritual articles do not promote idolatry, although they serve in the ceremonial law, so that Mendelssohn's theory of idolatry cannot be true.

RITUAL ARTICLES

Not only in ancient times were objects in Judaism ascribed magical powers or holiness. This also occurs in modern times. Especially troubling for the enlightener is that the use of ritual objects may lead to the conception of the regular service as a magical performance.

In Judaism, two kinds of "ritual articles" are distinguished: those in which the tetragrammaton is mentioned (or objects that are contiguous with them; although these rank lower) (sacred articles, תשמישי קדושה) and those that serve in the performance of precepts and deserve respect but on which the name of God is not written (ritual articles, תשמישי מצווה). When the former cannot be used any longer, they are put in special repositories (גניזה) and kept there or buried in a Jewish cemetery. These are above all sheets with sacred text but also the objects in close contact with them enjoy a similar status: not only the Torah scroll but also its cloth cover; not only the parchment in the phylacteries but also the case, the straps, and so on. This is Halakhah.[2] It is easy to see that it is not the divine message alone that is venerated but the "real symbol." The meaning of the text is here inseparably connected with the material article. An electronic medium with the entire text of the Bible, whether in Hebrew or in Hebrew letters and with the cantillations, does not enjoy respect; the same text written on parchment does. Simple ritual articles that are not ascribed intrinsic sanctity but merely serve the fulfillment of a mitzvah may be disposed of—but in fact they are not. While religious law does not forbid putting a broken shofar or a worn-out *tsitsit* in the garbage, this is not done. They are put in the same repositories as the sacred articles or used for a "dignified" purpose, until they "disappear." Both kinds of ritual articles may be and often are venerated. Torah scrolls are shown respect according to religious law: people should rise when in the presence of a Torah scroll and not turn their backs to it, and so on. This is Halakhah. But the custom does not stop there: Torah scrolls are kissed (not directly— the scroll is touched with the *tsitsit,* and the *tsitsit* is kissed), mezuzot are kissed (not directly—the mezuzah is touched with the hand, and the hand is kissed) and are often believed to have magical powers—as are phylacteries.[3] In general, all ritual articles are handled with special respect that often turns into veneration.

This is not a reflection on Jewish practices from today's perspective. In his *Vindiciae Judaeorum* (Defense of the Jews, 1656), Menasseh ben Israel defends Judaism against the allegation that the veneration shown towards the Torah scroll in ceremony is, in fact, idolatry. His answer consists in distinguishing between showing respect and worshiping; between *venerari* and *adorare* (*JubA* 8, 44–46). But this is a defense Mendelssohn cannot use! His entire theory of idolatry consists exactly in the thesis that there is no sharp distinction between the two and, moreover, that it is even very likely that what begins as innocent veneration will turn into adoration. The sin of the golden calf teaches exactly this. No wonder that in his preface to the German translation of Menasseh's book, Mendelssohn does not touch at all on this specific point or on Jewish ritual articles in general.

Indeed, there is no clear-cut distinction between respect shown to a religious symbol and superstition. Consider the story about the shofar in Solomon Maimon's autobiography. Maimon reports a dispute with a rabbi whose authority he refused to accept. The rabbi reproaches Maimon for his impious conduct, and Maimon shows no insight. The rabbi

> began to cry aloud, "*Shophar! Shophar!*" This is the name of the horn which is blown on New-Year's day as a summons to repentance, and at which it is supposed that Satan is horribly afraid. While the chief rabbi called out the word, he pointed to a *Shophar* that lay before him on the table, and asked me, "Do you know what that is?" I replied quite boldly, "Oh yes! it is a ram's horn." At these words the chief rabbi fell back upon his chair, and began to lament over my lost soul.[4]

Maimon's answer is "bold" because he refuses to acknowledge the shofar as a religious symbol of the New Year and repentance. His answer degrades it to a material object of dubious origin—the carcass of an animal. Even in enlightened circles, rejecting the "superstitious belief" that Satan is horribly afraid of the shofar, Maimon's answer would count as sacrilege—this although a shofar is not a "sacred article" but merely a "ritual article." The technique is well known since the prophets (see esp. Isaiah 44). In Hermann Cohen's words, "The material out of which the image is made condemns the end for which it was formed."[5]

This theme is, of course, not new in Judaism. Maimonides polemicized against the use of Torah scrolls and phylacteries as magical utensils and considered these practices idolatrous,[6] and the very same controversies are still with us today. A brief look at rabbinic pronouncements concerning the magical efficacy ascribed to ritual articles (especially mezuzot) shows that little or no progress has been achieved since the eighteenth century.

It is certainly not incidental that Mendelssohn did not explicitly discuss religious articles and that his discussion of Jewish ceremonies does not devote a single word to the existence of such articles. His conception of idolatry makes very clear what he thought of them. Inasmuch as they are considered "real symbols" and not merely "signs," they are a possible source of idolatry. But it is here that his skepticism concerning the objects of the inner sense, a fortiori those of other people, renders good services: We see people participating in ceremonies and demonstrating respect to religious articles. But we cannot know whether they consider these articles sacred in themselves or whether they intend the divine when showing respect to these material objects. In consequence of the discussion above, we may also say that in all likelihood the practitioner himself does not know the full answer either: the objects of the inner sense are evasive, and we cannot know that our beliefs today are precisely the same as yesterday, and a fortiori in the case of symbols that essentially involve ambiguity. There are no special sign-vehicles for "real symbols." The same sign-vehicle can be conceived as an indexical or symbolic representation, sometimes also as an icon. We need not and should not inquire into what people believe. We should be content that they participate in the common ceremonies and that these do not explicitly profess idolatry. This suffices to form with them a religious community.

Moreover, *in dubio pro reo:* Mendelssohn says of alien so-called primitive religions that one must "take care not to regard everything from one's own parochial point of view, lest one should call idolatry what, in reality, is perhaps only script (*Jerusalem,* 113). Indeed, he applies this principle to ancient Judaism itself.

> In plundering the Temple, the conquerors of Jerusalem found the cherubim on the Ark of the Covenant, and took them for idols of the Jews. They saw everything with the eyes of barbarians, and from their point of

view. In accordance with their own customs, they took an image of divine providence and prevailing grace for an image of the Deity, for the
Deity itself, and delighted in their discovery. (*Jerusalem*, 114)

Mendelssohn's apology here undermines his entire project. If indeed the
use of images may not be condemned as such because it is the interpretation that counts, then his entire argument for the superiority of Judaism
over Christianity and for the ceremonial law over a cult that involves
images collapses. Even Judah Halevi and Mendelssohn's mentor, Israel
Zamosc, acknowledged that the installment of the cherubim would have
counted as a transgression of the Second Commandment if it were not
explicitly ordained by God.[7] Moreover, Mendelssohn consciously distorts the reason for the dismay of the heathens.[8] The Babylonian Talmud
tells us that the cherubim symbolized God and the people of Israel and
that "[w]hen the Israelites came up on the Pilgrim Festivals the curtain
would be removed for them and the cherubim shown to them, their bodies interlocked with one another, and they would say to them, 'Look, you
are beloved before God as the love between man and woman'" (Babylonian Talmud, *Baba Batra*, 99a; *Yoma*, 54a).

   Salomon Maimon was more candid than Mendelssohn. He reports
this talmudic passage without reservation and says that the cherubim
were found "engaged in intercourse" ("in dem Vereinigungsakt beg-
riffen"), adding, "in order to guard against abuse [this likeness] had to
be withdrawn from the eye of the common people, who cling to the
symbol, but do not penetrate its inner meaning" (*GW* 1, 250–51; Murray, 181). Maimon was also bold in his conduct towards his coreligionists. He jeopardized his position in Posen, the place where he spent the
two happiest years of his life, by ridiculing the superstitions of the Jews
there, for example, the alleged lethal consequences of touching a stag
horn fixed at the entrance to the community hall.[9] Needless to say,
Mendelssohn would have said nothing in these cases.

Sacred Language and Ritual in Kabbalah

Mendelssohn suggested that the idolatry of the Egyptians was promoted by hieroglyphics and that the Hebrew alphabet derives from

hieroglyphics. His interpretation of the classical case of idolatry, the sin of the golden calf, exemplified his conception. A pictogram of a calf (or an ox) or the corresponding hieroglyphic sign, or the very similar Hebrew letter aleph deriving from it (*aleph* is not only the name of the letter but also the Hebrew term for an animal called "eleph" or "aluph," meaning "ox" ; see chapter 5), was used to practice astral magic and draw powers from the constellation Taurus. The pictogram, the hiero-glyph, and the Hebrew letter were understood as "real symbols," not as signs, as connected to the constellation of celestial bodies and sharing essence or powers with them. However, such understanding of symbols does not depend on similarity between sign and signified or on the usage of signs for astral magic. In his discussion of language and script, Mendelssohn also mentioned the Pythagoreans, who believed "that all mysteries of nature and of the Deity were concealed in these numbers; one ascribed miraculous power to them" (*Jerusalem,* 117). But the same holds also in other traditions. Roman numerals may be similar to what they represent, but Arabic numerals are not, and yet they were thought to be a code concealing natural and metaphysical arcane knowledge and endowed with magical powers. The same is true of spoken and writ-ten language. Mendelssohn passes in silence over the fact that major currents in Judaism (and not only in Judaism) hold such views, in fact are based on them.[10]

Historians of religion, who sympathize with their subject matter, re-mark that asking how it is possible that language is ascribed reality as if it were a causal agent is the wrong question. Language, they emphasize, is originally and essentially powerful and efficacious, it has life and power of its own, and it is we, in modern times, who degrade language to a mere conventional representation. The question should hence be asked how we brought about "the great crisis of language in which we find our-selves."[11]

In Jewish tradition (as also in others) language stands at the be-ginning of everything: the world is created by means of language (Genesis 1). The name of something is conceived as attached to its es-sence and expressing it. This is especially true of the name of God. The name of God is secret. God reveals himself in naming his name (Exodus 3:13), which must not be pronounced.[12] A new divine revelation in a new capacity requires a new name: "And I appeared unto Abraham, unto Isaac, and unto Jacob, by the name of God Almighty, but by my name JEHOVAH was I not known to them" (Exodus 6:3). Mendelssohn ingeniously translates here "name" with "essence" (*Wesen*)![13] And of course, a special commandment forbids taking "the name of the LORD in vain" (Exodus 20:7). The people of Israel are also warned of God's angel: "Beware of him, and obey his voice, provoke him not; for he will not pardon your transgressions: for my name is in him" (Exodus 23:21). God's name also dwells in the temple (e.g., Deuteronomy 12:11; 14:23; 16:2, 6, 11; 26:2). The name of the Lord is holy: "You are holy, and Your Name is holy, and holy ones every day praise You, sela" (this is the third blessing of the Amidah prayer). And in Christianity: "Our Father, who art in heaven, Hallowed be thy Name" (see Matthew 6:9–13; Luke 11:2–4). Also, the names of persons partake in their essence. When a person acquires a new essence, this is expressed by a new name: Abraham (Genesis 17:5), Sarah (Genesis 15), Jacob (Genesis 32:38), and Joshua (Numbers 13:16). The change of name does not merely reflect a change in essence or destiny but can also effect it: a seriously ill person is given an auspicious name such as Chaim (life) or Refael (may God heal): *Nomen est omen*. To many, names are inseparable from their bearer.[14] Lev Vygotsky, the renowned Soviet psychologist, tells the following anecdote, which he (in all likelihood erroneously) attributes to "Humboldt": After the eminent astronomer had given a peasant a brief introduction into astronomy, the peasant observed, "I think I understand how we found out the size of the stars and how far away they are, but what I can't fathom is how we discovered their names."[15]

Often it is not, or not only, the meaning of words and sentences that is important but rather the sensual sign itself, the sign-vehicle: the sounds or the script. This is the basis for the survival of expressions in ancient languages in rites conducted in modern languages (Hallelujah, Kyrieleison, Amen, om) and the pedantic repetition of formulas word by word and in the prescribed intonation. This is presumably also the basis of the sacredness of some languages and the refusal to allow service in another. It also stands behind the reluctance to permit the translation of the Holy Scriptures (the Bible, the Qur'an) into other languages.[16]

In Judaism the ascription of all these nonsemantic properties to language reaches a peak in Kabbalah.[17] Its hermeneutics of Scripture and its understanding of the ritual depend on ascribing an intrinsic significance and metaphysical efficacy to ceremonies, ritual articles, uttered words, even to single letters of the Hebrew alphabet and to numbers. From a modern point of view, these beliefs seem to depend on an assumed mutual essential connection between sign and signified, such that prayers and rituals and other practices with spoken or written linguistic signs are conceived not only as embodying holy reality but as influencing it as well.

Moshe Idel discusses these phenomena under the title "Reification of Language."[18] He distinguishes four major forms of such reification and religious practices based on them. According to one conception, language, especially the letters of the Hebrew alphabet, served as the building blocks of reality in God's creation of the world; according to another view, the graphic facets of the letters are images of divine attributes and therefore bestow holiness on Hebrew texts in general. Moreover, proper practices with the letters influence the divine spheres. Finally, the "talismanic conception of language" views Hebrew letters as vessels into which the divine influx can be captured and used: "Letters become entities that enable the mystic to come in direct contact with the divine in the mundane world, while at the same time they are viewed as vehicles for an ascent to the divine in the transcendental world" ("Reification of Language in Jewish Mysticism," 69). Reviewing these four kabbalistic conceptions, Idel concludes that "we may regard Jewish mysticism as viewing language as a reality in itself, generally fraught with divine features, bridging the gap between the corporeal—or the human—plane and the divine plane" (45). Whereas in some of these forms of "reification" of language, there obtains an "organic link between the symbol and the object it symbolizes," in others the symbol comes into the foreground and becomes "a reality in itself" (44–45); even the single letter becomes a holy symbol due to its "intrinsic value" (60).[19] Idel characterizes Kabbalah in exactly the terms with which Mendelssohn characterized idolatry.

But did Mendelssohn also have Kabbalah in mind when he formulated his criterion of idolatry? There can be little doubt that this is so.

Compare Mendelssohn's words on idolatry and understanding signs as "things themselves" with what Maimon writes about Kabbalah.

> Originally Kabbalah was presumably nothing else than psychology, physics, ethics, politics, and so on, represented by means of symbols and hieroglyphics, fables and allegories, whose secret meaning was revealed only to those apt to it. With time, perhaps through some revolutions, this secret meaning was lost and the *signs were taken for the designated things themselves* (*GW* 1, 127; Murray, 94–95; emphasis mine).

Note that Maimon uses the very same words to characterize Kabbalah that Mendelssohn used to characterize idolatry. Maimon also explains theurgical practices of Kabbalah on the basis of the mistake by which Mendelssohn characterized idolatry: taking the signs for things themselves. In Kabbalah "the holy names [of God] are considered not merely as arbitrary, but as natural signs, such that whatever operation is done with the signs must effect the objects themselves which they represent" (*GW* 1, 127; Murray, 94–95).

We will see below that here Maimon criticizes his own juvenile kabbalistic practices. But this semiotic characterization of Kabbalah also applies to contemporary number mysticism of non-Jews. In his critique of a contemporary "kabbalistic" work in which some number system is presented as a key to arcane metaphysical truths, Maimon characterizes Kabbalah as built on a principle and an idea. The principle is that "'[a]ll objects of nature, taken as things in themselves, stand with each other in Real-Relations." This means that everything is represented by something else, which is its natural sign on which it can also act. "The idea is that of a universal characteristics," that is, a system of signs that is supposed to apply to "all thinkable objects." Whereas algebra is applicable to magnitude only, this universal characteristic is supposed to apply to all properties of all objects (Ehrensperger, "Salomon Maimon als Rezensent," 252).

This interpretation of Kabbalah as a system of "real symbols" is shared by contemporary historians and is not a fancy of "enlighteners." None other than Gershom Scholem, the very sympathetic doyen of Kabbalah historians, characterized Kabbalah in almost the same way, and other historians of Kabbalah followed him. For the main constituent of the Kabbalists' faith and their method, says Scholem, we must look at the attention they gave to the symbol of the divine.

> In the mystical symbol a reality which in itself has, for us, no form or shape becomes transparent and, as it were, visible, through the medium of another reality which clothes its content with visible and expressible meaning, as for example the cross for the Christian. The thing which becomes a symbol retains its original form and its original content. It does not become, so to speak, an empty shell into which another content is poured; in itself, through its own existence, it makes another reality transparent which cannot appear in any other form. . . . If the symbol is thus also a sign or representation it is nevertheless more than that.[20]

In an interpretation of Scholem's conception of symbol, Nathan Rotenstreich suggests that symbols are "saturated with meaning to such an extent, that finally it is impossible to distinguish between their sensual appearance and the meaning contained in it." These two form a "synthesis" in the symbol.[21] Joseph Dan, another interpreter of Scholem and himself a historian of Jewish mysticism, emphasizes that the "mystical symbol is tightly conjoined with the hidden signification and together they form a whole of one piece that cannot be taken apart."[22] This insoluble connection between symbol and symbolized is the basis of theurgic or simply magical practices. Also, Maimon's words on the name of God as a "natural symbol" and on the role of the names of God in "magical" practices find confirmation in modern scholarship.[23] The same goes for the fulfillment of the Jewish religious mitzvoth that are ascribed theurgic power due to their nature as real symbols.[24] No wonder that the first reform of the Jewish prayer book "purged the distortions it suffered under kabbalistic influence" and that the prime reformer, Wolf Heidenheim, was named "Mendelssohn of the prayer book."[25] It is hence not only the case that Mendelssohn and Maimon perfectly agreed in their understanding of Kabbalah, but they succinctly formulated what remains today the accepted view of Kabbalah scholars.

Why does Mendelssohn also mention the Pythagoreans in this context (*Jerusalem*, 117)? Consider again Maimon, who equates the "Pythagorean" mysticism of numbers with Kabbalah. In a review of a book by a contemporary German mystic, Karl von Eckarthausen (1752–1803), *Zahlenlehre der Natur* (1794), Maimon characterizes the author as a reincarnation of Pythagoras and the work as "cabbalistische Schwärmerey."[26] Now, this association of Kabbalah with Pythagoras was not an innovation of either Mendelssohn or Maimon but rather had already been suggested by Johann Reuchlin in the sixteenth century.[27] Speaking of Pythagoras hence also evokes Kabbalah without naming it explicitly and may serve two purposes: caution in respect to the Jewish reader and safeguarding the image of "pure Judaism" that Mendelssohn wishes to promote.

Maimon's conception that Kabbalah was a system of knowledge expressed in pictorial language perfectly agrees with Mendelssohn's. Mendelssohn said:

> The kabbalistic philosophy of the Hebrews is due to the poverty of Hebrew in philosophical terminology combined with the figurative speech typical of oriental languages. It has a rational kernel, but understood verbatim it yields the "grossest nonsense and enthusiasm." (*Schwärmerey*)[28]

What is this "rational kernel"? Consider Mendelssohn's discussion of Plato's *Meno*, discussed in chapter 1 above. Plato maintains that learning is in truth "recollection." The very same doctrine, he says, was conceived by "oriental sages" (in fact, the sages of the Talmud). However, they expressed it in a myth "that the soul grasped the entire world prior to this life but then forgot everything when it entered this world." Everything that the soul learns in this world is in fact recollection of what it had once known. The moderns "have merely removed the mystical aspect that lends it so absurd an appearance" (*JubA* 2, 275–76; Dahlstrom, 258–59).[29] Now, as Mendelssohn told Nicolai, if the figurative language of Kabbalah is interpreted verbatim it yields "commentaries replete with images," "grossest nonsense and enthusiasm (*Schwärmerey*)."[30] If the image, the sign, is understood to be similar to its referent or essentially connected with it, we obtain idolatry. Maimon suggests that once the knowledge of Kabbalah was forgotten—presumably because of the misfortunes of Exile ("revolutions")[31]—these symbols became meaningless, an "empty vehicle" as Mendelssohn said of the hieroglyphics (*Jerusalem*, 115). Later a fantastic meaning was imputed to them, and thus a pseudoscience was formed.[32]

We see that Mendelssohn and Maimon agree on several issues. They agree in their view on Kabbalah as having (had) a rational kernel and that, when its figurative language is understood verbatim, it is nonsense and *Schwärmerey*. They also perfectly agree in their formulation of a basic mistake of Kabbalah: "If signs are taken for the designated things themselves," then signs are understood as "real symbols." The difference is merely that Maimon introduces this as a characteristic of Kabbalah, whereas Mendelssohn presents it as a criterion of idolatry. This difference is easily explained by the respective contexts of these formulations. Mendelssohn's criterion is part of an extended discussion of idolatry, whereas Maimon formulates his criterion in an autobiography in which he reports his experiences with Kabbalah. However, their views complement each other if we draw the obvious conclusion that in Mendlessohn's eyes Kabbalah is one form of idolatry among others. This would also explain his judgment, quoted at the beginning of this book, that in contemporary Judaism "enthusiasm and superstition" abound and that Jews would stone him if they understood his *Jerusalem*.[33] In view of his principle not to criticize idolatry if it contributes to social morality, it is not surprising that Mendelssohn did not spell out his critique. However, his critique of idolatry is not confined to Kabbalah, or to Judaism. It is a commonplace in scholarship that in "primitive cultures" intrinsic meaning is often ascribed to signs and that language especially is ascribed efficacious power over the signified; "word magic" (spells, etc.) testifies to this. However, similar phenomena are present also in modern culture.[34] Kabbalah is hence a classical example of ascribing intrinsic meaning to what enlighteners take to be merely conventional signs. In some conceptions, these "real symbols" can also influence their referents and therefore serve in verbal magic or theurgy (as in Maimon's narration). However, Kabbalah is certainly not the only example of such an understanding in Judaism, although it is certainly the most explicit.

The conclusions drawn from the critique of Kabbalah apply to other areas as well, with some reservations also to the claim that translation is impossible. Enlighteners do not accept this. In their view, a translation may need additional explanations to compensate for differences in the concept formation in different languages, and the poetic qualities of a text may lose (or gain!) in translation, but the same cognitive meaning can be conveyed in more than one language. Nothing holy adheres to the Hebrew language as such, certainly not to the graphic shape of its letters. Whatever does not survive translation and transliteration, perhaps with additional explanation, is not part of the text's plain meaning. This, of course, also justifies the translation of the Torah into German since the text loses nothing of its holiness by translation. Holiness pertains to the meaning of the text, not to the body of the text or its language or, finally, the shape of the letters. With this, much of homiletic and kabbalistic biblical exegesis loses its ground.[35]

Irreconcilable differences between conceptions ascribing intrinsic value to representations and those that do not recur in history. Mendelssohn here plays the role Maimonides played six centuries earlier. Maimonides, too, denied that linguistic expressions have an intrinsic value in addition to their semantic meaning, and his arguments for the superiority of Hebrew over other languages are not metaphysical but simply that Hebrew has no words for "indecent" issues (related to sex and bodily secretions) (*Guide of the Perplexed*, III, 8). Maimonides also permitted praying and saying the benedictions in other languages than Hebrew. Of course, he also polemicized against magic by means of linguistic formulas and of talismans (usually using the names of God).[36] The various kabbalistic techniques of prayer do not survive a critique along Maimonides' or Mendelssohn's lines.

We immediately recognize the radical consequences: properly understood, religious cult loses its value as actions in divine realms and therefore sacred in themselves—much to the disappointment of some of Mendelssohn's readers. Alexander Altmann missed in Mendelssohn's understanding of religious ceremonies the sense of the "truly symbolic" central to Kabbalah (more on this in the appendix). Indeed, the "truly symbolic" is not only absent from Mendelssohn's understanding, but its critique is the import of his semiotics, his philosophy of language, his conception of religion and idolatry, of common sense and myth. Mendelssohn's entire worldview aims at and results in the deliberate dissipation of the "truly symbolic."

Mendelssohn's semiotic distinction between sign or symbol and "real symbols" is a philosophical criticism of idolatry. It uncovers the single principle underlying and generating very different superstitions and idolatrous doctrines and practices.[37] It seems to me that this insight of Mendelssohn remains of paramount importance today.

THE IDOLATRY OF THE WORLDLY KINGDOM

Mendelssohn is famous for his stance that the state should not interfere with religious affairs and that the "church" should have no coercive power. I argued above that this is not Mendelssohn's ideal but rather his choice for the time being. His ideal is the Mosaic constitution, the direct reign of God over his people, the identity of religious and worldly rule. Here I wish to argue that this was not merely a slogan but Mendelssohn's sincere view. It is based on his notion of idolatry, and it has implications for the messianic age. In fact, Mendelssohn sees no justification for the separation of state and church; it is rather another case of idolatry and revolt against God. Moreover, Mendelssohn repeatedly alludes to the restitution of the Mosaic constitution in the messianic age in which the pluralism of different creeds will also be realized.

I will first present Mendelssohn's answer to Cranz's allegation that Judaism is a theocracy and then Mendelssohn's allusions to the messianic age in *Jerusalem*.

Cranz's *The Searching for Light and Right* (Das Forschen nach Licht und Recht) placed Mendelssohn in an extremely delicate situation. Cranz claimed that "the whole ecclesiastical system of Moses did not consist only of teaching and instruction in duties but was at the same time connected with the strictest ecclesiastical laws. The arm of the church was provided with the sword of the curse" (*JubA* 8, 79; quoted by Mendelssohn in *Jerusalem*, 85). It was a "theocratic government" (*JubA* 8, 78). Cranz then directly challenged Mendelssohn: this "ecclesiastical law armed with power has always been one of the principal cornerstones of the Jewish religion itself, and a primary article in the credal system of your fathers. How, then, can you, my dear Mr. Mendelssohn, remain an adherent of the faith of your fathers . . . when you contest the ecclesiastical law that has been given through Moses and purports to be founded on divine revelation?" (*JubA* 8, 80; quoted by Mendelssohn in *Jerusalem*, 85).[38]

Mendelssohn admits that "this objection cuts me to the heart," and then he ventures into a lengthy discussion to explain what the Mosaic constitution really was, discusses the revelation on Sinai, develops his semiotics and the place of idols in antique religions, discusses the sin of the golden calf, and finally summarizes again his conception of the Mosaic constitution (*Jerusalem*, 85–130). Now, in this lengthy discussion Mendelssohn says nothing to contradict *The Searching for Light and Right*. On the contrary: he fully endorses Cranz's *factual* findings, but he *interprets* them not as acts of the church authorized to punish heretics but as an act of the state/religion. In the original Mosaic constitution "every sacrilege against the authority of God, as the lawgiver of the nation, was a crime against the Majesty, and therefore a crime of state" (*Jerusalsem*, 129–30). It seems that the only objection he raises against Cranz concerns the naming of this constitution. What Cranz presented as "theocratic government," Mendelssohn insists on naming the "Mosaic constitution" since it was unique and not an instantiation of a kind. However, the difference suggests different historical lessons for the present. If we can identify in the past the same institutions that we know today and if the Jewish church was authorized to punish, why would a refusal to accept this authority not imply that Judaism is forsaken? In present locution, Mendelssohn's answer can be summarized thus: Cranz's view is anachronistic and therefore distorted. In the Mosaic constitution there were no church and state but one entity only, the kingdom of God, and every commandment was issued by the sacred, almighty ruler: it was religiopolitical. Transgression was punished as a rebellion against the God-King, not by the church for disbelief. Commandments refer to actions, not to beliefs. Since this constitution has long ceased to exist, and at present we have two institutions, "post-Mosaic" Judaism and the state, Mendelssohn does not forsake Judaism in denying the right of the church to punish transgressions of the commandments. He merely accepts the post-Mosaic status quo.

Another important point of difference shows concerning the question when this constitution ceased to exist. Mendelssohn simply states his view and does not polemicize against Cranz. The latter believed that the constitution ended with the destruction of Jerusalem and the exile of the people (*JubA* 8, 78);[39] Mendelssohn states that it ended with the anointing of King Saul—in a rebellion against the kingdom of God driven by the same motives that produce idolatry, analogous to the sin of the golden calf!

> I have said that the Mosaic constitution did not persist long in its erstwhile purity. Already in the days of the prophet Samuel the edifice developed a fissure which widened more and more until the parts broke asunder completely. The nation asked for a *visible king* as its ruler, a king of flesh and blood. (*Jerusalem,* 132; my emphasis)

It is obvious that Mendelssohn's explanation of the nation's desire parallels his explanation of the sin of the golden calf. People need visible representations to refer to invisible reality and then tend to take the symbol for the symbolized. And as the Israelites wished the calf to replace Moses who did not yet return from the Mount and guide them through the desert, so here they allegedly wished a "visible king," not only an invisible God-King. The call for a visible king was an act of rebellion against God, the real invisible king, and sprang from the same need as the idolatry of the golden calf.

This is not the biblical story. The biblical narrator points out that Samuel appointed his sons judges and that these "took bribes, and perverted judgment." The elders of Israel therefore asked Samuel to appoint a king "to judge us like all the nations" (1 Samuel 8:3–5). God himself refers to the wish of the people as an act of rebellion and treason, not as a semiotic aberration. To Samuel, God says that the people "have not rejected thee, but they have rejected me, that I should not reign over them" (1 Samuel 8:7–8), and Samuel makes the same point (1 Samuel 12:12). Mendelssohn hence applied his semiotic theory in variance with the biblical text to explain the rebellion of the people against a constitution that in his eyes had no fault. We recall that also in his translation and commentary on the sin of the golden calf he accused the people of rebellion. In a remark on his translation of "the people gathered themselves together unto Aaron" (Exodus 32:1), Mendelssohn comments that the verb *gathered* when used with the preposition *unto* means "mutiny" (מרידה).

The rebellion against God was foretold in the Pentateuch, and there God commands (in response to the wish of the people) the installment of a king once the people settle in the Promised Land. Herz Homberg, who authored the commentary on *Deuteronomy* for Mendelssohn, comments on 17:15 that the judges and elders were commanded to install a king when "the multitude of Israel wishes a king and when it seems to them as a blessing (הצלחה) and an act of grace (טובה) to watch the beauty and glory of a king . . . since this is the way of the multitude (המון) . . . and so it was in the days of Samuel the prophet. . . . [I]t is a commandment to install a king, although asking for one is rebellious." Homberg hence fully adopts Mendelssohn's explanation that heavenly and worldly rule were separated due to the demand of the multitude to have visible rulers. The separation of powers, of religious and state rule, is a rebellion against God and derives from the same semiotic aberration that led to the idolatry of the golden calf.

In his interpretation of the Mosaic constitution, Mendelssohn finds himself here in full agreement not only with Cranz but also with Hobbes. Hobbes opposes the interpretation of the expression "kingdom of God" as a metaphor for "eternal felicity" and insists that it means "a kingdom properly so named," that is, here on Earth. God was the king, and after the death of Moses the high priest was "his sole Viceroy, or Lieutenant." This kingdom ended with the revolt of the Israelites against God in Samuel's time, and the prophets foretold its restitution here on Earth on Mount Zion, in Jerusalem (Hobbes, *Leviathan*, III, 35). Among Mendelssohn's few extant preparatory notes for *Jerusalem* we find a reference to this chapter of *Leviathan*: "Regnum Dei quid sit in Scriptura sacra" (*JubA* 8, 97), in English: "Of the Signification in Scripture of Kingdome of God, of Holy, Sacred, and Sacrament," in which Hobbes also refers to 1 Samuel 12:12! Understandably, Mendelssohn does not quote Hobbes here. After all, together with the Catholic Church, Hobbes serves on the first pages of *Jerusalem* as the backdrop named "absolutism" to present the tolerant alternative (*Jerusalem*, 35–37). But Mendelssohn is by no means a convinced liberal. He does not believe that the functions of state and church can or should be really separated.

In the Mosaic constitution "state and religion were not conjoined, but *one;* not connected, but identical. Man's relation to society and his relation to God coincided and could never come into conflict" (128; original emphasis). But in consequence of the people's rebellion, "the constitution was undermined, the unity of interests abolished. State and religion were no longer the same, and a collision of duties was no longer impossible" (132). Mendelssohn's *Jerusalem* develops at length his view of how these collisions of duties should be attenuated. However, because of the inherent possibility of conflict of interests and because these contrary interests are rooted in the "relations of societal man," the conflict cannot be really resolved, although here and there people succeeded in resolving it "practically" rather than "theoretically," that is, in principle (33). Therefore Mendelssohn's own theory is also destined to show inconsistencies. However, Mendelssohn's ideal, to which he alludes in *Jerusalem* but does not explicitly discuss, is not a liberal state with a separation of powers but, on the contrary, the restitution of the Mosaic constitution, the identity of state and religion. It is in this constitution that no conflict between church and state can arise: "What divine law commands, reason, which is no less divine, cannot abolish" (130).

Mendelssohn begins *Jerusalem* with a discussion of "despotism"; Catholicism and Hobbes are examples of this system (*Jerusalem,* 33 ff.), and he is careful not to classify the Mosaic constitution as theocracy so as to sever it from such an association. It was and remained a unique phenomenon, says Mendelssohn, "and only the Omniscient knows among what people and in what century something similar will again be seen" (131). Note that this possibility is not excluded, not even preceded by a "whether." Now, the separation of political and religious issues is nothing but human institution: "It was thought proper (*man hat für gut befunden*) to separate these different relations of societal man into moral entities" (33; translation altered), Mendelssohn says with no approval of this view.[40] On the contrary, this separation is not based on the nature of these relations: "Rather, all men's duties are obligations toward God. . . . [T]o the man who is convinced of the truth that the relations obtaining in nature, are but expressions of the divine will, both principles will coincide" (58; cf. 41). Also in their functions we find no difference of principle: both are responsible for the "formation of man," such that his actions and convictions will accord with his felicity. In the ideal case *all* actions of man are governed by education that enhances social felicity (41) such that no coercion of the state is called for. In the less ideal case, Mendelssohn does not respect the division of competences but recommends that, when necessary, the state interfere in religious matters: atheism and fanaticism should be (indirectly) checked by the state "from a distance," "and only with wise moderation," but the state should by all means promote the fundamentals of natural religion: God, providence, and future life on which morality is based (63).[41]

Accordingly, Mendelssohn finds also no justification for Locke's severing the state, as responsible for the promotion of the temporal welfare of men, from religion, which is concerned with their eternal felicity. Mendelssohn opposes this suggestion, which is "neither in keeping with the truth nor advantageous to man's welfare" (*Jerusalem*, 38–39). The original Mosaic constitution was a kingdom of God; this identity of holy and worldly rule is rooted in the nature of the functions involved. As long as we have two different institutions, the state and the church, a conflict of interests may occur, and we should find ways to avoid such conflicts or resolve them.

On the basis of his semiotic principle, Mendelssohn succeeded to develop both an explanation of idolatry and an explanation of the origins of the worldly kingdom. Both are explained as resulting from the difficulty in accepting invisible entities as real and efficacious. All human beings need symbols to refer to invisible entities, and less educated peoples (ancient people, the multitude) tend to mistake the symbols for the represented invisible entity. Since symbols are indispensable for human thought, they are both the blessing and the predicament of the human race. The discovery of a basic principle of human thought that is at the basis of the development of human culture as well as most of its aberrations is a remarkable achievement indeed.

MENDELSSOHN: THE JEWISH LUTHER?

Two generations after Mendelssohn's death, Heinrich Heine characterized his reform of Judaism as analogous to Luther's revolt against Catholicism.

As Luther had overthrown the Papacy, so Mendelssohn overthrew the Talmud, and in the very same way, namely by repudiating tradition, by declaring the Bible to be the source of religion and by translating the most important part of it. But by so doing he destroyed Judaic catholicism, as Luther had destroyed Christian catholicism.[42]

Now, whereas there is an obvious analogy between Luther and Mendelssohn in that they are both great translators of the Bible into German, it is certainly false that Mendelssohn abolished tradition or wished to overthrow the Talmud. And yet, Heine's intuition is correct: Irrespective of Mendelssohn's intentions, his reform of Judaism acquired exactly this meaning and was conceived as an anti-rabbinic revolt analogous to Luther's overthrow of the papacy. The emphases on the Bible (and not on the Talmud), on Hebrew grammar as a means of biblical literal exegesis, and on the command of the vernacular as a key to modern (secular) culture were major goals of Haskalah and were conceived as a threat to traditional rabbinic culture and authority. Since 1779 it had been known that r' Raphael Cohen of Altona threatened to ban readers of Mendelssohn's translation of the Bible (which appeared in full only in 1783 but had already been announced), and r' Ezekiel Landau of Prague, the foremost rabbinic authority of the time, evidently aired misgivings that Mendelssohn did not ask for his "imprimatur" (הסכמה), although initially he presumably did not object to the project itself.[43] In addition to the nature of Mendelssohn's biblical project itself, it became a symbol of Jewish modernization due to its association with Naphtali Herz Weisel's (Wessely) reform project for Jewish schools in response to Joseph II's edict of tolerance.

Suggesting a reform of Jewish schooling, Weisel's booklet *Divrey Shalom ve-Emet* (Words of Peace and Truth)[44] of 1782 elicited fierce reactions from important rabbinic authorities. Weisel enthusiastically endorses Joseph II's edict to establish Jewish schools in which German and secular knowledge are taught.[45] These belong to the knowledge of man as such (תורת האדם), Jewish lore is God's knowledge (תורת ה׳) and concerns Jews only. He deplores the negligence of general secular knowledge among the European Jews, above all in Germany and Poland (chap. 3, 7–8), and sees the principal problem in lacking command of the vernacular, which prevents Jews from studying the books of secular knowledge (chap. 3, 10–11). This is a specific problem of Jews in Germany, whom Weisel unfavorably compares to Jews in other countries who speak their country's language properly (chap. 7, 24–25). Mendelssohn, says Weisel, translated the "Torah of our God" (תורת אלוהינו) into "very pure and clear German," (chap. 5, 16; chap. 8, 26) with the purpose of teaching the Jews German and enabling them to appropriate their country's culture and secular knowledge. But Weisel also criticizes the stammering Hebrew of talmudic scholars and (Polish) teachers of the youth. Pupils should learn proper Hebrew and grammar, and to this end Weisel recommends Mendelssohn's translation (chap. 7, 25; chap. 8, 26). Mendelssohn's Bible is thus given a central place in Weisel's plan for Jewish schooling. As if all this were not enough to associate Mendelssohn's Bible with Weisel's reform project, he also mentions that he himself was the author of the commentary on Leviticus in this Bible (chap. 7, 24). Of course, Mendelssohn's Bible was introduced by Weisel's poetic eulogy on Mendelssohn and his enterprise (מהלל ריע).

Weisel's booklet was received as a major offense against traditional, rabbinic authority and culture. A few days after its publication, on January 16, 1782, r' Ezekiel Landau ("הנודע ביהודה") practically banned Weisel in a sermon. This ban was repeated in a circulated letter of Landau's, written shortly after this sermon. Landau explains that he did not formally ban Weisel only because this would require the consent of a state official, but he nevertheless demands that nobody should host Weisel or buy any of his publications.[46]

Three times in the very first lines of the letter, Landau calls Weisel "*hediot*," that is, "unlearned," and ignoramus. R' David Tewel (Katzenelbogen) of Lissa used the same expression—and topped it: "*hediot shebaherdiotot*," or an ignoramus of ignoramuses, a "despicable ignoramus who did not serve talmudic scholars and learn from them," a "man lacking sublime wisdom except Hebrew grammar and literary exegesis of Scripture according to first truths of reason, and who has no share and heritage in the depth of the Talmud." Landau, Tewel, and other rabbinic figures were enraged that this nobody dared to advise learned talmudic scholars about the proper education of Jewish youth.[47]

Another aspect of Weisel's offense and his opponents' outrage concerns the relative importance of Jewish lore compared with secular knowledge. Weisel was explicit and bald: general education benefits all

humankind, but Jewish lore concerns Jews only. He then added his un-
orthodox interpretation of a traditional saying that was understood as
an unforgivable insult: "A talmudic scholar (he who knows God's laws
and teachings) but has no education (deah, דעה), proper manners and
occupation (נמוסיות ודרך ארץ) is worse than a carcass" (*Divrey Shalom
ve-Emeth*, chap. 1, 4).[48] With the translation of *deah* דעה as unequivo-
cally secular knowledge, Weisel turned the well-known saying into a
direct attack on talmudic scholars and an insult.

In his Passover sermon of the same year, r' Ezekiel Landau referred
to this sentence thus: "and an evil person of our people impudently said
that the Torah is not at all important and that a carcass is better than
Torah scholars and that the laws of nature and society are more important than the Torah, and this person's words return upon him, and he is
worse than a carcass and he will end as a carcass, dung on the field."[49]
The substance of his objection to Mendelssohn's Pentateuch is that to
understand Mendelssohn's "high" German, the pupils will be required
to study grammar and the "maiden" (the vernacular, secular knowledge
in general) will assume the place of the "mistress" (Jewish lore).

In short, the rabbinic elite correctly judged that the Jewish reformers
in Berlin promoted an understanding of Judaism that threatened theirs
and their authority. However, there was nothing heretical in Mendelssohn's translation or commentary as such, and it seems that the attacks
on him were of short duration. This is well illustrated by the endorsement
of Mendelssohn's Pentateuch by one of Landau's sons, and also by the
fact that r' Elazar Flekles, Landau's heir, printed an anti-kabbalistic letter
of Weisel's at the end of his introduction to his own anti-kabbalistic
book, *Ahavat David* (1800). Flekles introduced this letter with high praise
for Weisel and without any reservations.[50] Whereas in Weisel and Mendelssohn the assault on rabbinic authority was not direct, the much more
radical Salomon Maimon explicitly accused the rabbis of abusing the
Jewish lore to establish their rule. In his interpretation of the revelation
on Sinai, Maimon suggested that Moses was a lawmaker who gave divine authority to his creation using the same method as Egyptian priests:
he showed the illiterate people a natural image and claimed that it was
script and that it contained laws revealed to him by God (*GM*, 99–100).
A similar technique was used later by the rabbis. They, too, were law-

makers who wished to give their laws (mediated) divine authority and "abused" for this purpose natural religion and Scripture:

> The rabbis look upon the Holy Scriptures, not only as the source of the fundamental laws of Moses, and of those which are deducible from these by a rational method, but also as a vehicle of the laws to be drawn up by themselves according to the wants of the time. (*GW* 1, 166; Murray, 122)

And for this purpose they distort the proper meaning of the text by an "artificial" hermeneutics, designed to bring the new laws at least into an "external connection" with the text. Like Moses before them, they are lawgivers who deceive the multitude into believing in the divine origin of the law. What appears as a "Jewish theocracy" is, in fact, "rabbinic despotism" (*GW* 1, 538; Murray, 266), a "perpetual aristocracy," the rule of the learned nobility. The rabbis "have been able, for many centuries to maintain their position as the legislative body with so much authority among the common people, that they can do with them whatever they please" (*GW* 1, 570–71; Murray, 285–86). Their authority is based on their command of the talmudic literature and their ingenuity in deducing new laws from the extant corpus—or rather in giving the new laws they contrive the appearance of a deduction from the Holy Scriptures.

Mendelssohn never said similar things, and Heine's judgment presumably does not do justice to his intentions. And yet it was certainly correct in respect to the impact of Mendelssohn's reform: as Luther rebelled against the papacy, so the Maskilim (Jewish enlighteners) rebelled against the rabbis and the central place the Talmud occupied in Jewish culture and curricula. Moreover, the introduction of the Jews to the vernacular—among other means, through Mendelssohn's translation of the Pentateuch—enabled them to appropriate general culture and contribute to it. Modern Judaism was created and with it its integration into general society.

There is yet another "protestant" aspect to Mendelssohn's reform of Judaism: his criticism of "real symbols." Van der Leeuw aptly exemplified this crucial difference between the "sign" and the (real) "symbol" with the conception of the Eucharist: do bread and wine "signify" only the body and blood of Christ—as in reformed Protestantism—or are they these too—as in Catholicism?[51] Mendelssohn clearly sides with this "Protestant" reading.[52] Heine does not mention symbols when he compares Mendelssohn with Luther, and the historical Luther did not in fact take the stance Heine attributes to "the protestant," but he brilliantly captured the dividing line between Catholicism on the one hand and reformed Protestantism and Judaism (in Mendelssohn's spirit) on the other.

In his *The Baths of Lucca* (1829), Heine portrays two converted Jews, an "enthusiastic" (*schwärmerisch*) Catholic Don Quixote and a down-to-earth Protestant Sancho Panza. While the Catholic master kneels before the Madonna and the Crucifix, the servant polishes his master's spurs, and when the master has finished his prayers, the servant polishes the crucifix "with the same rag and with the same diligence and spittle with which he had just cleaned his master's spurs." "I dare say that the old Jewish religion suits you much better, my friend," says Heine to the servant.[53]

It is all here: unsophisticated enthusiastic Catholicism and its symbols (the Crucifix and the Madonna) and the refusal of the Jewish/Protestant servant to acknowledge the sacred nature of the symbol: As a Protestant, he polishes it like any other metal object;[54] as a Jew, he spits on the crucifix, the foremost example of idolatry for Jews in Europe, fulfilling the mitzvah "but thou shalt utterly detest it, and thou shalt utterly abhor it; for it is a cursed thing" (Deuteronomy 7:26).

CHAPTER 8

Philosophy of Enlightened Judaism

Mendelssohn's Judaism is based on "natural religion," the belief in God, in providence, and in afterlife. He adopts this conception of natural religion that was widely accepted in the eighteenth century and does not substantially add to it. The truths of natural religion seemed obvious to him. As a rule, it was not necessary to argue for them; it sufficed to remind people of these truths. Proofs of the existence of God and of the immortality of the soul belonged to metaphysics, a special occupation of specialists, designed to answer skeptics and sophists.

On the presupposed basis of natural religion, there are two further steps to take in order to justify Judaism: an argument for religion as a social practice and for Judaism rather than for another religion. The necessity of the first step is usually overlooked. This is presumably so because the argument for a specific religion normally implies *eo ipso* an argument for religion as such. However, the argument cannot be reversed: on the basis of natural religion, we may argue that religious practice is not meaningful or that it is meaningful in principle but that no extant religion is adequate. Mendelssohn believed both that religious practice is meaningful and that (his understanding of) Judaism was adequate. Differently put, he thought that no present religion is adequate but that Judaism is least inadequate and can be reformed to become adequate. Maimon, on the other hand, believed that no religious practice can in principle be adequate. I will consider their positions in turn.

The term *natural religion* is somewhat misleading. It refers to certain beliefs but not to a religious practice of a community, an order of life, and a cult. It is, therefore, not an existing, independent religion but a part or an aspect of a religion. How, then, is the transition from certain truths to practice conceived? What is religion as distinguished from so-called natural religion?

In his autobiography, Maimon answers the question twice. He first defines religion as "the expression of gratitude, reverence etc., which arise from the dependence of our weal and woe on one or more powers to us unknown" (*GW* 1, 150; Murray, 111), but with specific reference to Judaism, Maimon defines true religion (natural as well as revealed) as consisting "in a contract . . . between man and the Supreme Being" (*GW* 1, 245; Murray, 177).

Whereas Mendelssohn might have endorsed Maimon's first definition, they both believed that the second is a misunderstanding. The thoughtful reader, comments Maimon, understands that this idea of a covenant between God and man is to be taken "merely analogically" and is based on anthropomorphism: "the Supreme Being has no wants" (*GW* 1, 246; Murray, 178). And Mendelssohn explains: "God is not a being who needs our benevolence, requires our assistance, or claims any of our rights for his own use, or whose rights can ever clash or be confused with ours" (*Jerusalem*, 57, 58–59; see also the definition of a contract, 54–55). There cannot be a contract between God and a human being. So-called duties toward God are, in reality, duties toward ourselves and our fellow men. Moral philosophy and religion coincide in their content; religion "only gives those same duties and obligations a more exalted sanction" (*Jerusalem*, 58) and a motivation to act upon them. How does religion do this? First by supporting the truths of religion with arguments—rigorous or not—that are "not only convincing, but edifying, moving the mind and spurring conduct conforming with this knowledge" (*JubA* 2, 311; Dahlstrom, 293, translation modified); and second by "mutual edification," which is the "most essential purpose of religious society"; "by the magic power of sympathy," which transfers "truth from the mind to the heart" (*Jerusalem*, 74). This, hence, is the justification of religious practice in addition to natural religion. Religious practice forms a community, is the medium of education, and motivates the practitioners to act according to ethical-religious truths. It allows the expression of emotions, and it should also arouse them. The question is, though, whether the character of communal religious practice does not undermine other essential purposes, above all enlightenment. Maimon has already answered this question. Religious rite and anthropomorphism are inseparable. An enlightened person cannot participate in a religious rite—and Maimon didn't. Mendelssohn would have agreed that many practitioners understand the religious rite in a way that implies anthropomorphism. In fact, Mendelssohn, like many predecessors and successors, invested much effort in the critique of idolatry and anthropomorphism but, as discussed above, accepted that very different views may coexist in the same community.

Concerning Judaism in particular, Maimon opposes Mendelssohn both on the validity of the rabbinic law and on its purpose in society. Maimon distinguishes between "natural" and even "positive" (revealed) religion on the one hand and "political" religion on the other. Natural and positive religion have the same content, but the latter is more distinct than the former and its application completely defined. Both are different from political religion, the purpose of which is "civil felicity," or the welfare of the state (*bürgerliche Glückseligkeit*), and the individuals are made to believe that they act in their own interest (*GW* 1, 154–57; Murray, 114–15). Judaism is from its inception with the patriarchs monotheistic, and in its Mosaic form it seems to be a theocracy that serves both private and social interests. However, since the fall of the Jewish state and until today, Judaism "in its origin *natural* and *conformable to reason*, has been abused" by the rabbis. They added innumerable new laws, which they allegedly deduced from Scripture. "A Jew dare not eat or drink, lie with his wife or attend to the wants of nature, without observing an enormous number of laws" (*GW* 1, 164; Murray, 121; see also *GW* 1, 160; Murray, 117–18; original emphasis). These are purported to be deduced from Scripture but are in fact the work of the rabbis and referred to Scripture by an "artificial method" of expounding the Holy Scriptures (*GW* 1, 165; Murray, 122). This is the "great mystery" of political religion, namely, that the real purpose of the law is to serve the welfare of society, and it is referred to Scripture in the first place in order to imbue it with divine authority (*GW* 1, 156–57; Murray, 115), or, as

Mendelssohn said, to give it "exalted sanction." But even this is not all. In fact, Maimon believes that Judaism is not a theocracy. It is rather "a perpetual aristocracy under the appearance of a theocracy. The learned men, who form the nobility, have for many centuries been able to maintain their position as the legislative body with so much authority among the common people that they can do with them whatever they please" (*GW* 1, 570–71; Murray, 185). This is not very different from Mendelssohn's view of the Egyptian sages. Mendelssohn may have shared some or all of Maimon's observations, but he chose to stay in the community and participate in its reform.

RAMBAM AND RAMBAMAN, MAIMONIDES AND MENDELSSOHN

Mendelssohn was concerned that religious practice may elicit and facilitate wrong beliefs concerning the nature of the divine. This topic is at the core of Judaism from the very beginning. There is a continuous tradition of critique of inadequate rite beginning with the Second Commandment ("Thou shalt not make unto thee any graven image," etc.; Exodus 20:4); over the prophets' critique of sacrifice at the Temple (e.g., Isaiah 1:10–20; Jeremiah 7:22; etc.) and of idolatry (Isaiah 44); and leading to Maimonides and Mendelssohn (and continuing to Hermann Cohen). Inadequate service and idolatry are usually regarded as two separate issues, but I suggest that there is an important connection between them.

In the case of idolatry, the religious offense is straightforward: a false God is adored instead of the one true God (idolatry), or in addition to him (by association, שיתוף). However, since we cannot directly refer to God, that is, by ostension, we have to refer to him in such a way that the meaning of the expressions we use is true of him and him alone: "the most perfect being," "the infinite being," "the creator of the world," and so on. Conversely, traditionally "an impotent being," "a created being" cannot refer to God.

Similar considerations apply to service. Suppose that the religious service is a service *to* God and should be adequate to him. It is clear that, if taken at face value, animal sacrifice cannot intend the God of Mendelssohn or Maimon because it implies that God is a sensual being. Mendelssohn's and Maimon's God is not corporeal and has no senses, hence does not smell or eat the offering burned. In his translation of Genesis 8:21–22 and elsewhere, Mendelssohn is careful to remove any such corporeality from God. The verses read:

> And Noah builded an altar unto the LORD; and took of every clean beast, and of every clean fowl, and offered burnt offerings on the altar. And the LORD smelled a sweet savour.

Following Onkelos, who is repeatedly lauded by Maimonides for eradicating anthropomorphism from his translation of the Pentateuch,[1] Mendelssohn translates: "Der Ewige nahm den lieblichen Duft mit Wohlgefallen an . . ."; "nahm . . . an" (Onkelos: וקביל) means "accepted," not "smelled." The commentator (Shlomo Dubno) quotes Mendelssohn to the effect that "to smell" means at times "to remember." Proof texts are adduced, and then the phrase can be rendered thus: "God remembered the offering and the offerer favorably" ("favorably" for "*mit Wohlgefallen*"). Mendelssohn thus cleansed the text from the ascription of corporeal properties to God. But Noah's family, who observed the action itself and did not read its description in Mendelssohn's rendition, may well have understood that God has a body and senses similar to humans. This concept cannot refer to (Onkelos's or Mendelssohn's) God. Inadequate service may thus lead to idolatry if it is not tantamount to it.

With many philosophers of the Enlightenment, Mendelssohn attributed anthropomorphism and mythical thought to the lower classes, the more sophisticated understanding of signs to the learned upper classes. This perspective entails important consequences. First, concerning the different understandings of the same religious symbols: We may simultaneously find in the same community enlightened and unenlightened practitioners, religion and myth. The same symbols are used by all members of the community, enlightened and unenlightened alike, yesterday and today. Observing the ceremony, it is as a rule not possible to say what exactly the practitioners believe they are doing in applying them. Do they believe that the cult is an act of magic or theurgy? Or an act of communication with God or other invisible powers (prayer)? Or are they simply following tradition, or consciously contributing to the formation and subsistence of the social community? Or a mixture of some or all of these? A ceremony can be interpreted in any of these possibilities and more.

Mendelssohn's effective remedy for misunderstandings in verbal communication is to no avail here: pointing to the sign-vehicle to resolve uncertainty concerning reference cannot resolve the ambiguity of sense and interpretation, or of reference to the unique God. We can point to the sign-vehicle, not to the mode of signification. Moreover, it is certainly possible that a practitioner is not even aware of the distinctions between different modes of signification of the symbol he is using: most people who rely on the adequacy of photographic representation are certainly not aware of the difference between the iconic and the indexical mode of representation and, if asked, would smoothly move from one mode to the other. The same pertains to religious symbols. When we point to the sign-vehicle—say, a cross—and demonstrate its proper use in a ceremony, we do not resolve the ambiguity whether the practitioner believes that the material cross is physically or metaphysically *effective* by its very *form,* or because it was *sanctified* (by a priest or by contact with a holy object, say, the Holy Sepulcher), or, finally, whether it is not effective in itself but *signifies* the belief and intention of its holder who addresses the divine in prayer. These different possible modes of signification of the same sensuous sign and the vagueness of beliefs of the practitioners reinforce each other. Moreover, a religious ceremony that arouses religious emotions confers an aura on whatever partakes in it. Thus also all ritual articles are likely to be considered more or less sacred. There is, however, also a more general reason to be worried. Mendelssohn feared that Enlightenment and progress are not irreversible processes, that idolatry may return after it has been overcome, and that enlightening is a permanent task. He criticizes in *Jerusalem* Lessing's conception of progress as expressed in his "The Education of the Human Race" and maintains, instead, that the human race "never took a few steps forward without soon afterwards, and with redoubled speed, sliding back to its previous position." When one nation progresses, the next regresses thus that the human race as a whole maintains the same amount of "religion and ir-

religion, of virtue and vice, of felicity and misery" (*Jerusalem*, 96–97)—
and we may surely add: of enlightenment, enthusiasm, and superstition.
Enlightenment is always necessary, now in this society, then in another,
and, one should think, always in all societies to a greater or lesser degree.
The role of the enlightener in his community and of Judaism within the
nations is to defend true monotheism against the threat of polytheism,
anthropomorphism, and so on.[2] This function is not temporary but will
remain necessary until the Messiah comes. This conception is the mirror image of Mendelssohn's account of Egyptian idolatry. The priests deceived the inclined multitude into believing that hieroglyphics had "an
intrinsic meaning and attributed to them occult qualities and false effects." The ceremonial law was given to the Jewish people "to safeguard
them from those revolting things."[3] The mission of the enlightener is
exactly opposed to the doing of the Egyptian sages: he informs the multitude that religious symbols have no intrinsic meaning and thus opposes idolatry, and he promotes the ceremonial law as a proper religious
service. Enhancing Enlightenment in the Jewish community does not
mean that it turns to be an enlightened religion, and certainly not forever and everywhere. It rather means participating in the internal discussion of this community and advancing Enlightenment—as Mendelssohn attempted—while others (comparable to the Egyptian sages)
advance their own—in Mendelssohhn's view, idolatrous—versions of
Judaism. Thus conceived, Judaism (and all other religions) appears as a
platform and medium of discussion rather than as a definite position.
This is so at any given time, and so it is historically, that is, with successive periods of Jewish history.

Looking at Jewish religious history from this point of view is reward-
ing. Maimonides for example appears as engaged in a struggle similar to
Mendelssohn's. He, too, criticized conceptions of "real symbols," and this
project has lost nothing of its actuality to the present day. "Anyone familiar with contemporary Jewish life, especially within Orthodoxy,
will see immediately that the Maimonidean reform . . . has failed to take
hold," writes Kellner.[4] Indeed, the sequence: Myth—Maimonides—
Kabbalah—Enlightenment—Jewish Counter-Enlightenment ("ultra-
orthodoxy" and much of contemporary orthodoxy), and so on, beautifully illustrates Mendelssohn's view that superstition and idolatry on

the one hand, Enlightenment on the other, alternate in the career of a people. No wonder that Mendelssohn was named by his contemporary admirers "Rambaman" (r' Moshe ben Menachem) in clear allusion to "Rambam" (Maimonides); no wonder also that Shlomo ben-Yehoushua named himself "Maimon"—after Maimonides—when he needed a German surname.

This does not mean, however, that there is nothing new under the sun. Maimonides, for example, has no theory of ceremonies. Rather he accepts the existence of ceremonies (among other peoples) as given and explains the specific Jewish precepts as a means to distinguish the Jews from other peoples: People were accustomed to (idolatrous) ceremonies, and "man, according to his nature, is not capable of abandoning suddenly all to which he was accustomed." It would have been futile, and it still is futile today, to call upon the people: "Your worship should consist solely in meditation without any works at all" (*The Guide of the Perplexed,* III, 32; Pines, 526), although Maimonides believes that exactly this is the proper service of those "who have apprehended the true realities," that is, the most adequate service both to God and man (III, 51; Pines, 620). In other words: Maimonides has no theory of ceremonies, semiotic or other, but rather explains on the background of historical circumstances why God used such a "ruse" (III, 32; Pines, 527, 528) to direct human beings from idolatry to his service. Enlightenment is a continuous project, but the means and theoretical depth of the undertaking develop in history, and this was also Mendelssohn's view of philosophy in general.

The Critique of Christianity: Mendelssohn, Maimon, and Cassirer

In his philosophy of religion Ernst Cassirer appears as the limit of Jewish Enlightenment and his insights put in relief those of his predecessors. Cassirer structures his magnum opus, the *Philosophy of Symbolic Form,* according to a series of cultural spheres, "symbolic forms," beginning with the most elementary (language and myth) and concluding with science. This series presents a developmental order not only in the chronological sense of their emergence but also in the sense of progress from "lower" to "higher" culture. The hierarchy is determined by the mode of signification dominant in each form and by the more or less clear distinction between the sign-vehicle and its meaning. Cassirer elaborates three forms of signification. The expression (*Ausdruck*), representation (*Darstellung*), and purely symbolic meaning, pure significance (*reine Bedeutung*). Cassirer does not correlate these forms of signification with kinds of signs: the same sign-vehicle can serve all three forms of signification. Myth (and the associated level of language) is characterized by "expression" and "the naive indifference (*Ungeschiedenheit*) of image and thing," of the "real" and the "ideal."[5] The same holds for the primitive forms of language in which a part is taken for the whole thing (*pars pro toto*), or when similarity (established, e.g., in a metaphor) is understood as identity, and so on.[6]

> Whatever has been fixed by a name, henceforth is not only real, but is Reality. The potential between "symbol" and "meaning" is resolved; in place of a more or less adequate "expression," we find a relation of identity, of complete congruence between "image" and "object," between the name and the thing.[7]

This, of course, is exactly what Mendelssohn says of the great multitude: They "saw the signs not as mere signs, but believed them to be the things themselves" (*Jerusalem*, 110–11). As I suggested earlier, we need not assume an "identity" of sign and signified; a community of essence suffices (see chap. 6, above).

Cassirer further suggests that religion works the emancipation from myth—in Mendelssohn's words, of overcoming idolatry. It is religion that "actually introduces the opposition between 'meaning' and 'existence' into the realm of myth," "in its use of sensuous images and signs it recognizes them as such (*weiß sie sie zugleich als solche*) [i.e., as representations, not as their referents]."[8] Religion is constituted in this critique of myth. Cassirer argues that religious critique is necessarily limited. If the critique were thoroughly successful, if religious symbols were understood as entirely conventional, religion would uproot itself. Reducing religious symbols to conventional signs is where philosophy goes but not religion: "The striving beyond the mythical image world and an indissoluble attachment to this same world constitute a basic factor of the religious process itself," says Cassirer.[9]

Religion thus cannot do with pure signs and without "real symbols" (this is not Cassirer's term) and myth; that is, it cannot completely emancipate from the "nutrient medium" (*Nährboden*) of myth, and it cannot entirely succumb to it without relapsing into myth.[10] The discussion above also clarifies why the same sign-vehicle enables this continuous process. Using the same sign-vehicles, the same sensuous symbols, we are not committed to this or the other mode of signification. The same symbols can thus serve a mythical and an enlightened interpretation, and also enable the smooth transition from one to the other—and back. Religion consists in the tension between "real symbol" and symbol, between myth and philosophy; it must not collapse into myth, but it may also not complete its emancipation from it. Cassirer's conclusion can be succinctly formulated: No religion without idolatry! The struggle is over the extent. It is here that Jewish enlighteners see the advantage of Judaism over Christianity: Christianity is essentially dependent on the notion of "real symbol," Judaism not so.

Mendelssohn's critique of Christianity as it appears in unpublished writings and in letters is principled and radical. Mendelssohn refers even to Lutheran Christianity (and a fortiori to Catholicism) as "a yoke in spirit and in truth" (draft of *Jerusalem*, 248).[11] He enumerates the dogmas that "seem to blatantly contradict the first principles of human knowledge": trinity, incarnation, self-sacrifice of God, placation of the first Person of God by the suffering of the Second, and so on.[12] Judaism is the guardian of monotheism. In Mendelssohn's conception, Judaism figures in relation to Christianity as reason and Enlightenment to myth and idolatry. But within Judaism, Mendelssohn portrayed "ancient" and "original" Judaism as reason and Enlightenment in opposition to "enthusiasm and superstition," which were pervasive in the Judaism of his day.

Maimon's judgment of Christianity is similar to Mendelssohn's. As usual, he expresses it in a much bolder fashion. In the entry *"Wahnwitz"* (lunacy) of his *Philosophisches Wörterbuch*, he gives as an example somebody who believes he is "God's son" and attempts to explain how this lunacy develops (*GW* 3, 180–82). Consider also Maimon's report on his alleged attempt to convert to Christianity. He informs the clergyman as follows: "The Jewish religion, it is true, comes, in its articles of faith, nearer to reason than Christianity. . . . I hold the mysteries of the Christian religion for what they are, that is, allegorical representations of the truths that are most important to man [i.e., morality—G.F]. . . . I cannot believe them according to their common meaning" (*GW* 1, 521–22; Murray, 254–55).

The core of the conflict with Christianity is the dogma of the two natures of Christ, the divine and the human, the worldly and the transcendent. Jesus himself can be conceived as a "real symbol" in the most eminent sense: He is a worldly human being and at the same time divine and holy; he is his human self and also divine. Mendelssohn has high praise for Jesus as an exemplary moral person (as also for Socrates), but he vehemently rejects the notion that Jesus was divine. His respect is contingent on the fulfillment of the conditions that Jesus 1) "never meant to regard himself as equal with the Father; 2) that he never proclaimed himself as a person of divinity; 3) that he never presumptuously claimed the honor of worship; and 4) that he did not intend to subvert the religion of his fathers." But "had he proclaimed himself a divine person or the sole mediator between God and men, I would have had to deny him all respect. . . . [P]retensions of this sort appertain to the moral character."[13]

But exactly this is the Christian dogma. Mendelssohn says that Jesus is conceived as "Mangod, or Godman" ("Menschgott, oder Gottmensch"; *Gegenbetrachtungen* §5; *JubA* 7, 92). Hermann Cohen emphasizes over and over again that the essential contribution of Judaism consists in clear separation of the worldly realm from transcendence and that the person of Christ, even if considered merely as a symbol of divinity, is an obstacle to truth (e.g., *Religion der Vernunft*, 485; Kaplan, 496). Cassirer includes in myth not only the sacraments, particularly baptism and Eucharist (*The Philosophy of Symbolic Forms*, vol. 2, 247–49), but also the person of Christ, in which "the difference between God and man has vanished" (251). And Cassirer also suggests that Christianity prevailed over other oriental religions in late antiquity precisely because of its "mythical indigenousness" ("*mythische 'Bodenständigkeit'*") (249). This core doctrine of Christianity is thus unacceptable to Jewish enlighteners, but also the Eucharist is a "real symbol" in the Catholic and Lutheran confessions. The consecrated bread and wine are intrinsically different from bread and wine that are not consecrated. To a greater or lesser degree this is true of other symbols as well.

Mendelssohn argued that idolatry consists in mistaking the sign for the signified, attributing properties of the signified to the sign itself, that is, when the symbol itself is considered as sacred and not only what it stands for. I named such a symbol "real symbol" and following van der Leeuw characterized it as an object, in which "two realities coincide, God and Man encounter each other." Gerschom Scholem made a similar formulation for Kabbalah, and I argued that Kabbalah is Mendelssohn's case in point for idolatry within Judaism. More recently, and from within Christianity (Catholicism), Paul Moyaert stated, "symbols are replete with and permeated with the reality to which they refer; they are full of the reality that is expressed in them; they are not only signs, they are also partially what they signify." Whether naturally given (e.g., relics) or man-made (e.g., painted icons), "the power of symbols derives entirely from the divine reality. The reality, Christ, communicates himself in the symbol and this is how the symbols come to be. Icons are a divine self-expression."[14] Moyaert opposes the allegation that this practice depends on confusing the sign and the signified; this would be "too grotesque to be credible."[15] Indeed, Mendelssohn also said this of the Israelites who adored the golden calf. However, the conception of "real symbols" is not dependent on the *identity* of the sign and the signified. It suffices that their community of essence is maintained—and this is what Moyaert and Mendelssohn emphasize. An ordinary material object is thus transformed into a "real symbol." As van der Leeuw put it: "A transformation of the meaning of an object, whether by touching or by holy gestures and formulas, can indeed penetrate into the object's deepest fibers and smallest particles."[16] So much for a contemporary sympathetic view of "real symbols." In creating an opportunity for a religious experience, "real symbols" guarantee that the rite is meaningful. However, this very same nature of the symbol as a manifestation of the divine embodies the danger of idolatry, in Mendelssohn's sense.

Can religion do without such symbolization? Is religion essentially dependent on myth? Is the religious enlightener insincere or naive?

Doesn't he know that in enlightening he undermines his own religion, or does he rely on unenlightened members of the community who will contaminate and animate his fading enlightened religion with enough myth to keep it alive? Practitioners whose views are more enlightened or more mythical consider each other foes, but in fact each side may be essential to the existence of the other, and the existence of both may be essential to the subsistence of the community. No religion without idolatry and enlightenment? In this view, the essential tension and coexistence of these opposite poles constitute the medium in which community and religion exist. This, I suggest now, was also Mendelssohn's view.

THE CURSE AND BLESSING OF IDOLATRY

Idolatry is a necessary component of religion. Without idolatry religion would dissolve. It seems that Mendelssohn alluded to this contribution of idolatry to religion in his critique of Lessing's posthumous *The Education of the Human Race*. There are good reasons for Mendelssohn's objection to the idea of historical religious progress, obvious and less obvious.

The obvious reason why Mendelssohn cannot accept Lessing's idea of religious progress in history is, of course, that Judaism thus appears as the "childhood of the human race" and Christianity as its more advanced "boyhood" and that the Hebrew Bible is labeled a first "primer," the New Testament "the second, better primer" (Lessing, *The Education of the Human Race*, §§ 70, 71). Mendelssohn, of course, does not accept the superiority of Christianity over Judaism, reason enough to reject the identification of what is later with what is better in general. But there is a deeper reason for his reaction, and he alludes to it in *Jerusalem*. In Lessing's conception, says Mendelssohn, the human race is pictured "as an individual person" that grows from childhood to manhood, whereas in reality "progress is for the individual man" (*Jerusalem*, 95–96).

The mistake hence consists in attributing perfection to humanity instead of to the individual. And yet, why should they not both progress in perfection? The answer is that if the process is finite, then the perfection of the human race comes at the expense of individual perfection. The superiority of one revelation over another (whether earlier or later) may be detrimental to the individual in that it detracts from his possibility to perfect himself. Consider the beginning of Lessing's treatise:

> § 1: What education is to the individual human being, revelation is to the whole human race.

> § 2: Education is revelation imparted to the individual; and revelation is education which has been, and still is, imparted to the human race.

Both education and revelation hence refer to the same scale: what is lacking in revelation can be compensated for by education but also vice versa. This, however, implies that with the perfection of the human race the later-born individuals have an advantage and a disadvantage compared to previous generations. They have an advantage because they begin on a higher level of perfection; and they are disadvantaged because, if the process of perfection is finite, they have less opportunity for self-perfection. Both consequences are unacceptable to Mendelssohn because they violate his basic tenet that revelation—and a fortiori progress of science and culture—is irrelevant to eternal human felicity and human morality.

Consider first the alleged advantages of the member of a more advanced society over his predecessors. Mendelssohn writes: "One man's path takes him through flowers and meadows, another's across desolate plains, or over steep mountains and past dangerous gorges. Yet they all proceed on their journey, making their way to the felicity for which they are destined" (Jerusalem, 96). What counts is not the stage reached but the progress made, the process itself. This is so between given limits or when the progress is—as is the case with knowledge—infinite.

> Everything that lives and thinks must unavoidably exercise its intellectual faculties, and improve and strengthen them, in order to advance with more or less speed towards perfection. . . . [C]reated beings can never attain the ultimate peak of perfection. . . . By imitation of God man may gradually come closer to this perfection; and in this progress the happiness of spirits consists. But the way to them is infinite. (JubA 3.1, 113)

Ultimate perfection is not the lot of humans, but the progress of religion may nevertheless be finite. In Cassirer's language we can say that when symbols are understood to represent conventionally, when the philosophical content has been extracted from myth, then the opposition between myth and philosophy ceases and religion dissolves. Fully enlightened religion is no longer religion but philosophy. Without myth and idolatry, there is neither room nor motivation for enlightenment. The education of the human race directly undermines the possibility of the individuals to participate in the religious process that takes place between the mythical and the philosophical pole. Mendelssohn explicitly says so much about enlightenment in general, and we may surely ascribe it to religious enlightenment in particular. Consider the opening paragraph of his votum concerning an optimal constitution:

> Neither states nor individual persons can be happy without exercising their powers. The powers must encounter resistance if they are to be aroused. As soon as the spring has overcome the resistance and has extended itself, then the tension is gone, and it ceases to be aroused. The circulation lies in the nature of things. Once the fathers have acquired their honor and fortunes and bequeathed them to their children, there is nothing left but to enjoy without acquiring. Once the latter have won their freedom and secured it against all attack, indolence, slavishness sets in among the children. *Once all prejudices are contradicted and exterminated, the love of truth is extinguished and goes cold, and the children have no spur to enlightenment.* With regard to entire states, then, where happiness goes from fathers to children, stagnation and relapse seem inevitable. The highest degree of perfection threatens relapse in order that the spring receive some tension again.[17]

This is exactly what Mendelssohn advanced against Lessing, namely, that "each individual man advances, but mankind continually fluctuates within fixed limits," and that on the whole "the same amount of religion and irreligion, of virtue and vice" obtains (*Jerusalem*, 97). In the text quoted from his votum on the optimal constitution we also learn that this is not only negative: it keeps alive the individual human struggle for enlightenment. Mendelssohn also argues against Herder's thesis that "the human soul decreases in the measure in which it increases on the opposite side" and maintains that the individual always leaves the Earth more perfect than he entered it, and be it only the acquired ability of a baby to turn its eyes to light.[18] Lessing hence attributes to the human race what pertains to an individual, whereas Herder attributes to the individual what pertains to the human race.

Mendelssohn even has an idea of the mechanism governing such fluctuations. He compared a stage when people are still "left to brute nature" and cannot express themselves properly in words and speech with a society in which "science and art shine brightly through words, images, and metaphors, by which the perceptions of the inner sense are transformed into a clear knowledge of signs" (*Jerusalem*, 94). The clarity of thought is here achieved by the use of signs. However, signs are inevitably also conducive to idolatry. We can now see why—taken as a whole—the more educated society (or person) may be not more advanced, at least in religion, than the lesser educated. Both clarity of thought and increasing idolatry are the outcome of the use of signs, and they trade off against each other.

It seems paradoxical, but concerning religious progress, Mendelssohn is more loyal to Lessing's famous dictum concerning truth than Lessing himself. Lessing famously formulated:

> If God held fast in his right hand the whole of truth and in his left hand only the ever-active quest for truth, albeit with the proviso that I should constantly and eternally err, and said to me: 'Choose!', I would humbly fall upon his left hand and say: 'Father, give! For pure truth is for you alone!'[19]

This is what Mendelssohn could have said of religion: enlightened religion, free of all idolatry, is not for humans. The human condition is inseparably intertwined with sign-use and therefore also with idolatry to a greater or lesser extent, and it is therefore also the arena of individual progress and self-perfection. The mission of Judaism is to defend pure monotheism against more idolatrous religions in its neighborhood, the mission of the enlightener in all religions is to critique idolatry and uphold enlightenment in his own community, and the same holds for the individual development of each person. "No Religion Without Idolatry!"

is not only the human predicament but also the human chance, not only a curse but also a blessing: it is a necessary condition for the ever active quest for truth and enlightenment. However, I suggest that the dimension spanning between "real symbols" and "conventional arbitrary signs" is not the only religious semiotic dimension. There are more dimensions in the medium of religious life. One such dimension was decisive for Mendelssohn (and of rather marginal importance for Maimon): aesthetics. And here, too, man occupies a position peculiar to him, in between the extremes.

THE REPRESENTATION OF THE PERFECT BY THE BEAUTIFUL AND THE SUBLIME

The principal question is whether there can be a religious practice that escapes the alternative between arbitrary conventional symbols and "real symbols," between Wolff's ironic suggestion to substitute the cross with a "snuffbox" (see the introduction) and sacraments. Is there a third way to conceive of religious symbols? Mendelssohn suggests such a way: symbols that do not present the divine but are adequate human responses to him, a representation of divine perfection by human perfections such as beauty, goodness, sublimity. The precise nature of the symbols used may be conventional, but they all have to express human perfections and therefore be of a specific value, not entirely arbitrary.

Here we see why Christian Wolff's ironic suggestion to use a snuffbox instead of a cross as a symbol of Christianity misses the point. It is ridiculing religious practice, not criticizing it. As an object of everyday usage, the snuffbox is excluded in principle from serving in a religious ceremony irrespective of its indexical, iconic, or symbolic mode of signification. Religious rites and the ritual articles serving in these are identifiable first of all by their detachment from everyday practical purposes. The snuffbox would certainly be a conventional symbol only if it served to remind us of the way of life befitting a Christian, but it is not only not a "real symbol" but also presents a "category mistake": it is an object serving a daily practical purpose, and as such it is excluded from the religious sphere. But in fact, Wolff has also other suggestions concerning ceremonies. He sketched a "scientia ceremoniarium" as part of his general theory of signs.[20] Although he maintains that in general ceremonies are as arbitrary as words, he also believes that they better serve their mnemonic purpose when similarity obtains between sign and signified. Moreover, ceremonies that not only remind us of what they signify but also motivate us to do it are preferable to those that do not. In his German book on ethics, Wolff gives an example: "The music in churches on Sunday and holidays is a sign of the joy that we should experience over the benefits that God bestows on us."[21] But music, so Mendelssohn maintains, is not only a sign, but in fact brings about joyous feelings and can motivate us to action. How does music function as a symbol?

An adequate enlightened religious representation need not share essential properties with the represented, but it should be a representation that is *adequate* to the religious realm. But more than this: a religious ceremony is not an instinctive animal *reaction* to a stimulus but a human *response,* mediated by reflection and culture. A religious ceremony should indicate the *value* that we ascribe to the divine, although we do not wish to claim that it shares a *property* with it or is produced by it.[22] I believe that this conception captures best Mendelssohn's intentions. Religious service should involve representations that do not share an objective *property* with the divine or are connected with it by convention only. Rather, religious representations should merit — to an infinitely lesser degree, of course — the kind of *value* we ascribe to the most perfect being: they should partake in "perfection." Now, in Mendelssohn "perfection" refers to all higher faculties of the mind: "Man searches for truth, approves the good and beautiful and does the best."[23] Knowledge, morality, and aesthetics are all aspects of human perfection.

Mendelssohn turns to art, specifically to the beautiful and the sublime, as representations of God's perfection and infinity. Beauty also arouses emotions and motivates to action.

> Beauty is the sovereign ruler of all our sentiments, the cause (*Grund*) of all our natural drives and the vivifying spirit that transforms speculative knowledge of truth into sentiments, and urges to active decision.[24]

As such it serves the "most essential purpose of religious society." On the other hand, beauty is a "sensuous emulation" of "heavenly most splendid perfection" (*JubA* 1, 251; Dahlstrom, 23). None of these perfections is sensuous. Therefore, only reason can conceive "heavenly most splendid perfection." However, beauty can represent metaphysical perfection to the senses. Heavenly perfection consists in the harmony of multiplicity;[25] beauty consists in the unity of multiplicity. Beauty is the limited sensuous form in which perfection is perceived by human beings (*On Sentiments,* fifth letter, *JubA* 1, 250–53; Dahlstrom, 22–24). "*Beauty rests,* in the opinion of every philosopher, *on the indistinct representation of a perfection*" (second letter, *JubA* 1, 240; Dahlstrom, 12). Neither the angels nor God know beauty. This is so because higher beings can grasp perfection itself, a harmonious multiplicity of distinct components that refers to unity, whereas humans perceive the same indistinctly (fourth letter, *JubA* 1, 247–49; Dahlstrom, 19–20). However, we should not forget that beauty neither *depicts* nor represents metaphysical perfection in a form adequate to its *object;* this is so above all because the *sign* is sensuous, the signified not. The philosopher

> must beware of confusing this heavenly *Venus* [perfection] with the worldly, namely with *beauty*. The latter rests upon limitation, inability, but the enjoyment of the harmony of a multiplicity of things or features is based upon a positive power of the soul. . . . [A]nd to the extent that a positive power is elevated above the limitation, the pleasure of the intellectual perfection is far and away superior to pleasure of the sensuous perfection or, as we earthly creatures call it, the pleasure of *beauty*. (fifth letter, *JubA* 1, 252; Dahlstrom, 23–24)

This superior pleasure is reserved to angels and God. Human beings make do with its worldly appearance: beauty. As we will see, the difference also sheds more light on Mendelssohn's theory of idolatry. Mendelssohn maintains that every human being has adequate common-sensical knowledge of natural religion. The Greenlander points to dawn and says, "See, brother, the young day! How beautiful must be its author!"[26] However, the example shows not only that an uneducated human being can infer the existence of God from the beauty of the world but also that simple people tend to mistake the sign for the signified. God himself cannot be beautiful because he is not an object of sense perception. The philosopher should insist that the "earthly" Venus, *beauty* (standing for sensuous perfection), should not be mistaken for the "heavenly *Venus*," metaphysical perfection. But the Greenlander's mistake is so natural. The inference from the beauty of the world to the existence of God is based on their causal connection: The beauty of the world testifies to its creator and his perfection. However, whereas the structurally similar inference from smoke to fire establishes that the cause exists and ipso facto also belongs to the same realm as the effect (both are physical phenomena), here the inference to the existence of the cause should obtain but not the classification in the same (sensuous) realm. Although a category of the physical world is used (causality), it should also apply to a relation between a metaphysical agent and its sensuous effect—and yet strictly sever these two realms. These are subtle distinctions indeed that do not easily square with common sense (or scientific thought), perhaps too subtle for most people to be respected at all times, perhaps even inconsistent. It seems that in his joy over this testimony of innocent belief, even Mendelssohn himself overlooked the fact that it is a case in point for his understanding of idolatry.

Artistic beauty, sensuous perfection, should symbolize metaphysical perfection. The sign-vehicle used should not be determined by its referent, hence arbitrary, and yet constrained: it must partake in "perfection." The symbol need not be similar to the referent—only adequate. Consider an interesting example from an entirely different realm. In the 1920s, Wolfgang Köhler conducted experiments in which participants were shown two figures, one of angular, the other of rounded shape. One looks like an inkblot and the other like a jagged piece of shattered glass. The participants were asked to name the figures "Maluma" or "Takete"— two nonsense words. The effect is now called the bouba/kiki effect. It shows that more than 95 percent of the test persons name the rounded figure "bouba," the angular figure "kiki." The result is especially important because this seems to be valid transculturally.[27] Now, although "kiki" is as conventional as "bouba" (and both can, therefore, be replaced by innumerable other names), there evidently are some constraints on the choice of "adequate" representations. Not all words are adequate. Analogously, the divine should be represented by a "perfection," not by an "imperfection," but the choice of the concrete symbol or even of its kind is arbitrary. Mendelssohn prefers music to other arts as a representation of the divine. To Mendelssohn, music is the most beautiful and the most enlivening of arts. Music, as it were, affects directly the chords of the soul. It "tames coarse and uncivilized people, calms the enraged, and enlivens the melancholic."[28] But music alone does not suffice. It may arouse certain emotions, but if it cannot fix their referent or the intention of the believer, what makes it a specifically *religious* experience, different, for example, from national feelings arising in appropriate ceremonies? Both the kind of emotion and its object should be further determined. The representation should refer specifically to the object of religion: God. The music in a religious service is not *prescribed* by the object or content of the service, but it should be *adequate* to its addressee and to the purpose of the service; that is, it should be solemn and not a jingle, and it usually uses language to clearly refer to the divine.

Art and informative text should, therefore, unite here. Poetry, for example, can integrate informative text and artistic means (rhythm, rhyme, etc.). Metaphors, too, distinguish natural language from purely arbitrary signs as used in algebra.[29] The very same reason that renders natural language detrimental to metaphysics (see chap. 1, above) is conducive to its function in religious practice. A poetic text addresses the understanding, the imagination, and the emotions at the same time. This is of course enhanced by its synthesis with music. Vocal music, the synthesis of a poetic text and music, is most appropriate to religious practice.

The text of a hymn fixes an intentional object and a specific cognitive content. As far as we know, a solemn piece of religious vocal music in C minor does not *resemble* in any way the divine, nor is it naturally connected with it (as is, e.g., smoke to fire), but it evokes and forms in members of a given culture an *adequate* response and disposition *intending* the divine.

Mendelssohn praised the ancient art of hymns that used music to engrave religious truths onto the heart and arouse in the listener the emotions proper to the intention. We should not "compare the art of music that we have today with that magnificent art." In ancient times, the pleasure of music was conjoined to the "pleasantness of the meaning and intention of the text, not of the expression of lips and the sound of voice" (עריבת ענין דבק במובן וכוונת המאמר לא במבטא שפתים והברת הקול); today "it is merely pleasant to the sense." This synthesis of content and form is the reason that even if ancient Hebrew poetry loses in translation from its aesthetic beauty, it nevertheless does not cease to please by virtue of its content; not so foreign poetry.[30] Text convinces and moves, and music alone arouses emotions without content. Ethical and religious motivation intending the proper divine referent is best achieved by a synthesis of text and an adequate artistic effect on the soul, especially musical. "The meaning (*Verstand*) of the words commands the soul; and the pleasant tones supporting them set our senses in the condition of the specific affect that should be aroused."[31] Although Mendelsssohn does not mention this, it is obvious that music and recited text are least prone to idolatry. Like ceremonies, they exist as long as they are performed, and they leave behind no object that would lend them to idolatry.[32]

The Sublime

The representation of God by beauty does not suffice. Also, God's omnipotence and transcendence must be represented. This is the role of the sublime. Whereas beauty may represent harmony of perfections, it cannot represent the infinite power of the divine, the infinite distance between God and creature. This purpose is served by the "sublime," namely, by what "is or appears immense as far as the degree of its perfection is concerned." The immensity of perfection arouses awe. We can, therefore, define the sublime thus: "It is something sensuously perfect in art, capable of inspiring awe." And in the supreme degree this is true of God. "The properties of the Supreme Being which we recognize in his works inspire the most ecstatic awe and admiration because they surpass everything that we can conceive as enormous, perfect, or sublime." God is therefore said to be "the most sublime being" (*JubA* 1, 457–59; Dahlstrom, 195–96). Like beauty, the sublime, too, does not adequately represent the divine perfections; but both elicit an adequate human response to the divine. The difference between the representation and the represented follows necessarily from the difference between God and man.

As far as their nature is concerned, some things are so perfect, so sublime that they cannot be reached by any finite thought, cannot be adequately intimated by means of any sign and cannot be represented as they are by any images. Among such things are God, the world, eternity, and so on. Here the artist must exert all the powers of his spirit to find the most worthy signs by means of which these infinitely sublime concepts can be aroused in us intuitively. [33]

Although religious rites, signs, and symbols, as well as beliefs, must *in principle* be inadequate *presentations* of the divine, simply because he is not sensuous and infinite, they may nevertheless arouse adequate human *responses* to the divine, humanly adequate *representations* of him.[34] Immensity arouses a "sweet shudder," a "mixed sentiment" of pleasure experienced when something painful, terrifying, or ghastly is observed.

What blissful sentiments surprise us when we consider the immeasurable perfection of God! Our inability accompanies us on this flight, to be sure, and drags us back into the dust. But the ecstasy over that infinity and the displeasure with our own nothingness blend together into a holy shudder. (*Rhapsody, JubA* 1, 399; Dahlstrom, 145; translation modified)[35]

A religious rite or sign is in principle inadequate *a parte objecti,* that is, to the referent of religion, and yet may be adequate *a parte subjecti,* that is, to the religious practitioner. A crucial question is hence whether a religious practice must be justified with reference to the nature of God only, or whether it may be justified with reference to the specific human nature responding to the divine. Mendelssohn's view is clear and resolute. In the letter to Sophie Becker quoted in part above, Mendelssohn also says that "we sing for our own sake," not for God's, and then he elaborates on his own practice and on its relation to Enlightenment:

I believe that many Psalms are of a kind that, sung by the most enlightened person, they must effect true edification. . . . So much is certain, the Psalms sweetened for me some bitter hour, and I pray and sing them whenever I sense a desire to pray and sing.[36]

Not only the form but the very performance of a religious act is justified with reference to human needs. Human needs, whether individual happiness or social stability, may very well recommend religion. These needs may serve as a psychological or political but not as a philosophical justification of religion and religious service. They would remain in place even if we had conclusive reasons to believe that God does not exist or that no service is adequate to him. Mendelssohn's argument presupposes here the truths of natural religion, and this is perfectly reasonable since his interlocutor is credulous and asks for religious advice. Moreover, his interlocutor does not question the sense of religious expression but only its form. And regarding the form, Mendelssohn shifted the justification of religious practice from adequacy to the divine object of religion to adequacy to the human response to the divine. The practice suggested here, the chanting of (many, not all) psalms, is certainly an adequate service according to Mendelssohn's criteria, and from time immemorial they were an important part of prayer in Judaism and Christianity. In Mendelssohn, religion is a worldly human institution, albeit its referent is transcendent. On the background of Mendelssohn's conception of man and of aesthetic pleasure as defining man's unique place in the universe, on the one hand, and of God as the most perfect being, on the other, it is easy to see that his advice to Sophie Becker is not a casual remark but an integral component of his entire philosophy. To accept human value judgment as a philosophical (not psychological or sociological) justification of religious rite presupposes a basic agreement between human and divine value judgments. This is an optimistic outlook that expresses a basic trust in the world.

Now, on the basis of these tacit presuppositions, Mendelssohn's view supports religious pluralism and religious reform. If symbols need not present or represent the divine, but it suffices that they belong to the sphere of perfection and sublimity, then doubts concerning their "adequacy" to their object lose their importance. And if they are not necessary and therefore universal human *reactions* to the divine but human *responses* mediated by culture, then they may and even must be as different as cultures are. As long as they do not violate the principles of natural religion and the notion of God as the most perfect being (in Mendelssohn's interpretation) they are all legitimate religious expressions.

This is an argument for religious pluralism. For the very same reason we may change symbols to make them more adequate to our changing culture, in which also our "responses" to the divine change. And this is the justification of religious reform. Reform depends on the fact that the symbol is conventional, although it is not entirely arbitrary but must fulfill some conditions, that is, belong to a certain sphere of values and be compatible with tradition. But if the symbol has no "real connection" with its referent and is not a "real symbol," then it also lacks binding force. A unique obligatory practice cannot entirely forsake "real symbols" and its anchor in myth.

Finally, the limitations of proper forms of service must be remembered. Chorales and other religious music are appropriate ceremonies, but they are not more than that. If they are performed without religious intention, they are not a religious action. Religious music played in the concert hall proves the point. Certainly, we can experience a concert as a religious service and a service as a concert, but the distinction remains in place. It depends on the intention. Conversely, there is nothing binding in the specific form of service.

Again, concerning perfection and beauty and their relation to religious practice, Maimon is a clear alternative to Mendelssohn. Surprisingly, it seems at first sight that Mendelssohn and not Maimon follows Maimonides. Discussing different kinds of service, Maimonides characterizes them as relating to different faculties of the soul. He includes among them vocal music, the affection and fraternity arising from the gathering of the pilgrims (*The Guide of the Perplexed,* III, 46; Pines, 591–92), and even incense (III, 45; Pines 578). In this he seems closer to Mendelssohn than to Maimon, who exclusively concentrated on the intellect.

However, for Maimonides all aesthetic means are there to soften and touch the hearts of the multitude so that they "become submissive . . . so that they accept God's guiding commands and fear Him" (*The Guide of the Perplexed,* III, 45; Pines, 580). But these means address the low faculties of the soul, and obeying the precepts is a low grade of perfection, the highest being pure intellectual apprehension of the divine, open to the few only: "He who knows God *finds grace in His sight* [Exodus 33:13] and not he who merely fasts and prays, but everyone who has knowledge of Him" (I, 54; Pines, 123). The intellect, Maimonides repeatedly says, is the "bond" between man and God, and only those who attain the highest metaphysical knowledge and complete concentration reach union with God. Others, those who follow all precepts included, do not even enter the palace of God's dwelling.[37] In his attitude to the intellect, to emotions and aesthetics, Maimon, not Mendelssohn, closely follows Maimonides—at least before he conceived of God as a mere "idea."[38]

In Maimon, aesthetic pleasure and emotions certainly belong to worldly life, but they are the human predicament, not worthy of God and his service. Thus Maimon used to sing to himself and others Jewish religious hymns, "although he lived already for many years as a non-Jew," and when a converted Jew once played Maimon the tune of a solemn Jewish hymn, Maimon even broke down in tears.[39] However, Maimon did not ascribe to this practice or to his emotions any religious meaning. The power of religious emotions or the longing for the lost family and home once associated with the hymns and the communal-religious life does not disappear with the rational conviction of their vacuity. And, on the other hand, this emotional effect of the ceremonies implies nothing concerning their truth or adequacy. Only philosophical contemplation was judged adequate to God and man, the infinite and the finite intellect. Although God faded to a mere idea, Maimon nevertheless retained the value judgment concerning the intellectual striving of man.

Again, Maimon is an excellent observer, and he precisely diagnoses the roots of his disagreements with Mendelssohn. When he met Mendelssohn, says Maimon, he himself was philosophically a Maimonidean, and a stoic in moral theory. Mendelssohn thought differently: "All natural impulses, capacities and powers, as something good in themselves (not merely as means to something good), were to be brought into exercise as realities. The highest perfection, was the idea of the maximum, or the greatest sum, of these realities" (*Lebensgeschichte, GW* 1, 481–82; Murray, 227–28).

Mendelssohn and Maimon hence mark opposed positions in Jewish Enlightenment vis-à-vis worldly life. Mendelssohn's values "all natural impulses, capacities and powers," which are the human finite representation of the divine infinite "highest perfection"; Maimon values strict "reason" alone. This shows, of course, also in their attitude to literature and poetry. "For *belles lettres* I discovered not the slightest inclination," reports Maimon. And when Mendelssohn recommended a poet to him, Maimon answered, "What is a poet but a liar?" Although Maimon changed his attitude and learned to appreciate poetry, he nevertheless reprimands Homer for his "fairy tales," and his own writings on aesthetics betray his distance from such matters.[40] But Maimon's rationalistic stance is much more radical than the dismissal of art or his remaining alienation from it. He opposes "common sense" to rational knowledge, dismisses knowledge dependent on the senses as nonsense, which is as irrational as category mistakes, and disqualifies even geometry as merely subjectively necessary knowledge because it depends not on logic alone but also on spatial imagination.[41] There obtains a clear correlation between Mendelssohn's and Maimon's respective ideas of Enlightenment, ideals of the good life, and concept of God: In Mendelssohn "sound reason" is a legitimate source of valid knowledge, and all "perfections" are legitimate sources of eudemonia (*Glückseligkeit*); in Maimon pure reason is the only source both of valid knowledge and of eudemonia; Mendelssohn's God is the *ens perfectissimum;* Maimon's God is the infinite intellect. Mendelssohn wishes to reform Judaism and enrich its practice with the arts; Maimon wishes to replace religion by science and philosophy, that is, by reason. This, however, does not at all mean that Maimon is simply an atheist or indifferent to questions of belief and religion; on the contrary.

SALOMON MAIMON: THE RELIGIOUS SEEKER

In Maimon we encounter a radical alternative to Mendelssohn's conception of Jewish Enlightenment. Maimon began his career as a religious seeker and enthusiast, exploring the possibilities within rabbinic Judaism, Asceticism, Kabbalah, and the Chassidic movement. Finally, as an enlightened philosopher in Germany, he no longer lived in a Jewish community or practiced Judaism. His religion, if it was one, was a "philosophical mysticism" of sorts, which I will briefly address below.[42] However, Maimon not only changed his personal way of life but also reflected on the course he had taken and on the cultures he encountered. He now understood his own development as progress from "primitive" to "developed" culture, from obscure to enlightened stages in different aspects: cognitive, moral, aesthetic, emotional, and religious.

From this "enlightened" vantage point he summarizes the transformation he underwent thus:

> The conception of intermediate causes [studied by the sciences] replaced by and by the conception of the first cause [God] which transgressed its proper limits and set it back to its true designation, namely the idea to search for such intermediate causes *in infinitum.*— Melancholic and enthusiastic religion was transformed by and by into a religion of reason; the place of slavish religious service was taken by a free development of the cognitive faculty and moral; I understood that perfection was a condition of true *felicity (Glückseligkeit). (GW* 1, 306–7)

The Rationalist and the Skeptical Version

Once Maimon replaced the "slavish service" of Judaism with the "free development of the cognitive faculties," he practiced no religion, nor did he belong to a community or celebrate a religious ceremony: "It was the love of truth and the reluctance to do anything inconsistent, that made it impossible for me, without manifest aversion to say prayers which I regarded as a result of an anthropomorphic system of theology" (*GW* 1, 508–9; Murray, 246).

Maimon recounts some anecdotes on his changing attitudes to religious practice. Here is the first about the time when he was still practicing regularly:

> It is remarkable, that at the time when I still observed the rabbinical regulations with the utmost strictness, I yet would not observe certain ceremonies which have something comical [i.e., ridiculous] about them. . . . A blush of shame came over me, when I was to undertake such performances. I sought therefore, if I was pressed on the subject, to free myself by the pretext, that I had either already attended to it, or was going to attend to it, in another synagogue. (*GW* 1, 185–87; Murray, 135–36)

At stake were two ceremonies before New Year's Eve and the Day of Atonement, in which a person is symbolically beaten to atone for his sins or sits aside barefoot on the floor as a symbol of exile awaiting to be freed from vows he did not fulfill during the now ending year.[43] Maimon does not consider these ceremonies symbolic actions and judge the idea they stand for; he rather takes them at face value and finds them ridiculous.

What religious ceremony is not ridiculous? An act that is not merely symbolic, but has an intrinsic value, a ceremony that is itself also a religious experience, in short: practice with "real symbols." This demand is fully fulfilled in kabbalistic practices. As an adherent of Kabbalah, Maimon believed in the effect of religious action on the divine realm. In retrospect, he narrates one such practice. The biblical phrase "Koh amar Jehova" (כה אמר יהוה; Thus saith the Lord) is interpreted by one Kabbalist thus: "Jehova" represents the masculine aspect of the Godhead, "Koh" (English, "thus") refers to the *Shekhina,* the feminine aspect, and "amar" (English, "saith") stands for sexual union. The entire phrase hence means "the masculine and feminine aspects of God unite in intercourse":

> Accordingly, when I read this passage in the Bible, I thought nothing else, but that, when I uttered these words, and thought their occult meaning, an actual union of these divine spouses took place, from which the whole world had to expect a blessing. (*GW* 1, 134–35; Murray, 100–101)

In retrospect, Maimon asks rhetorically: "Who can restrain the excesses of imagination, when it is not guided by reason?" (*GW* 1, 135; Murray, 101).

But soon Maimon found the true form of service, adequate to reason: philosophizing. Still living in Lithuania, he spent every free minute with his bosom friend, neglecting the prescribed prayers. Maimon's friend relied on God's mercy, whereas Maimon gave a principled justification:

> I had by this time obtained from Maimonides more accurate ideas of God and of our duties towards Him. . . . "Our destination" [says Maimon to his friend] is merely the *attainment of perfection through*

the knowledge of God and the imitation of His actions. Prayer is simply the expression of our knowledge, is intended merely for the common man who cannot of himself attain to this knowledge; and therefore it is adapted to his mode of conception. But as we see into the end of prayer, and can attain to this end directly, we can dispense altogether with prayer as something superfluous. (*GW* 1, 196–97; Murray, 143; original emphasis)[44]

Maimon's adoption of the kabbalistic conception of prayer and his later purely intellectualistic conception of "service" have something in common: in both cases he demands that the act be justified in itself, not merely symbolize something else. Prayer is justified if it effects a physical or metaphysical change in the world or the divine; metaphysical studies are justified because they bring the student closer to perfection and God. Thus conceived, these practices do not stand for anything else, let alone for something of a different kind. Symbolic activity as such is not justified. And this attitude remained unchanged in Maimon. Throughout the series of his conversions from rabbinic Judaism to Kabbalah to Chassidism and finally to the "religion of reason," his expectations from actions remained invariant: an action should be meaningful in itself, that is, have an intrinsic value, not merely conventionally symbolize some meaningful content. Religious service is here conceived as a "real symbol" in the sense of van der Leeuw, as a tertium quid in which God and man encounter each other. Understood this way, religious practice fulfills Mendelssohn's criterion of idolatry or Cassirer's criterion of myth. Religion cannot be enlightened. Or differently again: Maimon rejects ceremonies as such, that is, as symbolic actions. Religious practice should consist in real religious experience, not in merely symbolic actions that have no intrinsic value.

Now, Mendelssohn would certainly object and maintain that prayer is an enlightened religious practice, theurgy not. But to Maimon prayer is either committed to theurgy or committed to anthropomorphism. Theurgy, the belief in the efficacy of prayer (not mediated by God's will) is a kind of superstition, as is the belief in talismans, amulets, blessings, and curses applying words, hieroglyphics, writ, or other signs. They are all based on a mistaken belief in the efficacy of mere signs motivated by fear or hope:

> In ancient times it was believed that a blessing or curse, expressed with ardent passion, will not fail to bring about the desired effect. But words are mere signs and have no necessary causal connection with the signified things themselves. (*GW* 3, 26)

However, if we understand prayer as an appeal to God, then we are committed to an "anthropomorphic system of theology" (*GW* 1, 508–9; Murray, 246). This is so because the "belief in the power of prayer" presupposes on the one hand that man is independent from the laws of nature and on the other that God is a being "that acts upon [his] mere arbitrary will (*Willkür*)" and that prayer may serve as a means "to influence this arbitrary will according to our purpose" (*GW* 3, 29). But ascribing a will to God implies already an anthropomorphic (and therefore wrong) conception of God, because it presupposes a striving for something that is not yet real—whereas for God everything that is possible "must permanently be real" (*GW* 3, 35–36).[45]

This is a philosophical critique of prayer, but in Maimon it is accompanied by an aversion to perform it. When in the Hague and invited for dinner, he not only doubts other guests' reports on miracles performed with Kabbalah and is, therefore, suspected of heresy but also refuses the honor of saying the blessing on the wine after dinner because of "reluctance to be guilty of inconsistency, that made it impossible for me, without manifest aversion, to say prayers which I regarded as a result of an anthropomorphic system of theology" (*GW* 1, 508–9; Murray, 245–46).

Symbolic action and prayer are thus disqualified as proper religious practice. The action he approves of is nothing less than mystical unification with God. We encounter two versions in Maimon, in his early Chassidic phase and in his mature philosophical period.

In the late 1760s Maimon heard of the Chassidim and wandered to the court of the *"groisse maggid"* of Mesritch. He decided to go there upon hearing homiletic interpretations of a biblical verse and of a Mishnah *locus* that reached him by hearsay: the point of both is "the self-annihilation before God." Also in his description of their religious practices, Maimon concentrates on self-annihilation and mystical union with God: "Their worship consisted in a voluntary elevation above the body, that is, in an abstraction of the thoughts from all created things, even from the individual self, and in union with God" (*GW* 1, 220; Murray, 160–61). Maimon approves of the purpose of this service but maintains that the "self-annihilation before God is only then well-founded, when a man's faculty of knowledge, owing to the grandeur of its object, is so entirely occupied with that object, that he exists, as it were, out of himself, in the object alone."

> Some simple men of this sect, who sauntered about idly the whole day with pipe in mouth, when asked, what they were thinking about all the time, replied, "We are thinking about God." This answer would have been satisfactory, if they had constantly sought, by an adequate knowledge of nature, to extend their knowledge of the divine. (*GW* 1, 223; Murray, 163)

This is written from his mature, enlightened vantage point, from which only intellectual perfection is of worth. Maimon conceives of God as an infinite intellect. It is the human intellect that justifies the notion that man was created in the "image" of God (*GM*, 32–34), either because the human intellect is a "schema" of the infinite (*Tr*, 65) or because they are "same in kind" (*GM*, 34), or—as Kant suspected that Maimon believed—that the finite intellect is conceived as "part" of the infinite (Kant's letter to Marcus Hertz, May 26, 1789; *AA* 11, 48–55), or, in Maimon's wording, that the human intellect is an "offspring" of the "pure intellects" (*Versuch einer neuen Logik, GW* 5, 266 f.). The differences between these versions are not important in our context.

And indeed, from this vantage point, if we proceed from a proper concept of God as the most perfect being, then true "prayer" (*Gebet*) and true worship (*Andacht*) consist not in religious ceremonies but in "abstracting from all contingent beings and concentrating on the necessary, infinite perfect being and on the dependence of all things—including ourselves—on the laws of nature which are identical to the wisdom and goodness of the most perfect being" (*GW* 3, 28–29, 33–34). True worship consists, in other words, in a comprehensive apprehension of the entire structure of the world and the awareness that we are part of it. The infinite intellect is hence the formal structure of the universe. Since in the framework of the Maimonidean (Aristotelian) philosophy, apprehension involves the identity of the intellect with its object, the "form" of the object known, knowledge of God is tantamount to the unity of the human intellect with him. Maimon upheld this metaphysical-epistemological Maimonidean thesis in different versions all his life. In all these versions, the peak of apprehension is an experience of mystical union with the infinite intellect, "philosophical mysticism." This is real "prayer" (*GW* 3, 32–39).

In a philosophy that takes this tack, cognition of the divine, worship, and religious experience coincide. Rational philosophy and mysticism are not opposed to each other, nor do they merely coexist; they are two aspects of the same contemplative activity. Maimon explicitly draws this conclusion: "If we think that our actual thought reached its highest grade, we obtain the idea of Deity with which we then unite" (*GW* 7, 354). Then, alas, it is no longer "we," since human individuality dissolves in this unification. This religious ideal of uniting with God is—partially—achieved by the philosophers already in this life.[46] This sounds deeply religious, and it certainly is so as far as the frame of mind, the sense of facing infinity, is concerned. In fact, it is an enlightened version of the Chassidic "self-annihilation before God" ("*die Zernichtung des Ich*")[47] that appealed to Maimon in his youth.

It may seem that Maimon turned to a very narrow intellectualistic view that is diametrically opposed to Mendelssohn's emphasis that truth should also be transferred from the mind to the heart (*Jerusalem*, 74), but Maimon in fact attaches strong emotions to apprehension (in fact, mystical elation). Speaking of the infinitesimal calculus, that "divine spark" and "patent of nobility" testifying to the origin of the human spirit in the "pure intelligences," Maimon writes, "Who can call the exercise of the faculties of the soul as such, and be it without ulterior benefit, futile? And who can reason out (*wegräsonieren*) the felicity (*Glückseligkeit*) connected to it? Certainly only someone who never enjoyed it" (*GW* 5, 325).

Although religious zeal is also present in Maimon's maturity, it is now outweighed by skepticism. Maimon's philosophy combines "dogmatic rationalism and empirical skepticism." Human knowledge proceeds in two ways: from sense experience "upward" to ever more general abstract concepts and from the most general concept(s) and categories "downward" to empirical objects. The problem is that neither method reaches its ultimate destiny, and moreover, we do not know whether they can complement each other. In fact, concepts and intuitions are so heterogeneous that it is inconceivable that concepts can apply to intuitions and that a judgment can be a synthesis of logic and perception. Certain empirical knowledge is impossible. Knowledge is either pure or real, either certain or empirical, but not both. The unique feature of Maimon's philosophy is that he upholds both opposed possibilities at once. We encountered this trait in his philosophy of language. The formation of language in its present form can be explained by empiricism, beginning with names of individual objects; and it can also be explained beginning with the most general abstractions (from objects) and categories (of relations). There is no way to decide which is true, nor that they complement rather than contradict each other. Finally, Maimon follows the program of rationalism and criticizes it with skeptical arguments.[48] This is of direct import for our problem here. Maimon adds to the God with whom one can unite the notion of God as a "regulative idea," which does not refer to an existing entity. Here God is the idea of the unity of all natural causes. Of an idea we may neither say that it "exists" nor that "it does not exist" any more than we may say of a geometrical line that it is sweet or not sweet.[49] Maimon offers this insight into the different senses of "there is" as a platform for peace between theists and atheists. Even if this suggestion were to resolve this controversy, it certainly cannot substantiate any religion or religious cult.[50] In his essay on theodicy (*GW* 3, 309–33), Maimon opposes Kant's characterization of God as a "necessary idea of reason" of the "supreme order and purposefulness" and suggests instead that it is based merely on the human "drive towards supreme perfection." It is hence based on "a subjectively necessary idea of supreme perfection" to which "nothing objective must fully correspond" (*GW* 3, 311–12). This idea of God is a far cry from any religious creed,[51] and it cannot anymore support Maimon's philosophical mysticism. The idea of God to which "nothing objective must fully correspond" is not a reality that can be approached although not reached; it may not be a reality at all. The infinite progress of apprehension itself towards some existing or nonexisting vanishing point replaces here religion. Maimon concluded his *Transcendentalphilosophie* with a talmudic quotation that he also used on two other occasions:

Our Talmudists (who at times certainly expressed thoughts worthy of a Plato) say: "Scholars find no peace, neither in this life nor in the hereafter." And this is how they interpret in their way the words of the Psalter (84:7/8) "They go from strength to strength, every one of them in Zion appeareth before God." (*Tr*, 444)[52]

Maimon adopts without any doubt the maxim that "scholars find no peace" in this life, but whether "every one of them in Zion appeareth before God" as "our Talmudists" believe is finally doubtful. We are left with two radically opposed alternatives, and we cannot decide which of them is true. In the "dogmatic" version, the striving for apprehension is the highest human end, and its peak is also the peak of religious experience: the mystical union with the infinite intellect. In the skeptical version, this striving for metaphysical apprehension and unification with God appears as a misconceived, futile, and meaningless Sisyphean undertaking.

JUDAISM: ETHOS OF A FAMILY OR STATUTES OF A VOLUNTARY ASSOCIATION?

Another important difference between Mendelssohn's and Maimon's stance is their attitude towards community and society at large. This issue has direct import for their opposing positions concerning religion. In theory and practice Mendelssohn demonstrates his view that community is the adequate form of human life, an essential condition of attaining personal and religious perfection. Belonging to a community is not only a necessity of man's worldly life, but also of his eternal life: without society man would remain a beast.[53] Not so Maimon. In his view, society exists only in order to cater to the necessities of material life and support the learned elite. Here, too, he agrees with Maimonides. Maimon begins the introduction to his juvenile *Hesheq Shelomo* with a very long quotation from Maimonides' introduction to the Mishnah. Maimonides there raises the question to what purpose God created humans who do not engage in studies as is proper to the vocation of the *animal rationale*. The principal reason is said to be the production of the necessities of life for the sake of the philosopher.[54]

Maimon's and Mendelssohn's different attitudes towards the community can be seen in their answers to two practical questions: May the Jewish community exclude or ban a member, and may Jews exempt themselves from the ceremonial law? Mendelssohn's stance is well known. He maintained that a religious community may not exclude one of its members: "no society can exercise a right which is diametrically opposed to the primary purpose of the society itself. To exclude a dissident . . . is like forbidding a sick person to enter a pharmacy" (*Jerusalem*, 74).

Maimon answers Mendelssohn in his autobiography. The case in point occurred in Hamburg. A Jew who overtly transgressed the rules of the community in public was banned by the local zealous rabbi, Raphael Cohen. Maimon's response to Mendelssohn's objection is formulated in the words that the community could have spoken to the transgressor: "'So long as you put yourself in opposition to the laws of our communion, you are excluded from it; and you must therefore make up your mind whether this open disobedience or the privileges of our communion can more advance your blessedness'" (*GW* 1, 488; Murray, 231).

The mirror image of the obligation of the community towards its members is the obligation of all members to keep the ceremonial law. Mendelssohn famously said, "In fact, I cannot see how those born into the House of Jacob can in any conscientious manner disencumber themselves of the law." As long as God himself does not abolish the law in a second revelation, as authentic as the first on Sinai, "no sophistry of ours can free us from the strict obedience we owe to the law" (*Jerusalem,* 133).

Maimon draws the opposite conclusion, although he accepts Mendelssohn's opinion that the Jewish religious laws are the laws of the Jewish state:

> They must therefore be obeyed by all who profess to be members of this state, and who wish to enjoy the rights granted to them under condition of their obedience. But, on the other hand any man who separates himself from this state, who desires to be considered no longer a member of it, and to renounce all his rights as such, whether he enters another state or betakes himself to solitude is also in his conscience no longer bound to obey those laws. (*GW* 1, 484–85; Murray, 229; translation slightly altered)

How can Mendelssohn and Maimon draw these opposing conclusions concerning the mutual obligations of the community and its members? This is easy to understand once we realize that they argue from different presumptions concerning the nature of the community. Maimon considers it a contractual voluntary association; Mendelssohn considers it a family. Maimon argues that a member enjoys privileges and assumes the obligation to abide by the statutes. Both sides can terminate membership. The community may exclude a member who violates the statutes; an individual may resign if he no longer wishes to belong to the community. The law is binding for "all who profess to be members of this state" and not binding for those who profess not to be members and forsake the privileges dependent on membership. In contrast, for Mendelssohn a Jew does not have to profess anything. The law is binding for all those "born into the House of Jacob." One is born into the Jewish community as into a family. Membership in a family is not voluntary and cannot be ended by any side. No wonder Mendelssohn repeatedly speaks of the "religion of my fathers," a formula that is not only the most significant way to address God in Judaism but also expresses the sense of being "born into the House of Jacob" as into a family.[55]

I argued above that belonging to the Jewish community as to a family has epistemic implications. We tend to and are entitled to trust in the first place "familiar" informants, hence prefer the tradition of our own community or society. This is Lessing's justification of pluralism without relativism, and this can be Mendelssohn's argument for his preference of the revelation on Sinai over others. But why should this historical event obligate persons born many centuries later? Irrespective of what God and the ancient Israelites promised each other upon their bonds, and even if the ancestors agreed to obligate not only themselves but also all generations to come—why should their obligation and promises be accepted by posterity? After all, do the oaths of our ancestors obligate us, or can an heir not decline the inheritance? In fact, according to Jewish law, oaths do not obligate posterity, but debts of the ancestors are inherited by their successors and inheritance cannot be declined![56] The present obligation to fulfill the Jewish law on the basis of the revelation on Sinai presupposes that the membership in the Jewish community is accepted as unconditional, by "tacit consent," as it were. Mendelssohn

clearly distinguishes in the name of the entire Jewish community between the unconditioned belonging to the Jewish community and the
voluntary citizenship:

> [I]f civil union cannot be obtained under any other condition than
> our departing from the laws which we still consider binding on us,
> then we are sincerely sorry to find it necessary to declare that we must
> rather do without civil union. (*Jerusalem,* 135)

The "civil union" can be chosen or declined, but Judaism cannot. Being
a (in fact, the only) ceremonial law that conforms to reason and to the
other demands from an adequate rite, we may grant this tradition our
trust. We do not choose our tradition any more than we choose our parents or mother tongue. If we believe that some detail of our tradition is
not adequate to the necessities of life or not an adequate human response
to the divine, we may reform it, as Mendelssohn suggested concerning the precepts of burial. But as we have seen, this reform has been suggested and argued for on traditional Jewish grounds, in a traditional
Jewish fashion: reliance on traditions and authoritative texts. Of course,
a reform must also be consistent with the rest of the traditional lore. This
again is similar to the case of our native tongue. We may reform this or
that grammatical rule or the orthography, and we may, of course, introduce new words and meanings of old ones, but we cannot invent a new
language from scratch.

This is entirely different in Maimon, both philosophically and practically. Maimon regarded the community as a voluntary association
and cancellable on both sides every moment. He was not committed in
any way to tradition but to his own reason alone. *"Selbstdenker,"* an
independent thinker, is the highest praise in his dictionary. Moreover,
he himself left the community into which he was born and wandered
to Germany, then also left the Jewish community in Berlin and lived
outside of any religious community.

We thus end this exploration into the philosophy of enlightened
Judaism with a set of alternatives for which two persons could stand:
Maimon or Mendelssohn? A justification of religion *ab ovo,* and pro-
ceeding from the presumption of disbelief, or a critical successive ex-

amination of religious teachings and practices from within community and religion? Does the burden of proof fall on the proponent of religion or on the opponent? Should the justification be a rigorous proof of all propositions accepted, or may it grant trust to tradition accepted by the community as long as this is not refuted? Must justification proceed by strict reasoning and exclusively cognitively, or by common sense and also on the basis of aesthetic experience and emotions? Is religion to be justified in respect to its referent, or does it suffice that it is an adequate human response to the divine and excludes idolatry? These alternatives form clusters of interdependent arguments.[57] There is also no external point from which we could compare these clusters and make an argued choice. The controversy between common sense, aesthetics, and community on the one hand and strict logic and rationality and autonomy on the other cannot itself be adjudicated. What criteria should be applied: those of Mendelssohn or those of Maimon? Here this or the other reason are not judge but party. Elaborating the alternatives is certainly the task of philosophy. The choice between the clusters is rather en bloc and depends on what forms of life are historically possible, and on our scale of values and our choice of the form of life we wish to endorse.

CHAPTER 9

Conclusion

In this book on the philosophy of the Jewish Enlightenment I attempted
to place Mendelssohn's views of Judaism within his general philosophy. I
also endeavored to show that Mendelssohn's philosophy in general and
his philosophy of religion in particular are based on semiotics and that
also Salomon Maimon's reflections on religion were fundamentally semiotic. I examined religion, not faith. I did not scrutinize Mendelssohn's
and others' commonsensical or metaphysical arguments for the existence of God, or theological deliberations concerning the nature of God,
his attributes, theodicy, or providence. I rather concentrated on religious
practice. There is, however, one theme that belongs both to practice and
to theology and which takes a prominent place in this study: idolatry.
This seems to be of special concern in Judaism.

There is a continuous tradition of criticizing idolatry or practices
that do not befit the notion of a monotheistic transcendent God, beginning with the Second Commandment, over the prophets' critique of
idolatry and many loci in the sages and leading to Maimonides and then
to Mendelssohn, Hermann Cohen, and in a way even to Ernst Cassirer.
Mendelssohn's interest in semiotics and the precedence he ascribes to
practice over theory, to common sense over metaphysics, "predestined"
him to develop the philosophy of Jewish religious enlightenment.

Mendelssohn emerges from this study as an original philosopher,
not a shallow popularizer of Wolffian metaphysics, as he has been hitherto portrayed. The kernel of his philosophy is the claim that commonsense knowledge, which is based on sense experience, is reliable and that

natural language represents it sufficiently well when accompanying practice or language of action, that is, gestures, in a shared practice. Concerning our own inner life, thoughts, wishes, and emotions, and a fortiori
that of others, Mendelssohn was a skeptic, as he was also a skeptic concerning our knowledge of abstract objects that necessarily relies on metaphors if it is not aided by a specially adequate symbolism, as in mathematics. Both these characteristics unite in Mendelssohn's philosophy of
religion, especially of Judaism. Mendelssohn's philosophy of language
implies that metaphysics and rational theology depend on metaphors
and are unreliable, when they depart considerably from experience and
common sense. It is therefore that we should restrict our truth claims to
"natural religion," to the certain and not controversial basic truths (the
existence of God the creator of the universe, his providence, and afterlife), and to those indubitable historical truths that answer the criteria of
empirical truth in the most eminent way (as the revelation on Sinai).

More reliable than conventional language is the synthesis of language of action and spoken language. Religious ceremonies apply a
segment of such language; here meaning and reference are least ambiguous, but this does not apply to theology and subtle metaphysics and
need not do so. A practitioner knows the eternal and historical truths
of his religion above all because he knows the core meaning of the ceremonies that are their symbols. Sabbath commemorates creation and Exodus, Passover commemorates Exodus, and so on. He can answer relevant questions without entering into intricate questions concerning
metaphysics. Religious practice should therefore consist in ceremonies
guided by the basic religious thoughts of the practitioners. Further theological thoughts are not only uncertain but also changing, and of no
practical import.

Turning to religious practice and the ceremonial law, the basic dilemma is the nature of religious symbols. Here Mendelssohn's semiotics again proves powerful. There are first two opposite poles: a "real
symbol," which is sacred in itself, and a conventional sign without intrinsic value. The crux is this: In the real symbol "two realities coincide, God and Man encounter each other."[1] In creating an opportunity
for a religious experience, "real symbols" guarantee that the rite is
meaningful. However, this very same nature of the symbol as a mani-

festation of the divine embodies the danger of idolatry. It is difficult to see how the cult with "real symbols" can be clearly distinguished from fetishism. On the other hand, a conventional sign is ideally transparent; we look through it, as it were, at what it stands for. The meaning of the sign is of interest, not the sign (sign-vehicle) itself. Thus the rite is immune to idolatry but also lacks intrinsic religious meaning. If its function is to remind us of some religious truth, then an inscription on the wall or an electronic buzz may do just as well. Moreover, whoever is permanently engaged with metaphysics or religious questions, a philosopher or a religious functionary, needs no reminder at all. In short: understanding religious symbols as conventional and not real deprives the ceremony of its meaning and sense.

I suggested above yet another possibility to conceive the religious symbol, and I argued that it captures Mendelssohn's suggestions concerning the use of aesthetic perfection in ceremonies. All perfections in the world are symbols of God's perfections, and religious service can use sensuous perfection, beauty, and sublimity to address God. The religious symbol should be an *adequate human response to the divine*. A religious ceremony should indicate the *value* that we ascribe to the divine, although we do not wish to claim that it shares a *property* with it or is produced by it. It should express and help revive human religious experience rather than represent the "wholly other." An encounter with the perfection of beauty and the sublime or of apprehension arouses in us the adequate human response to the divine, but this does not mean that beauty or natural immensity are similar to God.

In Mendelssohn's conception religious ceremonies must be accompanied by religious thoughts, but no specific theology should be prescribed. On the contrary: this should be left to the living discourse of the practicing community, thus enabling a continuous adjustment of religious thought and life. Whenever a definite theology is written down, it must be divorced from social life because time and mores change. Judaism consists in the ceremonial law. Judaism is the religion of actions, of precepts and ceremonies, and in that it is distinctly different from both Catholicism and Protestantism: Catholicism is the religion of "real symbols" (images, reliquia, sacraments); reformed Protestantism, the religion of the word (*sola scriptura*).

Finally, it seems to me that we can now see how fruitful Mendelssohn's principle is to attend to the observable action and avoid speculations as to people's beliefs. Complemented by the insight that the very same sign-vehicle may serve very different kinds of representation, ritual law enables the coherence of a community in spite of diverging opinions. Irrespective of how many people in fact shared Mendelssohn's understanding of the ceremonial law ("Fanaticism and superstition exist among us to a most abhorrent degree"), these two principles enabled him to be part of a community in which fanatics, superstitious believers, and atheists were also members—and to fulfill a meaningful function in bringing into the religious discourse of the community as much enlightenment as possible.

Of course, this rejection of a definite theology does not mean that "Judaism" has no content. Mendelssohn accepts and emphasizes the tradition that had begun with Abraham, was reestablished with the revelation on Mount Sinai and codified in the "Mosaic constitution," and has been continued in the "Oral Law" until his own time. Judaism needs coherence and continuity of tradition, but it need not be uniform. Thus the precise interpretation of the rites will differ from person to person, but as long as the rites and their basic meaning remain the same, and as long as the religious discourse in the community continues, the rites can serve as the skeleton of the community of believers. Mendelssohn presumably also trusts that the ongoing discourse in a coherent community will reproduce one religion, in spite of differences of opinion. It should "stimulate and encourage rivalry and emulation" (*Jerusalem*, 128) but not lead to schisms and excommunication.[2] The ceremonial law hence fulfills two communal functions with the same end: As a strange idea or practice without practical purpose, it prompts questions concerning its meaning and gives occasion to religious education; as a communal practice, it is the backbone of a community that makes possible self-perfection and the religious life of the individual. In both ways the ceremonial law is the medium of communal and individual religious life. Man cannot "fulfill his duties toward himself and toward the author of his existence" in isolation (*Jerusalem*, 40).

The religious ceremony not only serves education and the formation of the community. It also serves the needs of the individual practitioner.

The "most essential purpose of religious society," says Mendelssohn, "is mutual edification. By the magic power of sympathy one wishes to transfer truth from the mind to the heart; to vivify, by participation of others, the conceptions of reason, which at times are lifeless, into soaring sensations" (*Jerusalem*, 74). And of course, it also sweetens "some bitter hour" of the practitioner: It is the medium in which a person experiences and assimilates the worldview of his community and expresses his own worldview and existential frame of mind.

Mendelssohn's idea concerning the mechanism of tradition by means of interpreted communal practices is so happy because it does not import into Judaism a new and strange practice. It simply puts in focus an extant practice as it is manifested and explicitly stated, for example, in the ceremony of Passover (see chap. 6), and, moreover, it explicates its implicit or latent religious function. The same technique can be observed in Mendelssohn's interpretation of the precepts. He concentrates on the precepts that in the Pentateuch itself are interpreted as memorials—the phylacteries, the mezuzah, the *tsitsit,* the Shabbat, and so on—and he says next to nothing about the hundreds of remaining precepts. This is a showcase innovation within tradition. The technique consists first in changing the relative importance of components of the system in question. In concentrating on the commandments mentioned in the "Hear O Israel," he *eo ipso* marginalizes the others. But Mendelssohn neither erases nor adds anything of himself, and personally he keeps the prescriptions. However, his justification of the precepts applies best to the solemn ceremonies performed during communal service, much less so to the precepts one observes when alone in the course of daily life. Second, Mendelssohn introduces more or less radical innovations by means of commentaries on canonical texts and practices. This technique, too, is typical of Judaism. The role of the sacred text as the source of authority is thus enforced, and the innovation is introduced as its real (not necessarily unique) meaning, not as a new invention. The same holds true for the content. Philosophical reflection in Jewish culture has been concerned with idolatry before. Mendelssohn joins and strengthens the trend opposing the ascription of arcane or "symbolic" meanings to the precepts. The reform is presented as an obvious consequence of an accepted practice, while it significantly changes the dominant character of

Judaism accepted at the time. This traditional method of reform, however, does not mean that no theoretical innovation is involved. On the contrary, Mendelssohn's semiotic theory, his theory of language and religious symbols, is innovative and based on the philosophy of the Enlightenment in his age.

Mendelssohn presents his view of Judaism in the descriptive mood. He claims that this, in fact, is Judaism, at least "original" Judaism. And yet every reader of the Bible knows that Mendelssohn suppressed the magical powers ascribed to the brass serpent or the Urim and Thummim, to name just those examples he himself discusses; and every practicing Jew will notice, of course, that Mendelssohn circumvented the issue of religious articles. Mendelssohn introduces a reform of Judaism in a tacit way, by emphasizing some trends and passing in silence over others, and by introducing criteria of "true" Judaism that exclude interpretations opposed to his (e.g., Kabbalah), but he does not name them. Introducing radical change in this form that avoids controversy is certainly a hallmark of Mendelssohn's writing and personality.

Mendelssohn's justification of Judaism is twofold. It proceeds on the one hand in the traditional path from the truth of its origin (the revelation on Sinai) and the authenticity of its transmission. But Mendelssohn also argues for Judaism on the basis of its quality as an adequate response to the divine, as promoting morals, social and individual felicity, and as opposed to idolatry and myth. Mendelssohn favors further reforms of Judaism in this spirit and also acknowledges the merits of other creeds. His is a distinctly enlightened philosophy of religion and Judaism.

Furthermore, Mendelssohn justified religious ceremonies *a parte subjecti*, with reference to human nature and to human needs. In his view, the rite is no "service" to God, and Mendelssohn explicitly said so: God has no needs, and religious practice is for man's, not God's, sake. But exactly this is the basis of Maimon's critique. Maimon demands that an action be intrinsically meaningful. If it purports to be a religious action, it should involve the divine and be of proper efficacy, either theurgic or a religious experience. But it may not merely involve psychological means and serve human needs. In his youth he therefore endorsed the kabbalistic, theurgic notion of prayer, in his maturity philosophy and philosophical mysticism, but he never endorsed "symbolic action," ceremonies. All merely symbolic action and ceremonies must have been "empty puppetry" in his eyes. Many of these questions are relevant to all monotheistic religions. However, the central role given to idolatry in Mendelssohn's thought is specific to Judaism in a Christian environment and serves to segregate the former from the latter.

An important concern of this study has been the presumptions concerning the Jewish community. I argued that belonging to a community has a genuine philosophical import on the questions debated. Historical knowledge depends on tradition, and tradition depends on trust. Trust is not fully justified epistemically (and need not be; otherwise it would be an inductive conclusion, not the granting of trust) but has epistemic implications. As Nathan argues in Lessing's play, we grant "familiar" people trust more easily than foreigners. Belonging to a community has another important implication. It determines the allocation of the burden of proof. The burden of proof is not equally distributed: the defender of an accepted position merely needs to fend off critique, not substantiate it. The critic has both to refute the accepted position and to substantiate his own view. If we are born into a religious community, it is the "fall from faith" that requires arguments; if into a secular society, it is the assuming of faith that calls for reasons. The difference is much more important than the difference between individuals. In Mendelssohn's time, and especially among Jews, belonging to a religious community was the rule. I believe that much injustice has been done to Mendelssohn when current scholars expected him to convince the reader to assume faith. In his own time, he merely needed to refute the arguments to the contrary. This injustice points to something that is much more important than Mendelssohn's reputation: the disintegration of communities in modern societies, especially in the cities. Socioeconomic development, especially since the middle of the nineteenth century, dissolved communities and atomized individuals. These isolated individuals seem so natural to us that we no longer share important tacit and self-evident presuppositions of Mendelssohn's thought and therefore fail to appreciate the sincerity and force of his arguments.

There is no doubt, however, that individual differences are also important. Maimon, for example, showed no interest in the formation of a community; on the contrary: he was not only a "lone wolf," but a notorious provocateur. He showed no consideration for a person or community but for philosophy alone. His thought certainly earned the epitaph *"Consequenzerey,"* (unconditional acceptance of implications from one's presuppositions) derogatory in Mendelssohn's eyes. And, on the other hand, Maimon praised Mendelssohn's "prudence" (*Weltklugheit*) (Wolff, *Maimoniana,* 117) but also accused him of being a "philosophical hypocrite" (see chap. 2, above). In Maimon's view, prudence and philosophical hypocrisy are two sides of the same coin; and this is also one way in which the conflict between Maimon's philosophy and way of life on the one hand and Mendelssohn's on the other can be seen: rigorous philosophy and imprudence on Maimon's side versus prudence and less rigorous philosophy (disparagingly dubbed *Consequenzerey*), on Mendelssohn's.

Maimon's philosophy was not studied in this book but not because it is not worth the effort; on the contrary: I consider Maimon's philosophy to be of singular value. But Maimon did not develop a philosophy of Judaism. He rather turned his back not only on Jewish religion and community, but on all practiced religion. I hope that the confrontation of Mendelssohn's and Maimon's views shows how their different worldviews are coherent in themselves. We may thus see more clearly the alternatives that were relevant at the time and, I believe, today, too.

MIRROR IMAGES:

MOSES MENDELSSOHN AND ALEXANDER ALTMANN

In his insightful and sensitive paper "Moses Mendelssohn's Concept of Judaism Reexamined," Alexander Altmann voices doubts concerning Mendelssohn's understanding of the role of the "chosen people" and the ceremonial law. In Mendelssohn the "mystery of Israel" (the special mission of the Jews) is "reduced to its most attenuated form" (247–48), that is, to safeguard monotheism (cf. *Jerusalem*, 226). It is even worse with the ceremonial law. Understood in Mendelssohn's way, so Altmann believes, the ceremonial law may have a "sociological" function in contributing to the formation of the community, but "the piety expressed by such language sounds hollow." One misses "a sense of the truly symbolic" of the ceremonies, what the "Kabbalists understood by *Sitrey Torah* (mysteries of the Torah)" (245–47). And yet Altmann also writes, "Mendelssohn, though remote from kabbalistic thought, nevertheless reflects some of the religious emotion of awe that characterizes its approach to the commandments" (Commentary, *Jerusalem*, 226). Mendelssohn's overt emotional attachment to the Jewish rite is indeed obvious. What then? Is Mendelssohn opposed to Kabbalah and his piety hollow, or does his piety express religious awe similar to the Kabbalist's? Altmann's answer is clear: Mendelssohn himself observed the Jewish ceremonial law, but his philosophy undermines it. He was "a false messiah," as Altmann once casually remarked.[1]

In fact, Altmann knows that Mendelssohn is not only remote from kabbalistic thought, but strictly opposed to it. Efforts should be made, says Mendelssohn, to rediscover the authentic meaning of the rites, to make the script legible again, after its having been rendered illegible by "hypocrisy and priestcraft"—"a reference, probably, to kabbalistic interpretations of the meaning of the commandments," says Altmann (see Altmann, *Moses Mendelssohn: A Biographical Study,* 551)! Indeed, Altmann also knows that "the Kabbalists speak of the fulfillment of the divine commandments as acts that have an impact on the realm of the *Sefirot,* answering a divine 'need' (*tsorekh gavohah*),"[2] hence that the performance of religious commandments is understood as theurgy, as effecting the divine. And he comments that Mendelssohn "most certainly" opposed this view.

So where does Altmann's Mendelsson stand? Does he believe that the Kabbalist interpretation of the commandments is "hypocrisy and priestcraft" and theurgy and is left with a "hollow" religious emotion, or does he reflect the "emotion of awe"—which Altmann, not Mendelssohn!—ascribes to Kabbalah only? Or does it rather depend on whether Altmann himself stands with Enlightenment or with Kabbalah? The question is quite natural since the essay "Moses Mendelssohn's Concept of Judaism Reexamined" is unmistakably autobiographically tinted, as Isidore Twersky observed as well in his obituary on Altmann.[3]

In his "A Filial Memoir" on his father, the rabbi of Trier, Adolf Altmann (1879–1944),[4] Alexander Altmann writes about the mystical leanings of his father that impressed him as a child. "It was undoubtedly because of his father's influence," comments Paul Mendes-Flohr, "that Altmann did not share in the prevailing Kabbalah-Angst. His father, as noted, imbued in him an affection for the Hasidim and their mystical piety, especially as manifest in prayer."[5] There are many examples of Altmann's sympathies with mysticism, for example, his lecture "Jewish Mysticism" (Die jüdische Mystik) given in Berlin in June 1935. "Altmann concluded his oral presentation by exclaiming that although modern Jews are decisively beyond the world of myth, nonetheless 'we can and should return to mysticism,' for it is 'one of the sources out of which Judaism can renew itself.'"[6]

I suggest that Mendelssohn and Altmann shared a commitment to both religion and enlightenment. However, they are mirror images of each other. Whereas Mendelssohn lived in a world still dominated by religion and emphasized enlightenment to reduce superstition and myth, Altmann lived in a dominantly secular world and emphasized mysticism to save and restore religion. No wonder he had little sympathy for Mendelssohn's theory of idolatry. Perhaps, therefore, this great scholar put so little effort into understanding it but rather dismissed it without further ado as "the least substantiated of all theories he ever advanced."[7]

MENDELSSOHN'S MESSIANIC ALLUSIONS

The Search for Light and Right called upon Mendelssohn to forsake the Jewish ceremonial law that hinders closer bonds between Christians and Jews, and thus lay the foundations for the fulfillment of the prophecy that "there will be only one shepherd and one flock" (John 10:16; *JubA* 7, 86). In response, Mendelssohn addresses the Christian "dear brothers" with much pathos: "in order to be under the care of this omnipresent shepherd the entire flock need . . . not enter and leave the master's house through a single door" (*Jerusalem,* 135). Religious pluralism is not opposed to the prophetic messianic vision. Mendelssohn, too, refers to a prophetic vision associated with shepherd and sheep: "The wolf also shall dwell with the lamb, and the leopard shall lie down with the kid; etc. [and the calf and the young lion and the fatling together; and a little child shall lead them] (Isaiah 11:6) (*Jerusalem,* 134). Now, Mendelssohn used the same biblical verse in his unpublished *Gegenbetrachtungen über Bonnets Palingenesie* of 1770. It is there that he also answers the question whether it is possible that the Mosaic law will be abolished or changed. As in *Jerusalem,* here, too, Mendelssohn argues that only God has the authority to change his law. Will this happen? Opinions in Jewish tradition differ, and here Mendelssohn upholds the view he was later to reject in *Jerusalem.*

> All prophets of the Old Testament agree and reason acquiesces extraordinarily in this hope that the difference of religions will not be for ever, and that once there will be one shepherd and one flock and knowledge of the true God will cover the earth, *as the waters cover the sea.* (Isaiah 11:9; *JubA* 7, 98)

And Mendelssohn adds: "This vision is so delightful to the human soul that it joyfully dwells on it, and enjoys the imagination of the bliss expecting the human race after such salutary revolution" (*JubA* 7, 98).

However, Mendelssohn evidently changed his mind between 1770 and 1783, or even 1782, when he already voiced religious pluralism in his *Vorrede zu Menasse ben Israels Rettung der Juden*. This was the text to which *The Search for Light and Right* responded and Mendelssohn reciprocated with his *Jerusalem*. Mendelssohn argues there against the right to ban a member of a religious community, as he does in *Jerusalem*. In support of his position, he quotes the "sublime prayer" of King Solomon at the consecration of the Temple, which clearly reaches far beyond the topic discussed. It therefore seems that he seized the opportunity to make a point dear to him:

> Moreover concerning a stranger, that is not of thy people Israel, but cometh out of a far country for thy name's sake; (For they shall hear of thy great name, and of thy strong hand, and of thy stretched out arm;) when he shall come and pray toward this house; Hear thou in heaven thy dwelling place, and do according to all that the stranger calleth to thee for: that all people of the earth may know thy name, to fear thee, as do thy people Israel. (1 Kings 8:41–43)

The "stranger" at that time, so Mendelssohn explains, refers to the idolater,[8] and he adds that the rabbis adopted this stance of King Solomon. This is not a prophecy, but "Jerusalem" clearly stands here for religious pluralism, which Mendelssohn also advocates in *Jerusalem*. But also the classical prophetic visions are not absent from Mendelssohn's writings.

The visions of a united monotheistic faith and of religious pluralism were explicitly formulated in Isaiah (2:1–4) and Micah (4:1–5). Hobbes referred to these loci in his discussion of the "Kingdom of God" in *Leviathan,* and Mendelssohn referred to this discussion.[9] Mendelssohn himself did not mention these loci; but the vision is also present in Zechariah (8:19), and to this text Mendelssohn refers twice in *Jerusalem*. Moreover, the association between "Solomon's prayer" and the prophetic visions of religious pluralism is a commonplace in Jewish lore, and Mendelssohn's close associate, Herz Homberg, also makes the connection. I will first quote Homberg and then discuss a possible reason why Mendelssohn did not explicitly discuss messianism.

In his book *Imrei Shefer* (אמרי שפר) (Flowery Words), Homberg comments on the twelfth of Maimonides' "Thirteen Principles," namely, the belief in the advent of the Messiah and the messianic era. He mentions the return from exile where Israel is dispersed since "we were exiled from our ancestors' land and lost temple, priest and prophet" (note that the king is not mentioned!). The return involves the rebuilding of the Temple (again, the restitution of the kingdom of David is not mentioned!), "for mine house shall be called an house of prayer for all people" (Isaiah 56:7). The messianic vision appears here in purely religious, not national, terms.[10] Homberg also wrote the commentary on Isaiah accompanying Meyer Obernik's German translation of the book, and there we find this verse translated into German: "meinen Tempel nennt man dann:

"HAUS DER ANDACHT ALLER VÖLKER."

These are the only words in the translation of Isaiah that are printed in boldface and capital letters. In the commentary on this verse, Homberg refers to Solomon's prayer (1 Kings 8:41) quoted by Mendelssohn in his introduction to his *Menasse ben Israels Rettung der Juden*!

Why didn't Mendelssohn also quote in *Jerusalem* the verse from 1 Kings 8:41–43 that he quoted in his *Vorrede zu Menasse Menasse ben Israels Rettung der Juden,* although he discusses in both loci the very same point? And supposing that he held the same view as Homberg concerning the messianic age, why didn't he also quote the verses of Isaiah or Micah (Isaiah 2:1–4; Micah 4:1–5)? There was a good reason not to do this. In the very same year in which *Jerusalem* was published, Mendelssohn was engaged in a controversy with Johann David Michaelis, who opposed the initiative to grant Jews full civil rights, and in this controversy the messianic vision concerning Jerusalem was openly raised. Michaelis argued that the Jews expect their return to Palestine in accord with their understanding of the messianic vision of the prophets. Therefore, they consider their homelands only as a "temporary residence" and therefore lack the "patriotic love to the parental land" (*Liebe zum väterlichen Acker*) and therefore should not be granted full citizenship. Mendelssohn responded that human beings love the land in which they live well[11] and that the prophetic vision of return to Palestine refers to the messianic age; religious convictions that do not accord with civil life are reserved for the synagogue and prayer (not forsaken).[12]

The controversy is of interest here not only because it shows that the prophetic promise of a return to Zion is also alive in the discourse of non-Jews. It also shows why Mendelssohn could have been reluctant to openly voice the messianic vision associated with Jerusalem: Mendelssohn wished to procure civil rights for the Jews in Germany and had to counter the view that Jews are merely temporary residents in their fatherland; and this discriminatory view was justified with reference to the messianic vision—reason enough not to shout it from the rooftops![13]

However, there are numerous allusions to the messianic age even in *Jerusalem*. Consider first a remarkably clear allusion to an obscure referent. Mendelssohn maintains that religion may not be conceived as a contract between God and man. "God does not need our assistance. He desires no *service* from us." All this, says Mendelssohn, is plain to right reason. And yet men have acted in opposition to these self-evident principles: "Happy will they be if in the year 2240 they cease to act against them" (*Jerusalem*, 58–59). Why 2240? There can be no doubt that Mendelssohn planted here a riddle to raise the curiosity of the reader and signal that there is more in the text than meets the eye. The enigma posed by this remark is resolved when we calculate the Hebrew date for the year 2240. It coincides with the year 6000 of the Jewish chronology. According to a tradition recorded in the Babylonian Talmud (*Sanhedrin*, 97a–b; *Avodah Zarah*, 9a), this world is to exist 6,000 years. The year 2240 (6000) signifies therefore the end of the world. Mendelssohn "was justified in assuming that some Christian readers would understand the eschatological meaning of the date," writes A. Altmann (note on *Jerusalem*, 185). Altmann does not consider the possibility that *Jerusalem* also addressed the Jewish reader—although Mendelssohn's words to Sophie Becker clearly show he believed that Jews read his *Jerusalem*. Jewish or Gentile, Mendelssohn obviously sent the reader to consider what is beneath the surface, and this was eschatology. Moreover, as we shall see, some non-Jewish readers also understood the messianic message of the very title *Jerusalem*. But there are two other clear yet not elaborated references to the messianic vision associated with "Jerusalem."

In the second part of *Jerusalem* Mendelssohn argues that Judaism has no authoritative theology. Maimonides formulated thirteen principles of faith, and Albo differs, yet neither of them has been accused of heresy. "In this respect, we have not yet disregarded the important dictum of our sages: 'Although this one loosens and the other binds, both teach the words of the living God.'" Mendelssohn added a footnote and referred to "many a pedant" who quoted this saying to prove that the rabbis do not believe in the principle of contradiction. These "pedants" evidently believe that plurality of views is tantamount to a logical contradiction—a view that would incriminate religious pluralism: if one religion of revelation is true, the others must be false. This Mendelssohn does not accept. The "master's house" has more than a single door. However, here Mendelssohn uses the opportunity he gave himself to establish a connection between his religious pluralism and messianism. He answers the allegation that the rabbis are inconsistent thus: "I hope to live to see the day when all the peoples of the earth will admit this exception to the universal principle of contradiction: 'The fast of the fourth month, and the fast of the fifth, and the fast of the seventh, and the fast of the tenth, shall be to the house of Judah joy and gladness, and cheerful feasts; therefore love the truth and peace'" (*Jerusalem*, 101, quoting Zechariah 8:19).[14]

Why is the fact that days of mourning will turn into days of joy a contradiction? And why does Mendelssohn express the wish to witness this event? These four fast days (10th of Tevet, 17th of Tamuz, 9th of Av, 3rd of Tishrey (Fast of Gedaliah) commemorate the destruction of the first Temple and were renewed after the destruction of the second. Provided that the people "love truth and peace," so the verse is understood, God promises the rebuilding of the Temple and these fast days will turn into "cheerful feasts." Again, as when mentioning the year 2240, the messianic age has little to do with the issue discussed here by Mendelssohn.

It seems that Mendelssohn inserted without real need semicovert references to the messianic age. This surmise is corroborated by the fact that Mendelssohn also concludes the book with the fanfare "*Love truth! Love peace!*" taken from the same locus, Zechariah 8:19, referring to the messianic age. But in the very same locus not only the messianic age and the rebuilding of the Temple are promised, but also the vision of monotheistic pluralism is clearly expressed, and this vision may also explain why Mendelssohn addressed in his note the "peoples of the earth" and not "people," although he speaks of the ways people, not peoples, think:

> Thus saith the LORD of hosts; It shall yet come to pass, that there shall come people, and the inhabitants of many cities:
>
> And the inhabitants of one city shall go to another, saying, Let us go speedily to pray before the LORD, and to seek the LORD of hosts: I will go also.
>
> Yea, many people and strong nations shall come to seek the LORD of hosts in Jerusalem, and to pray before the LORD.
>
> Thus saith the LORD of hosts; In those days it shall come to pass, that ten men shall take hold out of all languages of the nations, even shall take hold of the skirt of him that is a Jew, saying, We will go with you: for we have heard that God is with you. (Zechariah 8:20–23)

It seems most improbable if not straightforwardly impossible that Mendelssohn inserted without intention the reference to the year 2240 and to the biblical loci with prophecies of the messianic age. It rather stands to reason that he alluded to the messianic age, when the Mosaic constitution and pluralistic monotheism will obtain in Jerusalem. This also sheds light on the continuity and change in his thought: Both in 1770 and in 1782–83 he seriously contemplated the question whether in the messianic time the plurality of religions will endure. What changed was the answer he gave to this question. In 1770 he envisaged the union of faith; in 1782–83 he endorsed religious pluralism. Is this also the reason why he titled the book *Jerusalem*?

The Title *Jerusalem*

Mendelssohn's book is titled *Jerusalem. Or on Religious Power and Judaism.* Why "Jerusalem"? The choice of title is not explained in the book or elsewhere in Mendelssohn's extant writings. Whatever may be suggested to explain the choice of this title will remain an assumption.[15] My own suggestion concentrates on Mendelssohn's usage of "Jerusalem" in various contexts, and the evidence adduced remains valid and relevant to the understanding of Mendelssohn's thought irrespective of whether it also explains the choice of the title *Jerusalem*. In my interpretation, "Jerusalem" stands for the messianic age in which no human rule exists but God alone directly reigns over all peoples united in monotheistic religious pluralism.

The writing of *Jerusalem* was prompted by the pamphlet *The Search for Light and Right* (1782) by August Friedrich Cranz. The pamphlet called on Mendelssohn to join Christianity, now that he had liberated himself from "coercion and burdensome ceremonies, and attaches true service of God neither to Jerusalem nor to Samaria."[16] The title *Jerusalem* can be understood as Mendelssohn's negative answer to this calling: The Jews will remain a distinct "nation" and stick to their particular creed and serve God in their particular way. Alexander Altmann suggested that this is the meaning of Mendelssohn's title.[17] This is certainly plausible. However, in Judaism and European culture in general, and also in Mendelssohn's writings in particular, the connotations of "Jerusalem" are much richer than merely a metaphor for Jewish ceremonial law. For this alone, the titles "Sinai" or "Moses" would have been better. After all, when Jerusalem became the capital of David's kingdom, the Mosaic constitution was no longer valid.

In the Jewish historical context, Jerusalem is both the site of the Temple and the capital of the kingdom of David and Solomon. In Jewish religious practice, "Jerusalem" or "Zion" is also a metaphor for the messianic age in which the Jews and all other peoples will pray to the same God in one temple. As we have seen, there are two versions of this vision: a unified monotheistic religion or a (monotheistic) plurality of religions. But there are also two versions of the restitution of the "Kingdom of God" that are rarely distinguished. In one of them God will directly reign in Jerusalem; in the other the "house of David," hence the Jewish Kingdom, will be restored. Mendelssohn's choices are significant. As we will see, he decidedly advocates the direct reign of God and considers a worldly kingdom in Jerusalem as idolatry. Mendelssohn refers to the prophets' vision of the messianic age, in which "the earth shall be full of the knowledge of the LORD, as the waters cover the sea" (Isaiah 11:9). The prophecy to which he refers here is presented in these well-known and moving images:

The word that Isaiah the son of Amoz saw concerning Judah and Jerusalem.

And it shall come to pass in the last days, that the mountain of the LORD's house shall be established in the top of the mountains, and shall be exalted above the hills; and all nations shall flow unto it.

And many people shall go and say, Come ye, and let us go up to the mountain of the LORD, to the house of the God of Jacob; and he will teach us of his ways, and we will walk in his paths: for out of Zion shall go forth the law, and the word of the LORD from Jerusalem.

And he shall judge among the nations, and shall rebuke many people: and they shall beat their swords into plowshares, and their spears into pruninghooks: nation shall not lift up sword against nation, neither shall they learn war any more. (Isaiah 2:1–4)

The "word of the LORD from Jerusalem" is opposed to the present state in which even the land of the house of Jacob "is full of idols; they worship the work of their own hands, that which their own fingers have made" (Isaiah 2:8) (And remember Mendelssohn's words that at present Judaism is full of "enthusiasm and superstition"). The vision hence presents the victory of Judaic monotheism over Jewish and Gentile idolatry.

More or less verbatim, Isaiah's prophecy quoted above is repeated in Micah 4:1–5—and this prophetic image of reinstalling of the "Kingdom of God" in Zion and Jerusalem is quoted in chapter 35 of Hobbes's *Leviathan,* a chapter to which Mendelssohn refers in his notes for *Jerusalem* (*JubA* 8, 97). The last verse, however, adds the new vision compared to Isaiah. The Gentiles retain their own religions, at least their external forms:

For all people will walk every one in the name of his god, and we will walk in the name of the LORD our God for ever and ever. (Micah 4:1–5)

In messianic Jerusalem it should hence be possible that all peoples hold fast to the same "law" and "word" as these go forth from Jerusalem and yet walk each in the "name of his god" as the Jewish people will "walk in the name of the LORD . . . for ever and ever." This, of course, coincides with Mendelssohn's vision of pluralistic monotheism.

Now, are there any indications that Mendelssohn mentions "Jerusalem" to refer to this messianic vision? Indeed, there are several such indications and even to a specific version of this messianic vision. I have shown above that in his interpretation of the "sublime prayer" of King Solomon at the consecration of the Temple in the preface to Menasseh ben Israel's *Vindicia Judaeorum*, Mendelssohn clearly endorsed religious pluralism, which he also advocated in *Jerusalem*. It is thus clear that he shares the vision in Micah 4:5.

One issue remains to be clarified. To what concrete vision of the "Kingdom of God" does Mendelssohn refer? In both Judaism and Christianity the messianic vision is often expressed by the metaphor of the descent of "heavenly Jerusalem" on Earth.[18] Turned towards Jerusalem, Jews pray several times daily for the rebuilding of the Temple and the return to Zion from exile. But in some contexts, the restoration of the kingdom of the house of David is foreseen; in others God himself is addressed as the sole king.[19] There can be little doubt what Mendelssohn prefers. As we have seen, Mendelssohn considers the anointing of King Saul as a rebellion against the kingdom of God driven by the same motives that produce idolatry, analogous to the sin of the golden calf! (See above, chap. 7, "The Idolatry of the Worldly Kingdom.") It stands to reason that his Jerusalem is the holy city of God rather than a capital of a worldly kingdom. But there is also direct evidence that Mendelssohn held this view.

Mendelssohn began his literary career with the translation of Judah Halevi's poem "Zion, won't you ask for your captives" (1755).[20] The translation is rather a free adaptation. Mendelssohn's significant changes to the original consistently stress that "Jerusalem" is not a worldly capital of a kingdom but God's dwelling place. One example will suffice. Halevi writes:

אַתְּ בֵּית מְלוּכָה וְאַתְּ כִּסֵּא אֲדֹנָי וְאֵיךְ
יָשְׁבוּ עֲבָדִים עֲלֵי כִסְאוֹת גְּבִירָיִךְ

Gabriel Levin translates thus:

You are the royal house, the Lord's throne,
though drudges sit on the thrones of your princes.[21]

Mendelssohn:

> Seliger Ort! der, irdischen Thronen zu heilig, Dem Throne der Herrlich-
> keit Gottes nur eingeweihet war. Ach jetzt haben verwegene Knechte
> dein Heiligthum entweihet.

> (Blessed Site! too holy for worldly thrones, it was consecrated to the
> throne of God's glory alone. But now insolent servants desecrated your
> sanctuary.)

Whereas Halevi speaks of Jerusalem both as an earthly royal palace
and the throne of God and laments how it came to pass that drudges sit
on the thrones of the princes of Jerusalem, Mendelssohn explicitly de-
clares Jerusalem to be "too holy for worldly thrones" and adds of his own
a line that transforms the national humiliation into a religious desecra-
tion. He repeats the same practice in many more loci of his translation.[22]

The same tendency shows in Mendelssohn's translation of the
Psalms. The translation appeared at the same time as his preface to
Menasseh Ben-Israel's *Vindicia Judaeorum* and can be seen as a "coun-
terpart" to it.[23] Consider first Mendelssohn's translation of the famous
verses of Psalm 137:4–5:

אֵיךְ--נָשִׁיר אֶת-שִׁיר-יְהֹוָה: עַל, אַדְמַת נֵכָר.

אִם-אֶשְׁכָּחֵךְ יְרוּשָׁלָ‍ִם-- תִּשְׁכַּח יְמִינִי.

King James:

> "How shall we sing the LORD's song in a strange land? If I forget thee,
> O Jerusalem, let my right hand forget her cunning."

Mendelssohn:

> "Können wir Gesang des Herrn singen auf entweihtem Erdreich?"
> (Luther: "in fremden Landen"; Philippson "auf fremder Erde.")[24]

Mendelssohn changes "foreign land" to "desecrated soil," exile into
idolatry, as he also changed in the previous verse the expression: "שובינו",

"they that carried us away captive," to "die uns ins Elend trieben," that is, "those who have driven us into misery." "Jerusalem" is turned here from a name of a town and a synecdoche for the lost kingdom and homeland into an antonym of idolatry. This usage accords with Mendelssohn's explanation quoted above that נכרי (foreigner, stranger) means idolater. "Jerusalem" is hence a metaphor for the friendly convention of all peoples and religions.[25] Note that his translation of Halevi's *Zion, Won't You Ask,* his quotation of 1 Kings 8:41–43, and his translation of the Psalms predate *The Search for Light and Right*!

We have seen that Mendelssohn consistently has "Jerusalem" stand for the direct kingdom of God as opposed to worldly kings. We have also seen that he has "Jerusalem" stand for pluralistic monotheism. And we also know that these two conceptions agree with Mendelssohn's own views. Whether he chose the title *Jerusalem* to allude to this messianic image must remain an open question, although the allusions to the year 2240 and his repeated reference to Zechariah 8:19 strongly suggest that this was the case. However, it should be clear that the messianic vision of *Jerusalem* at the end of days perfectly fits Mendelssohn's own views: the direct reign of God as in the time of the Mosaic constitution (for the Jews) and pluralistic monotheism for which he pleads at the end of *Jerusalem*.

Introduction

1. "Das wahre Judentum ist nirgend mehr, Schwärmerei und Aberglauben ist bei uns in der größten Abscheulichkeit. Wenn meine Nation nicht so dumm wäre, so würde sie mich wegen meines 'Jerusalems' steinigen, aber sie verstehen mich nicht." Mendelssohn in conversation with Sophie Becker. See Becker, *Briefe einer Kurländerin*, 172 ff.; New expanded edition: *Vor hundert Jahren*, 196 (November 27, 1785), 217–18, 225, 232–33. Partially quoted in Badt-Strauss, *Moses Mendelssohn. Zeugnisse, Briefe, Gespräche*, 148–50. Translation according to Altmann, *Moses Mendelssohn: A Biographical Study*, 722.

2. Santayana, "Reason in Religion," 180.

3. Cohen, *Religion der Vernunft*, 235.

4. This was formulated at the Second Council of Nicaea (787) and at the Council of Trent (1543). An extended and enlightening discussion (with rich documentation) can be found in *On Holy Images*, by St. John of Damascus (675–749).

5. Wolff, *Philosophia practica universalis*, vol. 2, § 441. Cf. Krochmalnik, "Das Zeremoniell als Zeichensprache," 257–58.

6. Moses de León, *Sefer ha-Rimmon*, quoted in Matt, "The Mystic and the Mizwot," 375. The article provides plenty of examples of blatant magical and theurgic and of course also anthropomorphic interpretations of the Mitsvot. See also Scholem, *Major Trends in Jewish Mysticism*, 397–98. The critic of the mystical view of the phylacteries supports Mendelssohn's view that philosophy develops in its methods rather than in its content.

7. Shakespeare, *Romeo and Juliet* II, 2, 1–2.

8. "Im Kult spricht und handelt der Mensch, aber auch Gott. Das kann nur geschehen, wenn göttliches und menschliches Handeln eine Gestalt bekommen, wenn es sichtbar, hörbar, tastbar wird. Und dies ist nur möglich mittels eines dritten, das von der Welt ist, aber im Kult geheiligt und aus der Welt genommen wird. Wir nennen dieses dritte: Symbol, nicht in dem abgeschwächten, modernen Sinn des Wortes, sondern in dem echten, antiken: im Symbol fallen zwei wirklichkeiten zusammen, begegnen Gott und Mensch

einander." Van der Leeuw, *Einführung in die Phänomenologie der Religion,* 189, cited in Hubbeling, "Der Symbolbegriff bei Gerardus van der der Leeuw," 29.

9. See van der Leeuw, *Religion in Essence and Manifestation,* 448.

Friedrich Theodor Vischer already defined the religious symbol as "mistaking the symbol for the thing" [signified] and maintained that it is essential to religion. Like van der Leeuw, he, too, adduces the Eucharist as the example of a religious symbol. See Vischer, "Das Symbol," 159.

Halbertal and Margalit, *Idolatry,* 40 (without reference to van der Leeuw), refer to icons only. "Not mere transparent signs, icons have independent power; they heal and perform miracles and therefore are addressed and worshiped. Their unique power is due not to the identity between God and the material makeup of the icon, but to the special relationship between the two. . . . The icon also shares some of the features of the thing it represents. . . . Thus there is a 'substitution' in idol worship of the symbol for the thing symbolized, in which some of the traits of the symbolized thing are transferred to the symbolizing thing."

The conceptions above share one deficit in my view. They identify the modes of representation with kinds of signs. However, most signs signify in more than one mode. Moreover, I will argue below that exactly this ambiguity is essential to religion and idolatry.

10. "Rambaman" is an acronym for "Rabbi Moshe ben Menachem," i.e., the son of Mendel, i.e., Mendels-Sohn. "Rambam" is an acronym for "Rabbi Moshe ben Maimon," i.e., the son of Maimon, i.e., Maimonides. Mendelssohn once rendered Maimonides' name "Maimonsohn."

11. In 1854 Hirsch published an attack on the term *"Ceremonialgesetze,"* which allegedly Mendelssohn coined for the religious law, and attacked Mendelssohn himself without naming him. The name of the person who coined the expression (i.e., Mendelssohn—or Spinoza?), says Hirsch, should flourish as long as there are Jews "who violate their most holy duties." This term "gnaws away the entire holiness of our religious law." The "natural consequence" of its usage is that one may abstain from observing it. See "Die jüdischen Ceremonialgesetze," 70, 72, 71. The essay was reprinted as the first issue of the series *Schriften des Vereins zur Erhaltung des überlieferten Judentums.*

In *Jeschurun* 2, no. 12 (September 1857): 615–30, the first essay in a long series of Hirsch's "Jewish Symbolism" appeared under the title "Grundlinien einer jüdischen Symbolik," which later appeared in English under the title, "Outlines of a Jewish Symbolism." In these Hirsch neither differentiates between symbolic and expressive actions or magic, nor between signs and symbols. His "Jewish Symbolism" is rather a collection of homilies.

By the way, the description "the person who coined the expression 'Ceremonialgesetz,'" fails to refer to Mendelssohn. Altmann suggested that Mendelssohn may have adopted the term from Spinoza (see his commentary to Mendelssohn, *Jerusalem*, 220–21), but in fact it was already used in 1423 by Simeon Duran in *Magen Avot*, II, chap. 4, 219; and Joseph Albo, *Sefer ha-Iikkarim*, III, chap. 25. See Cohen, *Religion der Vernunft*, 415. John Spencer uses it in the title of his important book *De Legibus Hebraeorum Ritualibus*, the 1732 edition of which was in Mendelssohn's possession! See *Verzeichnis der auserlesenen Büchersammlung des seeligen Herrn Moses Mendelssohn, Berlin*, 4, no. 58. See too the remark made by Christoph Starke, a learned and widely read exegete, in his commentary on Exodus 32: "Das Sittengesetz hat Gott selbst mit lauter Stimme ausgesprochen, das Ceremenialgesetz und die Risse und Zeichnungen der Stiftshütte durch die Engel dem Mosi gegeben." Starke, *Synopsis bibliothecae exegeticae in Vetus Testamentum*, vol. 1, 1209.

12. "Wenn man Mendelssohn in seiner theoretischen Schwäche begreifen will, muß man ihn in seiner geschichtlichen Kraft zu verstehen suchen. Ihm kam es in erster Linie nicht auf die Philosophie der Religion, noch selbst auf die des Judentums an, sondern er wollte eine Vereinbarung herbeiführen zwischen dem Judentum in seinem Fortbestande und der modernen Kultur." Hermann Cohen, *Deutschtum und Judentum*, 24. Reprinted in *Jüdische Schriften*, vol. 2, 259–60.

Cohen criticizes Mendelssohn's alleged constriction of Judaism to the ceremonial law (without religious content) (*Religion der Vernunft*, 415 f.). This interpretation is clearly influenced by Kant. In fact, Cohen's own view of the law perfectly agrees with Mendelssohn's view (see *Religion der Vernunft*, 427). The basic difference between their views consists in the theoretical foundation. Mendelssohn concentrates on the notion of symbol, whereas Cohen has no definite view of semiotics and reaches some of Mendelssohn's conclusions only after various meanders (see *Religion der Vernunft*, 430; and see "symbol" in the index).

A laudable exception from this series of critics is Abraham Wolf (1876–1948). In his *A History of Science, Technology, and Philosophy in the Eighteenth Century*, 778–81, Wolf gives an unusually favorable exposition of Mendelsson's philosophy. It is little known that prior to his eminent career as a historian and philosopher of science, Wolf served as rabbi of a Jewish congregation in Manchester and was a partisan of Jewish reform. See on him, Haberman, "Abraham Wolf: A Forgotten Jewish Reform Thinker," 267–304; on Wolf's view of Mendelssohn, see 275–76.

13. Chatam Sofer coined the rhymed saying, "Don't reach for Mendelssohn's books, and then you will not stumble in all eternity!" [ר׳] ד״רמי ובספרי"]
[.עד לעולמי ימעד לא רגליכם אז יד תשלחו אל [דסאו משה]

See Solomon Sofer, *Chut ha-Meshulash* (Hebr.), 52b.

14. Guttmann, *Die Philosophie des Judentums*, 315.

15. Ibid., 313–17.

16. Altmann, *Moses Mendelssohn: A Biographical Study,* 518. Similarly Fox, "Law and Ethics in Modern Jewish Philosophy: The Case of Moses Mendelssohn,"1–13.

Allan Arkush adopted Altmann's judgment and suspected also Mendelssohn's personal integrity: "One is consequently forced to conclude that the apologetical arguments with which he defended Judaism were intended not so much to establish a solid rational foundation for his religion as to give the appearance of doing so." Arkush, *Moses Mendelssohn and the Enlightenment,* 230.

17. In a later essay titled "Mendelssohn's Concept of Judaism Reexamined," 245, and in a comment to his edition of Mendelssohn's *Jerusalem,* 223, Altmann noted that Mendelssohn did not invent this theory but took it over from Warburton (and Tindal). However, he did not attempt to understand its rationale.

Arnold Eisen follows Altmann in his judgment on Mendelssohn's semiotics. See his "Divine Legislation as 'Ceremonial Script,'" 239–67. He finds the discussion of hieroglyphics "painfully weak." He also finds that it is beside the point: "Canaan, Greece, and Rome—the idolatrous cultures of most concern to Jewish tradition—all had alphabets" and not hieroglyphics (255). Arkush follows and finds the theory "purely conjectural" (Arkush, *Moses Mendelssohn and the Enlightenment,* 211). Lawrence Kaplan ("Maimonides and Mendelssohn on the Origins of Idolatry, the Election of Israel, and the Oral Law,"423–45), speaks of the "evident weaknesses of Mendelssohn's theory" (425) and finds Altmann's point "well taken." He explains the "weaknesses in Mendelssohn's thesis" as resulting from the "disparity between limited means and grandiose ends" (440–41), since Mendelssohn also undertook to explain by the same theory the superiority of the oral law. Robert Erlewine follows Arnold Eisen and Alexander Altmann and finds Mendelssohn's account of idolatry "frustratingly arbitrary and problematic," of "dubious philosophical status," and the "site of his greatest weakness." Erlewine, *Monotheism and Tolerance,* 54; see also 65, and 198–99 n. 97. None of these scholars consulted either Warburton's or Mendelssohn's commentary on the Pentateuch, and none of them paid attention to Mendelssohn's semiotics.

Neglecting the *Bi'ur* proves here especially detrimental to the understanding of Mendelssohn. On abstracting from Mendelssohn's Hebrew writings, see Sorkin, "The Mendelssohn Myth and Its Method," 7–28. As Sorkin remarks, even Altmann hardly considered the *Bi'ur* (20).

There are notable exceptions to this disregard for Mendelssohn's semiotics. See Krochmalnik, "Das Zeremoniell als Zeichensprache," 238–85; Hilfrich,

'Lebendige Schrift'; Batnitzky, *Idolatry and Representation*, 32–40; and Fenves, *Arresting Language: From Leibniz to Benjamin*, 80–97. Bruce Rosenstock's *Philosophy and the Jewish Question: Mendelssohn, Rosenzweig, and Beyond* appeared after the completion of my manuscript. Krochmalnik's helpful and learned discussion of Enlightenment semiotic theories of ceremonies are consulted below. Hilfrich's intellectual orientation is very different from mine, and our interpretations do not at all overlap; to a lesser extent this is also true of Rosenstock. The purpose of Batnitzky's discussion is to give some background to her discussion of Rosenzweig and is, naturally, brief and general. It is nevertheless precise and sympathetic. Goetschel's "Langage et écriture dans la Jérusalem de Moise Mendelssohn," 491–500, is the text of a brief oral presentation on Mendelssohn's views on the Jewish law as a "lebendige Schrift." None of these works considers the *Bi'ur* or the translation of the Torah; Mendelssohn's general philosophy is hardly considered in most of them.

Chapter 1. Mendelssohn: Common Sense,
Rational Metaphysics, and Skepticism

1. *Abhandlung über die Evidenz in metaphysischen Wissenschaften, JubA* 2, 267–330; Dahlstrom, 251–306.

2. Note, however, that Julius Guttmann repeatedly addresses Mendelssohn's trust in sound reason and does not at all mention Wolffian metaphysics.

The best discussion of common sense and metaphysics is in Leo Strauss's introduction to the *Morgenstunden* in *JubA* 3.2, lxvii–lxix. However, Strauss pays no attention to language.

Wolfgang Vogt, *Moses Mendelssohns Beschreibung der wirklichkeit menschlichen Erkennnens,* suggests that Mendelssohn was "eclectic," that is, that Mendelssohn considers metaphysical propositions irrespective of their origin and admits them only if they stand the test of common sense.

3. See, for example, Arkush's *Moses Mendelssohn and the Enlightenment,* in which the assertion that Mendelssohn was a disciple of the Leibniz-Wolff school is already made in the first paragraph of the introduction and the first chapter is titled "The Leibniz-Wolffian Background." Arkush raises the question how this tallies with Mendessohn's commonsense philosophy but does not resolve it; see xiii, 70, 75–79. For a useful survey of the discussion in Mendelssohn's age and in subsequent scholarship, see 79–97. David Sorkin, on the other hand, does not analyze Mendelssohn's philosophy but follows the received view—however, with certain unelaborated reservations concerning

the relation of speculation and practice, theoretical reason and common sense. See Sorkin, "The Mendelssohn Myth and Its Method," 6–14.

4. See Beck, *Early German Philosophy. Kant and His Predecessors*, 335. This is also Altmann's view. See his introduction to *JubA* 3.2, lxiv–lxxi: "Mendelssohn hat also im Laufe seines Lebens der Kritik an der Zulänglichkeit der demonstrativen Philosophie immer mehr nachgegeben" (lxvii).

Ernst Cassirer believes that Mendelssohn followed other philosophers, and attributes Locke's *Essay on Human Understanding* and English empiricism in general an influence on Mendelssohn's psychology and aesthetics, whereas in logic and methodology he follows Christian Wolff. My discussion in the following shows that this is not the case. See "Die Philosophie Moses Mendelssohns," 40–41. Furthermore, Cassirer reduces the role of common sense in Mendelssohn to facilitate the distribution of metaphysical truths (51).

5. "An affirmation is true if its predicate is in its subject; thus, in every true affirmative proposition, necessary or contingent, universal or singular, the concept of the predicate is somehow contained in the concept of the subject, in such a way that anyone who understood the two concepts as God understands them would *eo ipso* perceive that the predicate is in the subject" (Leibniz, *Opuscules et fragments inédits*, 16–17). I quote the translation of Benson Mates, *The Philosophy of Leibniz: Metaphysics and Language*, 84. This locus was unknown in Mendelssohn's time, but there are many equivalent loci in Leibniz's published writings.

6. The qualification, "explained either absolutely or under certain assumed conditions," should account for contingent propositions and need not be discussed here.

7. The thesis that the same faculty is active in both forms of knowledge is not specific to Mendelssohn. See, e.g., Tetens, "Kein Seelenvermögen wirket in den höhern Wissenschaften mehr, als in den niedern. Nur wirken sie in verschiedenen Graden!" (*Philosophische Versuche über die menschliche Natur und ihre Entwicklung*, Achter Versuch, 575).

8. Descartes, *Discours de la Méthode*, VI, 1–2.

9. See also Mendelssohn's letter to Raphael Levi, in which he insists that his popular arguments in the *Phaedon* can be translated from the language of common sense to that of rigorous metaphysics. Quoted by Altmann, *Moses Mendelssohn: A Biographical Study*, 162–63. Altmann's discussion of this essay by Mendelssohn in his *Moses Mendelssohns Frühschriften zur Metaphysik* is of little help concerning metaphysics and common sense. Julius Guttmann maintains that "plain common sense is a source of religious, not scientific, knowledge." See "Mendelssohn's *Jerusalem* and Spinoza's *Theologico-Political*

Treatise," 369. The references Guttmann names do not support this claim, and I believe that the evidence to the contrary adduced above and in the following is overwhelming. Michah Gottlieb, in "Mendelssohn's Metaphysical Defense of Religious Pluralism," 205–25, stresses more than all previous commentators the importance of common sense in Mendelssohn and its role in the argument for religious tolerance. Gottlieb sees that this claim raises the question how common sense relates to metaphysics but leaves the discussion of this "complex issue" to another opportunity (212).

10. Mathematics is a special case in this respect since the distinction between mathematics and meta-mathematics is blurred and changing in time.

11. *Morgenstunden, JubA* 3.2, 50.

12. With mathematical propositions (not axioms or postulates), knowing the fact includes a standard proof on the basis of accepted presuppositions (definitions, axioms, postulates) and with the help of an appropriate symbolism (on this more in the next section). The philosophical business here is the justification of these fundamentals.

13. A famous similar case in the twentieth century sheds light on the difference between mathematics and its foundation. In July 1943, more than forty years after the event, Bertrand Russell recalled that in June 1901 [in fact: June 1902—G.F.], he had discovered the famous paradox in Frege's *Grundgesetze der Arithmetik*. "I wrote to Frege, who replied with the utmost gravity that "die Arithmetik ist ins Schwanken geraten" (Russell, "My Mental Development," 13). Again more than twenty years later, in 1966, Russell returned to this letter of Frege in a letter to Quine. "You say that Frege is said to have commented 'Arithmetic totters.' In fact, in a letter to me he says 'Die Arithmetik ist ins Schwanken geraten.' The comment of Frege is, therefore, quite authentic" (Quine, "Logical Correspondence with Russell," 230).

Russell's memory failed twice. What Frege really wrote was: "Ihre Entdeckung des Widerspruchs hat mich auf's Höchste überrascht und, fast möchte ich sagen, bestürzt, weil dadurch der Grund, auf dem ich die Arithmetik . . . aufzubauen dachte, ins Wanken gerät" (Frege, *Wissenschaftlicher Briefwechsel*, 213). There is all the difference in the world between saying that arithmetic totters or that the (philosophical) foundations totter, which Frege conceived for arithmetic that already existed independently from his philosophical efforts.

14. See on this my discussion in *Definition and Construction: Salomon Maimon's Philosophy of Geometry.*

15. *An die Freunde Lessings, JubA* 3.2, 197; 198. Mendelssohn quotes Psalms 94:9–11 as another natural conclusion: "He that planted the ear, shall

he not hear? he that formed the eye, shall he not see? he that teacheth man knowledge, shall not he know?" In verse 11 Mendelssohn omits the words, "He that chastiseth the heathen, shall not he correct?" This translation differs from Mendelssohn's published translation of the Psalms.

Mendelssohn's words on the the role of philosophy have a Wittgensteinian ring. In a book that appeared after the completion of my manuscript, Bruce Rosenstock (*Philosophy and the Jewish Question: Mendelssohn, Rosenzweig, and Beyond*) argues that the positions of these philosophers are very similar. I rather fear that the apparent similarities cover decisive differences. Thus Rosenstock argues that Wittgenstein appeals to ordinary language "to provide an exit from skeptical doubt and the metaphysical errors it engenders" and credits Mendelssohn for inaugurating this position: "I read Mendelssohn as one of the inaugural voices in this philosophical recuperation of ordinary language, tied closely to what he calls "common sense," against the threat of skepticism" (30). However, as we will see, to Mendelssohn it is, on the contrary, the threat of skepticism that is the raison d'etre of metaphysics!

16. The end of *Abhandlung über die Evidenz, JubA* 2, 267–330, is missing from Dahlstrom's English translation.

The opposed characterizations of "raw" and "vigorous" on the one hand, "refined" and "weak" on the other, correspond to the opposition between the young, coarse native of moderate intelligence and a gaunt woman of "enthusiastic physiognomy" in Mendelssohn's allegory quoted below.

17. See also *An die Freunde Lesssings, JubA* 3.2, 198–99. Mendelssohn makes exactly the same distinction in his *Phaedon*. There, Mendelssohn's Simmias, the first contester of the doctrine of immortality, says, "If I raise doubts against the immortality of the soul, this is not against the truth of this divine doctrine, but against its provability by reason, or rather against the way, which you, oh Socrates, have chosen to convince us by reason" (*JubA* 3.1, 79). The proof is, here too, necessary to refute recent sophism, not per se (*JubA* 3.1, 149). See also the introduction by Leo Strauss, *JubA* 3.1., xviii, xxiv–xxv.

18. See his letters to Raphael Levi (end of 1767), to von Platen (April 7, 1769), and to Herder (May 2, 1769); *JubA* 3.1, xxv.

19. In this Mendelssohn differs from, for example, Tetens's view. In cases of conflict, says Tetens, "We must investigate both the judgments of common sense and those of reason. On principle, none of them is more or less suspicious." See Tetens, *Philosophische Versuche über die menschliche Natur und ihre Entwicklung*, Achter Versuch, IV, 573.

20. "So bald sie sich entzweyen: so suche ich mich zu orientieren, und sie beide, wo möglich, auf den Punkt zurückzuführen, von welchem wir ausge-

gangen sind. Da Aberglaube, Pfaffenlist, Geist des Widerspruchs und So-
phisterey uns durch so vielerley Spitzfindigkeiten und Zauberkünste den Ge-
sichtskreis verdreht, und den gesunden Menschenverstand in Verwirrung
gebracht haben; so müssen wir freilich wieder Kunstmittel anwenden, ihm zu
Hülfe zu kommen" (*JubA* 3.2, 82, 198).

Isaac (Itzig) Euchel testifies to Mendelssohn's attitudes toward metaphysics
and common sense in his biography of Mendelssohn, *A History of our Teacher
and Sage, Moses b. Menachem* (Hebr.), 115:

"שכלו היה צרוף מאד לרדת אל מעמקי החקירה בכל דבר נשגב, ואהב מאד את החריפות
בעניני המדע, אבל יותר ממנה אהב את הסברא הישרה . . . וכה אמר לפעמים אל רעיו: הזהרו
מאד במשפטי השכל הפשוט, כי הוא שופט צדק אשר לא ישא פנים ולא יקח שוחד, הוא
ירחיק שקר מגבולו, אף אם תעותהו ותתהכשהו [ותכחשהו!] בכל הלמודיות והמושכליות
שבעולם, סופך לתת דין וחשבון לפני כס משפטו."

21. *Die Bildsäule* (1784), *JubA* 6.1, 79–87. See Altmann, *Moses Mendelssohn: A Biographical Study,* 660. The friends of common sense named there are
James Beattie and Thomas Reid. In 1770 Mendelssohn asked Nicolai to obtain
for him Reid's *An Inquiry into the Human Mind on the Principles of Common
Sense* (1764). See Altmann, *Moses Mendelssohn: A Biographical Study,* 285. Mendelssohn also recommended the study of Reid in his *Anweisung zur spekul. Philosophie, für einen jungen Menschen von 15–20 Jahren, JubA* 3.1, 305.

22. The latter misunderstanding originated in a polemical rhetorical
move of Jacobi in his controversy with Mendelssohnn and was adopted by a
contemporary critic of Mendelssohn, Thomas Wizenmann. Jacobi answered
Mendelssohn's contention that Judaism knows no obligation to believe in particular eternal truths (in this significantly different from Christianity) with the
following ambiguous usage of "belief" (*Glauben*), in which "belief that," "belief
in," and "faith" are hopelessly confused: "We all are born into belief (*Glauben*)
and must stay in belief (*Glauben*), as we are all born into society." "It is through
belief (*Glauben*) that we know that we have a body and that besides us, there are
also other bodies and other thinking beings. A true, wonderful revelation!"
"Thus we have a revelation of nature that not only ordains, but forces each and
every man to believe (*zu glauben*), and by this belief (*Glauben*) to accept eternal
truth." See Jacobi, *Über die Lehre des Spinoza* (1786), quoted in Scholz, *Die
Hauptschriften zum Pantheismusstreit,* 168–69. In the second edition (1789) Jacobi quoted in a footnote to this locus pages 173–77 of Wizenmann's book
(1786)! On the basis of this argument, Jacobi formulated as one of his "principles" (*Lehrsätze*) the following: "The element of all human knowledge and
activity is belief" ("Das Element aller menschlichen Erkenntnis und Wirksam-
keit ist Glaube") (180). In the first edition of his book he quoted here Lavater on

"Intuitionssinn," "dies Etwas" or "Wahrheitssinn," which is the "Element und Prinzipium des Glaubens." Since the demonstrations of reason lead to fatalism, Jacobi commends a *salto mortale* to faith. (See Scholz, *Die Hauptschriften zum Pantheismusstreit*, 81, 91, for Jacobi; and 114 for Mendelssohn's answer.)

Wizenmann adopted Jacobi's argument: "In spite of the terminological difference between faith and the utterances of a sound understanding, Jacobi and Mendelssohn were in perfect agreement that conviction of the fundamental truths of religion is possible and real even without demonstration and without what one usually and more properly calls grounds of reason (*Vernunftgründe*)." See Wizenmann, *Die Resultate der Jacobischer und Mendelssohnischer Philosophie*, 47. Quoted from Arkush, *Moses Mendelssohn and the Enlightenment*, 83; translation altered. Arkush translated *Vernunftgründe* with "rational grounds"—but common sense is by all means "rational," although it is different from systematic philosophical "reason." I believe that Arkush adopted Wizenmann's (mis)understanding of Mendelssohn's "common sense" and therefore also, although with some reservations, most of Wizenmann's critique and suspicions (See Arkush, *Moses Mendelssohn and the Enlightenment*, 91–93). For a more balanced view, see Beiser, *The Fate of Reason*, 109–13. However, Beiser, too, shares the common misunderstanding of common sense.

Kant had better insight, I believe. He correctly criticized Wizenmann and maintained that "daß es in der That bloß die Vernunft, nicht ein vorgeblicher geheimer keine überschwengliche Anschauung unter dem Namen des Glaubens, worauf Tradition oder Offenbarung ohne Einstimmung der Vernunft werden kann, sondern, wie Mendelssohn standhaft und mit gerechtem Eifer behauptete, bloß die eigentliche reine Menschenvernunft sei, wodurch er es nöthig fand und anpries, sich zu orientiren; obzwar freilich hiebei der hohe Anspruch des speculativen Vermögens derselben, vornehmlich ihr allein gebietendes Ansehen (durch Demonstration) wegfallen und ihr, so fern sie speculativ ist, nichts weiter als das Geschäft der Reinigung des gemeinen Vernunftbegriffs von Widersprüchen und die Vertheidigung gegen ihre eigenen sophistischen Angriffe auf die Maximen einer gesunden Vernunft übrig gelassen werden muß" (Kant, *Was heißt: Sich im Denken orientiren?* [1784], *AA* 8, 134). See the entire text (131–48), as well as *Einige Bemerkungen zu Ludwig Heinrich Jakob's Prüfung der Mendelssohn'schen Morgenstunden* (*AA* 8, 149–56). See also Kant's enlightening discussion of common sense in his *Kritik der Urteilskraft,* §40; *AA* 5, 293–96; Guyer and Matthews, 173–76.

23. The legend told by the "oriental sages" is found in the Babylonian Talmud, *Nidah,* 30b.

Julius Guttmann suggested that Mendelssohn "asserted, with Enlighten-ment-nourished pride" that "especially the philosophy of his age has risen far above the level attained by the Greeks" ("Mendelssohn's *Jerusalem* and Spi-noza's *Theologico-Political Treatise*," 369–70). The sole reference is the intro-duction to the essay on evidence and does not necessarily contradict what was said above. Guttmann does not differentiate progress in the sense of enlarging the body of knowledge and progress in the refinement of arguments. In the introduction, Mendelssohn says that the sciences extended their body of knowl-edge (*JubA* 2, 270), but he does not say so of philosophy. However, the argu-ments of Descartes and Leibniz are superior to those of Aristotle.

24. "Truth is very often in conflict with bon-sens; and in this case it can be reached only by reason; e.g. the shape of the globe, its motion, the distance of the fix stars, the infinite divisibility of matter" (Mendelssohn, *Verwandtschaft des Schönen und Guten, JubA,* 2, 185).

25. See Mendelssohn's review of J. H. Lambert's *Neues Organon* (1764), in *Allgemeine deutsche Bibliothek* 3, no. 1 (1766): 1–23; and his review of the second volume, 4, no. 2 (1767): 1–30 (quote on p. 3).

Compare this with Heinrich Hertz's famous introduction to his *Mechanik* (1894): "We form for ourselves internal images (*innere Scheinbilder*) or symbols of external objects; and the form which we give them is such that the neces-sary consequences of the images in thought are always the images of the nec-essary consequents in nature of the things pictured" (Hertz, *The Principles of Mechanics Presented in a New Form,* 1).

26. See, e.g., Leibniz, *GP* 6, 423; *GP* 7, 204–7. Mendelssohn showed in-terest in and admiration for Lambert's and Plouquet's attempts to construct symbolic logical notations. See Altmann, *Moses Mendelssohn: A Biographical Study,* 121.

27. Immanuel Kant, "Some Remarks on Ludwig Heinrich Jakob's Ex-amination of Mendelssohn's *Morgenstunden* (1786)," 180–81 (*AA* 8, 152).

28. The difference between the Spinozist and the Wolffian version—in Wolff's and Mendelssohn's view—is that *Spinoza* understands the *summa re-alitatis* in extensive terms, whereas Wolff and Mendelssohn do so in intensive terms. On the latter view, Kant's concept of the (intensive) magnitude of reality can then be identified with his category of "reality," comprising "reality," "ne-gation," and "limitation," which also corresponds to the degree of reality expe-rienced in sensation.

Paul Franks suggested that Kant changed the views he held in the first edi-tion of the *Critique of Pure Reason* and moved towards a "monistic" position. See Franks, *All or Nothing,* 64–79. Anneliese Maier, *Kants Qualitätskategorien,* interpreted Kant's category of "reality" as indebted to the conception of "summa realitatis." For Christian Wolff's criticism of Spinoza, see his *Theologia naturalis*, §§ 671–716; for his criticism of Spinoza's notion of infinity in particular, see § 706. Mendelssohn adopts Wolff's position. See *Morgenstunden, JubA* 3.2, 110–11; and Jacobi, *Über die Lehre des Spinoza*, 116–19. On both interpretations, Mendelssohn is the "critical" philosopher who limits metaphysics to an immediate inference from experience whereas Kant is the true metaphysician. It seems to me that Kant's evaluation of Mendelssohn's position is correct.

29. It seems that Kant was not consistent in his views on the role common sense can fulfill. In the *Prolegomena* he maintains that common sense cannot guide the speculative use of reason (*AA* 4, 259), whereas in his lectures on logic, he appreciates its role as a "Probirstein" to discover the mistakes of the artificial use of reason—exactly as Mendelssohn did (*AA* 9, 57).

30. See Hume, *Enquiry Concerning Human Understanding*, VII, 1, § 48, 60:

> The great advantage of the mathematical sciences above the moral consists in this, that the ideas of the former, being sensible, are always clear and determinate, the smallest distinction between them is immediately perceptible, and the same terms are still expressive of the same ideas, without ambiguity or variation. An oval is never mistaken for a circle, nor an hyperbola for an ellipsis. The isosceles and scalenum are distinguished by boundaries more exact than vice and virtue, right and wrong. If any term be defined in geometry, the mind readily, of itself, substitutes, on all occasions, the definition for the term defined: Or even when no definition is employed, the object itself may be presented to the senses, and by that means be steadily and clearly apprehended. But the finer sentiments of the mind, the operations of the understanding, the various agitations of the passions, though really in themselves distinct, easily escape us, when surveyed by reflection; nor is it in our power to recall the original object, as often as we have occasion to contemplate it. Ambiguity, by this means, is gradually introduced into our reasonings: Similar objects are readily taken to be the same: And the conclusion becomes at last very wide of the premises.

The insecurity concerning thoughts and beliefs of others is also one of Mendelssohn's reasons for pluralism. See on this, Witte, "Jüdische Aufklärung. Zu Moses Mendelssohns Schrift Jerusalem oder über religiöse Macht und Judentum," 415–28; and Azuelos, "Le judaïsme en question à l'époque des Lumières: Christian Konrad Wilhelm von Dohm (1751–1820), Moses Mendelssohn (1729–1786), Wilhelm von Humboldt (1767–1835)," 19.

31. As is well known, Maimonides dedicated the first part of *The Guide of the Perplexed* to a critique of the anthropomorphic idea of God due to the literal understanding of biblical expressions.

32. "Überhaupt is die Sprache eines Volks die beste Anzeige seiner Bidlung, der Kultur sowohl als der Aufklärung, der Ausdehnung sowohl als der Stärke nach" (Mendelssonn, *Über die Frage: Was heißt aufklären?*, JubA 6.1, 116; Schmidt, 54).

33. For some references to other philosophers, see Altmann, *Moses Mendelssohn: A Biographical Study*, 677, 688, and 866 n. 20. See also the discussion of the topos "*l'abus des mots*," in Rosenfeld, *A Revolution in Language*, 14–27.

34. Condillac, *Essai sur l'origine des connaissances*, 91–92; Aarsleff, 171–72.

Mendelssohn "used commonly to close a discussion with the words 'We must hold fast, not to words, but to the things [they signify]'" (Maimon, *Lebensgeschichte*, GW 1, 478; Murray, 225).

In his *Lebensgeschichte*, Maimon calls Mendelssohn twice a "philosophischer Heuchler," a philosophic hypocrite. See on this my "Radikale und Kompromißler in der Philosophie—Salomon Maimon über Mendelssohn, den 'philosophischen Heuchler,'" 369–85.

35. "Language is the element in which our abstract concepts live and thrive. . . . [Y]ou cannot forsake it without running the danger of surrendering the spirit (*Geist*) as well" (*Morgenstunden*, JubA 3.1, 61).

36. These words were directly criticized by Kant: "Ich bin hingegen einer ganz entgegengesetzen Meinung und behaupte, daß in Dingen, worüber man, in der Philosophie, eine geraume Zeit hindurch gestritten hat, eine Wortstreitigkeit zum Grunde gelegen habe, sondern immer wahrhafte Streitigkeit über Sachen. Denn obgleich in jeder einige Worte in mehrerer und verschiedener Bedeutung gebraucht werden so kann es doch gar nicht lange währen, bis die, so sich im desselben Anfangs veruneinigt haben, den Mißverstand bemerken und an deren Statt anderer bedienen: daß es also am Ende eben so wenig wahre Homonyma als Synonyma giebt" (Kant, *Einige Bemerkungen zu Ludwig Heinrich Jakob's Prüfung der Mendelssohn'schen Morgenstunden*, AA 8, 152). Of course, Kant was notoriously not interested in philosophical problems of language.

37. *Morgenstunden*, JubA 3.2, 124. Translation adapted from Vallée, ed., *The Spinoza Conversations between Lessing and Jacobi*, 65.

38. More on the danger of idolatry involved in an unclear distinction between the properties of the sign and the signified below in the discussion of the sin of the golden calf.

39. In his famous critique of Heidegger, Rudolf Carnap observes that "pseudo-concepts," "the meaningless words of metaphysics usually owe their

origin to the fact that a meaningful word is deprived of its meaning through its metaphorical use in metaphysics." See Carnap, "The Elimination of Metaphysics through Logical Analysis of Language" (1932), 62, 71.

40. Ralph Cudworth, *True Intellectual System of the World* (1678), 113, characterizes hieroglyphics as "[f]igures not answering to sounds or words, but immediately representing the Objects and Conceptions of the Mind." Quoted from Assmann, *Moses the Egyptian*, 84. Mendelssohn owned Cudworth's book in the Latin translation. See *Verzeichnis der auserlesenen Büchersammlung des seeligen Herrn Moses Mendelssohn*, 4, nos. 67–68.

41. See Quine, *Word and Object*.

42. This metaphor can also be taken seriously. See below the discussion of the "language of action." Ernst Cassirer maintained that "the relation of body and soul (Leib und Seele) represents the prototype and model for a purely symbolic relation which cannot be converted into a relation between things or into a causal relation." *The Philosophy of Symbolic Forms*, vol. 3, 100. See on this, Krois, "Cassirer's 'Prototype and Model' of Symbolism," 531–47.

43. והקשר הזה שבין הרוחני והגשמי הוא ענין נפלא עד מאוד שעליו אנו מברכים בכל
יום ומפליא לעשות כמ״ש הרמ״א בא״ח ס״ו ע״ש [כמו שכתב ר' משה איסרליש באורח חיים,
סימן ו', עיין שם.]

44. "Blessed are You, the Lord, our God, King of the universe, Who formed man with wisdom and created within him many openings and many hollows (cavities). It is obvious and known before Your Throne of Glory that if but one of them were to be ruptured or if one of them were to be blocked it would be impossible to survive and to stand before You (even for a short period of time). Blessed are You, God, Who heals all flesh and acts wondrously."

45. ועוד יש לפרש: ש״מפליא לעשות״ במה ששומר רוח האדם בקרבו, וקושר דבר
רוחני בדבר גשמי. והכל הוא על ידי שהוא ״רופא כל בשר״, כי אז האדם בקו הבריאות
.ונשמתו משתמרת בקרבו

46. Maimon, too, uses "wind" and "mind" (*Geist*) as an example of a term for a sensual object to name an abstract concept (*GW* 3, 10). It is clear that he thinks of the Hebrew רוח. See also Spinoza, *Tractatus Theologico-Politicus*, 24–27.

47. Mendelssohn to Abbt, July 12, 1764, quoted from Altmann, *Moses Mendelssohn: A Biographical Study*, 121.

No doubt, however, that Maimonides' discussion of anthropomorphism resulting from metaphors when speaking of God was an excellent preparation for Mendelssohn's understanding of metaphors in the context of the philosophy of the Enlightenment. Note, however, that speaking of an "influence" would here be even more vacuous than usual: Mendelssohn believed that we can ascribe to God as attributes our powers of the intellect that we know by introspection, of course: with infinite degree (*Abhandlung über die Evidenz, JubA* 2, 310–11; Dahlstrom, 291).

Wolff, too, contributed importantly to a theory of scientific language and also discussed metaphors. See Ricken, "Zum Thema Christian Wolff und die Wissenschaftssprache der deutschen Aufklärung," 41–90.

48. "Diese Gesinnnungen habe ich seit vielen Jahren angenommen, und daher zwischen Dogmatiker und Skeptiker eine Art von Mittel zu halten gesucht. Dogmatisch, in dem strengsten Verstande, in Absicht auf mich, habe ich, was die wichtigsten Punkte der Religion und Sittenlehre betrifft, meine Partey genommen, und stehe unverrükt auf der Seite, wo ich die meiste wahrheit zu finden glaube; aber eben so skeptisch, wenn ich meinen Nächsten richten soll. Ich räume einem jeden das Recht ein, das ich mir anmaße, und setze das größte Mistrauen in meine Kräfte, irgend jemanden, der auch Partey genommen hat, von meiner Meinung überführen zu können. Es kann mir also nicht anders, als sehr angenehm seyn, daß Hr. L.[avater] zufrieden ist, den öffentlichen Briefwechsel hiermit zu beschliessen" (Mendelssohn's *Nacherinnerung, JubA* 7, 47).

49. Translation of the first sentence changed.

50. Arkush airs similar suspicions. He suggestively asked whether the reason for Mendelssohn's position is not "because he would greatly have preferred not to have had to discuss such matters in public?" (*Moses Mendelssohn and the Enlightenment,* 258).

51. *Phaedon, JubA* 3.1, 88.

52. Lessing, *Nathan the Wise,* third act, seventh entry.

53. Similarly, in his controversy with Emden about the afterlife of non-Jews, Mendelssohn's first argument (!) against the opposite view is that the consequence is morally unacceptable to him! See his letter to Jacob Emden of October 26, 1773, *JubA* 16, 178; see the discussion in chapter 5 under "Gentile Idolatry, Jewish Idolatry."

Ernst Cassirer distinguishes (and separates) "theoretical justification" (*Begründung*) and "standing the test of practice" (*Bewährung*). He ascribes the first to Mendelssohn, the "rationalist" of Enlightenment philosophy, the second to Lessing, who heralds a historical understanding of human perfection and religion. Hermann Cohen is said to synthesize some 140 years later both threads in his "Religion of Reason" in which Messianism (i.e., the orientation towards future) is at the core. Cassirer's sympathies are clearly with Cohen and therefore with Lessing. He accepts the claim to truth of both conceptions, and his concept of "truth" is, therefore, rather vague. See Cassirer, "Die Idee der Religion bei Lessing und Mendelssohn," 37 f., 41.

54. There is also an enlightening although only partial analogy between this relation of philosophy to first-order knowledge on the one hand and the

study of the Talmud vis-à-vis Jewish religious law (Halakhah) on the other: The valid law is given in the relevant codex (*Shulchan 'Arukh*) and subsequent rulings of established authorities, but the practitioner may study Talmud and other sources and engage in debates over the foundations of this or that ruling. This intellectual exercise does not impinge on the practice of the practitioner, which is guided by valid law alone.

55. See *JubA* 12, 13 f.

56. Mendelssohn, "On the Question: What Is Enlightenment?" 55; *Über die Frage: Was heißt aufklären? JubA* 6.1, 118.

57. "On the Question: What Is Enlightenment?" 55; *JubA* 6.1, 118. In the text above, I translated verbatim the title of Mendelssohn's essay.

See the discussion in Altmann, "Das Menschenbild und die Bidlung des Menschen nach Moses Mendelssohn," 14.

However, Mendelssohn also maintains that "Under all circumstances," "the containment of enlightenment is much more pernicious than untimely enlightenment." Letter to Hennings, September 21, 1784; quoted in Kayserling, *Moses Mendelssohn. Sein Leben und Wirken*, 536–37.

58. This Hobbesian view finds support in one of the most popular Hebrew sources. "Rabbi Chanina, deputy to the kohanim (priests), would say: Pray for the integrity of the government; for were it not for the fear of its authority, a man would swallow his neighbor alive" (*Ethics of the Fathers*, 3:2).

59. Letter to August von Hennings, September 21, 1784; in Kayserling, *Moses Mendelssohn. Sein Leben und Wirken*, 536.

60. "The common people are convinced through superstitions of very important truths, without which they cannot be happy in social life" (*JubA* 7, 74).

61. The essays submitted to the academy were recently published. See Adler, ed., *Nützt es dem Volk, betrogen zu werden?*

62. See the discussion in Arkush, *Moses Mendelssohn and the Enlightenment*, 116–21. Discussing the notorious question whether atheism is detrimental to morals, Mendelssohn does not deny that an atheist society can be moral; he does maintain, however, that ceteris paribus the pious society is superior since belief in God provides a powerful motivation for moral behavior which the atheist society lacks. See "Zu Bayles *Pensées diverses sur les comètes*," *JubA* 2, 25.

63. See Sigad, "Moses Mendelssohn—Judaism, Divine Politics, and the State of Israel" (Hebr.), 93–103. Arkush argues that Mendelssohn's liberalism is incompatible with his support of the Mosaic constitution and concludes that the latter must be insincere. *Mendelssohn and the Enlightenment*, 222–29; 267–70. See Gottlieb, *Faith and Freedom*, 56–58 and 154 n. 196: "I do agree with Arkush that if pressed Mendelssohn probably would have conceded that the separation of civil and religious law in the modern state was preferable to their

unification in the ancient Israelite state. Nevertheless, I do not think that Mendelssohn is disingenuous in his treatment of the Mosaic state. While there are various aspects of the Mosaic state that Mendelssohn praises, I do not find any place where he praises the unification of civil and religious law in it."

None of these authors noticed Mendelssohn's reservation concerning the separation of church and state at the beginning of *Jerusalem*, or Mendelssohn's interpretation of Saul's anointment, or finally his clear partisanship for the direct rule of God in Jerusalem in the messianic time. See on this the appendix "Mendelssohn's Messianic Allusions" and "The Title *Jerusalem*."

64. In some present Western societies, religious creeds that are not part of the established social order are named "sects" and their freedom is restricted. And in these very days the question is often discussed by what means "from afar" the state should influence "extreme" Islam, at least in Europe.

65. See Mendelssohn to Lessing, August, 2, 1756, *JubA* 11, 55.

66. *On Sentiments* (Dahlstrom), second letter, 12; fourth letter, 20.

67. *On Sentiments,* fourth letter, 18–19; fifth letter, 22–24. The same view is already expressed in *Kohelet Mussar,* the Hebrew journal published by Mendelssohn. See pt. 4, lines 64–65; Gilon, *Kohelet Musar Le-Mendelssohn,* 170. See also Cassirer, "Die Philosophie Moses Mendelssohns," 61; and Karp, "The Aesthetic Difference: Moses Mendelssohn's *Kohelet Musar* and the Inception of the Berlin *Haskalah*," 93–120.

68. *On Sentiments,* first letter, 10–11.

69. *On Sentiments,* second letter, 12–13; fifth letter, 23.

70. Sophie Becker to Mendelssohn, December 24, 1785, *JubA* 13, 331. On Mendelssohn's interchange with Sophie Becker, see Altmann, *Moses Mendelssohn: A Biographical Study,* 716–23. The translation of the following quotations of the correspondence are taken from Altmann.

71. Mendelssohn to Sophie Becker, December 27, 1785, *JubA* 13, 333.

72. See Maimon, *Lebensgeschichte, GW* 1, 196–97; and compare Maimonides, *Guide of the Perplexed,* I, 18, 54; III, 51, 52.

73. See Altmann, *Moses Mendelssohn: A Biographical Study,* 130–40.

74. Mendelssohn to Sophie Becker, December 27, 1785, *JubA* 13, 334.

75. "la *perfection* n'étant autre chose que la grandeur de la realité positive prise precisement, en mettant à part les limites ou bornes dans les choses qui en ont." Leibniz, *La Monadologie,* § 41. Leibniz gives no examples of comparing magnitudes of perfection of different values. For the conception of "realitas" as quantified in the Wolffian school, see Maier, *Kants Qualitätskategorien.*

76. Mendelssohn's commentary in *Bi'ur Millot ha-Hahigayyon, JubA* 14, 29–30. "Since it is not dependent on discretion and on the balance of reason" (my translation).

אחרי שאינן תלויות בשקול הדעת ובפלס הסברא. The term סברא can also mean "opinion," "accepted view," etc.

77. "For the common saying is true enough—rationes non esse numerandas sed ponderandas; [reasons are not to be counted but weighted]. But no one has as yet pointed out the scales, though no one has come closer to doing so and offered more help than the jurists. I have therefore thought a good bit about this matter and hope sometime to fill this need." Leibniz to Gabriel Wagner (1696), *GP* 7, 521; Loemker, 467. As far as I know, Leibniz never made good on this promise.

Mendelssohn: "Ich denke nicht, daß Ihr Freund, der Wahrheitsforscher, Stimmen sammeln will, um sie zu zählen. Sie wollen gewogen und nicht gezählt sein" (*Über Freiheit und Nothwendigkeit*, 4; *JubA* 3.1, 346). Maimon refers to this expression in *GW* 2, 433.

78. This problem has been extensively discussed under the heading "Judicial Discretion." The expression "weighing alternatives" is a widespread metaphor for comparing alternatives, insinuating that these are products of the values involved and their degrees. "The law characteristically includes only incomplete indications as to their [the principles'] relative weight and leaves much to judicial discretion to be exercised in particular cases. The scope of discretion is in fact doubly extended, since not only must the relative importance of principles be determined, but also the importance relative to each principle of deviating from it or of following it in particular occasions. The matter is usually entrusted to juridical discretion" (Raz, "Legal Principle and the Limits of Law," 846, quoted by Aharon Barak, *Judicial Discretion* [Hebr.], 104). Barak insists that his book is not philosophical (14). He attempts to clarify judicial discretion by means of a "balance" between values and adopts the metaphor of the "weight" of values (in Hebrew the term for "discretion" in "judicial discretion" is derived from "weighing") (*Judicial Discretion*, 103–7). However, he does not explicate any transformation rules of different values to one standard measure. Barak concludes: "Indeed, judicial discretion reaches its peak when the judge determines a balance between competing principles according to their weight and fortitude at the point of disagreement" (107).

Chapter 2. Salomon Maimon: The Radical Alternative to Mendelssohn

1. See his introduction to *Cheshek Shlomo*, 18, 19. Of true philosophers Maimon says:

"ולזה מאסו האנשים הנז׳[כרים] בהבלי העולם וחמודותיו ושמו כל מגמתם בעסק התורה
והמצוות לשמו לא להתפרנס בם ולא לקנות הכבוד ושבח בני האדם כי זה נמאס בעיניהם
ולא יחפצו בו . . . "

And of himself:

"ואני שלמה באא׳ [בן אדוני אבי] מוהר״ר [מורנו הרב רבי] יהושע ממדינת ליטא מעודי מאסתי
עסקי העולם ותענוגות בני אדם והחזקתי בתורת ה׳ התמימה ולדרוש ולתור בחכמה . . . "

2. See on this my "Maimon's Subversion of Kant's *Critique of Pure Reason*," 144–75.

3. Julius Guttmann suggests that Mendelssohn "asserted, with Enlightenment-nourished pride," that "especially the philosophy of his age has risen far above the level attained by the Greeks" ("Mendelssohn's *Jerusalem* and Spinoza's *Theologico-Political Treatise*," 369–70). The sole reference is the introduction to the essay on evidence and does not necessarily contradict what was said above. Guttmann does not differentiate progress in the sense of enlarging the body of knowledge and progress in the refinement of arguments. In the introduction to *Abhandlung über die Evidenz*, Mendelssohn says that the sciences extended their body of knowledge (*JubA* 2, 270), but he does not say this of philosophy. As to the arguments, Mendelssohn indeed claims that they are superior to those of Aristotle (Plato is not mentioned!), but his essay shows that in the last analysis metaphysics is dependent on metaphors. Surely, Mendelssohn never sided explicitly with skepticism, but I do claim that he argues to this effect without using the title. Friedrich Niewöhner suggested that Mendelssohn imported into general culture the traditional Jewish method of intellectual innovation: the commentary. On this interpretation, the work commented on is not chosen because the commentator agrees with all its theses but because it suits his purposes. The commentator should share the basic orientation of the work on which he comments (e.g., rationalism) and believe that the topics discussed are important and that the work is "rich" enough to call for a commentary in which he can develop *his* views without abusing the text. On this interpretation, Mendelssohn wrote commentaries mainly on Leibniz (and Wolff) because this was the foremost philosophy in his society and times and because it suited his purposes, but this would not make him a "Leibnizian." See Niewöhner, "Mendelssohn als Philosoph — Aufklärer — Jude. Oder: Aufklärung mit dem Talmud," 119–33. Niewöhner writes:

Sein Erstlingswerk, die 'Philosophischen Gespräche', sind im Grunde ein Kommmentar zu Leibniz, die 'Morgenstunden', sein letztes Werk, ein Kommentar zu Spinoza. 'Pope, ein Metaphysiker' ist ebenso ein Kommentar wie Mendelssohns Bemerkungen zur Logik des Maimonides oder seine 'Anmerkungen zu Abbts freundschaftlicher Correspondenz'. Die öffentlichen Briefe sind fast Zeilenkommenatre, und was sind die Rezensionen in den Literaturbriefen anders als Kommentare? Ich könnte noch den 'Phädon' als einen erneuten Kommentar zu Platon characterisieren oder die 'Sache Gottes' als einen erneuten Kommentar zu Leibniz. Kurz: Mendelssohn kommentiert. (124)

I attempted to substantiate a similar thesis for Salomon Maimon. See my "Salomon Maimon: A Philosopher between Two Cultures," 1–17. For a more elaborate discussion of this genre, see my "Salomon Maimon: Commentary as a Method of Philosophizing" (Hebr.), 126–60.

4. For a more detailed treatment of these questions, see my "Radikale und kompromißler in der Philosophie—Salomon Maimon über Mendelssohn, den »philosophischen Heuchler«," 369–85.

5. See also Maimon's *GM,* 161.

6. Mendelssohn himself explicitly warned against the imputation of hypocrisy to a teacher who mixes "into his otherwise salutary exposition of truths beneficial to the public some untruth. . . . I would, at any rate, be careful not to accuse, on this account, an otherwise honest teacher of hypocrisy or Jesuitry" (*Jerusalem,* 72).

7. See on this in brief my entry "Salomon Maimon," in *Metzler Lexikon jüdischer Philosophen,* 198–202; and extensively in my *Definition and Construction: Salomon Maimon's Philosophy of Geometry.*

8. *Bi'ur Millot ha-Hahigayyon, JubA* 14, 44, 65, 69, 95. Lazarus Bendavid shared this view: "Essence and properties are here one and the same" (*Versuch einer logischen Auseinandersetzung des mathematischen Unendlichen,* xxvii). As an example of "logical truth," Wolff once gave the proposition "Triangulum habet tres angulos" (*Philosophia rationalis sive Logica* [1728], pt. 2, 1, § 505, quoted in German translation in Maimon, *GW* 1, 600).

9. All things are contained virtually in Alexander's concept, as "the properties of the circle are contained in its essence (nature)." Leibniz, *Philosophical Papers and Letters,* 310; Mugnai, "Leibniz on Individuation," 46. On formal and virtual identity, see Kauppi, *Über die Leibnizsche Logik,* 71–76.

10. Kant, *What Real Progress Has Metaphysics Made in Germany since the Time of Leibniz and Wolff,* 404; *AA* 20, 323.

11. "Antwort des Hrn. Maimon auf voriges Schreiben," 52–80; *GW* 3, 198–99. See also *GW* 4, 449–50.

The same criticism also applies to Mendelssohn, who gives this example for properties following with "absolute necessity" from the definition. Men-

segulaempirischersegularationalerBegriffzac

delssohn also considers the possibility of reversing the order of the *differentia* and *proprium* (*segula*) using such properties in the definition itself and inferring those now serving as defining properties.

12. "Die Zusammennehmung dieser Qualitäten ist bloß eine Synthesis der Einbildungskraft, wegen ihres Zugleichseyns in Zeit und Raum . . . nicht aber eine Synthesis des Verstandes: man kann so wenig einen rothen Körper als eine süße Linie denken" (*GW* 2, 92–93). On the synthesis of the imagination that produces "fictions," see "fiction" (Erdichtung), in *Philosophisches Wörterbuch*, 36–49.

13. This was clearly seen by Ernst Cassirer. Maimon's skepticism "folgt lediglich aus der Strenge, mit der er, im Widerstreit zu allem Sensualismus, das rationale Ideal des Wissens aufgestellt und innherlab der Logik und der reinen Mathematik in seiner Notwendigkeit erwiesen hatte. Er ist 'empirischer Skeptiker', weil und sofern er—nach seinem eigenen Ausdruck—'rationaler Dogmatiker' ist (*Tr*, 436 ff.), d.h. weil er die Erfahrung der unbedingten Forderung, die sich aus dem Erkenntnisbegriff der exakten Wissenschaft für ihn ergibt, niemals gewachsen findet" Cassirer, *Das Erkenntisproblem in der Philosophie und Wissenschaft der neueren Zeit*, vol. 3: *Die Nachkantischen Systeme*, 101.

14. For Maimon's views on language, see especially his *Über die symbolische Erkenntnis und philosophische Sprache,* in *Tr*, 263–332; "Sprache," *Philosophisches Wörterbuch, GW* 3, 135–45; "Sprache in psychologischer Hinsicht," *GW* 4, 593–98; "Die philosophische Sprachverwirrung," *GW* 6, 406–52.

The most extensive and accurate presentation of Maimon's philosophy of language is Zac, "Salomon Maimon et les malentendus du langage," 181–202. See also Atlas, "Solomon Maimon's Philosophy of Language Critically Examined," 235–88. In a yet unpublished paper, Dan Dahlstrom compared some aspects of Maimon's and Mendelssohn's philosophies of language. All discussions of Maimon's philosophy of language develop only the rationalist alternative.

15. The Counter-Enlightenment's theory of language formation in dance and poetry intends to undermine the validity of knowledge and not only to clarify its origin. Thus the famous dictum of J. G. Hamann in his *Aesthetica in nuce* (1762), in *Werke*, vol. 2, 197: "Poesie ist die Muttersprache des menschlichen Geschlechts; wie der Gartenbau älter als der Acker: Malerei—als Schrift: Gesang—als Deklamation: Gleichnisse—als Schlüsse: Tausch—als Handel. Ein tieferer Schlaf war die Ruhe unserer Urahnen und ihre Bewegung ein taumelnder Tanz. Sieben Tage im Stillschweigen des Nachsinns oder Erstaunens faßten sie—und taten ihren Mund auf—zu geflügelten Sprüchen."

A late enlightener like Ernst Cassirer adopts this view and yet continues to construct from this "Ausdrucksfunktion" the "Bedeutungsfunktion" that can raise claims to objective knowledge. In his conception, the origin of language and its validity are clearly severed. See, e.g., his *Language and Myth*, 34–35.

16. He refers to the alternatives with reservations. The empiricist version "can be cast in doubt." Or, introducing the rationalist alternative with a question mark: isn't it possible that the word designating genera "could be predicated" of their "common genus"? See *GW* 1, 322–23 n. Early in his career, Mendelssohn also suggested this possibility. See his "Sendschreiben an den Herrn Magister Lessing", *JubA* 2, 108–9.

17. Another example is the term "תפס", "to grasp" (in German, *fassen*). In his commentary on the *Guide of the Perplexed*, he suggests that the term was transferred from grasping an empirical object to intellectual apprehension (*GM*, 88). In his *Versuch über die Transcendentalphilosophie*, he uses "fassen einen Körper und fassen einen Gedanken" as an example of a transcendental concept with two applications (*GM*, 306). A good example of Maimon's new conception is his discussion of relational terms. See his discussion of "high" and "low," "left" and "right" (*GM*, 44).

18. In his commentary, Maimon translates the first meaning with *verzehren* (consume), the second with *nähren* (nurture) (*GM*, 60).

19. "Die philosophische Sprachverwirrung" (*GW* 7, 409).

20. On Maimon's principle of determinability, see Schechter, "The Logic of Speculative Philosophy and Skepticism in Maimon's Philosophy: *Satz der Bestimmbarkeit* and the Role of Synthesis," 18–53.

Chapter 3. The Truth of Religion

1. Mendelssohn quotes also the following psalm as an example: "He that planted the ear, shall he not hear? he that formed the eye, shall he not see? . . . [H]e that teacheth man knowledge, shall not he know?" (Psalms 94:9–10; *An die Freunde Lessings, JubA* 3.2, 198). In verse 11 Mendelssohn omits the words "He that chastiseth the heathen, shall not he correct?" The translation in *Jerusalem* differs from Mendelssohn's published translation of the Psalms.

2. "I do not esteem the use of an endeavor, such as this present one, so highly as to suppose that the most important of all our cognitions, *there is a God*, would waver or be imperiled if it were not supported by deep metaphysical investigations. It was not the will of Providence that the insights so necessary to our happiness should depend upon the sophistry of subtle inferences. On the contrary, Providence has directly transmitted these insights to our natural common sense. And, provided that it is not confused by false art, it

does not fail to lead us directly to what is true and useful, for we are in extreme need of these two things" (Kant, *The Only Possible Argument in Support of a Demonstration of the Existence of God*, 111; *AA* 2, 265; original emphasis).

3. "I consider none of all systems of philosophy to be correct and reliable enough to base on it teachings of such importance as those of religion. In my investigations of religion, I made it a rule to base them on nothing but propositions about which all men on the entire globe have always been unanimous, and which have such content that mere reason suffices to judge them, and which, finally, do not flatter human inclinations, but rather derogate them" (Bolzano, "Mein Glaube," 209–10).

4. For Mendelssohn's discussion of the different kinds of truths, see *Jerusalem*, 90–94. It is often maintained that Mendelssohn adopted Leibniz's distinction between *verités de raison* and *verités de fait*. However, there are important differences. The first is that Mendelssohn presents three truths, whereas for Leibniz there are only two. In Leibniz, historical truths are not distinguished from other contingent truths.

Note that for Mendelssohn religious truths in themselves are eternal *necessary truths*, although we learn of them as we learn of *contingent eternal truths*, namely, from experience and by common sense. For example, if correct, the ontological proof is an analytic and therefore necessary truth. However, metaphysics is a very specialized cultural practice. The vast majority of people learn of God's existence, providence, and afterlife (with or without guidance) from observation of inner and outer nature and an inference (of common sense) (*Jerusalem*, 94–95). (See Leibniz, *Discours de métaphysique*, §9; and Mendelssohn's commentary in *Bi'ur Millot ha-Hahigayyon*, chap. 8, *JubA* 14, 71–72).

Moreover, Mendelssohn's orientation is epistemological, not semantic. This shows, for example, in his characterization of necessary truths. They are necessary because God thinks them so. In Leibniz, God thinks them so because they are necessary. Mendelssohn is here closer to Descartes.

5. "der Gesetzgebende Gott unserer Väter, oder wie die Modesprache lieber will, der Gesetzgeber Moses" (Vorrede zu Menasse ben Israel, *Rettung der Juden*, *JubA* 8, 10).

6. This is the argument of Judah Halevi in his *Kuzari*, I, § 86–91. Mendelssohn introduces this argument as well in his commentary on *Millot ha-Higayyyon* of Maimonides. Maimonides demands only that the witness be "one or many" "excellent persons" (נבחרים) as a condition of their credibility (which Efros translates, "from a chosen person or from a chosen assembly" [*Maimonides' Treatise on Logic*, 47]). Mendelssohn, in contrast, does not qualify the witnesses as excellent but as "trustworthy" (נאמנים), nor does he say "one or

many" but that the revelation on Sinai took place "with great publicity and [in the presence of a] great audience" (בפרסום גדול ובהמון רב). See Mendelssohn's commentary on *Millot ha-Higayyon,* chap. 8, *JubA* 14, 71–72.

7. "were his witnesses"—"waren seine Zeugen"—plural also in German. This stance accords with Maimonides' position in *Mishneh Torah,* Book of Knowledge, Basic Principles, 8,1.

8. Mendelssohn's Commentary on *Millot ha-Higayyon,* chap. 8, *JubA* 14, 70–72.

9. Maimon was such a skeptic and sophist. "Die geoffenbarte Religion, insofern sie auf dem Glauben an Wunderwerke beruht, kann, vorausgesetzt daß die Fakta, die man zu ihrer Unterstützung annimmt, wahr sind, dennoch in Zweifel gezogen werden. Denn gesetzt, daß diese Fakta sich nicht nach den bisher bekannten Naturgesetzen erklären lassen, so ist doch immer möglich, daß es noch Naturgesetze gäbe, die uns bis jetzt unbekannt sind, woruas sich dergleichen Fakta erklären lassen; und folglich wir zu keinen übernatürlichen Gesetzen unsre Zuflucht zu nehmen brauchen" (*GW* 3, 242).

10. Bachya ben Joseph ibn Pakuda's *Duties of the Heart,* pt. 1, chap. 7, brings a series of arguments for the uniqueness of God. Among them is a version of Occam's razor: "Since it has been established that the world has a creator . . . there is no need to consider the possibility that there is more [or less] than one [creator]. For there could not be a world without even one creator," nor should more than one creator be assumed: "For in the case of things that are verifiable by way of adducing proofs, when their existence is proved conclusively, we need not assume them to be more than is necessary to account for the phenomenon that constitutes their proof" (Haberman's translation, 98–99). Mendelssohn's mentor, Israel Zamosc, also wrote a commentary to this book under the title *Tov ha-Levanon.*

11. One of the requirements that hypotheses must fulfill in order to be recognized as empirical truths is that they "explain and determine cases of a kind different from those which were contemplated in the formation" of those hypotheses. (See Whewell, *Novum Organon Renovatum,* 88).

12. For a short presentation of the similar medieval arguments, see Arkush, *Moses Mendelssohn and the Enlightenment,* 170–73.

13. Arkush, *Moses Mendelssohn and the Enlightenment,* 167; see also 255. For the opposite view, see David Sorkin, "Moses Mendelssohn's Biblical Exegesis," 243–76. Sorkin agrees with Franz Rosenzweig that Mendelssohn "had grasped the torch of the great medieval commentators and rekindled it" (265). Specifically, Sorkin argues that Mendelssohn answered the challenge of the "historical-critical school of Biblical study" (above all Eichhorn's *Einleitung ins Alte Testament*) with his introduction to the translation of the Pentateuch

(*Or la-Netivah*) that was "an innovative defense of the traditional Jewish view" (267). Sorkin likens Mendelssohn's approach to that of the Wolffian theologist Sigmund Jacob Baumgarten two generations earlier (273). Thus, compared with the Enlightenment of the 1770s and 1780s, Mendelssohn appears as a conservative in his biblical studies as well as in his philosophy. For a detailed treatment of the context of Mendelssohn's translation and commentary of the Pentatuech, see Breuer, *The Limits of Enlightenment*. See Breuer's discussion of Mendelssohn's defense of the authenticity of the biblical text (*The Limits of Enlightenment*, 147–75). My discussion concentrates on the philosophical justification of Mendelssohn's position, which was not addressed in these studies.

14. Arkush disregards this context and measures Mendelssohn's argument against those of Deists and Spinoza's (*Moses Mendelssohn and the Enlightenment*, 133–65, 177–80). Moreover, I believe that he argues from the presumption of the inauthenticity of revelation and demands a proof to the contrary. It seems to me unjustified to put on Mendelssohn this heavy burden of proof rather than the lighter burden required by the opposite assumption.

15. See Carolyn McLeod, "Trust," in *The Stanford Encyclopedia of Philosophy* (Fall 2008 ed.), http://plato.stanford.edu/archives/fall2008/entries/trust (last accessed June 2010).

16. Acknowledging that the truth of revelation and the binding force of the mitzvoth cannot be justified on the basis of rational principles alone, Daniel Rynholds advances a "non-argumentative foundation": "The practice itself rather than any alleged propositional representation of it, contains its own rationality, a non-discursive form of rationality that is irreducibly practical. . . . Actual practice rather than abstract theorizing is the mode of access to a practical form of rationality. . . . [P]ractice yields a reasoned confidence in a practice." Rynhold, *Two Models of Jewish Philosophy*, 174–75. The immediate consequence is the suspicion of relativism (206–9). The way out seems similar to Mendelssohn's. We should accept that we are born into a given community (218–19): "You are born into the Jewish religion, into a certain pre-existing framework, and practically habituated into the norms of that framework. . . . We do not start from a neutral standpoint and simply choose a certain way of life from an array of theoretical options set before us, in accordance with which we work out which is the best way to live" (219). Although the consequences may seem similar to Mendelssohn's, there is an all-important difference between them: Whereas "habituation" is prima facie a sociological category and introduced as an epistemological category for ethical and religious principles only, "trust" is a presupposition of all knowledge and, moreover, open to revision! (222).

Chapter 4. The Language of Action in Biblical Times

1. See Mendelssohn's discussion in *Or la-Netiva.* Solomon Dubno added a *Tikkun Sofrim* (text critical notes) to Genesis that was intended to supersede all hitherto available editions. Also in the discussion over the *Aleinu* prayer, Mendelssohn argued that the text suffered no change because all its syllables were counted and thus reliably bequeathed to posterity (*JubA* 10.1, 307–9).

2. Condillac, *Essay on the Origin of Human Knowledge,* 6. On "language of action" and pantomime, see Rosenfeld's chapter, "Pantomime as Theater, 1760–1789," in *A Revolution in Language: The Problem of Signs in Late Eighteenth-Century France,* 57–85. In particular, body language is ascribed high expressive qualities.

3. See also on this topic, Jospe, "The Superiority of Oral over Written Communication: Judah Ha-Levi's Kuzari and Modern Jewish Thought," 127–56.

4. Presumably referring to the Babylonian Talmud, *Gittin,* 71a.

5. See the pioneering study of Peretz Sandler, *Mendelssohn's Edition of the Pentateuch* (Hebr.). On Mendelssohn's view of the importance of the oral tradition in the transmission of the biblical text, on the cantillations and other aspects of his commentary, see Sorkin, "Moses Mendelssohn's Biblical Exegesis," 243–76. See also the discussion of Mendelssohn's defense of the authenticity of the biblical text and of his claim that not only the entire text but also the vowel points and the cantillations were revealed to Moses on Sinai (Breuer, *The Limits of Enlightenment,* 147–75, 165–66). To Breuer's discussion we should add the function of these means in transmitting the Pentateuch also as an oral text. They save it from corruption, which, as Mendelssohn says, frequently happens with secular texts as a result of mistakes and deliberate changes introduced by copyists.

6. "מעתה אין ספק שמרע״ה [משה רבינו עליו השלום] שמע את כל דברי התורה מפי הגבורה עם כל הדר ותקון הנקודות והטעמים המיוחסים להן, בדקדוקיהן וצרופיהן לא נעדר מהם דבר, וכן מסרה ליהושע ויהושע לזקנים וכן נשתלשלה הקבלה ההיא דור אחר דור."
Or la-Netiva, JubA 15.1, 25; German translation, *JubA* 9.1, 16.

7. *Or la-Netiva, JubA* 15.1, 25. See also Jospe, "The Superiority of Oral over Written Communication: Judah Ha-Levi's Kuzari and Modern Jewish Thought," 139–40.

8. A modern scholar even successfully interpreted Mendelssohn's works on language — including the important passages in *Jerusalem* — without recourse to the Jewish lore or to Mendelssohn's work on the translation of the Bible and the *Bi'ur,* that is, as if it exclusively belonged to the philosophy of the

Enlightenment. See Ricken, "Mendelssohn und die Sprachtheorien der Auf-klärung," 195–241, esp. 208–9, 232–33.

Ricken points to Christian Wolff's elaboration of Leibniz's semiotics, to Locke's *Essay Concerning Human Understanding,* to Condillac's *Essai sur l'origine des connaisances humaines,* and to William Warburton's *The Divine Legation of Moses Demonstrated.* Now, Leibniz (respectively Wolff) and Locke are obvious sources of Mendelssohn's thought. Wolff is Mendelssohn's first recommendation for the study of logic and metaphysics, and of Locke's *Essay* together with Leibniz's *Nouveaux essais,* he says that they "almost suffice to educate a philosophic mind." Condillac's *Essai sur l'origine des connaissances humaines* follows immediately Locke and Leibniz in this list. See *Anweisung zur spekul. Philosophie, für einen jungen Menschen von 15–20 Jahren, JubA* 3.1, 305–7, esp. 305.

Of special interest is William Warburton's *The Divine Legation of Moses Demonstrated.* Although Mendelssohn doesn't mention Warburton in the context of the philosophy of language, there is no doubt whatsoever that Mendelssohn knew his work. Condillac says that Warburton is the major source of his discussion of script and extensively quotes him, and Warburton was also extensively discussed by Christoph Meiners in his *History of Ancient Egyptian Religion,* a book that (like Condillac's) was in Mendelssohn's library and that he repeatedly quotes in *Jerusalem.* See Meiners, *Versuch über die Religionsge-schichte der ältesten Völker, besonders der Egyptier;* and especially Warburton's elaboration of hieroglyphics, 217–23.

Mendelssohn knew of Warburton very early in his career, when he penned with Lessing *Pope ein Metaphysiker* and referred to a previous contro-versy over Pope's philosophy in which Warburton took part. See *JubA* 2, xvi; *JubA* 4, 322–24.

It is also noteworthy that Warburton's book, which first appeared in 1737–38, was translated into German in 1751–53 (and reached a tenth edition by 1846), and part of it was translated even earlier into French. See Warbur-ton, *The Divine Legation of Moses Demonstrated.* A reprography of the famous fourth part of the fourth book appeared in 1980 in Frankfurt under the title, *Versuch über die Hieroglyphen der Ägypter.*

Moreover, Reimarus quotes Warburton's in the fourth "Wolffenbütteler Fragment," and Lessing discusses him in his *The Education of the Human Race,* §24, 25. Warburton is omnipresent in Mendelssohn's intellectual environment.

For a discussion of the "language d'action" not only in Condillac but also in Rousseau and Diderot, see Sophia Rosenfeld, *A Revolution in Language,* 27–56.

9. This form of posing the question and answering it is condensed in Charles Peirce, "What Is a Sign?" (1894) into one paragraph, §4. Note also that here, too, the development leads to hieroglyphics:

> Imagine two men who know no common speech, thrown together remote from the rest of the race. They must communicate; but how are they to do so? By imitative sounds, by imitative gestures, and by pictures. These are three kinds of likenesses. It is true that they will also use other signs, finger-pointings, and the like. But, after all, the likenesses will be the only means of describing the qualities of the things and actions which they have in mind. Rudimentary language, when men first began to talk together, must have largely consisted either in directly imitative words, or in conventional names which they attached to pictures. The Egyptian language is an excessively rude one. It was, as far as we know, the earliest to be written; and the writing is all in pictures. Some of these pictures came to stand for sounds,—letters and syllables. But others stand directly for ideas. They are not nouns; they are not verbs; they are just pictorial ideas. (*The Essential Peirce*, vol. 2, 6–7)

10. Condillac, *Essai sur lorigine des connaissances*, 62; Aarsleff, 116–18. Condillac did not quote the first two sentences. He quoted the French translation, # 8, 9. I quote Warburton's original English according to the reprint of the second English edition (1741), *The Divine Legation of Moses Demonstrated*, vol. 2, 81–83. I omitted two long footnotes that Condillac did not quote.

11. See, e.g., his view that the controversy between materialists and dualists is not real: *JubA* 3.2, 61.

12. See de l'Epée, *Institution des Sourds et Muets*. See also Knowlson, "The Idea of Gesture as a Universal Language in the XVIIth and XVIIIth Centuries," 495–508.

13. Presumably, Mendelssohn has the word גזירה in mind. It derives from the verb "to cut" and means "decree."

14. On these practices in the Near East, see H. Tadmor, "Treaty and Oath in the Ancient Near East: A Historian's Approach," 127–52.

15. See Shalom Albeck, "Acquisition, Kinyan," in *Encyclopedia Judaica*, vol. 2, 210–21.

16. See J. L. Austin, *How to Do Things with Words*.

17. *Or la-Netiva*, 23b. See also *Bi'ur* to Genesis 2:19. Here Mendelssohn follows Nachmanides (who deviates from Rashi and Radak) and writes: "in their names it was explained who can be of help to the other, i.e., can procreate with each other." This idea, too, can be found in the *Kuzari*. See *Kuzari*, IV, 25. See also Mendelssohn's early *Kohelet Mussar* (in Gilon's edition, 160):

"לה"ק [לשון הקודש] . . . הוא מבלי ספק השלימה מכל הלשונות והנאותה לקרואיה יותר מכלם.
כמו שאמר וכל אשר יקרא לו האדם נפש חיה הוא שמו [בראשית ב' י"ט] ר"ל שהוא ראוי לשם
הזה ונאה לו ומלמד על טבעו (ר"ל כי אף ביתר הלשונות קראו בשמות לכל דבר אך לא יסכים
שמם לטבעם יותר משם אחר. לא כן בלה"ק אשר הונחו השמות מסכימים לטבעי הדברים . . . ".
See Sorkin, *Moses Mendelssohn and the Religious Enlightenment*, 38–40.

18. Although cantillations determine the declamation of the text as much as possible, there are nevertheless gestures and mimicry that cannot be represented by signs. The "wise reader" will therefore supplement these by means of voice, gestures, movement of the eyes, and so on, according to his imagination and his emotions. For this reason, direct oral teaching is always to be preferred to the study of books (53b). In this and in the following discussion, Mendelssohn closely follows Judah Halevi. See *Kuzari*, II, 67–76.

Chapter 5. Idolatry: Egyptian and Jewish

1. This is also Warburton's opinion: *The Divine Legation of Moses Demonstrated*, vol. 2, 138–40. The English transliteration is misleading. Since the Hebrew alphabet contains only consonants, the spelling of the name of the letters and of the corresponding words is exactly the same.

2. See his judgment on C. de Pauw's *Recherches philosophiques sur les Américains*, in Letter to J. D. Michaelis, April 10, 1771, *JubA* 12.2, 8–10. Mendelssohn owned de Pauw's books and knew him personally.

3. Here Mendelssohn obviously draws on Lessing's theory of fables. In representing abstract concepts, these "things themselves" are not vulnerable to Swift's critique of the referential theory of language in *Gulliver's Travels*. There Swift ridicules this view by reductio ad absurdum: "since Words are only Names for Things, it would be more convenient for all Men to carry about them, such Things as were necessary to express the particular Business they are to discourse on." Jonathan Swift, *Gulliver's Travels*, bk. 3, chap. 5, 172.

4. This suggestion is rehearsed in Homberg's commentary on *Deuteronomy* 4:16: "*temunah*" is a nonexistent imagined figure, combined from existing parts. Once this is executed, for example, in metal, it is called "symbol" (סמל). "Since many of the worshiped idols were figures combined of different parts not found combined in one of the bodies, as is known."

5. Even such arbitrary signs as the numbers of the *Pythagoreans* could be misunderstood. The followers of Pythagoras believed "that all mysteries of nature and of the Deity were concealed in these numbers; one ascribed miraculous power to them" (*Jerusalem*, 117).

6. Consider, for example, what Thomas Spart writes on the wisdom of the ancient orientals in *The History of the Royal Society of London* (1667), 5: "It was the custom of their Wise men, to wrap up their Observations on Nature, and the Manners of Men, in the dark Shadows of Hieroglyphic; and to conceal them, as sacred Mysteries, from the apprehensions of the vulgar. This was a sure way to beget a Reverence in the Peoples Hearts towards themselves: but not to advance the true Philosophy of Nature."

7. The golden calf has been identified by "ancient sources such as Philo, Lactantius, Hieronymus, and the *Targum Hierosolymitanis*," as the Apis Bull. These sources are quoted by John Spencer, *De legibus hebraeorum ritualibus et earum rationibus*. See Assmann, *Moses the Egyptian*, 72, 234 n. 68.

8. In this, too, Mendelssohn follows Zamosc in his commentary *Otsar Nechmad* on *Kuzari*, I, 98:

"ולשון המקרא מסייע לזאת הסברא במה שנאמר אלה אלהיך ישראל אשר העלוך מארץ מצרים, כשהוא אומר העלוך לשון רבים משמע דהיינו כבוד ה' השוכן על הצורה ההיא, שודאי לא נשתגעו כל כך שיאמינו כי הפסל נסך אשר עצבו ידם בין לילה, הוא הוציאם ממצרים."

See Zamosc, *Otsar Nechmad*, in *Sefer ha-Kuzari be-Chamisha Ma'amarim* (Hebr.), 65b.

9. Van der Leeuw, *Religion in Essence and Manifestation*, 448; emphasis in the original.

10. See Mendelssohn's commentary on *Exodus* 20:2. In this he clearly opposes the view of Maimonides, who considered the knowledge of God's existence one of the thirteen principles of Judaism and also as a positive commandment. See Maimonides, *Mishneh Torah*, Book of Knowledge, Basic Principles, chap. 1,1.

11. This is also Maimonides' notion of idolatry. See *Mishneh Torah*, Book of Knowledge, Laws Concerning Idolatry and the Ordinances of the Heathens, chaps. 1–3.

12. This has been a controversially debated question for centuries. The great rabbinic authority, Ezechiel ben Judah Landau, who, at one point, also opposed Mendelssohn's translation of the Pentateuch, rejected the view Mendelssohn and Homberg expressed. See his *Noda bi-Yehuda*, 2nd ed., Yoreh Deah, §148. But Mendelssohn's view was not at all an exception. See Shochet, *Beginnings of the Haskalah* (Hebr.), 67–71, 288 nn.

13. *Mishneh Torah*, Book of Judges, Laws of Kings and Wars, chap. 8, 14 (11). The wording of this sentence was corrupted in earlier prints, but the change does not affect the conclusion relevant here. Compare Maimonides' *Eight Chapters*, his introduction to *Pirkei Avot*, chap. 6, quoted in *A Maimonides Reader*, 376.

14. In his letter to Jacob Emden of October 26, 1773 (*JubA* 16, 178–79), Mendelssohn refers to the previously cited Maimonidean law in *Mishneh Torah,* Laws of Kings and Wars, chap. 8, 14 (11), and writes:

"והזכרתי לפני אדמו״ו בעת ההי׳ שכדומה לא יצאה הסברא הזאות להרב ז״ל כי אם ממה שגזר במקומות רבי׳ מספריו שאין הטוב והרע כי אם מהמפורסמות, ושאין להם שורש ועקר במושכלות כלל, ואם כן הוא אין לסמוך בצדק ועול, טוב ורע נאה ומגונה על נטית הדעת ופלס השכל, כי אם צריך שיהיו מן המקובלות . . . ונראה שלדעת הרב גם הידיעות שקראום המפורסמות לא נתפרסמו באומות כי אם ע״י הקבלה, היו בתחלה קבלה מאדה״ר ומבני נח ואחרי שנשכח לבניהם אחריהם עקר וראש הקבלה, נשאר הדבר אליהם כמפורסם ביניהם ולא ידעו מבטן מי יצא. ועתה אף שהדברים הללו מקובלי׳ על הדעת וקרובי׳ אל האמת הנה כתבתי עוד לאמו״ו נ״י שבעיני דרך הרב ז״ל בידיעת הטוב והרע והצדק והעול הנאה והמגונה והיותה בלתי מושכלות זר מאד, ולי מופתי׳ ברורי׳ ונכוחים על ענין הטוב והרע הצדק והעול הנאה והמגונה והיותם מן המושכלת באמת . . . "

Emden sided with Maimonides. See his answer of November 1773, *JubA* 16, 179–83. See also the discussion in Stanislawski, "Towards an Analysis of the *Bi'ur* as Exegesis: Moses Mendelssohn's Commentary on the Revelation at Sinai," 135–52.

15. Letter to Herz Homberg, September 22, 1783, *JubA* 13, 132–34.

16. On the opposition of Halevi, Abrabanel, and Nachmanides to idolatrous forms of astral magic and to their leanings toward those forms that accord with their understanding of Judaism, see Schwartz, *Astral Magic in Medieval Jewish Thought* (Hebr).

17. In *Jerusalem* the accent is slightly different. Mendelssohn writes there that the people "purported" or "pretended" (*Ihrem Vorgeben nach*). In *JubA* 8, 185, this has been misread as *Vorgehen* (the way of action, behavior), to wish an image "not really to worship it as a deity" but rather as a guide, a replacement for Moses. Be it as it may, the commentary on Exodus presents in detail the view that the aberration developed successively.

18. *Bi'ur* on Exodus 32:4.

19. This is also an explanation Maimonides gives in his interpretation of the word *Tselem* (image, form, but also idol). Idols are called "Tselem," says Maimonides, not due to their shape, but due to their (Aristotelian) "form," their essence, which—so idolaters believe—attracts the "affluent emanation" of the stars. The image serving in astral magic need not be similar to the stars referred to. See his *Commentary on the Mishnah*, Avodah Zarah, chap. 3, 3. However, in man-made objects the "form" is much more dependent on the shape than in natural objects. The "purpose" of the object puts constraints on the shape but does not determine it. The seat of a chair may be round, triangular, or square, and yet its shape has to fit the purpose of sitting (e.g., be nearly

flat, not cone-shaped). See Maimonides, *Treatise on Logic,* chap. 9. Moreover, in the case in point, the "similarity" between image and constellation may be mediated by language: A man-made image of a calf, a calf, and the symbol of the constellation Taurus may each be named "ox," and therefore associated with each other, yet the image of an ox is not similar to the word *ox.*

On the term *Tselem* in Maimonides, see Klein-Braslavy, *Maimonides' Interpretation of the Adam Stories in Genesis* (Hebr.), 13–22. Hannah Kasher draws attention to Maimonides' qualification that if the shape of the device used in such sympathetic magic is necessary for its function, then Tselem means both the shape and the (Aristotelian) "form" and is, therefore, an equivocal term (*The Guide of the Perplexed,* I, 1; Pines, 22). See Kasher, "To the Forms of the *Tselamim* in Maimonides" (Hebr.), 31–42.

There are a number of similarities between Maimonides' and Mendelssohn's views of idolatry. See Kaplan, "Maimonides and Mendelssohn on the Origins of Idolatry, the Election of Israel, and the Oral Law," 424–55. I doubt, however, that "Maimonides' Laws Concerning Idolatry and the Ordinances of the Heathens," chap. 1, in *Mishneh Torah,* Book of Knowledge, constitutes the basic source underlying Mendelssohn's discussion in *Jerusalem* about divine legislation as "ceremonial script" (439). Kaplan discussed only Mendelssohn's *Jerusalem* and not his interpretation of the sin of the golden calf or contemporary discussions like Warburton's. Above all, however, Maimonides has no theory of religious semiotics, therefore also no comprehensive theory of idolatry, but only singular circumstantial explanations for individual cases of idolatry.

20. Psalms 106:20: "They made a calf in Horeb, and worshipped the molten image. Thus they changed their glory into the similitude of an ox that eateth grass."

21. Ibn Ezra, Halevi's close friend, also explains the sin as an attempt at astral magic. In his short commentary he suggests that the form of a calf was chosen because "in India there are people who think that this form receives supreme power" and that "he who understands astronomy knows why they chose the form of a calf." In his long commentary, he first relates the view of astrologers who explain that at the time the connection between the planets was in Taurus—and now rejects it (commentary on Exodus 32:1). See, for details, Sela, *Astrology and Biblical Exegesis in Abraham's Ibn Ezra's Thought* (Hebr.), 291–99.

22. Commentary on Exodus 32:4. See Kasher, ed., *Torah Shlemah,* notes to *Exodus* 32, vol. 6, 90. This view was shared by others. See Kasher, *Torah Shlemah,* Supplementa, vol. 6, 206–12. See also Maimonides, *Mishneh Torah,* Book of Knowledge, Laws Concerning Idolatry and the Ordinances of the Heathens, chap. 1.

Nachmanides offers an alternative interpretation. Drawing on Ezekiel 1:10 (and on *Shemot Rabbah*, 42, 5), he suggests that the figure of the ox is derived from one of the four figures of the divine carriage that the people of Israel attempted to draw down towards them, in order that these will guide them through the desert as did the columns of cloud and fire (Exodus 14:19).

23. "ויהיו בוחרים במעשה ידי אדם, כעין תרפים אשר עשו להם בימים ההם להגיד להם צרכיהם, כי היי הדבר הזה מפורסם בימים ההם שידבק ענין אלהי בצורות התרפים ההם, ויגבא אותם."

See also the commentary to Genesis 31:19.

והנה יעשו אותם [התרפים] קטני אמנה להם לאלהים לא ישאלו בשם הנכבד ולא יתפללו אליו רק כל מעשיהם בקסמים אשר יגידו להם התרפים

The commentary was penned by Solomon Dubno, but Mendelssohn says the same things in his commentary on Exodus 32:1.

24. Halbertal and Margalit say very similar things on Maimonides. See their *Idolatry*, 42–44.

25. See *Bi'ur* on Exodus 32:1 and Genesis 31:19.

26. Warburton, *The Divine Legation of Moses Demonstrated*, vol. 2, 170.

27. In Luther's translation: "Ihr sollt euch keinen Götzen machen noch Bild, und sollt euch keine Säule aufrichten, noch keinen Malstein setzen in eurem Lande, daß ihr davor anbetet; denn ich bin der HERR, euer Gott."

28. See Mendelssohn's addition in brackets to the commentary *ad locum*:

"ואבן משכית [א"ה, הרד"ק בשרש ש.כ.ה. כתב שהוא מעניין ציור, מלשון הבטה שהדב' המצוי' יביט בו האדם, ויתכן שהוא האבן אשר עליו חרטו צורות משונות, נקראות (היעראגליפען, בילדערשריפט), זכרתי ענינם אצל חרטומי מצרים, והיו הצורות ההם לכהניהם ולחכמיהם כמו מכתב, רשמו על ידם העניינים אשר רצו להעלימם מיתר העם, וכדי לכבדם בעיני ההמון אמרו עליהם שהן צורות נשגבות ראוי להשתחוות להן ולעבדם, ונשתיירו מן האבנים ההם עד היום הזה, והם אוס' לנו לקיים הצורות האלה בארצנו, אף לנוי או לזכ' בלבד, והטעם כמו שיזכי' הרב המבא'], לפי שהמעשים הללו מרגילין מחשבות הבל ומקרבין לע"ז, ולכן נסמך לכאן שלא יקימו הדברים הללו בארץ הקדושה, לפי שהפרשה כלה מדברת בקדושת הארץ שתנהוג בה שביעית ויובל, ושלא תמכ' לצמיתות כי לי הארץ, חתם הענין באזהרות הללו שמדרך הגוים לפאר בהן טירותם ועריהם שלא יעשו כן ישראל בארצם" . . .

29. Mendelssohn added an explanation of the latter word in brackets. These magicians change with their arcane crafts the "appearance of things" ("*die durch verborgene Künste den Schein der Dinge verändern können*"). Thus Mendelssohn severs their art from the (evidently: real) transformation of the rod into a serpent by God's wonder (through Moses and Aaron) reported in the previous verse. In this Mendelssohn follows Ibn Ezra, but he omits Ibn Ezra's interpretation of the "wise" who were also summoned by Pharaoh. Ibn Ezra suggests that these were astrologers (חכמי המזלות). See Ibn Ezra's long commentary on Exodus 7:11 and 7:22. Mendelssohn quotes Ibn Ezra's first commentary

in his. Moses is presented as an Egyptian sage in Acts of the Apostles 7:22 and in Philo's *De vita Mosis*. See also Exodus 11:3. For a detailed account of these traditions, see Assmann, *Moses the Egyptian*. In Jewish tradition, Egypt stands for a center of magic (e.g., Babylonian Talmud, *Kidushin*, 49b).

30. In the commentary Mendelssohn offers some German words as translations: Ziesel, Meissel, and Grabstichel.

31. Mendelssohn underlined the sentences "that the first intention of the Law as a whole is to put an end to idolatry" (in Pines's translation, 517) and "For the foundation of the whole of our Law and the pivot around which it turns, consists in the effacement of these opinions from the minds and of these monuments from existence" (521). See Rawidowicz, "Mendelssohns handschriftliche Glossen zum More Nebukim," 201.

32. Mendelssohn's note to the commentary on Numbers 15:37(8)–41.

33. The question is first discussed in the Babylonian Talmud, *Sanhedrin*, 21b.

34. Mendelssohn's *Bi'ur* on Exodus 31:18.

35. One way to understand the words "the tables were written on both their sides; on the one side and on the other were they written" (Exodus 32:15) is that the script was engraved through the entire thickness of the stone. But in this case, those letters that form a closed figure should fall out. The rabbis refer to the difficulty, saying that they "remained miraculously in place" (see Babylonian Talmud, *Shabbat* 104a; and *Sanhedrin* 21b). Mendelssohn, too, adopts this view. See his commentary on Exodus 32:15.

36. The Ark of the Covenant was clearly ascribed divine powers (1 Samuel 4:4–7), likely to help the Israelites win a war against their enemies (Numbers 10:35–36; 1 Samuel 4:1–11) as it itself overcomes alien Gods (1 Samuel 5:1–5). Again, in the tabernacle and the temple, the Ark of the Covenant was kept in the innermost sanctum (the Holy of Holiness, קודש הקודשים) (Exodus 26:34; 1 Kings 8:8) that only the High Priest entered once a year, and it was considered so holy that it was forbidden to touch and to see it. Nachmanides associated this prohibition with the prohibition to see God himself (Numbers 4:15, 20; see Ibn Ezra and Nachmanides *ad locum*). Even touching the Ark with the intention of preventing it from falling aroused the anger of God, who killed thereupon the person involved (2 Samuel 6:6–8).

37. There are of course many more such voices against the magical interpretation of ritual practices. Consider also the following story. R' Yochanan Ben-Zakkai is asked about the ritual purification after contact with the dead by means of being sprinkled by the ashes of a red heifer mixed with water. He answers, "Do me a favor! The dead does not render impure, nor the water

pure, but it is the discretion of the king of all kings" (*Midrash Tanchumah,* "Chukat," 8:8; *Bamidbar rabbah* 19:8). However, if the ceremony and all its details remain unchanging in history, then a person educated in this tradition cannot know whether the purported success of a ceremony depends on the intention of the practitioners or on the actions performed, hence whether it is a prayer or a magical act.

38. *Bi'ur* on Exodus 32:4.

39. The King James translation omits the definite article found in the original.

40. Exodus 28:30:

וְנָתַתָּ אֶל-חֹשֶׁן הַמִּשְׁפָּט אֶת-הָאוּרִים וְאֶת-הַתֻּמִּים וְהָיוּ עַל-לֵב אַהֲרֹן בְּבֹאוֹ לִפְנֵי יְהוָה וְנָשָׂא אַהֲרֹן אֶת-מִשְׁפַּט בְּנֵי-יִשְׂרָאֵל עַל-לִבּוֹ לִפְנֵי יְהוָה תָּמִיד."

(ל) "את האורים ואת התמים, לא פירש לנו הכתוב מה הם, אף לא צוה על עשייתן, כאשר צוה בשאר כלים, כי אם הזכירם עתה בפעם הראשונה בה"א הידיעה, את האורים ואת התמים, וכן במעשה לא נזכר אומן כי אם משה לבדו שאמר ויתן אל החשן את האורים ואת התמים, ויראה מזה שלא היו מעשה אומן חרש ולא הי' לבעלי המלאכה בהם מעשה, ולא לקהל ישראל בהם נדבה כלל, אבל הם סוד מסור מפי הגבורה למשה, והוא כתבו בקדושה, והם מעשה שמים, לכך יזכירם סתם ובה"א הידיעה, כמו וישכן מקדם לגן עדן את הכרבים (בראשית ג' כ"ד), והנה צוה השם את משה שיניח בין כפלי החשן את כתב האורים והתמים, ונקרא כך על שם שעל ידו הוא מאיר את דבריו ומתמם את דבריו, וכן נקרא משפט על שם אותו הכתב, שנאמר ושאל לו במשפט האורים (במדבר כ"ז, כ"א), לפי שעל ידו הוא מברר ומאמת את דבריו, כמ"ש למעל' בשם רש"י ז"ל (מדברי הרמב"ן ז"ל בבאור דברי רש"י): את משפט בני ישראל, הם האורים והתמים, דבר שהם נשפטים ונוכחים על ידו, אם לעשות דבר אם לא (רש"י)."

41. See, e.g., Maimonides, *Mishneh Torah,* Book of Love, Laws of Phylacteries, Mezuzah, and Torah Scroll, 4,2.

42. Reinhold, *Die Hebräischen Mysterien oder die älteste religiöse Freymaurerey* (1788). On the Urim and Thummim, see chapter 6, "Sechster Abschnitt. Von den Geheimnissen des Urims und Thummims," 102–14.

43. In the tefillin the following text is enclosed: Exodus 13:9 "And it shall be for a sign unto thee upon thine hand, and for a memorial between thine eyes, that the LORD's law may be in thy mouth: for with a strong hand hath the LORD brought thee out of Egypt." In the mezuzah (and also the tefillin) Deuteronomy 6:4–9 is included: "And thou shalt bind them for a sign (אות) upon thine hand, and they shall be as frontlets between thine eyes. 9: And thou shalt write them upon the posts of thy house, and on thy gates"—that is, install mezuzah. The Deuteronomy text (6:1–11) speaks of the land of Israel that God gives his people; verse 12 (not contained in the mezuzah and the tefillin) explicitly mentions the Exodus from Egypt.

Chapter 6. The "Ceremonial Law" of Judaism: Transitory Hieroglyphics

1. Mendelssohn's clear-cut distinction between "doctrinal opinions" and "commandments" may be contested. Mendelssohn claimed that the voice on Sinai did not proclaim, "I am the Eternal, your God, the necessary, independent being, omnipotent and omniscient, that recompenses men in future life according to their deeds" (*Jerusalem*, 97). This is certainly true. However, what about the verse Deuteronomy 6:4? "Hear, O Israel: The LORD our God is one LORD." Mendelssohn translates: "Höre Israel! Der Ewige unser Gott ist ein einiges, ewiges Wesen." This is certainly an assertion on God and an eternal truth, and yet it is considered a commandment. Indeed, *Sefer ha-Chinukh* counts it among the 613 commandments; see *Sefer ha-Chinukh*, Commandments 417–18; and Maimonides included it as his second of the thirteen principles.

2. Nicholas of Cusa, *De Pace Fidei*, chap. 1.

3. Cf. *Kuzari*, II, 24. See also *Jerusalem*, 40.

4. See "An die Freunde Lessings," *JubA* 3.2, 197.

5. For Spencer's understanding of the rite as representing arcane knowledge, see Assmann, *Moses the Egyptian*, 78–79.

6. Without reference to Mendelssohn and with a much less elaborated philosophy, an influential orthodox philosopher of Judaism of our time, Yeshayahu Leibowitz, advanced what appears to be a further development of Mendelssohn's position. He, too, defines Judaism as consisting in the observation of the ceremonial law without regard to theology, and he, too, bases his stance on a kind of linguistic skepticism. Some of Leibowitz's formulations are so close to Mendelssohn's that it seems plausible that they were consciously or unconsciously influenced by him (Mendelssohn is not mentioned in these contexts and with little respect in others): "It is impossible for one person to communicate to another exactly what he feels: except for the formally defined terms of scientific discourse, the meanings of words and expressions of our common language vary from person to person in communication and in private thought. Hence there can be no collectivity of ideas or feelings. Collectivity is limited to the field of action—to cooperation in performance and achievement. Of course people will often jointly say or declare something. But it is only as acts that these declarations may be considered collectively performed. Hence if Judaism is a collective reality, not as the set of beliefs and the religious experience of individual Jews but as the religion of the Congregation of Israel, it can only consist in the common religious action—the halakhic praxis." See Leibowitz, *Judaism, Human Values, and the Jewish State*, especially "Religious Praxis: The Meaning of Halakhah" (1953), 3–29.

In fact, Leibowitz's position is very different from Mendelssohn's. Leibowitz vehemently rejects a justification of religious practice in view of human needs (whereas Mendelssohn does exactly this), and yet he does not adduce a justification for the practices on the basis of revelation either. Leibowitz presents without further ado or justification the very performance of the ritual as the proper way of accepting "the yoke of His kingdom" resulting from a decision that cannot be further justified. Not surprisingly, the result is paradox, and it has resisted to date attempts at explication.

7. Wittgenstein appeals to the "mirroring" quality of hieroglyphics in order to illustrate his claim that a sentence is a mirror of reality. See *Tractatus Logico-Philosophicus*, 4.016, 4.02, 4.021.

8. Bacon, *The Advancement of Learning*, bk. 2, chap. 16, 3, in *The Advancement of Learning and New Atlantis*, 131.

9. Circumcision is of course an exception. It is an act of the ceremonial law that leaves a permanent sign (although not an object but rather its absence) in the world. And yet, although circumcision or foreskins are ascribed magical powers in the Bible (see Exodus 4:24–26) and in some folklore until today, I do not believe that circumcision can serve as a counterexample to Mendelssohn's principle. An idolatry of the missing foreskins is not likely to develop.

10. Israel Zamosc, *Otzar Nechmad* (Hebr.), 128 on *Kuzari*, I, 97, 128; Cf. Mendelssohn's commentary on Exodus 32:1; my emphasis.

11. See Mendelssohn's commentary on Genesis 2:4; and Exodus 3:13–15; 6:2.

12. "Das Kalb, welches sie gemacht hatten, nahm er, kaliznierte es im Feuer, zerrieb es bis es ganz fein ward, streuete den Staub auf das Wasser, und ließ die Kinder Jisrael davon trinken." I elaborated this point in my "Enlightenment in Gold."

13. Whereas in *Jerusalem* Mendelssohn does not introduce this distinction, he discusses the reason for commandments that are not "signs" in his commentary on the Bible, for example, the prohibition against cooking a kid in the milk of its mother (Exodus 23:19). He criticizes there the attempts to adduce rational reasons for this prohibition that are "but very subtle surmises based on nothing and not acceptable to the heart." Once we accepted the yoke of God's kingdom, says Mendelssohn, we are bound to do his will, and the benefit of the commandments lies in performing them rather than in knowing their reason.

In *Ritualgesetze der Juden* (1778) (*JubA* 7, 109–251) Mendelssohn deals under this title with heirship, tutelage, testament and property of spouses, and so on.

14. Mendelssohn's letter to H. Homberg, September 22, 1783; *JubA* 13, 134.

15. "All laws refer to, or are based upon eternal truths of reason, or remind us of them, and rouse us to ponder them. Hence, our rabbis rightly say: the laws and doctrines are related to each other, like body and soul" (*Jerusalem,* 99). Mendelssohn uses the simile of body and soul also in reference to words in the introduction to his commentary on *Millot ha-Higayyon* of Maimonides. An expression and thought, he says there, relate to each other as "body and soul . . . thus that if the soul separates from the body, the body will remain a mute stone; and the soul too, if not dressed in a body, will disappear and be invisible to the eye of the flesh" (*Bi'ur Millot ha-Higayyon* (Hebr.), *JubA* 14, 25; German translation, *JubA* 2, 199).

Mendelssohn uses the simile again when speaking of the worst cases of idolatry and superstition, leading even to human sacrifices. These developed because "the images lost their value as signs" (*Jerusalem,* 115) and were taken to be divine themselves. Some reformers attempted to "restore to the images their old meaning or to impart to them a new one, and thereby to reinfuse, as it were, the soul into the dead body" (*Jerusalem,* 115–16). In short: body and soul stand for a sign and its meaning. Idolatry consists in ascribing value to the sign itself, not to its meaning alone.

Note that Mendelssohn does not claim originality for his conception but ascribes it to "our rabbis." Presumably Mendelssohn had in mind Ibn Pakuda's statement (*Duties of the Heart,* pt. 8, chap. 3), ‏"ודע, כי המלות תהיינה בלשון‏ ‏והעיון בלב, והמלות כגוף לתפלה והעיון כרוח."‏

But he could also have meant r' Yitzchak Luria, Ha'ari: ‏"המצוה יש לה גוף דהיינו המעשה, ויש לה נשמה דהיינו הכוונה שאדם מכוון לעשותו‏ ‏בתיקונה. אם יעשה אותה בלי כוונה הצריכה, יהיה כגוף בלא נשמה" (שולחן ערוך של האר"י‏ ‏(תמ"א), לא ע"ד).‏

Cited by Scholem, *Basic Chapters for Understanding Kabbalah and Its Symbols* (Hebr.), 120.

16. Concluding commentary on Exodus.

17. See also *The Guide of the Perplexed,* II, 31 (speaking of Sabbath): "You know from what I have said that opinions do not last unless they are accompanied by actions that strengthen them, make them generally known, and perpetuate them among the multitude" (Pines, 359).

18. This is also Mendelssohn's interpretation of Sabbath in his commentary on Exodus 20:8: "Remember the Sabbath day, to keep it holy," he says. "It was custom in Israel to go just before the Sabbath to the prophets to hear the words of God" [referring to 2 Kings 4:23]. In general, the purpose of the commandments is to remind us of God and thus give opportunity to religious discourse.

19. The instrumental purpose of the Pesach rites in raising curiosity and prompting a theological explanation is explicitly expressed in *Shulchan 'Arukh, Orach Chayim,* §473, 6–7. See also the following tale in the tenth chapter of tractate *Pessachim* in the Babylonian Talmud, 115b:

> R. Shimi bar Ashi said: "Unleavened bread, bitter herbs, and Charoset [a dish] must be dealt out to each man separately, but immediately before the Haggadah is read, the tables on which the food is served should not be removed at once, but only from the man who is about to recite. . . .
>
> For what purpose were the tables removed? Said the disciples of R. Janai: "In order to excite the curiosity of the children present, and induce them to inquire into the reasons." Abayi while still a child sat at a table in the presence of Rabba, and observed that the table of Rabba was removed. Said Abayi: "We have not yet eaten our meal, why are the tables being removed?" and Rabba replied: "By thy question we are absolved from commencing with the passage: 'Wherefore is this night distinguished from all nights?' and we can immediately proceed with the answer: 'Because we were slaves,' etc.

20. See Rousseau, *Emile, or On Education,* bk. 4. Mendelssohn remarks that print enabled reading in isolation instead of instruction in direct intercourse— making us isolated literati (*Jerusalem,* 103–4). Mendelssohn was hence also on safe Enlightenment ground as he stood squarely within Jewish tradition.

21. See *Ramban (Nachmanides) Commentary on the Torah,* Exodus, 171–73.

22. *Sefer Ha-Chinuch* (Hebr.), commandment 16. Cf. Mitzvah 95; Wengrov, *Sefer ha-Hinnuch,* vol. 1: *Genesis and Exodus,* 118–21.

23. This distinction is similar to that between the interpretation of precepts in the late rabbinic *cheftza/gavra,* or "object/person," respects. It also has parallels in the Catholic distinction between *ex opere operato* and *ex opere operantis.*

24. See Seidel, Baskin, and Snowman, "Circumcision," in *Encyclopedia Judaica,* vol. 4, 730–35.

25. On the translation of the Torah, see Mendelssohn to Avigdor Levi, May 25, 1779; *JubA* 19, 251–53; on the *Morgenstunden, JubA* 3.2, 3–4.

26. In the King James Version the verse reads: "Ye shall do my judgments, and keep mine ordinances, to walk therein: I am the LORD your God."

27. Forbidden in Leviticus 11:7.

28. A mixture of wool and linen, forbidden in Leviticus 19:19.

29. Water mingled with the ashes of the red heifer, as described in Numbers 19:5–9.

30. For a similar view concerning another commandment of purification with the ashes of a red heifer for which no reason could be adduced, see

Bamidbar Rabbah, 19:8. See also the despair of the author of *Sefer Ha-Chinuch* (Hebr.), commandment 397.

In general we could say that Mendelssohn relativizes the distinction between mitzvoth that have a rational explanation (מצוות שכליות), for example, those that accord with universal moral, and mitzvoth that are valid simply on the ground that they were ordained by God (מצוות שמעיות). Even if a reason for precepts of the first kind is found to be invalid, the precept itself remains valid because it was ordained by God.

31. *Midrash Tanchumah,* Exodus, Mishpatim, §7: תלמוד לומר: אני ה׳ אני ה׳" חקקתים ואין לך רשות להרהר בהן."

See also Babylonian Talmud, *Yoma,* 67b. Compare Mendelssohn's Counter-Reflections on Bonnet's *Palingenesie philosophique, JubA* 7, 97.

32. The view that only a public revelation similar to that in which the law has been given can annul it is also Joseph Albo's view. See *Sefer ha-'Ikkarim,* III, chap. 19.

33. The same tendency shows in Mendelssohn's translation of Deuteronomy 33:2–3. This passage was interpreted by Warren Zev Harvey. I quote his interpretation in full:

> In Deuteronomy 33:2, as understood by Mendelssohn, it is stated that God came from Sinai with a "religion of fire" (*esh dat; Feuersglutreligion*) in His right hand. The following verse begins with the words "af hobeb 'amim," which is often translated: "Yea, He loveth the peoples"; i.e., God loves all the peoples of the world. However, Mendelssohn renders these words quite differently: "*welche die Völker verpflichtet*" (i.e., the Feuersglutreligion obligates the people of Israel). The subject is not God but the "religion of fire"; the plural direct object ('*amim*) is taken to refer to Israel (as in Deuteronomy 33:18; cf. *Sifre,* Deuteronomy, 344; and Rashi and Ibn Ezra, *ad loc.*); and most significantly, the verb (*hobeb*) is understood as "obligates," not "loves." God came forth from Sinai with a Torah which *obligates* the people of Israel. In his comment on Deuteronomy 32:43, Mendelssohn himself refers to God as *malkenu mehobebenu* ("our king our obligates"). ("Mendelssohn's Heavenly Politics," 406–7)

Harvey convincingly argues that not only the translation but also the commentary *ad locum* is Mendelssohn's, 410–11 n. 5.

34. Arkush finds all this suspicious. Mendelssohn "was surely aware" that with the progress of integration, "it would undoubtedly become much harder for a Jew to remain a Jew" (Arkush, *Moses Mendelssohn and the Enlightenment,* 222). And referring to religious compromises Jews would have to

make if summoned to military service in their home countries, compromises that Mendelssohn approved, he writes, "In fact, with the least amount of foresight he could have seen that his entire program of Jewish integration, if achieved, would necessarily entail many such compromises in all areas of life. Perhaps Mendelssohn saw all of this quite clearly. Perhaps it did not really bother him. Perhaps he was, at bottom, much less orthodox in his approach to the law than he often strives to appear to be (274). In all this, I see nothing that cannot be said of all orthodox reformers.

35. This argument is not at all new. It was raised already by Greeks against the Christians. See Rokeah, "Early Christian-Jewish Polemics on Divine Election" (Hebr.), 73–75.

36. Julius Guttmann ("Mendelssohn's *Jerusalem* and Spinoza's *Theologico-Political Treatise*," 376–77) claims that Mendelssohn "cannot reconcile God's goodness with the notion that He is supposed to have revealed the verities required for man's felicity to the Jews alone." Guttmann's conclusion does not take into account that natural religion alone suffices for man's felicity. Moreover, Guttmann presupposes that Mendelssohn is committed to an "undifferentiated sameness of all people and ages." I argued above that this is wrong.

The same presupposition underlies Robert Erlewine's discussion. Erlewine maintains that Mendelssohn cannot reconcile the idea of Israel's election with "cultural egalitarianism" (Erlewine, *Monotheism and Tolerance*, 69–78: "Monotheism and the Discernible Other"; quotation on p. 78). Both Guttmann and Erlewine presuppose as self-evident that nondiscrimination implies "undifferentiated sameness" or "egalitarianism."

Max Wiener criticizes Mendelssohn from the opposite perspective, namely, for forsaking his universalism for the unique value of the Jewish people and the ceremonial law. The "spirit of religious law" is not the special way of Jews only to attain the highest religious ideal but the only way. The righteous of other nations may share in eternal felicity, but there are also different grades of eternal felicity. Moreover, "the particularism represented by the ritual is so intimately integrated into the universally valid highest ethical demand, that perfection is attainable only on the basis of the [Jewish] religious law" (Wiener, *Jüdische Religion im Zeitalter der Emanzipation*, 23).

Alexander Altmann criticized Mendelssohn in the same spirit as Wiener. In Mendelssohn, claims Altmann, the "mystery of Israel" (the special mission of the Jews) is "reduced to its most attenuated form" ("Mendelssohn's Concept of Judaism Reexamined," 247–48). Wiener and Altmann correctly characterize Mendelssohn's position. Whether one endorses their value judgment is a different question. Altmann's position is discussed briefly in the appendix.

37. Mendlessohn's letter to Herz Homberg, September 22, 1783, *JubA* 13, 132–34. See also the letter to Homberg of March 1, 1784, *JubA* 13, 177–81, esp. 179. "The limited nature of the integration achieved by Mendelssohn and his group is best illustrated by the fact that the Gentile mind did not expect these enlightened Jews to continue remaining Jews" (Katz, *Out of the Ghetto,* 51). Katz points to exceptional "semi neutral" places where Jews and Gentiles could meet on equal terms: Mendelssohn's circle, Freemasonry, and the literary salons (42–56).

38. *An die Freunde Lessings, JubA* 3.2, 197.

39. See *Gegenbetrachtungen über Bonnets Palingenesie, JubA* 7, 91–94.

40. "Therefore, I am rather of the opinion that Moses Mendelssohn saw in pure Mosaism an institution which can so to say serve as Deism's last entrenchment." Heine, *Zur Geschichte der Religion und Philosophie in Deutschland,* in *Werke und Briefe,* vol. 5, 250.

This, I believe, is correct as far as the cognitive content of religion is concerned, but it pays no attention to the life of a religious community.

Chapter 7. Idolatry in Contemporary Judaism

1. In *Jerusalem* Mendelssohn once paradoxically mentions the mezuzah (not by name) in support of the purely oral nature of Jewish lore. In praise of the "living instruction from man to man" in the Jewish community Mendelssohn says, "In everything a youth saw being done . . . on all gates and on all doorposts . . . he found occasion for inquiring and reflecting, occasion to follow an older and wiser man" (119). The expression "on all gates and on all doorposts" is taken from the verse "And thou shalt write them [these words, which I command thee this day] upon the posts of thy house, and on thy gates" (Deuteronomy 6:9; 6) that is the prooftext for the precept of mezuzah. Mendelssohn blatantly passes over in silence the fact that the mezuzah is a material object, not a floating text. This is striking because the ascription of magical powers to the mezuzah is a permanent topic in Jewish tradition.

2. "Our Rabbis taught: 'Accessories of religious observances [when disused] are to be thrown away; accessories of holiness are to be stored away. The following are accessories of religious observances: a Sukkah, a Lulab, a Shofar, fringes. The following are accessories of holiness: large sacks for keeping scrolls of the Scripture in, Tefillin, and Mezuzot, a mantle for a *Sefer Torah* and a Tefillin bag and Tefillin straps'" (Babylonian Talmud, *Megillah,* 26b). See also *Shulchan 'Arukh,* Orach Hayyim, §154; and Yoreh Dea, §282.

3. See Sabar, "Torah and Magic: The Torah Scroll and Its Appurtenances as Magical Objects in Traditional Jewish Culture," 135–70. See Spinoza's critique in *Tractatus Theologico-Politicus*, chap. 12 in *Spinoza Opera*, vol. 3, 158–60.

4. Maimon, *The Autobiography of Solomon Maimon*, 261–62. The alleged fear of Satan refers presumably to the Babylonian Talmud, *Rosh Hashana*, 16b.

5. Cohen, *Religion der Vernunft*, 65–66; Kaplan, 57.

6. *Mishneh Torah*, Book of Knowledge, Laws Concerning Idolatry and the Ordinances of the Heathens, chap. 11, 12; and Kellner's comprehensive account on *Mishneh Torah*, Book of Love, Laws of Phylacteries, 5, 4.

7. *Kuzari*, I, 97; and Zamosc, *Otzar Nechmad, ad locum.*

8. John Spencer believed that the cherubim are the Egyptian heritage of the Hebrews. See Assmann, *Moses the Egyptian*, 73–74.

9. Maimon's *Lebensgeschichte*, GW 1, 289–93; Murray, 207–9.

10. Of course, I do not intend to give even a sketch of the meaning of language in religion. I merely wish to make the point that the kabbalistic notion of language is not an aberration from the main path of Judaism (and religion in general), although it emphasizes some aspects much more than the mainstream.

The following is mainly based on van der Leeuw, *Religion in Essence*, pt. 3, §58–64; and Heiler, *Erscheinungsformen und Wesen der Religion*, chap. 7, 266–339, and chap. 8, 339–64. For a useful short overview, see Wheelock, "Language: Sacred Language," in *The Encyclopedia of Religion*, vol. 8, 439–46.

11. See Scholem, "The Name of God and the Linguistic Theory of the Kabbala," pt. 1, *Diogenes* 79 (1972): 59–81; pt. 2, *Diogenes* 80 (1972): 194; and van der Leeuw, *Religion in Essence*, 457–58.

12. Enlightened commentators and translators had to navigate their way between the wording of the text and their views. Ibn Ezra (Long Commentary on Exodus 3:13 explicitly warns that "the change of name does not change the signified" and opposes word magic. In contrast, the Kabbalist Joseph ben Abraham Gikatilla maintains in the first part of his *Ginat Egoz* (1274), in which the meaning of the different names of God is discussed, that only the tetragammaton represents God's essence and is his name (שם). Other names are merely indications (כינוי). Maimonides (*Guide of the Perplexed*, I, 61) maintains that the uniqueness of the tetragammaton lies in its exclusive reference. God's other names may also refer to created beings. He also suggests that the name perhaps indicates "necessary existence." Mendelssohn famously translates the tetragammaton with *"der Ewige* or *das ewige Wesen."*

From this name, he suggests, necessary existence and permanent providence can be derived (see Mendelssohn on Exodus 3:13–15).

13. "Ich erschien dem Awraham, Jitzhak und Jakob als Gott der allmächtige; aber mit meinem Wesen, welches unendlich und allgegenwärtig heißt, bin ich von ihnen nicht erkannt worden."

14. See also Maimonides, *Mishneh Torah*, Book of Knowledge, Laws of Repentence, chap. 2, 4; and the discussion in Kadari, *Thought and Halakhah in Maimonides' Laws of Repentance* (Hebr.), 59.

15. Wygotsky, *Denken und Sprechen* (1934), 308.

16. For the controversies over translations of the Qur'an, see Meir Bar-Asher, "We have made it an Arabic Qur'an, so that you will understand it" (Hebr.), forthcoming.

17. For a concise discussion of this aspect of the kabbalistic conception of the Hebrew language (relying on Moshe Idel), see Eco, *The Search for the Perfect Language,* chap. 2: "The Kabbalistic Pansemioticism," 25–33. On its revival in the context of astral magic, see chap. 6, "Kabbalism and Lullism in Modern Culture," 117–43. For an extensive survey, see Andreas Kilcher, *Die Sprachtheorie der Kabbala.* Kilcher discusses not only Hebrew Kabbalah but also its reception by non-Jews from early modernity to German romanticism.

18. See Idel, "Reification of Language in Jewish Mysticism," 42–79.

19. Shlomo Naeh argues that in the Mishna the Hebrew script was not ascribed special significance, whereas later, in talmudic times, the letters were considered meaningful in themselves and the Hebrew script holy. This, he observes, is part and parcel of the view that the text is not merely a means of preservation and dissemination of the holy revealed message but a sacred object and that its sanctity depends on its physical form. Naeh argues that this conception arose because in the rabbinic Beit Midrash the Holy Scriptures were the one and only written text. A written text and a holy text were co-extensional terms, and the various ideas concerning the holy nature of the letters were attempts to ground and explain this fact. The unique status of the Scriptures also explains the refusal to commit the rabbis' words to script, a privilege reserved for the Holy Scriptures. See Naeh, "On the Torah's Script in the Thought of the Sages (II): Transliterations and Crowns of Letters" (Hebr.), forthcoming. I am grateful to Shlomo Naeh for allowing me to read his papers in manuscript.

20. Scholem, *Major Trends in Jewish Mysticism,* 27. See Moshe Idel's enlightening essay, "The Function of Symbols in Gershom Scholem's Thought" (Hebr.), 43–72.

21. Rotenstreich. "Symbolism and the Divine Realm: Following Two Unhistorical Articles by Gershom Scholem" (Hebr.), 40.

22. Dan, "From the symbol to the Symbolized, towards an Understanding of Gershom Scholem's 'Ten Unhistorical Aphorisms on Kabbalah'" (Hebr.), 378.

23. See Scholem, "The Name of God and the Linguistic Theory of the Kabbala."

It is important to note that Kabbalah merely pushes this conception of language to its very extreme but does not invent it. The mystery of the name of God is of course present in the Bible (in different books to a greater or lesser degree) and also in the thought of the ancient sages. See on this Urbach, *The Sages: Their Concepts and Beliefs,* chap. 7. See also Ogden and Richards, *The Meaning of Meaning,* chap. 2, "The Power of Words," 24–47.

24. "In Kabbalah the reasons for the commandments are integrated in the general system in relation to two basic principles: a symbolic view according to which everything in this world and all human acts, especially religious acts, are a reflection of divine processes and particularly those of the divine emanation; and the notion of reciprocal influence between the upper and lower worlds, which are not separated from each other but affect each other in all matters. Thus it appears that the commandments both reflect a mystical reality and the relations between heavenly forces, and also themselves influence this heavenly reality." Altmann, Scholem, and Blidstein, "Commandments, Reasons for," in *Encyclopaedia Judaica,* 2nd ed., vol. 5, 85–90. The text quoted is identical to that in the *Encyclopedia Judaica,* 1st ed. (1972). See also Scholem, *Elements of the Kabbalah and Its Symbolism* (Hebr.), 113–52.

Joseph Dan suggests that from the theurgic interpretation of the Jewish rite it follows that these symbols may not be replaced by others, and thus symbolism leads to orthodoxy. See his "From the Symbol to the Symbolized: Towards an Understanding of Gershom Scholem's 'Ten Unhistorical Aphorisms on Kabbalah'" (Hebr.), 378.

25. See Elbogen, *Der jüdische Gottesdienst in seiner geschlichtlichen Entwicklung,* 396–97. An important example of the theurgic understanding of prayer is the short formula introduced before the actual blessing of some mitzvoth: "For the sake of the Unity of Him may He be Blessed and His divine spirit (*Shekhina*) [literally, "presence"]" (לשם ייחוד קודשא בריך הוא ושכינתיה). The formula was reintroduced into most prayer books and is said or not said according to persuasion.

26. The review appeared anonymously in issues 111 and 113 of *Annalen der Philosophie* (1795). Reprinted in Ehrensperger, "Salomon Maimon als Rezensent," 249–62. Maimon gives on another occasion a concise (and humorous) judgment of Kabbalah: "Aus der Kabbala, wie wir sie jetzt haben,

kann man so wenig etwas vernünftig Theoretisches, als etwas nützlich Praktisches lernen. Sie besteht in einem bloßen Spiele mit Zahlen und Buchstaben, worin die Kabbalisten große Geheimnisse suchen, und wodurch (gleich Gott, der sich, ihrem Vorgeben nach, bei Erschaffung der Welt eben dieses Mittels bedient haben soll) sie alles nach Belieben hervorzubringen im Stande sind. Ich glaube aber schwerlich, daß Gott selbst in der Qualität als bloßer Mathematiker oder Kabbalist das kleinste Strohhälmchen hätte hervorbringen können" (*GW* 3, 460–61). See also Maimon's discussion of Pythagoras (and comparison to practical Kabbalah) in *GW* 4, 402–5.

27. "Kabbalah is simply (to use the Pythagorean vocabulary) symbolic theology, where words and letters are code for things, and such things are themselves code for other things. This drew our attention to the fact that almost all Pythagoras' system is drived from the Kabbalists, and that similarly he brought to Greece the use of symbol as a means of communication." Reuchlin, *On the Art of the Kabbalah*, 241.

28. Mendelssohn to Nicolai. See Meyer, *Moses Mendelssohn, Bibliographie*, 113. Moshe Idel remarks that the term "orieantalische Philosophen," which Mendelssohn also uses here for Kabbalists, appears in the Latin subtitle of the kabbalistic work *Imrei Binah*, published by Satanov, an acquaintance of Mendelssohn's, in Berlin: "*Metaphisica cabbalistica, sive Philosophia orienetalis antiqua*" (Idel, "Perceptions of Kabbalah in the Second Half of the 18th Century," 66 n. 52). Associating the Orient with rich figurative and metaphorical language was commonplace at the time.

Idel dedicated a section of his "Perceptions of Kabbalah in the Second Half of the 18th Century" to a comparison of Mendelssohn's and Maimon's view of Kabbalah (62–68). He reaches the conclusion that they are very similar and that—since Maimon voiced these views already in his early manuscript *Hesheq Shelomo*—it was Maimon who influenced Mendelssohn (66–67). Idel does not discuss their common philosophical criticism of symbolism and Kabbalah elaborated here.

29. This allegory appears in the Babylonian Talmud, *Niddah*, 30b.

30. Mendelssohn to Nicolai. See Meyer, *Moses Mendelssohn, Bibliographie*, 113, quoted more extensively above.

31. See on this *GM* 4.

32. Whereas radical enlighteners criticize Kabbalah in order to dispose of it, more conservative modern religious thinkers are ambivalent. Samson Raphael Hirsch, the leader of German strict orthodoxy, values Kabbalah as that which could have "imbued practical Judaism with spirituality," had it not been interpreted as "a form of magical mechanism, a means of influencing or

resisting theosophic worlds and anti-worlds." See Hirsch, *Nineteen Letters,* letter 18, pp. 267–68; see the editorial notes pp. 295 (for letter 18) and 153–55 (for letter 10). I discuss Alexander Altmann's similarly ambivalent view in the appendix.

33. Usually *Jerusalem* is read as addressing the Gentiles mainly because it was written in German. Mendelssohn's explicit words here refute this assumption.

34. From this vantage point, this community of essence between the sign-vehicle and the signified is an essential component of myth and the basis of magic. See Cassirer, *Language and Myth,* esp. chap. 4, "Word Magic," 44–62. See also Ogden and Richards, *The Meaning of Meaning,* chap. 2, "The Power of Words," 24–47; see also Ogden's "Word Magic," 19–126.

35. Mendelssohn once said that Jewish ritual law depends at times on the precise expression used, "which is inseparable from the language and cannot be translated into another language with the required precision." Mendelssohn admits that he, too, is uncertain whether some words have precisely the same meaning, extension, and connotations as in Hebrew. A judgment according to the Jewish law should, therefore, be passed by a judge who knows Hebrew and has diligently studied the Talmud. Note, however, that Mendelssohn writes this in the introduction to his *Ritualgesetze der Juden,* a compendium intended to serve Gentile judges in trials involving Jews. It should have sufficed to rule according to Jewish law, at least to understand the ruling of a judge who is versed in Hebrew and Talmud. In other words, the reasons for a ruling must be communicable in German to a person who does not understand Hebrew and has no firsthand knowledge of the Talmud. Cognitive content can be translated and explained.

Edward Breuer observes in *The Limits of Enlightenment* that in his discussion of the four methods of exegesis (*Pardes*), Mendelssohn subordinated *remez* and *sod* to *derash,* thus reducing these four methods to "a binary question of *peshat* and *derash*" (186–87). Breuer also remarks that the "brevity with which he glossed over *remez* and *sod* certainly made evident his distance from medieval Kabbalah" (186). This can be easily assimilated to a binary classification of "sound reason" and "mysticism."

36. Ravitsky, "Maimonides and His Disciples on Linguistic Magic and 'the Madness of the Writers of Amulets'" (Hebr.). See the recent comprehensive study of Menachem Kellner, *Maimonides' Confrontation with Mysticism.*

37. Horwitz, "Mendelssohn und die Kabbalah," 17–32, wishes to attenuate Altmann's judgment in his introduction to *Jerusalem* (22) that "it is the mystical domain that Mendelssohn sought to banish from Judaism" (17), but

her discussion (24–28) does not disprove Altmann. Zev Harvey observes that in none of Mendelssohn's quotations from the *Zohar* "does he refer to mythical or irrational elements," and "in some place the less relevant parts or the blatantly mythical parts are judiciously skipped." See Harvey, "Why Philosophers Quote Kabbalah: The Cases of Mendelssohn and Rosenzweig," 121. Harvey concludes that Mendelssohn quoted kabbalistic texts "when he thought they could support or enrich his own arguments" (125). It should, however, be kept in mind that this is not merely a tactic. Mendelssohn and others believed that Kabbalah contained true knowledge couched in figurative language. With proper knowledge and caution from the idolatrous danger lurking in its lacking distinction between signs and the signified, there was good reason to believe that it may truly enrich our knowledge.

38. The case in point is the sanctification of Sabbath. This is commanded in Exodus 31:12–18; 35:1–3; etc. In Numbers 15:32–36 we read of a perpetrator who was put to death on God's command.

39. Maimon agrees on both points with Cranz. He calls the Mosaic constitution "theocracy" and believes that it ended with the destruction of the Jewish state (*GW* 1, 159; Murray, 117).

40. In his preface to Menasseh ben Israel (*JubA* 8, 21), and concerning the church, Mendelssohn is even more reserved: "People seem to have settled to regard the external form of service, the *church,* as a moral person" ("*. . . scheinen sich geeinigt zu haben . . . als eine moralische Person zu betrachten*").

41. Altmann (*Moses Mendelssohn: A Biographical Study,* 529, 844 n. 104) suggests that "from afar" means that "the state should not concern itself with theological minutiae, but should pay attention to broad principles only." An alternative reading is that the state should not directly interfere with religious matters but favor state-supporting religious institutions. These readings do not exclude each other.

42. Heinrich Heine, *Concerning the History of Religion and Philosophy in Germany,* 193.

43. See Mendelssohn's letter of May 25, 1779 (י״י סיון תקל״ט) to Avigdor Levi, *JubA* 19, 251–53. For Landau's initial reaction to Mendelssohn's project, see *Samet,* "*Moshe Mendelssohn,* Naphtali Herz *Weisel,* and the Rabbis of Their Age," 74–78. For the entire affair, see Feiner, *The Enlightenement Revolution* (Hebr.), 164–87.

44. The expression is taken from Esther 9:30.

45. Chap. 4 (not paginated). Note that Weisel refers there to Emperor Joseph II's decrees as "divrey shalom ve-emet." He thus identifies his brochure

with the emperor's project—and gives both the tint of enthusiasm characteristic of the original missive of Mordechai and Esther in the Bible. The content
of the original message was to celebrate "the days wherein the Jews rested
from their enemies, and the month which was turned unto them from sorrow
to joy, and from mourning into a good day: that they should make them days
of feasting and joy, and of sending portions one to another, and gifts to the
poor" (Esther 9:30). Later Weisel also adds: "and the heart of every wise man
will rejoice when he hears of this directive" (chap. 8).

46. "ואלמלא הי׳ לנו חירות במדינה זו להחרים למי שהוא ראוי להחרימו הייתי
מחרימו אלא מחמת חקי המדינה שלא להחרים מבלי הרשות מאפלאציאן טיטול יר״ה חדלתי
מזה אמנם עכ״פ פרסמתי כבר שמו לרעה ומעתה לא אקוה שמי שהוא מעדת ישראל ויהי׳ לו
ידיעה מזה שיתן לינת לילה או יארחהו בביתו להרשע הרץ ויזל . . . וגם ח״ו לקנות שום חיבור
מהמחבר . . .".

Heschel, "The Opinions of the Age's Greatest Sages in Their Struggle
against the Maskil Naphtali Herz *Weisel (may his name rot)*" (Hebr.), pt. 1,
162–65, 166.

47. Heschel, "The Opinions of the Age's Greatest Sages in Their Struggle
against the Maskil Naphtali Herz *Weisel (may his name rot)*" (Hebr.), pt. 2,
122, 125, 127.

48. *Leviticus Rabbah*, 1, 15: הימנו טובה נבלה דעת בו שאין ת״ח כל :15.

49. Quoted from Heschel, "The Opinions of the Age's Greatest Sages in
Their Struggle against the Maskil Naphtali Herz *Weisel (may his name rot)*"
(Hebr.), pt. 1, 162–65, 166. Also r' David Tewel of Leszno was enraged by this
sentence. See his Passover sermon in "The Opinions of the Age's Greatest
Sages in Their Struggle Against the Maskil Naphtali Herz *Weisel (may his
name rot)*" (Hebr.), pt. 2, 125.

50. "האלקים אנה לידי דברי האגרת, מהמשורר שירי תפארת, הוא המליץ אחד מני
אלף, המהולל ונודע לרבים מימי נעוריו, עם חבוריו וביאוריו, אשר כתב וחתם בכתב ידו
לאחד מתושבי עיר פראג, ואמרתי דבריו ראוים להביאם בדפוס לחלקם בישראל, אוהבי אמת
יראו וישמחו וישרים יעלוזו, וזה לשונו אות באות."

The letter is dated September 3, 1792 (אלול תקנ״ב 'טי). In spite of Flekles's words,
a recent reprint of his book (*Ahavat David* [Hebr.], Brooklyn, NY: Goldenberg
Brothers, 1992), omitted Weisel's letter. The articles of Heschel cited above testify to the radicalization of ultraorthodox reactions to the Enlightenment. See
also the daily newspaper *Yated Ne'eman* of August 16, 2002, where Heschel's
articles are extensively quoted to explain the ultraorthodox (*Charedi*) prohibition against selling reprints of Weisel's books, which were prepared by (strictly
observant) circles.

51. Van der Leeuw, *Religion in Essence and Manifestation*, 448.

52. Consider Hume's scorn for this Catholic doctrine:

A famous general, at that time in the Muscovite service, having come to Paris for the recovery of his wounds, brought along with him a young Turk, whom he had taken prisoner. Some of the doctors of the Sorbonne (who are altogether as positive as the dervishes of Constantinople) thinking it a pity, that the poor Turk should be damned for want of instruction, solicited Mustapha very hard to turn Christian, and promised him, for his encouragement, plenty of good wine in this world, and paradise in the next. These allurements were too powerful to be resisted; and therefore, having been well instructed and catechized, he at last agreed to receive the sacraments of baptism and the Lord's supper. The priest, however, to make every thing sure and solid, still continued his instructions, and began the next day with the usual question, How many Gods are there? None at all, replies Benedict; for that was his new name. How! None at all! cries the priest. To be sure, said the honest proselyte. You have told me all along that there is but one God: And yesterday I ate him. (Hume, *The Natural History of Religion*, chap. 12 in *Principal Writings on Religion*, 167–68)

53. Heinrich Heine, *Works of Prose*, 110–13. Translation slightly altered.

54. This, of course, is the same attitude expressed by Maimon, who refused to acknowledge the sanctity of the shofar and related only to its natural properties, "a ram's horn."

Chapter 8. Philosophy of Enlightened Judaism

1. See, e.g., *The Guide of the Perplexed*, I, 21, 27, 28, 36, 48, and more.

2. Letter to Herz Homberg, September 22, 1783. In *Jerusalem* Mendelssohn says that the Jews were chosen to be a priestly nation, "a nation which, through its establishment and constitution, through its laws, actions, vicissitudes, and changes was continually to call attention to sound and unadulterated ideas of God and his attributes" (*Jerusalem*, 118).

3. Mendelssohn's note to the commentary on Numbers 15: 37(8)–41.

4. Kellner, *Maimonides' Confrontation with Mysticism*, 286. In fact, I believe that Kellner's interpretation goes too far in a "social-constructivist" direction and uproots Maimonides' religion. He suggests that it is best captured by Durkheim's understanding of religion as opposed to Rudolf Otto's, which is allegedly akin to the idolatrous view that Maimonides and Kellner reject (39–40). Durkheim's dictum, "I see in the Divinity only society transfigured and sym-

bolically expressed," suffices to see that this is a sociological reductive explanation of religion that undermines (although does not refute) its truth (Durkheim, "The Determination of the Moral Fact" [1906], 52). This cannot serve as an adequate philosophical explication of the religious thought of Maimonides. But neither are Kellner's own categories (e.g., 31–32, 36–37) satisfactory. The following alternative is presented: "Does Halakhah reflect an antecedently existing ontological reality, or does it constitute a social, institutional reality?" (36). A full-fledged Catholic sacrament is not captured by these distinctions: the bread and wine are not "antecedently" sacred, that is, before the ceremony, nor is their holiness after sanctification merely institutional; rather it is real. Also, Mount Sinai was not holy before revelation or after but only during revelation itself; and yet it was so holy that all living beings touching it would or should have been killed.

5. See *The Philosophy of Symbolic Forms,* vol. 2: *Mythical Thought,* 252, 238; and see 36 ff.

6. *The Philosophy of Symbolic Forms,* vol. 2: *Mythical Thought,* 237 f.; see vol. 1, 186 ff. See *Language and Myth,* chap. 6, "The Power of Metaphor," 83–99.

7. Cassirer, *Language and Myth,* 58. See also 94 n. 89: "for mythic and magical thought there is no such thing as a mere picture, since every image embodies the 'nature' of its object, i.e., its 'soul' or 'daemon.'"

8. *The Philosophy of Symbolic Forms,* vol. 2, 239.

9. *The Philosophy of Symbolic Forms,* vol. 2, 252. The last section of this volume is titled "The Dialectics of Mythical Consciousness."

10. "Der Begriff der symbolischen Form im Aufbau der Geisteswissenschaften" (1921–22), in *Wesen und Wirkung des Symbolbegriffs,* 188–89.

11. The draft appeared under the title "*Jerusalem* (Entwurf und Notizen)," JubA 8, 93–98, and was translated and added by Altmann and Arkush to their edition of *Jerusalem.* This was also Maimon's opinion. See *Giv'at ha-Moreh,* 25. See also my "'Die Philosophischen Systeme der Theologie,' nach Salomon Maimon," 87–106.

12. Response to the letter of the hereditary prince of Braunschweig-Wolfenbüttel from January 2, 1770. JubA 7, 301. Robert Erlewine, *Monotheism and Tolerance,* 43–68: "Mendelssohn and the Repudiation of Divine Tyranny" discusses the incompatibility of the dogmas of the original sin and the self-sacrifice of God with Mendelssohn's notion of man and the perfection of God.

13. Mendelssohn's letter to Lavater, January 15, 1771; JubA 3, 263; translation according to Altmann, *Moses Mendelssohn: A Biographical Study,* 262. Mendelssohn's notes on Lavater, March 9, 1770, JubA 7:59; translation (slightly changed) according to Altmann, *Moses Mendelssohn: A Biographical Study,* 204.

14. Moyaert, "The Sense of Symbols as the Core of Religion: A Philosophical Approach to a Theological Debate," 59, 61.

15. Paul Moyaert, "In Defense of Praying with Images," 607. I am grateful to Paul Moyaert for some clarification of his view in letters.

Michael Polanyi speaks of our "surrender" to a symbol and being "carried away" with it to explain reverence to symbols, e.g., to a national flag (Polanyi and Prosch, *Meaning*, chap. 4, "From Perception to Metaphor," 66–81.

16. Van der Leeuw, *Einführung in die Phänomenologie der Religion*, 189.

17. "Über die beste Staatsverfassung" (1785), *JubA* VI.1, 145–48; my emphasis.

18. See Altmann, *Moses Mendelssohn: A Biographical Study*, 169–73, 177.

19. Lessing, "A Rejoinder" (1778), in Philosophical and Theological Writings, 98.

20. See Krochmalnik, "Das Zeremoniell als Zeichensprache," esp. 255–59. Krochmalnik refers to Christian Wolff, *Philosophia practica universalis*, vol. 2, §442–512.

21. Christian Wolff, *Vernünftige Gedancken von der Menschen Thun und Lassen*, in *Gesammelte Werke*, pt. 1, vol. 4, §176.

22. Rudolf Otto conceived the relation between on the one hand human religious experience and its expression and on the other its "wholly other" referent as a "schematization" of the latter through the former. Now, a scheme—the concept is borrowed from Kant (see *CpR* B 176 ff.; B742, B746)—is a sensuous representation of what in itself is nonsensuous. The schema shares at least one characteristic property with its referent but not its essence, in that it is distinct both from a symbol and from an arbitrary sign. See Otto, *The Idea of the Holy*, chap. 7, "Analogies and Associated Feelings," 41–49. Otto explicitly remarks that the connection between the holy and the sublime is "intimate" (*innige Verbindng*) and not merely by the emotions they elicit. Kant himself maintains that religious symbols represent ideas of reason by analogy but do not present as intuitions present concepts of the understanding (see *Critique of the Power of Judgment*, §59, 225–27; *AA* 5, 351–53). Kant displays here his Protestant heritage.

23. Morgenstunden, JubA 3.2, 66. See Gottlieb, *Faith and Freedom*, 44.

24. *Über die Hauptgrundsätze der schönen Künste und Wissenschaften* (1757), *JubA* 1, 428.

25. "His independence, infinity, immensity, his supremely perfect will, unbounded intellect, and unlimited power, his wisdom, providence, justice, holiness, and so forth are grounded in one another in such a way that, without the others, each of these properties would be contradictory" (*JubA* 2, 297–98; Dahlstrom, 279).

26. *An die Freunde Lessings, JubA* 3.2, 198.

27. See Köhler, *Gestalt Psychology.*

28. *JubA* 1, 85, 280–81.

29. "Only symbolic knowledge, as in arithmetic and algebra, leaves the mind unmoved; it can produce neither love nor hate, neither fear nor sympathy, neither even pleasure nor displeasure. . . . But how is it possible that we can produce the greatest effects of this kind through words? Sentiments cannot deceive. Where a sentiment occurs, we can with the greatest certainty infer that there is intuitive, immediate knowledge (*anschauende Erkenntnis*)" (*JubA* 3.2, 42). Translation adopted from Hlobil, "Two Concepts of Language and Poetry: Edmund Burke and Moses Mendelssohn," 456. See the discussion on pp. 454–56.

30. Mendelssohn's introduction to his commentary on Exodus 15:1–19, first three paragraphs.

31. "Letters on Art," first letter; *JubA* 2, 168–69. On the role of music in Mendelssohn's conception of Judaism, see the informative paper by Daniel Krochmalnik, "Die Psalmen in Moses Mendelssohns Utopie des Judentums," 235–67.

32. Hermann Cohen: "Es ist schon auffällig, daß das Judentum seine vorzüglichen Quellendokumente in einer Literatur darstellt, während der Polytheismus sie vorzüglich in Denkmälern der Plastik besitzt. Die Plastik macht sich zur Analogie der Natur. Die Poesie dagegen, als die Ursprache der Literatur, macht den geistigen Gedanken auch durch die Form innerlicher, als er durch die bildende Kunst werden/kann" (*Religion der Vernunft*, 43–44; Kaplan, 37). Kenneth Seeskin ("Herrman Cohen on Idol Worship," 107–16, 112) asks: "Is a verbal description not also a representation?" Halbertal and Margalit believe that language is less conducive to idolatry because it does not determine the details, whereas a picture is fully determined. Mendelssohn's objection to all kinds of permanent objects captures of course all these possibilities but also offers an important insight into the inception of idolatry: a religious ceremony can sanctify any kind of object serving in it.

33. *On the Sublime and Naive in the Fine Sciences*, 202; *JubA* 1, 465; my emphasis. Translating *"Begriff"* with "idea" in this context is based on Mendelssohn's translation of Burke's "idea" with *"Begriff."* See *JubA* 3.1, 251. The German *"Begriff"* was also used to translate the Latin "idea." See on this Hlobil, "Two Concepts of Language and Poetry: Edmund Burke and Moses Mendelssohn," 455–56.

34. Edwyn Bevan proposes a similar conception: "Let us take the conception of God as a loving Father. Obviously such an idea of God is symbolic. . . . [T]he Theist or Christian . . . says: 'Act as if there were God who is a

loving Father, and you will, in so doing, be making the right response to that which God really is. God is really of such a character that, if any of us could know Him as He is (which we cannot do) and then had to describe in human language to men upon earth what he saw, he would have to say: 'What I see is undescribable, but if you think of God as a loving Father, I cannot put the Reality to you in a better way than that: that is the nearest you can get'" (*Symbolism and Belief*, 335–36).

35. Rudolph Otto named this the "creature feeling." *The Idea of the Holy*, chap. 3, 8–11.

36. Mendelssohn to Sophie Becker, December 27, 1785, *JubA* 18, 334.

37. *The Guide of the Perplexed*, III, 51; Pines, 619, 624. See on this my "The Philosophical Mysticism of Maimonides and Maimon." Mysticism is the reverse and complementary side of Maimonides' and Maimon's positions. Both of them insist that the essence of man is the intellect, on account of which man is said to have been created in the "image" of God. Adequate apprehension is conceived by both as unity of the understanding with its object achieved in knowledge. Complete concentration on the divine and pure intellectual apprehension of him are tantamount to conjunction with him. Disdain of ordinary religious cult therefore has two aspects: critique of all-too-human (idolatrous) ceremonies and a positive alternative that transcends human limitation.

38. In Mendelssohn, too, we find the notion that knowledge—but not exclusively knowledge—may have a function similar to religious service. Already in his early *On Evidence in Metaphysical Sciences* he writes that the knowledge of God "is supposed to be not only convincing, but edifying, moving the mind and spurring conduct conforming with it" *JubA* 2, 311; Dahlstrom 291; translation modified).

39. See *Maimoniana*, 87–88.

40. See *Lebensgeschichte*, *GW* 1, 491–92; Murray, 234–35.

41. See, e.g., "man kann so wenig einen rothen Körper als eine süße Linie denken," *Versuch über die Transcendentalphilosophie*, 93. On the qualification of synthetic geometry as only subjectively necessary because it depends on axioms and postulates that are imposed on us by intuition without insight of the understanding, see my *Definition and Construction: Salomon Maimon's Philosophy of Geometry*.

42. For a detailed elaboration of Maimon's philosophical mysticism, see my "The Philosophical Mysticism of Maimonides and Maimon," 113–52.

43. *GW* 1, 186–88; Murray, 135–37. See *Shulchan Arukh*, Orach Chayim, §607.6. Concerning the vows, see also the traditional *Hattarat Nedarim* (the release of vows) and *Kol Nidrei* (all vows) prayers recited respectively in preparation for and at the beginning of the Day of Atonement.

44. See Maimonides, *The Guide of the Perplexed*, I, 18, 54; and III, 51–52.

45. Anthropomorphism hence contradicts God's perfection. In fact, also "the existence of imperfect, limited deities, which relate to particular nations, can and must of course be denied, since their concepts are self-contradictory" (GW 3, 49). This excludes the Jewish God. The concept of a God as the most perfect being is not contradictory because all perfections are positive predications that cannot contradict each other; however, they may very well oppose each other in the object (as different colors exclude each other and not by logical contradiction) and therefore the concept will not be real. See GW 3, 49–51; and GW 1, 480–81. "Setting up some limited model for imitation instead of the ideal of the most perfect being is idolatry" ("Abgötterei," *Philosophisches Wörterbuch, GW* 3, 30).

46. "Der Weise genießt schon im diesseitigen Leben die Erhaltung der Seele und die Einheit mit Gott" (*GW* 7, 277). Interestingly, Mendelssohn entertains an idea that seems similar but is the exact opposite. With him the ideal of life and afterlife is not merely intellectual but involves senses and joy. See his *Sendschreiben an den Herrn Magister Lessing in Leipzig und Nachschrift,* JubA 2, 102:

> Ich glaube eine Menge trübsinniger Enthusiasten hat den Grund zu dieser wunderbaren Denkungsart gelegt. Sie haben sich beflissen, diese Welt mit verhaßten Farben abzuschildern. Sie haben sie einen Kerker, ein Jammerthal genannt, um durch deren Verdunkelung den Glantz einer herrlichen Zukunft desto mehr in unsern Augen zu erheben. Allein worin wird meine Glückseelgkeit in jenem Leben bestehen? In Erkenntnis der Wahrheit, in der Beschauung der göttlichen Werke, in der Freude an ihrer Vortrefflichkeit? Wohlan! So soll . . . meine Zukunft schon in diesem Leben anfangen. Der Vorgeschmack, den ich hienieden davon haben kann, macht mir die Welt zu einem Paradiese.

47. This homiletic exegesis, in Maimon's later judgment, "wrenched passages of the Holy Scriptures from their context," "which fitted best the principle of self-annihilation before God" (*GW* 1, 229; Murray, 166). On the "astounding" "exceeding precision and faithfulness" of Maimon's rendering of this exegesis some fifteen years after he had heard it and before it ever appeared in print, see Weiss, "On One Homily of the Maggid of Mesritsh" (Hebr.), 97; and "On a Chassidic Doctrine of the Maggid of Mesritsh" (Hebr.), 107–8. See also Assaf, "The Teachings of the Maggid r' Dov-Beer of Mesritsh in the Memoirs of Salomon Maimon" (Hebr.), 99–101.

48. For a brief discussion, see my "A Philosopher between Two Cultures," 1–17.

49. See *GW* 7, 424–27 (*GW* 3, 121–25). Compare Maimonides, *The Guide of the Perplexed*, I, 57. See also *GW* 3, 49–51. Fritz Mauthner was rather helpless when he read Maimon's entry "atheist" in Maimon's *Philosophisches Wörterbuch*. "Unklarheit bis zur völligen Konfusion möchte ich annehmen, wenn ich den kleinen Artikel Atheist (Gottesleugner) in Maimons "Philosophischem Wörterbuch" (25) lese. Es scheint zu einem Keulenschlag gegen den Atheismus auszuholen, um nachher schärfste Kritik an dem landläufigen Gottesbegriff zu üben." Having presented Maimon's arguments that "existence" cannot be predicated or negated by God, he concludes: "So ungefähr sagen die schlimmsten Atheisten auch. Und dennoch glaube ich in diesem krassen Falle sogar nicht an eine Unehrlichkeit." Mauthner, "Gott," in *Wörterbuch der Philosophie*, vol. 1, 456–57.

50. On the basis of the idea of God as a necessity of reason Kant expressed in rather harsh words (in a text, "Vom Gebet," which he did not publish) his view of prayer:

> Aber endlich ist auch bei dem Gebete Heuchelei; denn der Mensch mag nun laut beten, oder seine Ideen innerlich in Worte auflösen, so stellt er sich die Gottheit als etwas vor, das den Sinnen gegeben werden kann, da sie doch blos ein Princip ist, das seine Vernunft ihn anzunehmen zwingt. Das Daseyn der Gottheit ist nicht bewiesen, sondern es wird postulirt, und es kann also blos dazu dienen, wozu die Vernunft gezwungen war, es zu postuliren. Denkt nun der Mensch: Wenn ich zu Gott bete, so kann mir dies auf keinen Fall schaden; denn ist er nicht, nun gut, so habe ich des Guten zuviel gethan; ist er aber, so wird es mir nützen; so ist diese Prosopöia Heuchelei, indem beim Gebet vorausgesetzt werden muß, daß Derjenige, der es verrichtet, gewiß überzeugt ist, daß Gott existirt. Daher kommt es auch, daß Derjenige, welcher schon große Fortschritte im Guten gemacht hat, aufhört zu beten; denn Redlichkeit gehört zu seinen ersten Maximen—ferner, daß diejenigen, welche man beten findet, sich schämen. In den öffentlichen Vorträgen an das Volk kann und muß das Gebet beibehalten werden, weil es wirklich rhetorisch von großer Wirkung seyn und einen großen Eindruck machen kann, und man überdies in den Vorträgen an das Volk zu ihrer Sinnlichkeit sprechen und sich zu ihnen so viel wie möglich herablassen muß. (Kant, *Erläuterungen zu G. Achenwalls Iuris Naturalis, AA* 19, 637–38)

51. Whereas for Mendelssohn "[w]ithout God, providence, and immortality all the goods of this life have . . . a contemptible value" (*JubA* 3.2, 68; trans. Arkush, *Moses Mendelssohn and the Enlightenment*, 110–11), Maimon

rejects the idea of providence: it is based on the same idea that makes theodicy necessary: "Man is vain enough to consider himself the ultimate purpose of the entire creation" (*GW* 3, 313). Following Maimonides the philosopher (and not Maimonides the theologian), Maimon concludes that "divine providence is proportionate to the natural receptivity of things, and therefore awarded man according to the grade of his practical reason" (*GW* 3, 328). Maimon included in this essay extensive translations of Maimonides' discussion of providence in *The Guide of the Perplexed*, III, 12, 13, 14, 17, 18. See *GW* 3, 313–27.

52. Maimon added the verse in the margin of his early manuscript *Hesheq Shelomo*, 10, which remained hitherto unpublished, and quoted it also in his commentary on Maimonides' *The Guide of the Perplexed, GM*, 10. I published the introduction as an appendix to my essay "Salomon Maimon's Development from Kabbalah to Philosophical Rationalism" (Hebr.), in *Tarbiz* 79, no. 4 (2011).

53. *JubA* 8.109, 116; *Jerusalem*, 40, 47. And see Mendelssohn's commentary on Genesis 2:18:

לא טוב היות האדם לבדו והרצון בו אינו נאות לתכלית בריאת האדם שיהי׳ לבדו בלי עזר, כי האדם מדיני בטבעו, ולא יגיע אל ההצלחה בלי עזר מבני מינו, ואם ישאר לבדו לא יצאו כחות הנפש ומדותיה מן הכח אל הפועל ויהי׳ נמשל כבהמות הארץ, ואפשר שלא יגיע אל מעלתם, וגם חיי האדם ומזונו ובריאת גופו ושמירת איבריו הכל ע״י עזר מזולתו, וא״כ אין קיום לאדם לאמר עליו כי טוב בהיותו לבדו:

54. See the introduction to *Hesheq Shelomo*, 3–6. On the notion of perfection in Maimonides, see Kreisel, "Individual Perfection vs. Communal Welfare and the Problem of Contradictions in Maimonides' Approach to Ethics," 107–41.

55. The beginning of the *Amidah* prayer, recited at least three times a day, begins with the words, "Blessed are you, O Lord our God and God of our fathers, the God of Abraham, the God of Isaac and the God of Jacob."

56. "Upon death the estate passes automatically and immediately into the ownership of the heirs. Hence an heir cannot renounce his share by waiver thereof, since in Jewish law a person cannot waive something that already belongs to him but only that which is yet to come to him, and the heir can only transfer his share in the same way as any other property is transferred through one of the recognized modes for its assignment or alienation" (Shilo and Elon, "Succession," in *Encyclopaedia Judaica*, vol. 19, 287).

In fact, Abarbanel argues that later generations are compelled to follow the law not because of oaths taken but because of the debt to God assumed by the Israelites for delivering them from Egypt and giving them his lore and for giving them the Holy Land to serve God there. See Abarbanel on Deuteronomy 29:9–14. Now, in his commentary on Deuteronomy 29:14, Homberg indeed remarks that the next generations are obligated to follow the law because "the gift of the land and the other gifts of grace transferred to posterity are contingent upon observing the bond." This, of course, raises the question whether, when "the gift of the land" has been taken from the Jews in exile, they are still committed to observe the law. Writing to Jews who live in exile, Mendelssohn could not rely on this tradition to convince them that they are obligated to keep the law.

57. However, the relations between the proponents of these views are not symmetrical: The Mendelssohnian philosopher accepts the Maimonian position as a partial truth; the Maimonian philosopher cannot accept that emotional or aesthetical considerations count as counter-"arguments" to arguments of reason. In Maimon's view, Mendelssohn's philosophical position is hypocritical. See my "Radikale und Kompromißler in der Philosophie—Salomon Maimon über Mendelssohn, den 'philosophischen Heuchler,'" 369–85.

Chapter 9. Conclusion

1. Van der Leeuw, *Einführung in die Phänomenologie der Religion*, 189. For the full quotation, see chap. 8, above.

2. In fact, traditionally Jewish communities in Germany remained united in spite of very different coexistent persuasions. This changed only in 1876 when Rabbi Samson Raphael Hirsch split with the "*Grossgemeinde*" and founded his "*Austrittsgemeinde*." Not all orthodox rabbis agreed with this move.

Appendix

1. In response to Gershom Scholem's letter, in which Scholem remarked on the coincidence of publications of his own study of Sabbatai Zevi and Altmann's biography of Mendelssohn, Altmann noted, "It is, indeed, remarkable that at the same time extensive biographies have appeared on two such different figures, which, however, stand in hidden correspondence with each other. In a certain sense, Mendelssohn, too, was a 'false Messiah,' and, as you have shown, Sabetai Zevi finally paved the way to disintegration." See Altmann's letter to Scholem, December 2, 1973, in Scholem, *Briefe*, vol. 3 (1971–82), 377. Scholem's letter is from November 19, 1973, ibid., 87–88. I am grateful to Willi

Goetschel for this reference. I would not like to ascribe too much significance to this causal remark, surely also motivated by the wish to find some point of similarity between the two heroes (and their biographers); nevertheless, it is also not entirely meaningless.

2. See Altmann's note, *Jerusalem*, 184.

3. Twersky, "Alexander Altmann (1906–1987)," 1–7, esp. 7.

4. Altmann, "Adolf Altmann (1879–1944): A Filial Memoir."

5. Mendes-Flohr, "Theologian before the Abyss," xlii.

6. Mendes-Flohr, "Theologian before the Abyss," xlii. This turn to mysticism in order to enhance religiosity is not new with Altmann, and it is still used today. A "still valid" argument for distributing Kabbalah is "the emphasis on the spiritual conception of fulfilling the commandments"; see Halamish, 81.

7. Altmann, *Moses Mendelssohn: A Biographical Study*, 546.

8. Mendelssohn, *Vorrede zu Menasse ben Israels Rettung der Juden, JubA* 8, 22. Note that in his own words Mendelssohn refers to the "stranger" (נכרי) with the word *"Ausländer."* This is also the translation he chose in Deuteronomy 15:3 and 16:15.

9. Hobbes discusses the restitution of the kingdom of God foretold by Isaiah, Micah, and Ezekiel—and of course in the New Testament (*Leviathan*, pt. III, chap. 35). In his preparatory notes for *Jerusalem*, Mendelssohn referred to this chapter of Hobbes's *Leviathan*, but he did not use it in the work itself.

10. See Homberg, *Imrei Shefer*, 80. I am grateful to Rachel Manekin for this reference. See also Hermann Cohen, *Religion der Vernunft*, 124; Kaplan, 107.

11. Similarly Maimon: "The Polish Jews, who have always been allowed to adopt any means of gain, and have not, like the Jews of other countries, been restricted to the pitiful occupation of *Schacher* or usurer, seldom hear the reproach of cheating. They remain loyal to the country in which they live, and support themselves in an honourable way" (*GW* 1, 179; Murray, 130).

12. Michaelis's critique and Mendelsson's response are printed in Christian Wilhelm Dohm's *Über die bürgerliche Verbesserung der Juden*, pt. 2, 31–71, and 72–76. Michaelis's quotations are taken from pages 42–43 and Mendelssohn's from pages 74–76. Zev Harvey ("Moses Mendelssohn on Erez-Israel" [Hebr.], 301–12, esp. 307–9) refers to the controversy with Michaelis to explain why Mendelssohn does not air what Harvey calls his "proto-zionist" expectations. The evidence I quote below that in Mendelssohn's eyes all political rule desecrates Zion is incompatible with "proto-Zionism."

13. "Instead of Christians and Jews," Mendelssohn writes in the same context, "Mr. Michaelis constantly uses the expression Germans and Jews.... (He) wishes that we be looked at as strangers ... but I would also like to see the

following question discussed: how long, how many thousands of years, should this relation of proprietors of the country (*Landeigentümer*) and foreigner last?"

Suppression of messianism so as not to endanger civil rights for the Jews still occurs more than two generations later. When the "Neuer israelitischer Tempelverein" was founded in Hamburg in 1817, one of the two important changes it introduced into the prayer book was the change of the prayer for the advent of the Messiah. Wherever the return of the Jews to Zion had been prayed for, the text was changed to express a universal and symbolic meaning. The motivation was to counter the allegation of opponents of Jewish emancipation that the prayer for the restitution of the Jewish kingdom in the messianic age testifies to their lacking roots in their homeland. See Elbogen, *Der jüdische Gottesdienst in seiner geschlichtlichen Entwicklung,* 402–11.

14. On the sources to which Mendelssohn refers here, see Altmann's note, *Jerusalem,* 218–19. This quotation must have been very dear to Mendelssohn. Indeed, he chose to conclude *Jerusalem* with the exclamation "*Love truth! Love peace!*" taken from the same verses in Zechariah 8:19. Finally, at the same time (September 16, 1783) he again wrote the very same words into a "Poesiealbum" (*JubA* 6.1, 197).

15. Johann Georg Hamann believed that *Jerusalem* stands for the messianic vision. Mendelssohn, he says, "planted on the title of his book the pennon of his parental faith, a sign and landmark that the spirit of prophecy remained faithful to him" ("Fliegender Brief," in Reiner Wild, *Metacriticus bonae spei,* 59–60; quoted from Krochmalnik, "Die Zinnen Jerusalems," 238: "So sehr also auch der jüdische Weltweise dem Geiste der Weissagung zu entsagen meynete: so war doch das auf dem Titel ausgesteckte Fähnlein, das auf dem Giebel seines Buchs ausgehängte Lämpchen seines väterlichen Glaubens, ein Merkmal und Wahrzeichen, daß ihm der Geist der Weissagung nicht untreu geworden war, sondern ihn vielmehr in einer unsichtbaren Wolken- und Feuer-Säule begleitete."

Also, Johann Gottfried Herder seems to have thought so. On May 4, 1784, he criticized *Jerusalem* in a letter to Mendelssohn, saying, "Nobody will doubt your theory—up there or in future Jerusalem." Quoted from Kayserling, *Moses Mendelssohn. Sein Leben und Wirken,* 412–13.

16. See on this pamphlet, Altmann, *Moses Mendelssohn: A Biographical Study,* 502–13. It is reproduced in *JubA* 8, 73–92. Opposing true service to the service in Jerusalem (see *JubA* 8, 81) alludes to John 4:21–23.

17. See Altmann, "Mendelssohn's *Jerusalem* in a New Biographical Perspective" (Hebr.), 51. See also Michael Albrecht's claim in his introduction to the Meiner edition of *Jerusalem oder über religiöse Macht und Judentum* (xv):

"The title of the book is hence a straightforward avowal of Judaism (and at the same time also a reply to Cranz; see *JubA* 8, 81)." Compare *Jeursalem*, 86–87; and Feiner, *Moses Mendelssohn* (Hebr.), 134–35. Daniel Krochmalnik ("Die Zinne Jerusalems. Zum programmatischen Titel von Moses Mendelssohns Theologisch-Politischem Traktat," 227–39) interprets the name with reference to the first part of *Jerusalem,* which discusses the relation of church and state. However, there is no evidence in Mendelssohn for this interpretation.

18. On heavenly Jerusalem, see Babylonian Talmud, *Taanit,* 5a–b; *Sukkot,* 51b. See also Galatians 4:26; Book of Revelation 21.

19. Each of these conceptions can be found in various places in the prayer book. Here is one example in which both are in one and the same prayer for New Year's Day: "Lord our God, You are He who alone will reign over all Your works, in Mount Zion the abode of Your glory, in Jerusalem Your holy city, as it is written in Your holy Scriptures: 'The Lord shall reign forever, your God, O Zion, throughout all generations; praise the Lord' (Psalms 146:10)."

But in the same prayer it also says: "And thus shall Your Name, Lord our God, be sanctified upon Israel Your people, upon Jerusalem Your city, upon Zion the abode of Your glory, upon the kingship of the house of David Your anointed, and upon Your dwelling-place and Your sanctuary."

20. See *JubA* 14, 364–68. The translation first appeared in 1755. It was reprinted in 1778 at the end of *'Alim Li-trufah,* the pamphlet announcing Mendelsohn's Pentateuch, and has even been included in some later prayer books.

21. Judah Halevi, *Poems from the Divan,* 100.

22. The poem was often reprinted both in German and Jewish contexts. See the detailed analysis of the poem by Maren Niehoff, "Moses Mendelssohn's Translation of 'Zion' of Judah Halevi" (Hebr.), 313–23. Niehoff emphasizes that to Mendelssohn "Zion is apt for the 'rule of heaven' only, and whoever assumes there political rule desecrates Zion" (319). Zev Harvey's "Moses Mendelssohn on Erez-Israel" (Hebr.), 301–11, confirms these findings.

23. Altmann, *Moses Mendelssohn: A Biographical Study,* 501.

24. *Die Psalmen,* trans. M. Mendelssohn (1783).

25. Consider also Mendelssohn's translation of Psalm 122:3–4:

יְרוּשָׁלַם הַבְּנוּיָה כְּעִיר שֶׁחֻבְּרָה־לָּהּ יַחְדָּו. שֶׁשָּׁם עָלוּ שְׁבָטִים שִׁבְטֵי־יָהּ עֵדוּת לְיִשְׂרָאֵל לְהֹדוֹת לְשֵׁם יְהֹוָה.

King James:

Jerusalem is builded as a city that is compact together: Whither the tribes go up, the tribes of the LORD, unto the testimony of Israel, to give thanks unto the name of the LORD.

Mendelssohn:

> Jerusaelm du Wohlgebaute! Hauptstadt! wo alles sich gesellt; Wohin die
> Stämme Gottes wallen, Dem Herrn zu danken nach Gesetz;

> (Verbatim in English: "Jerusalem, you well-built [city]! Capital! in which
> all friendly convene; Whereto the tribes [resp. peoples] of God pilgrim,
> To thank the Lord according to Law.")

In his translation, Mendelssohn first replaces the unity of the town with the
"friendly convening" (*gesellen*) of the peoples. Moreover, he omits the name
"Israel"! He translates עדות לישראל, "testimony (or law) of (or for) Israel," with
the not further qualified and therefore universal "law" (not prefaced by a
definite article!), "according" to which thanksgiving to God is performed. Instead of the compact built town where the tribes of Israel unite three times a
year on the occasion of the annual pilgrimages, Jerusalem is here presented as
the place where all peoples friendly assemble (not unite) to thank the same God.

Adler, Hans, ed. *Nützt es dem Volk, betrogen zu werden? Est-il utile au Peuple d'etre trompé? Die Preisfrage der Preußischen Akademie für 1780.* Stuttgart–Bad Cannstatt: Frommann-Holzboog, 2007.

Albeck, Shalom. "Acquisition, Kinyan." In *Encyclopedia Judaica,* 1st ed. C. Roth and G. Wigoder. Jerusalem: Keter Publishing, 1972.

Albo, Joseph. *Sefer ha-'Ikkarim* (1485). Trans. and ann. Isaac Husik. Philadelphia: Jewish Publication Society of America, 1946.

Albrecht, Michael. "Einleitung." In *Moses Mendelssohn: Jerusalem oder über religiöse Macht und Judentum,* ed. M. Albrecht. Hamburg: Meiner, 2005.

Altmann, Alexander. "Adolf Altmann (1879–1944): A Filial Memoir." *Leo Baeck Institute Year Book* 26 (1981).

———. "Mendelssohn's Concept of Judaism Reexamined." In *Von der mittelalterlichen zur modernen Aufklärung: Studien zur jüdischen Geistesgeschichte.* Tübingen: J. C. B. Mohr, 1987.

———. "Mendelssohn's 'Jerusalem' in a New Biographical Perspective" (Hebr.). *Zion 33* (1967–68).

———. "Das Menschenbild und die Bildung des Menschen nach Moses Mendelssohn." In *Die trostvolle Aufklärung: Studien zur Metaphysik und politischen Theorie Moses Mendelssohns.* Stuttgart–Bad Cannstatt: Frommann-Holzboog, 1982.

———. *Moses Mendelssohn: A Biographical Study.* University: University of Alabama Press, 1973.

———. *Moses Mendelssohns Frühschriften zur Metaphysik.* Tübingen: J. C. B. Mohr, 1969.

Altmann, Alexander, Gershom Scholem, and Gerald Y. Blidstein. "Commandments, Reasons for." *Encyclopaedia Judaica,* 2nd ed., vol. 5, ed. M. Berenbaum and F. Skolnik. Detroit: Macmillan Reference USA, 2007.

Arkush, Allan. *Moses Mendelssohn and the Enlightenment.* Albany: State University of New York Press, 1994.

Assaf, David. "The Teachings of the Maggid r' Dov-Beer of Mesritsh in the Memoirs of Salomon Maimon" (Hebr.). *Ziyyon* 71, no. 1 (2006).

Assman, Jan. *Moses the Egyptian: The Memory of Egypt in Western Monotheism.* Cambridge, MA: Harvard University Press, 1998.

Atlas, Samuel. "Solomon Maimon's Philosophy of Language Critically Examined." *Hebrew Union College Annual* 28 (1957).

Austin, John L. *How to Do Things with Words.* Ed. J. O. Urmson. Oxford: Clarendon, 1962.

Azuelos, Daniel. "Le judaïsme en question à l'époque des Lumières: Christian Konrad Wilhelm von Dohm, Moses Mendelssohn, Wilhelm von Humboldt." *Etudes Germaniques* 59, no. 2 (2004).

The Babylonian Talmud. Ed. I. Epstein. London: Soncino Press, 1936.

Bacon, Francis. *The Advancement of Learning.* In *The Advancement of Learning and New Atlantis,* ed. A. Johnson. Oxford: Clarendon Press, 1974.

Badt-Strauss, Bertha. *Moses Mendelssohn, Der Mensch und das Werk, Zeugnisse, Briefe, Gespräche.* Berlin: Welt, 1929.

Barak, Aharon. *Judicial Discretion* (Hebr.). Tel Aviv: Papyrus, 1987.

Batnitzky, Leora. *Idolatry and Representation.* Princeton: Princeton University Press, 2000.

Beck, Lewis White. *Early German Philosophy: Kant and His Predecessors.* Cambridge, MA: Harvard University Press, 1969.

Becker, Sophie. *Briefe einer Kurländerin.* Vol 2. Berlin, 1791.

———. *Vor hundert Jahren, Elisa v.d. Reckes Reisen durch Deutschland nach dem Tagebuch ihrer Begleiterin S. Becker.* Stuttgart: Spemann, 1884.

Beiser, Frederick. *The Fate of Reason.* Cambridge, MA: Harvard University Press, 1987.

Bendavid, Lazarus. *Versuch einer logischen Auseinandersetzung des mathematischen Unendlichen.* Berlin: Petit und Schöne, 1789.

Ben Israel, Menasseh. *Vindiciae Judaeorum* (Defense of the Jews). London, 1656, 1708. German translation: *Rettung der Juden,* trans. and pref. M. Mendelssohn. *JubA* 8.

Bevan, Edwyn. *Symbolism and Belief.* New York: Macmillan, 1938.

Bolzano, Bernard. "Mein Glaube." In *Ausgewählte Schriften,* ed. E. Winter. Berlin: Union Verlag, 1976.

Breuer, Edward. *The Limits of Enlightenment: Jews, Germans, and the Eighteenth-Century Study of Scripture.* Cambridge, MA: Harvard University Press, 1996.

Carnap, Rudolf. "The Elimination of Metaphysics through Logical Analysis of Language" (1932). Trans. A. Pap. In *Logical Positivism,* ed. A. J. Ayer. New York: Free Press, 1959.

Cassirer, Ernst. "Der Begriff der symbolischen Form im Aufbau der Geisteswissenschaften" (1921–22). In *Wesen und Wirkung des Symbolbegriffs.* Darmstadt: Wissenschaftliche Buchgesellschaft, 1957.

————. *Das Erkenntisproblem in der Philosophie und Wissenschaft der neueren Zeit*, vol. 3: *Die Nachkantischen Systeme*. Berlin: B. Cassirer, 1920.

————. "Die Idee der Religion bei Lessing und Mendelssohn." In *Festgabe zum zehnjährigen Bestehen der Akademie für die Wissenschaft des Judentums, 1919–1929*. Berlin: Akademie-Verlag, 1929.

————. *Language and Myth*. Trans. S. K. Langer. New York: Dover, 1946.

————. "Die Philosophie Moses Mendelssohns." In *Moses Mendelssohn. Zur 200 jährigen wiederkehr seines Geburtstages*, ed. Encylopedia Judaica. Berlin: Lambert Schneider, 1929.

————. *The Philosophy of Symbolic Forms*, vol. 2: *Mythical Thought*. Trans. R. Manheim. New Haven: Yale University Press, 1955.

————. *The Philosophy of Symbolic Forms*, vol. 3: *The Phenomenology of Knowledge*. Trans. R. Manheim. New Haven: Yale University Press, 1957.

Cohen, Hermann. *Deutschtum und Judentum*. Gießen: Alfred Töpelmann, 1915.

————. *Jüdische Schriften*. Berlin: C. A. Schwetschke & Sohn, 1924.

————. *Religion der Vernunft aus den Quellen des Judentums* (1919). Frankfurt: Kauffmann, 1929. English translation: *Religion of Reason out of the Sources of Judaism*, 2nd ed., trans. Simon Kaplan. Oxford: Oxford University Press, 2000.

Condillac, Etienne Bonnot de. *Essai sur l'origine des connaissances*. In *Oeuvres philosophiques*, vol. 1, ed. G. Le Roy. Paris: Presses Universitaires de France, 1947. English translation: *Essay on the Origin of Human Knowledge*, ed. and trans. H. Aarsleff. Cambridge: Cambridge University Press, 2001.

Cranz, August Friedrich. *Das Forschen nach Licht und Recht in einem Schreiben an Herrn Moses Mendelssohn auf Veranlassung seiner merkwürdigen Vorrede zu Mannaseh Ben Israel*. Berlin: Maurer, 1782; reprint, *JubA* 8.

Cudworth, Ralph. *True Intellectual System of the World*. London: R. Royston, 1678.

Dahlstrom, Daniel O., trans. and ed. *Moses Mendelssohn, Philosophical Writings*. Cambridge: Cambridge University Press, 1997.

Dan, Joseph. "From the Symbol to the Symbolized: Towards an Understanding of Gershom Scholem's 'Ten Unhistorical Aphorisms on Kabbalah'" (Hebr.). *Jerusalem Studies in Jewish Philosophy*, no. 5 (1986).

Descartes, René. *Discours de la Méthode*. In *Oeuvres de Descartes*, vol. 6, ed. C. Adam and P. Tannery. Paris: J. Vrin, 1983.

Dohm, Christian Wilhelm. *Über die bürgerliche Verbesserung der Juden*. Pt. 2. Berlin und Stettin: Friedrich Nicolai, 1783.

Duran, Simeon. *Magen Avot* (1785). Reprint, Jerusalem: Makhon Haketav, 2003.

Durkheim, Emile. "The Determination of the Moral Fact" (1906). In *Sociology and Philosophy,* trans. D. F. Pocock. London: Cohen and West, 1953.

Eco, Umberto. *The Search for the Perfect Language.* Trans. J. Fentress. Oxford: Blackwell, 1997.

Ehrensperger, Florian. "Salomon Maimon als Rezensent, nebst einer bisher unbeachteten Rezension." In *Salomon Maimon: Rational Dogmatist, Empirical Skeptic,* ed. G. Freudenthal. Dordrecht: Kluwer, 2003.

Eichhorn, Johann Gottfried. *Einleitung ins Alte Testament.* Leipzig: Weidmanns Erben und Reich, 1780–83.

Eisen, Arnold. "Divine Legislation as 'Ceremonial Script': Mendelssohn on the Commandments." *Association for Jewish Studies Review* 15 (1990).

Elbogen, Ismar. *Der jüdische Gottesdienst in seiner geschichtlichen Entwicklung.* Leipzig: Gustav Fock, 1913.

l'Epée, Charles-Michel de (l'Abbé). *Institution des Sourds et Muets, par la voie des signes méthodiques: Ouvrage qui contient le Project d'une Langue Universelle, par l'entremise des Signes naturels, assujetis à une Méthode.* Paris: Nyon l'aine, 1776.

Erlewine, Robert. *Monotheism and Tolerance: Recovering a Religion of Reason.* Bloomington: Indiana University Press, 2010.

Euchel, Isaac. *A History of Our Teacher and Sage, Moses b. Menachem* (Hebr.). Berlin: Chinukh Ne'arim, 1788.

Feiner, Shmuel. *The Enlightenment Revolution* (Hebr.). Jerusalem: Zalman Shazar Center, 2002.

———. *Moses Mendelssohn* (Hebr.). Jerusalem: Zalman Shazar Center, 2005.

Fenves, Peter. *Arresting Language: From Leibniz to Benjamin.* Stanford: Stanford University Press, 2001.

Flekles, Elazar. *Ahavat David* (Hebr.). Reprint, Brooklyn, NY: Goldenberg Brothers, 1992.

Fox, Marvin. "Law and Ethics in Modern Jewish Philosophy: The Case of Moses Mendelssohn." *Proceedings of the American Academy for Jewish Research* 43 (1976).

Franks, Paul W. *All or Nothing: Systematicity, Transcendental Arguments, and Skepticism in German Idealism.* Cambridge, MA: Harvard University Press, 2005.

Frege, Gottlob. *Wissenschaftlicher Briefwechsel.* Ed. Gottfried Gabriel. Hamburg: Meiner, 1976.

Freudenthal, Gideon. *Definition and Construction: Salomon Maimon's Philosophy of Geometry.* Preprint 317. Berlin: Max Planck Institute for the History of Science, 2006.

————. "Enlightenment in Gold." In Studies in the History of Culture and Science, vol. 30 (2010): Studies in Jewish Culture and Science. Edited by Resianne Fontaine, Ruth Glasner, Reimund Leicht, and Giuseppe Veltri .

————. "Maimon's Subversion of Kant's *Critique of Pure Reason*: There Are No Synthetic A Priori Judgments in Physics." In *Salomon Maimon: Rational Dogmatist, Empirical Skeptic*, ed. G. Freudenthal. Dordrecht: Kluwer, 2003.

————. "The Philosophical Mysticism of Maimonides and Maimon." In *Maimonides and His Heritage*, ed. I. Dobbs-Weinstein, L. E. Goodman, and J. A. Grady. Albany: State University of New York Press, 2009.

————. "'Die Philosophischen Systeme der Theologie,' nach Salomon Maimon." In *Religious Apologetics — Philosophical Argumentation*, ed. Y. Schwartz and V. Krech. Tübingen: Mohr Siebeck, 2004.

————. "Radikale und Kompromißler in der Philosophie—Salomon Maimon über Mendelssohn, den 'philosophischen Heuchler.'" *Tel Aviver Jahrbuch für deutsche Geschichte* 30 (2002).

————. "Salomon Maimon." In *Metzler Lexikon jüdischer Philosophen*, ed. A. B. Kilcher and O. Fraisse. Stuttgart: J. B. Metzler, 2003.

————. "Salomon Maimon: Commentary as a Method of Philosophizing" (Hebr.). *Da'at* 53 (2004).

————. "Salomon Maimon: A Philosopher between Two Cultures." In *Salomon Maimon: Rational Dogmatist, Empirical Skeptic*, ed. G. Freudenthal. Dordrecht: Kluwer, 2003.

————. "Salomon Maimon's Development from Kabbalah to Philosophical Rationalism" (Hebr). *Tarbiz* 80, no. 1 (2011): 105–71.

Gilon, Meir. *Mendelssohn's Kohelet Mussar in Its Historical Context* (Hebr.). Jerusalem: Publications of the Israel Academy of Sciences and Humanities, 1979.

Goetschel, Roland. "Langage et écriture dans la Jérusalem de Moise Mendelssohn." *Revue des Études juives* 153, no. 3–4 (July–Dec. 1994).

Gottlieb, Michah. *Faith and Freedom: Moses Mendelssohn's Theological-Political Thought.* Oxford: Oxford University Press, 2011.

————. "Mendelssohn's Metaphysical Defense of Religious Pluralism." *Journal of Religion* 86, no. 2 (Apr. 2006).

Guttmann, Julius. "Mendelssohn's *Jerusalem* and Spinoza's *Theologico-Political Treatise*." In *Studies in Jewish Thought: An Anthology of German Jewish Scholarship*, ed. A. Jospe. Detroit: Wayne State University Press, 1981.

————. *Die Philosophie des Judentums.* München: Ernst Reinhardt, 1933.

Haberman, Jacob. "Abraham Wolf: A Forgotten Jewish Reform Thinker." *Jewish Quarterly Review*, n.s., 81, no. 3–4 (January–April 1991).

Halbertal, Moshe, and Avishai Margalit. *Idolatry.* Cambridge, MA: Harvard University Press, 1992.

Halevi, Judah. *The Kuzari: In Defense of the Despised Faith.* Trans. N. D. Korobkin. Northvale, NJ: Jason Aronson, 1997.

———. *Poems from the Divan.* Trans. G. Levin. London: Anvil Press Poetry.

Hamman, Johann Georg. *Aesthetica in nuce* (1762). In *Werke,* vol. 2, ed. J. Nadler. Vienna: Herder Verlag, 1949–57.

Harvey, Warren Zev. "Mendelssohn's Heavenly Politics." In *Perspectives on Jewish Thought and Mysticism,* ed. A. L. Ivry, E. R. Wolfson, and A. Arkush. Amsterdam: Harwood Academic, 1998.

———. "Moses Mendelssohn on Erez-Israel" (Hebr.). In *Erez-Israel in Modern Jewish Thought* (Hebr.), ed. A. Ravitsky. Jerusalem: Yad Itzhak Ben-Zvi, 1998.

———. "Why Philosophers Quote Kabbalah: The Cases of Mendelssohn and Rosenzweig." *Studia Judaica* 16 (2008).

Heiler, Friedrich. *Erscheinungsformen und Wesen der Religion.* Stuttgart: Kohlhammer, 1961.

Heine, Heinrich. *Zur Geschichte der Religion und Philosophie in Deutschland.* In Heinrich Heine, *Werke und Briefe,* ed. H. Kaufmann. Berlin:Aufbau-Verlag, 1961–64. English translation: *Concerning the History of Religion and Philosophy in Germany,* trans. H. Mustard, in *The Romantic School and Other Essays,* ed. J. Hermand and R. C. Holub. New York: Continuum, 1985.

———. *Works of Prose.* Ed. H. Kesten, trans. E. B. Ashton. New York: L. B. Fischer, 1943.

Hertz, Heinrich. *The Principles of Mechanics Presented in a New Form.* Trans. D. E. Jones and J. T. Walley. New York: Dover, 1956.

Heschel, Israel Nathan. "The Opinions of the Age's Greatest Sages in Their Struggle against the Maskil Naphtali Herz *Weisel (may his name rot)*" (Hebr.), pt. 1. *Kovetz Beit Aharon ve-Yisrael* 8, 1, vol. 43 (Tishrei-Cheshvan, 5753/1992).

———. "The Opinions of the Age's Greatest Sages in Their Struggle against the Maskil Naphtali Herz *Weisel (may his name rot)*" (Hebr.), pt. 2. *Kovetz Beit Aharon ve-Yisrael,* 8, 2, vol. 44 (Kislev-Tevet, 5753/1992–93).

Hilfrich, Carola. *"Lebendige Schrift": Repräsentation und Idolatrie in Moses Mendelssohns Philosophie und Exegese des Judentums.* München: Fink, 2000.

Hirsch, Samson Raphael. "Grundlinien einer jüdischen Symbolik." *Jeschurun* 2, no. 12 (Sept. 1857).

————. "Die jüdischen Ceremonialgesetze." *Jeschurun* 1, no. 2 (Nov. 1854). Reprint, *Schriften des Vereins zur Erhaltung des überlieferten Judentums,* no. 1–2. Halberstadt: H. Meyer, 1925.

————. *The Nineteen Letters.* Trans. Karin Paritzky. Rev. with commentary by Joseph Elias. Jerusalem: Feldheim Publishers, 1995.

————. "Outlines of a Jewish Symbolism." In *Collected Writings,* vol. 3. New York: Feldheim, 1984–86.

Hlobil, Tomáš. "Two Concepts of Language and Poetry: Edmund Burke and Moses Mendelssohn." *British Journal for the History of Philosophy* 8, no. 3 (2000).

Hobbes, Thomas. *Leviathan, with Selected Variants from the Latin Edition of 1668.* Ed. E. Curley. Indianapolis: Hackett, 1994.

Homberg, Naftali Herz. *Imrei Shefer: A Religious and Moral Reader for the Children of Israel, Boys and Girls* (Hebr. and Yidd.). Vienna: G. Hroshant-ski, 1808.

Horwitz, Rivka. "Mendelssohn und die Kabbala." In *Kabbala und die Literatur der Romantik: Zwischen Magie und Trope,* ed. E. Goodman-Thau, G. Mat-tanklott, and C. Schulte. Tübingen: Max Niemeyer Verlag, 1999.

Hubbeling, H. G. "Der Symbolbegriff bei Gerardus van der Leeuw." In *On Symbolic Representation of Religion: Groninger Contributions to Theories of Symbols,* ed. H. G. Hubbeling and H. G. Kippenberg. Berlin: de Gruyter, 1986.

Hume, David. *Enquiry Concerning Human Understanding.* Ed. L. A. Selby-Bigge, rev. P. H. Nidditch. Oxford: Clarendon, 1975.

————. *Principal Writings on Religion: Including Dialogues concerning Natural Religion and the Natural History of Religion.* Ed. J. C. A. Gaskin. Oxford: Oxford University Press, 1993.

Ibn Pakuda, Bachya ben Joseph. *Duties of the Heart.* Trans. D. Haberman. Jerusalem: Feldheim, 1997.

Idel, Moshe. "The Function of Symbols in Gershom Scholem's Thought" (Hebr.). Trans. A. Bar-Levav. *Mada'ey ha-Yahadut* 38 (1998).

————. "Perceptions of Kabbalah in the Second Half of the 18th Century." *Journal of Jewish Thought and Philosophy* 1 (1991).

————. "Reification of Language in Jewish Mysticism." In *Mysticism and Language,* ed. Steven T. Katz. New York: Oxford University Press, 1992.

Jacobi, Johann Georg. *Über die Lehre des Spinoza in Briefen an den Herrn Moses Mendelssohn.* In *Sämtliche Werke,* vol. 4. Zürich: Orell, Füßli und Compagnie, 1825.

John of Damascus, Saint. *On Holy Images.* Trans. M. H. Allies. London: Thomas Barker, 1898.

Jospe, Raphael. "The Superiority of Oral over Written Communication: Judah Ha-Levi's Kuzari and Modern Jewish Thought." In *Essays in Honor of Marvin Fox*, vol. 3, ed. J. Neusner, E. S. Frerichs, and N. M. Sarna. Atlanta: Scholars Press, 1989.

Kadari, Adiel. "Thought and Halakhah in Maimonides' Laws of Repentance" (Hebr.). Ph.D. dissertation, Ben-Gurion University of the Negev, 2000.

Kant, Immanuel. *Critique of Pure Reason*. Ed. and trans. P. Guyer and A. W. Wood. Cambridge: Cambridge University Press, 1998.

———. *Einige Bemerkungen zu Ludwig Heinrich Jakob's Prüfung der Mendelssohn'schen Morgenstunden. AA*, vol. 8. English translation: "Some Remarks on Ludwig Heinrich Jakob's Examination of Mendelssohn's *Morning Hours* (1786)." In *Anthropology, History, and Education*. Cambridge Edition of the Works of Immanuel Kant in Translation. Trans. R. B. Louden and G. Zöller. Cambridge: Cambridge University Press, 2007.

———. *Erläuterungen zu G. Achenwalls Iuris Naturalis. AA* 19.

———. *Gesammelte Schriften*. Königlich Preußische Akademie der Wissenschaften. Berlin: Reimer, later Walter de Gruyter, 1900.

———. *Kritik der Urteilskraft. AA* 5. English translation: *Critique of the Power of Judgment*, ed. Paul Guyer, trans. P. Guyer and E. Matthews. Cambridge: Cambridge University Press, 2000.

———. *The Only Possible Argument in Support of a Demonstration of the Existence of God*. In *Theoretical Philosophy: 1755–1770*, vol. 1, trans. and ed. D. Walford. Cambridge Edition of the Works of Immanuel Kant in Translation. Cambridge: Cambridge University Press, 1992.

———. *Was heißt: Sich im Denken orientiren? AA* 8.

———. "What Real Progress Has Metaphysics Made in Germany since the Time of Leibniz and Wolff." In *Theoretical Philosophy after 1781*, ed. H. Allison and P. Heath, trans. G. Hatfield, M. Friedman, H. Allison, and P. Heath. Cambridge: Cambridge University Press, 2002.

Kaplan, Lawrence. "Maimonides and Mendelssohn on the Origins of Idolatry, the Election of Israel, and the Oral Law." In *Perspectives on Jewish Thought and Mysticism: Proceedings of the International Conference Held by the Institute of Jewish Studies in Celebration of Its Fortieth Anniversary: Dedicated to the Memory and Academic Legacy of Its Founder Alexander Altmann, University College London, 1994*, ed. A. L. Ivry, E. R. Wolfson, and A. Arkush. Amsterdam: Harwood Academic, 1998.

Karp, Jonathan. "The Aesthetic Difference: Moses Mendelssohn's *Kohelet Musar* and the Inception of the Berlin *Haskalah*." In *Renewing the Past, Reconfiguring Jewish Culture*, ed. R. Brann and A. Sutcliffe. Philadelphia: University of Pennsylvania Press, 2004.

Kasher, Hannah. "To the Forms of the *Tselamim* in Maimonides" (Hebr.). *Da'at,* no. 53 (Winter 2004).

Kasher, Menachem Mendel, ed. *Torah Shlemah.* Jerusalem: Noam Aharon, 1992–96.

Katz, Jacob. *Out of the Ghetto: The Social Background of Jewish Emancipation, 1770–1870.* New York: Schocken Books, 1978.

Kauppi, Raili. *Über die Leibnizsche Logik, mit besonderer Berücksichtigung des Problems der Intension und der Extension.* Helsinki: Societas Philosophica, 1960.

Kayserling, Meyer. *Moses Mendelssohn. Sein Leben und Wirken.* Leipzig: Hermann Mendelssohn, 1888.

Kellner, Menachem. *Maimonides' Confrontation with Mysticism.* Portland, OR: Littman Library of Jewish Civilization, 2006.

Kilcher, Andreas B. *Die Sprachtheorie der Kabbala als ästhetisches Paradigma: die Konstruktion einer ästhetischen Kabbala seit der frühen Neuzeit.* Stuttgart: J. B. Metzler, 1998.

Klein-Braslavy, Sarah. *Maimonides' Interpretation of the Adam Stories in Genesis* (Hebr.). Reprint, Jerusalem: Rubin Mass, 1987.

Knowlson, James R. "The Idea of Gesture as a Universal Language in the XVIIth and XVIIIth Centuries." *Journal of the History of Ideas* 26, no. 4 (Oct.–Dec. 1965).

Köhler, Wolfgang. *Gestalt Psychology.* New York: Liveright, 1929.

Kreisel, Howard. "Individual Perfection vs. Communal Welfare and the Problem of Contradictions in Maimonides' Approach to Ethics." *Proceedings of the American Academy of Jewish Research* 58 (1992).

Krochmalnik, Daniel. "Die Psalmen in Moses Mendelssohns Utopie des Judentums." In *Der Psalter in Judentum und Christentum,* ed. E. Zenger. Herders Biblische Studien, vol. 18. Freiburg, 1998.

———. "Das Zeremoniell als Zeichensprache. Moses Mendelssohns Apologie des Judentums im Rahmen der aufklärerischen Semiotik." In *Fremde Vernunft,* ed. S. Josef and W. Stegmaier. Zeichen und Interpretation IV. Frankfurt: Suhrkamp, 1998.

———. "Die Zinne Jerusalems. Zum programmatischen Titel von Moses Mendelssohns Theologisch-Politischem Traktat." In *Religion und Politik,* ed. M. Walther. Baden-Baden: Nomos Verlagsgesellschaft, 2004.

Krois, John Michael. "Cassirer's 'Prototype and Model' of Symbolism." *Science in Context* 12, no. 4 (1999).

Landau, Yechezkel ben Yehuda. *Noda bi-Yehuda.* 2nd ed. Prague: M. Katz, 1811.

Leibniz, Gottfried Wilhelm. *Discours de métaphysique et correspondance avec Arnaut.* Ed. G. Le Roy. Paris: Vrin, 1957.

————. *La Monadologie*. Ed. E. Boutroux, Paris: LGF, 1991.

————. *Opuscules et fragments inédits. Extraits des manuscrits de la Bibliothèque royale de Hanovre*. Ed. L. Couturat. Paris: Félix Alcan, 1903.

————. *Philosophical Papers and Letters*. 2nd ed. Ed. and trans. L. E. Loemker. Dordrecht: Reidel, 1969.

————. *Die philosophischen Schriften von G. W. Leibniz*. Ed. C. I. Gerhardt. Berlin, 1849–55. Reprint, Hildesheim: Georg Olms, 1978.

Leibowitz, Yeshayahu. *Judaism, Human Values, and the Jewish State*. Ed. E. Goldman. Cambridge, MA: Harvard University Press, 1992.

Lessing, Gotthold Ephraim. "The Education of the Human Race." In *Philosophical and Theological Writings*, trans. and ed. H. B. Nisbet. Cambridge: Cambridge University Press, 2005.

————. *Nathan the Wise*. Trans. W. T. of Norwich. London: Cassell & Company, 1893.

————. "A Rejoinder." In *Philosophical and Theological Writings*, trans. and ed. H. B. Nisbet. Cambridge: Cambridge University Press, 2005.

Maier, Anneliese. *Kants Qualitätskategorien. Kant-Studien. Ergänzungsheft* 65. Berlin: Pan-Verlag Kurt Metzner, 1930.

Maimon, Salomon. "Antwort des Hrn. Maimon auf voriges Schreiben." *Berlinisches Journal für Aufklärung* 9, no. 1 (1790); *GW* 3.

————. *Gesammelte Werke*. Ed. Valerio Verra. Hildesheim: Olms, 1965.

————. *Giv'at ha-Moreh*. Ed. S. H. Bergman and N. Rotenstreich. Jerusalem: Publications of the Israel Academy of Sciences and Humanities, 1966.

————. *Hesheq Shelomo* (Hebr.). Posnan, 1778 (autograph, Jewish National Library, Jerusalem, MS 806426).

————. Introduction to *Hesheq Shelomo*. In Gideon Freudenthal, "Salomon Maimon's Development from Kabbalah to Philosophical Rationalism" (Hebr.). *Tarbiz* 80, no. 1 (2011), appendix.

————. *Lebensgeschichte*, *GW* 1. English translation: *The Autobiography of Solomon Maimon*, trans. J. C. Murray. Urbana: University of Illinois Press, 2001.

————. *Philosophisches Wörterbuch, order Beleuchtung der wichtigsten Gegenstände der Philosophie, in alphabetischer Ordnung*. Berlin: Johann Friedrich Unger, 1791.

————. *Versuch einer neuen Logik, oder Theorie des Denkens. Nebst angehängten Briefen des Philaletes an Änesidemus*. Berlin: Ernst Felisch, 1794; *GW* 5.

————. *Versuch über die Transzendentalphilosophie*. Berlin: Christian F. Voß und Sohn, 1790.

Maimonides, Moses. *The Code of Maimonides* (*Mishneh Torah*), vol. 2: *The Book of Love*. Ed. M. Kellner. New Haven: Yale University Press, 2004.

————. *Commentary on the Mishnah* (Hebr.). Trans. and ed. Y. Kapach. Jerusalem: Mossad ha-Rav Kook, 1987.

————. *The Guide of the Perplexed.* Trans. and ed. Shlomo Pines. Chicago: University of Chicago Press, 1963.

————. *A Maimonides Reader.* Ed. I. Twerski. Springfield, NJ: Behrman House, 1972.

————. *Maimonides' Treatise on Logic (Makalah fi-sinaat al-mantik): The Original Arabic and Three Hebrew Translations.* Ed. and trans. Israel Efros. New York: American Academy for Jewish Research, 1938.

————. *Mishneh Torah, Book of Knowledge.* Trans. Moses Hyamson. Jerusalem: Boys Town Jerusalem Publishers, 1962.

Maren, Niehoff. "Moses Mendelssohn's Translation of 'Zion' of Judah Halevi" (Hebr.). In *Erez-Israel in Modern Jewish Thought,* ed. A. Ravitzki. Jerusalem: Yad Itzhak Ben-Zvi, 1998.

Mates, Benson. *The Philosophy of Leibniz: Metaphysics and Language.* New York: Oxford University Press, 1986.

Matt, Daniel C. "The Mystic and the Mizwot." In *Jewish Spirituality: From the Bible through the Middle Ages,* vol. 1, ed. A. Green. New York: Crossroad, 1987.

Mauthner, Fritz. "Gott." In *Wörterbuch der Philosophie,* vol. 1. München: G. Müller, 1910–11.

McLeod, Carolyn. "Trust." In *The Stanford Encyclopedia of Philosophy* (Fall 2008 ed.), ed. E. N. Zalta. http://plato.stanford.edu/archives/fall2008/entries/trust (last accessed June 2010).

Meiners, Christoph. *Versuch über die Religionsgeschichte der ältesten Völker, besonders der Egyptier.* Göttingen: Johann Christian Dieterich, 1775.

Mendelssohn, Moses. *Abhandlung über die Evidenz in metaphysischen Wissenschaften. JubA* 2. English translation: "On Evidence in Metaphysical Sciences." In *Moses Mendelssohn, Philosophical Writings,* trans. and ed. D. Dahlstrom. Cambridge: Cambridge University Press, 1997.

————. *An die Freunde Lessings. JubA* 3.2.

————. *Anweisung zur spekul. Philosophie, für einen jungen Menschen von 15–20 Jahren. JubA* 3.1.

————. *Zu Bayles Pensées diverses sur les comètes. JubA* 2.

————. *Bi'ur Millot ha-Higayyon. JubA* 14.

————. *Gegenbetrachtungen über Bonnets Palingenesie* (1770). *JubA* 7.

————. *Gesammelte Schriften–Jubiläumsausgabe.* Ed. I. Elbogen, J. Guttmann, E. Mittwoch, A. Altmann, et al. Bad Cannstatt: Frommann-Holzboog, 1971.

————. *Jerusalem, or On Religious Power and Judaism.* Trans. Allan Arkush, introd. and comm. Alexander Altmann. Hanover, NH: Brandeis University Press, 1983.

————. *Jerusalem* (Entwurf und Notizen). *JubA* 8.

————. *Kohelet Musar*. Berlin, ca. 1755.

————. *Morgenstunden. JubA* 3.2.

————. *On Sentiments.* English translation in *Moses Mendelssohn, Philosophical Writings*, trans. Daniel Dahlstrom. Cambridge: Cambridge University Press, 1997. German original: *Über die Empfindungen* (1755), *JubA* 1.

————. *On the Sublime and Naive in the Fine Sciences.* In *Moses Mendelssohn, Philosophical Writings*, trans. and ed. D. Dahlstrom. Cambridge: Cambridge University Press, 1997. German original: *Über das Erhabene und Naïve in den schönen Wissenschaften. JubA* 1.

————. *Or la-Netivah*, introduction to *Netivot ha-Shalom* (Hebr.). Berlin: G. F. Starcke, 1780–83. Reprint, *JubA* 15.1.

————. *Phaedon, oder über die Unsterblichkeit der Seele. JubA* 3.1.

————. *Die Psalmen.* Trans. M. Mendelssohn. Berlin: Friedrich Maurer, 1783.

————. *Rhapsody, or Additions to the Letters on Sentiments.* English translation in *Moses Mendelssohn, Philosophical Writings*, trans. Daniel Dahlstrom. Cambridge: Cambridge University Press, 1997. German original: *Rhapsodie, oder Zusätze zu den Briefen über die Empfindungen* (1761). *JubA* 1.

————. *Ritualgesetze der Juden* (1778). *JubA* 7.

————. *Sendschreiben an den Herrn Magister Lessing in Leipzig und Nachschrift. JubA* 2.

————. *Über die Frage: Was heißt aufklären? JubA* 6.1. English translation: *On the Question: What Is Enlightenment?* In *What Is Enlightenment? Eighteenth-Century Answers and Twentieth-Century Questions*, ed. James Schmidt. Berkeley: University of California Press, 1996.

————. *Über Freiheit und Nothwendigkeit. Berlinische Monatsschrift* 7 (July 1783). *JubA* 3.1.

————. *Über die Hauptgrundsätze der schönen Künste und Wissenschaften* (1757). *JubA* 1.

————. *Verwandtschaft des Schönen und Guten. JubA* 2.

————. *Verzeichnis der auserlesenen Büchersammlung des seeligen Herrn Moses Mendelssohn.* Berlin, 1786. Reprint, Berlin: Soncino, 1926.

————. *Vorrede zu Menasse ben Israels Rettung der Juden. JubA* 8.

Mendelssohn, Moses (Solomon Dubno, Aaron Jaroslav, Naftali Herz Weisel, Herz Homberg). Commentary to the biblical text in *Netivot ha-Shalom* (Hebr.). Berlin: G. F. Starcke, 1780–1783. Reprint, *JubA* 15–18.

Mendes-Flohr, Paul. "Theologian before the Abyss." In Alexander Altmann, *The Meaning of Jewish Existence: Theological Essays, 1930–1939,* ed. A. L. Ivri, trans. E. Ehrlich and L. H. Ehrlich. Hanover, NH: Brandeis University Press, 1991.

Meyer, Herrmann M. Z. *Moses Mendelssohn, Bibliographie.* Berlin: de Gruyter, 1965.

Moyaert, Paul. "In Defense of Praying with Images." *American Catholic Philosophical Quarterly* 81, no. 4 (Fall 2007).

———. "The Sense of Symbols as the Core of Religion: A Philosophical Approach to a Theological Debate." In *Transcendence in Philosophy and Religion,* ed. J. E. Faulconer. Bloomington: Indiana University Press, 2003.

Mugnai, Massimo. "Leibniz on Individuation: From the Early Years to the Discourse and Beyond." *Studia Leibnitiana* 33, no. 1 (2001).

Nachmanides, Moses. *Ramban (Nachmanides) Commentary on the Torah.* Trans. and ann. Rabbi Dr. C. B. Chavel. New York: Shilo Publishing House, 1971.

Nicholas of Cusa. *Nicholas of Cusa's De Pace Fidei and Cribratio Alkorani,* 2nd ed. Trans. J. Hopkins. Minneapolis: Arthur J. Banning, 1994.

Niewöhner, Friedrich. "Mendelssohn als Philosoph–Aufklärer–Jude. Oder: Aufklärung mit dem Talmud." *Zeitschrift für Religions- und Geistesgeschichte* 41, no. 2 (1989).

Ogden, Charles Kay, and Ivor Armstrong Richards. *The Meaning of Meaning: A Study of the Influence of Language upon Thought and of the Science of Symbolism.* New York: Harcourt Brace & World, 1923.

———. "Word Magic." *Psyche* 18 (1933–52).

Otto, Rudolph. *The Idea of the Holy: An Inquiry into the Non-Rational Factor in the Idea of the Divine and Its Relation to the Rational.* Trans. J. W. Harvey. London: Oxford University Press, 1970.

Pauw, Cornelius de. *Recherches philosophiques sur les Américains, ou Mémoires intéressants pour servir à l'histoire de l'espèce humaine.* Berlin: G. J. Decker, 1768–69.

Peirce, Charles Sanders. *What Is a Sign?* In *The Essential Peirce: Selected Philosophical Writings, Volume 2 (1893–1913),* ed. Peirce Edition Project. Bloomington: Indiana University Press, 1998.

Polanyi, Michael, and Harry Prosch. *Meaning.* Chicago: University of Chicago Press, 1975.

Quine, Willard Van Orman. "Logical Correspondence with Russell." *Journal of Bertrand Russell Studies* 8, no. 1 (1988), art. 18, 230. http://digitalcommons .mcmaster.ca/russelljournal/vol8/iss1/18 (last accessed June 2010).

———. *Word and Object.* Cambridge, MA: MIT Press, 1960.

Ravitsky, Aviezer. "Maimonides and His Disciples on Linguistic Magic and 'The Madness of the Writers of Amulets'" (Hebr.). In *Jewish Culture in the Eye of the Storm: A Jubilee Book in Honor of Yosef Ahituv* (Hebr.), ed. A. Sagi and N. Ilan. Ein Tzurim: ha-Kibbutz ha-Meuhad and Merkaz Yaacov Herzog, 2002.

Rawidowicz, Simon. "Mendelssohns handschriftliche Glossen zum More Ne-bukim." *Monatsschrift für Geschichte und Wissenschaft des Judentums* 78, no. 1 (1934).

Raz, Joseph. "Legal Principle and the Limits of Law." *Yale Law Journal* 81 (1972).

Reinhold, Carl Leonhard [Br(uder) Decius, pseud.]. *Die Hebräischen Mysterien oder die älteste religiöse Freymaurerey* (1788). Ed. and comm. J. Assmann. Neckargemünd: Edition Mnemosyne, 2001.

Reuchlin, Johannes. *On the Art of the Kabbalah.* Trans. M. Goodman and S. Goodman, introd. G. Lloyd Jones; introd. to the Bison Book ed. Moshe Idel. Lincoln: University of Nebraska Press, 1993.

Ricken, Ulrich. "Mendelssohn und die Sprachtheorien der Aufklärung." In M. Albrecht and E. J. Engel, *Moses Mendelssohn im Spannungsfeld der Aufklärung.* Stuttgart–Bad Cannstatt: Frommann-Holzboog, 2000.

———. "Zum Thema Christian Wolff und die Wissenschaftssprache der deutschen Aufklärung." In *Linguistik der Wissenschaftssprache,* ed. H. L. Kretzenbacher and H. Weinrich. Berlin: de Gruyter, 1995.

Rokeah, David. "Early Christian-Jewish Polemics on Divine Election" (Hebr.). In *Chosen People, Elect Nations, and Universal Mission* (Hebr.), ed. S. Almog and M. Heyd. Jerusalem: Zalman Shazar Center, 1991.

Rosenfeld, Sophia A. *A Revolution in Language: The Problem of Signs in Late Eighteenth-Century France.* Stanford: Stanford University Press, 2001.

Rosenstock, Bruce. *Philosophy and the Jewish Question: Mendelssohn, Rosen-zweig, and Beyond.* New York: Fordham University Press, 2010.

Rotenstreich, Nathan. "Symbolism and the Divine Realm: Following Two Un-historical Articles by Gershom Scholem" (Hebr.). In Gershom Scholem, *'Od Davar* (Hebr.). Tel-Aviv: Am Oved, 1989.

Rousseau, Jean-Jacques. *Emile, or On Education.* Trans. A. Bloom. New York: Basic Books, 1979.

Russell, Bertrand. "My Mental Development." In *The Philosophy of Bertrand Russell,* ed. Paul Arthur Schilpp. Evanston: Northwestern University Press, 1944.

Rynhold, Daniel. *Two Models of Jewish Philosophy.* Oxford: Oxford University Press, 2005.

Sabar, Shalom. "Torah and Magic: The Torah Scroll and Its Appurtenances as Magical Objects in Traditional Jewish Culture." *European Journal of Jewish Studies* 3, no. 1 (2009).

Samet, Moshe Shraga. "Moshe Mendelssohn, Naphtali Herz Weisel, and the Rabbis of Their Age" (Hebr.). Reprint in *Chapters in the History of Ortho-*

doxy (Hebr.). Jerusalem: Merkaz Dinur Le-Cheker Toldot Yisrael and Karmel, 2005.

Sandler, Peretz. *Mendelssohn's Edition of the Pentateuch* (Hebr.). Jerusalem: Rubin Mass, 1940.

Santayana, George. "Reason in Religion." In *The Life of Reason: or, The Phases of Human Progress.* New York: Scribner, 1954.

Schechter, Oded. "The Logic of Speculative Philosophy and Skepticism in Maimon's Philosophy: *Satz der Bestimmbarkeit* and the Role of Synthesis." In *Salomon Maimon: Rational Dogmatist, Empirical Skeptic,* ed. G. Freudenthal. Dordrecht: Kluwer, 2003.

Schmidt, James, ed. *What Is Enlightenment? Eighteenth-Century Answers and Twentieth-Century Questions.* Berkeley: University of California Press, 1996.

Scholem, Gershom. *Basic Chapters for Understanding Kabbalah and Its Symbols* (Hebr.). Jerusalem: Mossad Bialik, 1976.

———. *Briefe,* vol. 3 (1971–1982). Ed. I. Sheldletzky. München: C. H. Beck, 1999.

———. *Elements of the Kabbalah and Its Symbolism* (Hebr.). Trans. J. Ben Shlomo. Jerusalem: Mossad Bialik, 1980.

———. *Major Trends in Jewish Mysticism.* New York: Schocken, 1946.

———. "The Name of God and the Linguistic Theory of the Kabbala." Trans. S. Pleasance. Pt. 1, *Diogenes* 79 (1972); pt. 2, *Diogenes* 80 (1972).

Scholz, Heinrich. *Die Hauptschriften zum Pantheismusstreit.* Berlin: Reuther und Reichard, 1916.

Schwartz, Dov. *Astral Magic in Medieval Jewish Thought* (Hebr.). Ramat-Gan: Bar-Ilan University Press, 1999.

Seeskin, Kenneth. "Herrman Cohen on Idol Worship." In *"Religion of Reason out of the Sources of Judaism": Tradition and the Concept of Origins in Hermann Cohen's Later Work,* ed. H. Holzhey, G. Motzkin, and H. Wiedebach. Hildesheim: Olms, 2000.

Sefer ha-Chinukh. Reprint, Jerusalem: Machon Yerushalayim, 1988–91. English translation: *Sefer haHinnuch: The Book of (Mitzvah) Education.* Trans. C. Wengrow. Jerusalem: Feldheim, 1992.

Seidel, Jonathan, Judith R. Baskin, and Leonard V. Snowman. "Circumcision." In *Encyclopedia Judaica,* 2nd ed., ed. M. Berenbaum and F. Skolnik. Detroit: Macmillan Reference USA, 2007.

Sela, Shlomo. *Astrology and Biblical Exegesis in Abraham's Ibn Ezra's Thought* (Hebr.). Ramat Gan: Bar-Ilan University Press, 1999.

Shilo, Shmuel, and Menachem Elon. "Succession." In *Encyclopaedia Judaica,* 2nd ed., ed. M. Berenbaum and F. Skolnik. Detroit: Macmillan Reference USA, 2007.

Shochet, Azriel. *Beginnings of the Haskalah* (Hebr.). Jerusalem: Bialik, 1960.

Sigad, Ran. "Moses Mendelssohn: Judaism, Divine Politics, and the State of Israel" (Hebr.). *Da'at,* no. 7 (1981).

Sofer, Solomon. *Chut ha-Meshulash* (Hebr.). Drohobitz, 1893.

Sorkin, David. "The Mendelssohn Myth and Its Method." *New German Critique,* no. 77, Special Issue on German-Jewish Religious Thought (Spring–Summer 1999).

———. *Moses Mendelssohn and the Religious Enlightenment.* Berkeley: University of California Press, 1996.

———. "Moses Mendelssohn's Biblical Exegesis." In M. Albrecht and E. J. Engel, *Moses Mendelssohn im Spannungsfeld der Aufklärung.* Stuttgart–Bad Cannstatt: Frommann-Holzboog, 2000.

Spart, Thomas. *The History of the Royal Society of London for the Improving of Natural Knowledge* (1667). London: J. Martyn. Reprint, ed. J. I. Cope and H.W. Jones. St. Louis: Washington University Press, 1966.

Spencer, John. *De Legibus Hebraeorum Ritualibus Earumque Rationibus Libri Quatuor Ad Nuperam Cantabrigiensem.* Canterbury: Crownfield, Jeffrey and Thurlbourn, 1732.

Spinoza, Benedictus de. *Tractatus Theologico-Politicus.* In *Spinoza Opera,* ed. C. Gebhart. Heidelberg: Carl Winter Press, 1925.

Stanislawski, Michael. "Towards an Analysis of the Bi'ur as Exegesis: Moses Mendelssohn's Commentary on the Revelation at Sinai." In *Neti'ot Ledavid. Jubilee Volume for David Weiss Halivni,* ed. Y. Elman, E. B. Halivni, and Z. A. Steinfeld. Jerusalem: Orhot Press, 2004.

Starke, Christoph. *Synopsis bibliothecae exegeticae in Vetus Testamentum, kurzgefaster Auszug der gründlichsten Auslegungen über alle Bücher Altes Testaments.* Berlin: Breitkopf, 1741.

Strauss, Leo. Introduction to Moses Mendelssohn, *Morgenstunden. JubA* 3.1.

Swift, Jonathan. *Gulliver's Travels.* Ed. R. DeMaria Jr. London: Penguin, 2003.

Tadmor, Haim. "Treaty and Oath in the Ancient Near East: A Historian's Approach." In *Humanizing America's Iconic Book,* ed. G. M. Tucker and D. A. Knight. Chico, CA: Scholars Press, 1982.

Tetens, Johann Nicolaus. *Philosophische Versuche über die menschliche Natur und ihre Entwicklung* (1775). Ed. Wilhelm Uebele. Reprint, Berlin: Reuther & Reichard, 1913.

Theodor, Friedrich. "Das Symbol." In *Philosophische Aufsätze: Eduard Zeller zu seinem fünfzigjährigen Doktor-Jubiläum gewidmet.* Leipzig: Fues, 1887.

Twersky, Isadore. "Alexander Altmann (1906–1987)." *Proceedings of the American Academy for Jewish Research* 55 (1988).

Urbach, Efraim Elimelech. *The Sages, Their Concepts and Beliefs.* Trans. I. Abrahams. Jerusalem: Magnes Press,1979.

Vallée, Gérard, ed. *The Spinoza Conversations between Lessing and Jacobi.* Trans. G. Vallée, J. B. Lawson, and C. G. Chapple. Lanham, MD: University Press of America, 1988.

Van der Leeuw, Gerardus. *Einführung in die Phänomenologie der Religion.* Munich: Reinhardt, 1925.

———. *Religion in Essence and Manifestation: A Study in Phenomenology.* Trans. J. E. Turner. New York: Harper & Row, 1963.

Vischer, Theodor Friedrich. "Das Symbol." In *Philosophische Aufsätze: Eduard Zeller zu seinem fünfzigjährigen Doktor-Jubiläum gewidmet.* Leipzig: Fues, 1887.

Vogt, Wolfgang. *Moses Mendelssohns Beschreibung der wirklichkeit menschlichen Erkennnens.* Würzburg: Königshausen & Neumann, 2005.

Warburton, William. *The Divine Legation of Moses Demonstrated.* London: F. Gyles, 1738–65. Reprint, New York: Garland, 1978. German translation: *Göttliche Sendung Mosis, aus den Grundsätzen der Deisten bewiesen,* ed. and trans. J. C. Schmidt. Frankfurt and Leipzig: Johann Gottlieb Vierling, 1751–53.

———. *Versuch über die Hieroglyphen der Ägypter. Mit einem Beitrag von Jacques Derrida.* Frankfurt: Ullstein, 1980.

Weisel, Naphtali Herz. *Divrei Shalom ve-Emet* (Hebr.). Berlin: Chinukh Ne'arim, 1782.

Weiss, Josef. "On a Chassidic Doctrine of the Maggid of Mesritsh" (Hebr.). *Ziyyon* 20 (1955).

———. "On One Homily of the Maggid of Mesritsh" (Hebr.). *Ziyyon* 12 (1947–48).

Wheelock, Wade T. "Language. Sacred Language." In *The Encyclopedia of Religion,* vol. 8, ed. M. Eliade. New York: Macmillan, 1987.

Whewell, William. *Novum Organon Renovatum: Being the Second Part of the Philosophy of the Inductive Sciences.* 3rd ed. London: J. W. Parker and Son, 1858.

Wiener, Max. *Jüdische Religion im Zeitalter der Emanzipation.* Berlin: Philo Verlag, 1933.

Wild, Reiner. *"Metacriticus bonae spei": Johann Georg Hamanns "Fliegender Brief."* Frankfurt am Main: Lang, 1975.

Witte, Bernd. "Jüdische Aufklärung. Zu Moses Mendelssohns Schrift Jerusalem oder über religiöse Macht und Judentum." In *Passerelles et passeurs. Hommages à Gilbert Krebs et Hansgerd Schulte.* Asnières: PIA, 2002.

Wittgenstein, Ludwig. *Tractatus Logico-Philosophicus.* Trans. C. K. Ogden. London: Routledge & Kegan Paul, 1922.

Wizenmann, Thomas. *Die Resultate der Jacobischer und Mendelssohnischer Philosophie von einem Freywilligen.* Leipzig: Göschen, 1786.

Wolf, Abraham. *A History of Science, Technology, and Philosophy in the Eighteenth Century* (1938). London: Allen & Unwin, 1952.

Wolff, Christian. *Philosophia practica universalis methodo scientifica pertractata.* Vol. 2. Frankfurt, 1738–39.

———. *Theologia naturalis.* Frankfurt: Renger, 1737.

———. *Vernünftige Gedancken von der Menschen Thun und Lassen, zu Beförderung ihrer Glückseligkeit.* In *Gesammelte Werke,* ed. J. École et al. Reprint of 4th ed. (Frankfurt and Leipzig: Renger, 1733). Hildesheim: Georg Olms, 1983.

Wygotsky, Lev Semyonovich. *Denken und Sprechen* (1934). Trans. G. Sewekow. Berlin: Akademie-Verlag, 1964.

Zac, Sylvain. "Salomon Maimon et les malentendus du langage." *Revue de Metaphysique et de Morale* 91, no. 2 (1986).

Zamosc, Israel. *Netzach Israel.* Frankfurt a. Oder, 1741.

———. *Otsar Nechmad.* In *Sefer ha-Kuzari be-Chamisha Ma'amarim. 'Im shnei ha-Biurim ha-Mefursamin Kol Yehudah, ve-Otsar Nechmad* (The Kuzari in Five Parts. With the Two Famous Commentaries, Kol Yehudah and Otsar Nechmad). Warsaw: r' Isaac Goldmann, 1879–80.

INDEX

The abbreviation "n" designates one or more notes on the indicated pages.

GIDEON FREUDENTHAL
is professor at the Cohn Institute for the History and Philosophy of Science and Ideas, Tel-Aviv University.